ISBN 978-1-5282-6013-8
PIBN 10925389

1 MONTH OF
FREE
READING

at
www.ForgottenBooks.com

By purchasing this book you are eligible for one month membership to ForgottenBooks.com, giving you unlimited access to our entire collection of over 1,000,000 titles via our web site and mobile apps.

To claim your free month visit:

www.forgottenbooks.com/free925389

English
Français
Deutsche
Italiano
Español
Português

www.forgottenbooks.com

Mythology Photography **Fiction**
Fishing Christianity **Art** Cooking
Essays Buddhism Freemasonry
Medicine **Biology** Music **Ancient
Egypt** Evolution Carpentry Physics
Dance Geology **Mathematics** Fitness
Shakespeare **Folklore** Yoga Marketing
Confidence Immortality Biographies
Poetry **Psychology** Witchcraft
Electronics Chemistry History **Law**
Accounting **Philosophy** Anthropology
Alchemy Drama Quantum Mechanics
Atheism Sexual Health **Ancient History**
Entrepreneurship Languages Sport
Paleontology Needlework Islam
Metaphysics Investment Archaeology
Parenting Statistics Criminology
Motivational

STATE OF WASHINGTON

SEVENTH BIENNIAL REPORT

OF THE

BUREAU OF LABOR STATISTICS

COMPLIMENTS OF

CHAS. F. HUBBARD

LABOR COMMISSIONER

CHARLES F. HUBBARD,
COMMISSIONER

OLYMPIA, WASH.;
E. L. BOARDMAN, PUBLIC PRINTER
1910

BUREAU OF LABOR

APPOINTMENT OF COMMISSIONER.—A commissioner of labor shall be appointed by the governor, and said commissioner of labor, by and with the consent of the governor, shall have power to appoint and employ such assistants as may be necessary to discharge the duties of said commissioner of labor; and said commissioner of labor, together with the inspector of coal mines, shall constitute a bureau of labor. On the first Monday in April, 1897, and every four years thereafter the governor shall appoint a suitable person to act as commissioner of labor, and as factory, mill and railroad inspector, who shall hold office until his successor is appointed and qualified. (L. '05, sec. 1, chap. 83).

DUTIES OF COMMISSIONER.—It shall be the duty of such officer and employes of said bureau to cause to be enforced all laws regulating the employment of children, minors and women, all laws established for the protection of the health, lives, and limbs of operators in workshops, factories, mills and mines, on railroads and other places, and all laws enacted for the protection of the working classes, and declaim it a misdemeanor on the part of the employers to require as a condition of employment the surrender of any rights of citizenship, laws regulating and prescribing the qualifications of persons in trades and handicrafts, and similar laws now in force or hereafter to be enacted. It shall also be the duty of officers and employees of the bureau to collect, assort, arrange and present in biennial reports to the legislature, on or before the first Monday in January, statistical details relating to all departments of labor in the state; to the subjects of corporations, strikes or other labor difficulties; to trade unions and other labor organizations and their effect upon labor and capital; and to such other matters relating to the commercial, industrial, social, educational, moral, and sanitary conditions of the laboring classes, and the permanent prosperity of the respective industries of the state as the bureau may be able to gather: In its biennial report the bureau shall also give account of all proceedings of its officers and employes which have been taken in accordance with the provisions of this act, or of any other acts herein referred to, including a statement of all violations of law which have been observed, and the proceedings under the same, and shall join with such accounts and such remarks, suggestions and recommendations as the commissioner may deem necessary. (Sec. 2, p. 132, '01).

LETTER OF TRANSMITTAL

OFFICE OF BUREAU OF LABOR STATISTICS AND FACTORY
INSPECTION.

OLYMPIA, WASHINGTON, Nov. 1, 1910.

To His Excellency, M. E. Hay, Governor of the State of Washington:

SIR—In accordance with chapter LXXIV, Laws of 1901, I have the honor to transmit herewith to you, and through you to the honorable legislature, this, the seventh biennial report of this bureau for the years 1909-1910. Respectfully yours,

CHARLES F. HUBBARD,
Commissioner.

INTRODUCTION

This report is designed to present in as brief compass as possible a review of conditions surrounding the wage-earners of Washington, with a resume of the various activities engaged in by the bureau of labor during the past biennium, as required by law. It is satisfactory to note that labor has been more generally employed than was the case during the preceding two years and that the state has not suffered to any great extent from any serious financial or industrial disturbances.

The panic of 1907, while severe in its immediate results, had no lasting adverse influence on the manufacturing and other labor-employing interests of the state, and at the beginning of the current biennium normal conditions had practically been restored. This satisfactory situation has been maintained up to the present time, and there is no substantial reason for anticipating any cessation of the uniform prosperity which the state is now enjoying.

The two years covered by this report have been marked by a more complete and thorough establishment of the factory inspection law and by an almost entire absence of hostility to its enforcement. Accidents in manufacturing plants have been greatly reduced, as will be seen by reference to the chapter dealing with that subject, and the receipts from inspection fees have exceeded by a considerable sum the amount appropriated for conducting the factory inspection work. Other state laws for the protection of wage-earners, including the eight-hour law for public works and the ten-hour law for females, have been carefully enforced and violations of same have been promptly investigated and corrected, as far as possible, and sanitary conditions generally improved.

By act of the last legislature, the position of female assistant labor commissioner was created, and was filled by the appointment of Mrs. Blanch H. Mason, of Seattle. Mrs. Mason's duties have taken her over the entire state in the work of inspecting establishments where female labor is employed, and she has been of much assistance in securing compliance with laws governing female and child labor and in improving the standard of conditions under which the women wage-earners of the state are called upon to work.

It is believed that the statistical features of this report are more complete and accurate than ever, and their importance as a basic source of information with reference to general labor conditions in Washington cannot be overestimated. Statistics have been compiled relating to practically all lines of labor employed in the state, and by comparison with reports of former years it is quite apparent that wage-earners are as uniformly employed and well paid as at any previous time since Washington was admitted to statehood. On the other hand, it will be observed from the chapter dealing with the cost of living that prices of food commodities exhibit a steady upward tendency, this being particularly true of a large list of staple articles which enter into common household use in all families. From all the facts assembled as the results of investigations by this bureau, and from reports of labor organizations, it is quite evident that wages have failed to keep pace with advanced living expenses. Some method of adjusting this unsatisfactory situation is a crying necessity.

Acknowledgement should be made here of the deep interest manifested at all times in the work of this bureau by the governor, Hon. M. E. Hay, and of invaluable assistance rendered on many occasions by the attorney general, Hon. W. P. Bell, and his deputies. Due credit should be assigned to the office and field employees, who are strongly and sincerely commended for their efficient and faithful services in the work of this bureau; also to employers of labor and to labor organizations for valuable statistics and suggestions they have cheerfully contributed on request of this department.

CHARLES F. HUBBARD,
Commissioner.

RECOMMENDATIONS

TO THE

LEGISLATURE

RECOMMENDATIONS TO THE LEGISLATURE.

FACTORY INSPECTION.

It is satisfactory to report that the factory inspection law has been more firmly established than ever during the past two years. The act as it now stands is a practical, working legislative enactment and its requirements are readily complied with by practically all of the manufacturing interests of the state, who recognize in it a power for good not only to themselves, but to the wage-earners in their employ. A few exceptional cases arise where difficulty is encountered in securing compliance with the terms of the law, but in no instance has it been necessary to resort to prosecution in order to secure payment of the inspection fee and the installation of necessary safeguards for the protection of employees.

The department has been, however, handicapped in its work by reason of a lack of sufficient inspectors to cover the state in a satisfactory manner. There are many classes of manufacturing enterprises in Washington, and these industires are scattered throughout all of its thirty-eight counties. To satisfactorily accomplish the purposes of the law it is essential that frequent reinspection of all plants should be made. With the present staff of four inspectors, it is a physical impossibility to do this in a proper manner. Certificates cannot be renewed as rapidly as they expire, and in fact lengthy delays sometimes occur while the inspectors are endeavoring to make the round of their respective districts.

Moreover, there is an element of injustice in the situation in this particular: that the receipts from the inspection exceed the amount appropriated for the work by several thousand dollars, which difference must be, under the law, converted into the general fund of the state treasury. The manufacturing interests therefore not only contribute their share of state revenues as levied under the general taxation laws, but a considerable percentage of the factory inspection fees paid by them for the exclusive purpose of maintaining factory inspection is diverted into the common treasury. It would seem no more than just that the full amount collected as inspection fees should be made available for increasing the efficiency of the inspection work, as was the original intent of this law. Two additional inspectors are needed, and the revenues of the department will admit of their being employed. It is strongly urged, therefore, that for the ensuing biennial period an appropriation of thirty thousand dollars be allowed, or such a sum under that amount as may be collected from inspection fees.

Although the manufacturing interests of this state have greatly increased since 1905, when this law went into effect, there has been no increase in the amount appropriated for inspection purposes. To remedy this condition, it is essential that all funds collected for inspection fees should be applied to the inspection service.

The recent nation-wide agitation regarding a uniform employers' liability law, whereby personal injury cases may be settled without resort to court proceedings, should awaken a renewed interest in the effective inspection of machinery by this department, and more attention by employers in maintaining safeguards. While splendid results have already been accomplished, as statistics presented in this report will indicate, a far better showing can be made if funds adequate to the necessities of the situation are made available for the inspection work.

REPORTS OF ACCIDENTS.

The existing law for securing reports of accidents in mills and other industrial establishments is highly unsatisfactory, and has failed almost entirely of accomplishing the purpose for which it was enacted. To be made properly effective, detailed reports of all accidents should be made to this bureau, immediately after their occurrence, and while the facts are fresh in the minds of the parties concerned. A requirement of this nature would enable the department to keep a more accurate record from year to year of all accidents, and this information properly tabulated would supply a reliable method of determining the effectiveness of existing laws for the prevention of accidents. Suitable action for the accomplishment of the above purpose is therefore recommended.

STEAMBOAT INSPECTION.

In accordance with the recommendation made to the legislature two years ago, an appropriation of one thousand dollars was granted for steamboat inspection purposes out of the general fund, in addition to the sum collected from inspection fees. With this amount available to start the work, it has been possible to make a complete and satisfactory inspection each season of all the steamers coming within the jurisdiction of the department. In every case there has been a thorough inspection, and in fact three inspections have been made this year. It is recommended therefore that the same amount be again appropriated from the general fund as was allowed two years ago.

DECREASE IN NUMBER OF WORKING HOURS.

The movement for a general eight-hour working day is annually growing in strength. The state itself has set an example in this direction by limiting the hours of service in connection with all classes of public work to eight hours out of the twenty-four. This applies not only to such wage-earners as are employed directly by the state, but extends also to county and city employees and to all those who are employed by contractors engaged in any line of public work.

Practically all skilled mechanics and those labor unions which have a complete organization of their craft also enjoy an eight-hour day.

On the other hand, it is found that unorganized labor and almost all female workers are still required to remain at their duties for ten hours out of each and every working day.

By reason of the conditions surrounding them it is undoubtedly true that the women wage-earners must look to the state for assistance in securing the benefits of a reduced working day.

Usually the nature of their employment, their fear of losing their positions and the fact that others are waiting to take their places combine to render it impossible for female wage-earners to perfect an organization possessing the strength or influence such as is wielded by the unions of skilled mechanics. It becomes of moment, therefore, to inquire whether the state itself should not enlist its aid in behalf of this class of toilers, who obviously are not in a position to undertake a struggle for an eight-hour day without assistance. Any argument that might be brought forward in support of an eight-hour day for men has two-fold weight when applied to women. The fact that many women, under existing conditions, are working continually on the verge of physical and nervous exhaustion cannot be con-tradicted. Their power of endurance is strained to the utmost at all times, and the element of recreation scarcely enters into their lives, for the reason that the hours not spent at their work must be devoted to an effort to regain their energy for tomor-row's toil.

Yet it is to these same women wage-earners that the state must look in large measure for the mothers of its future citizens, and it would appear, therefore, that the state has a vital in-terest in this phase of the situation. As a nation and as a state, we are now devoting a great deal of thought and en-deavor to the subject of conservation of our natural resources, and it is fair to ask if it is not worth while to give some atten-tion to the problem of conserving and protecting the physical strength of our wage-earning womanhood. That the adoption of an eight-hour day for women wage-earners of all classes would constitute a substantial step toward a satisfactory solu-tion of this problem all who have given time and earnest study to the question are agreed.

VIOLATIONS OF EIGHT-HOUR LAW FOR PUBLIC WORKS.

The extraordinarily large amount of public work that is now in progress in various sections of the state has been ac-companied by numerous violations of the eight-hour law. While this law has been thoroughly tested in the courts and convictions secured for its infraction in many cases, yet some contractors pay little attention to it. This is due primarily to the fact that in most instances the fine assessed is the minimum of $25.00 and costs. Such contractors are usually men of means, and influence in their community; convictions are secured with difficulty and the offender is ordinarily let off with the lightest punishment possible. To men of this class a fine of $25.00 is a small matter which they can readily pay from their added gains in working their men 9 and 10 hours per day. The knowledge that a heavier penalty would be incurred would doubtless deter many from violating this law, and it is therefore recommended that the minimum fine be raised to not less than $50.00 and costs.

PAYMENT OF WAGES.

In connection with the payment of wages to men who are discharged or leave their employment prior to regular pay days, a great many abuses occur. In fact, probably no other class of cases is more frequently brought to the attention of this bureau. It usually happens that the place where the work has been performed is remote from the point where the wages are paid. Men may be working in the timber or at railroad construction, 50 or 75 miles away from the headquarters of their employers. For some cause, voluntary or otherwise, their connection with the latter is severed. They are given a statement of their time, payable at headquarters, and are left to reach the location of same as best they may. Often they are without a dollar of ready money and are compelled to go the entire distance on foot, begging their meals and lodging, notwithstanding the fact that money honestly earned is due them. It not infrequently happens, also, that delay awaits them when the disbursing office is finally reached. Their time must be made up, or the return of some absent official awaited or some other reason for delay is advanced, all tending to work serious injury to those whose sole capital is their capacity for physical work.

So many cases of the above nature have been brought to the attention of the department, and the abuses are so flagrant, that

it seems imperative to adopt some legislative remedy. At the
very least, men leaving their employment or who are discharged
under such conditions as are described in the foregoing should
be entitled to their transportation and actual expenses of living
until the wages due them are paid.

EMPLOYMENT AGENTS.

As a measure of protection against the operations of dis-
honest employment agents, it is recommended that all persons
engaged in securing places of employment for wage-earners and
charging a fee for such services be required to issue duplicate
receipts or contracts. It frequently happens that men are
sent out to work, and on arriving at their destinations find the
place filled, or the conditions of employment not such as had
been represented. Usually the contract or receipt issued by
the agent is handed to the prospective employer by the applicant, and in a great number of cases the receipt is not returned
to him, even though he many not secure the place. Under such
conditions he is entitled to the return of his fee, but without his
receipt he is helpless, having no evidence with which to substantiate his claim. Possession of a duplicate receipt issued to the
applicant and to be retained by him and surrendered only on
return of his fee would prevent abuses of this nature, which are
of constant occurrence.

HOSPITAL FEES.

Frequent complaints arise among wage-earners in connection with hospital and similar fees which many large employers
of labor are accustomed to deduct from the earnings of their
employees. The objections made are directed not so much to the
system itself as to the methods of carrying it into effect. Often,
it occurs that the men do not know what they are entitled to
for the fee paid, and they are not informed in advance as to
the amount of such fee. In short, they are forced to pay what
the employer decides to hold out of their wages, and in case of
injury or sickness they receive such hospital care and medical attention as he may feel disposed to provide. Such abuses may be
remedied by requiring all employers operating the hospital or

sick fee system to post in conspicuous locations a full explanation of fees and benefits, so that every employee may understand in advance of accepting work the extent to which he obligates himself and the advantages that are to accrue to him in case he becomes sick or disabled. An enactment of this nature would work no hardship on the proprietor and would obviate a vast amount of misunderstandings and complaints.

INSPECTION OF BAKERIES.

One of the important duties placed by law upon this bureau is in relation to the inspection of bakeries. This is a work which should be carried on thoroughly and vigorously, and cases of violations of the law should be followed by prompt prosecution. Inasmuch, however, as no appropriation has been made available for the employment of inspectors and to meet other expenses, it has been impossible to give this work the attention it deserved. The plan of co-operation with local officials, as outlined in a previous report of this bureau, has been followed during the current biennial period and with a considerable degree of success. Without funds or state inspectors, it is impossible for this department to do justice to this extremely important work, and, moreover, the necessity of pure bakery products in protecting the health of the community suggests the propriety and desirability of transferring the inspection work to the State Board of Health. If it is desired that the work be continued under this bureau, the recommendation of two years ago for an adequate appropriation with which to conduct the inspection is respectfully renewed.

BOILER INSPECTION.

At the present time there is no state law for the inspection of boilers in operation in lumber mills, shingle mills and other similar enterprises in this state; most steam plants are insured and inspected by surety companies. By municipal laws steam plants located within city limits of cities of the first-class, however, are required to be inspected and a licensed engineer placed in charge. State license and inspection, and a requirement that at least one licensed engineer be employed in every plant, located outside the limits of cities and towns where local inspection in enforced, would undoubtedly prevent many accidents, and materially reduce the annual loss of life and property in the state. A suitable enactment, embodying the provisions indicated above, is urgently recommended.

LAWS TO BE POSTED.

Experience in securing compliance with the terms of the ten-hour law for females and other laws relating to female wage-earners has demonstrated conclusively that very few of the latter are aware of the enactments which have been adopted for their protection. By reason of this condition, it is undoubtedly true that frequent violations of the law occur of which the wage-earners concerned are themselves ignorant and which, in consequence, are not reported to this bureau. To overcome this condition, authority is requested for supplying all employers of female workers with copies of the laws in question, same to be posted in conspicuous locations in their establishments, with a suitable penalty for failure so to do. Legislation along the foregoing lines would greatly simplify the problem of enforcing these laws.

FACTORY INSPECTION LAW

—2

FACTORY INSPECTION LAW.

The work of inspecting the factories and other machinery-using establishments of the state has progressed steadily during the biennial period now closing, and the results have again demonstrated the wisdom of the important law under which this work is conducted. It is a matter of satisfaction to note the fact that there is no longer anything like organized opposition to the enforcement of this act. No instance has occurred during the entire two years in which it has been necessary to resort to prosecution to secure compliance with the requirements of the inspectors' orders or to insure payment of the inspection fee. It is true that individual opposition to the law manifests itself occasionally, but such instances are so rare as merely to emphasize the fact that the great body of manufacturers of Washington are cheerfully supporting the law and complying with its provisions. Moreover, it is quite apparent that they are doing this for sound business reasons. It is now beyond any question or doubt that the factory inspection law has been the direct cause of an extraordinary reduction in the number of accidents in manufacturing establishments throughout the state generally. Not only do all statistics bearing upon the subject indicate this to be the fact, but court records show that accidents for damages on account of injuries received in industrial establishments are far less numerous than formerly was the case. It is such practical results as the above that give the law its justification and explain why the manufacturing interests, almost without exception, readily comply with its provisions, even to the extent of paying, in the form of inspection fees, the cost of administration.

As was also the case two years ago, the department is able to report collections substantially in excess of the amount appropriated by the legislature to meet the expenses of the in-

spection work, notwithstanding the fact that several causes
have arisen as the result of which there has been more or less in-
activity in several lines of manufacturing enterprises.

The shingle business for a time became demoralized by reason of overproduction, and a general shut down followed, await-
ing a return of better prices. The lumber trade has also suffered from temporary depressions, and suspension of operations
has been frequently resorted to by the sawmill owners. Forest
fires and floods have also been effective in curtailing operations
in the above industries, and through these various causes the
average running period of the mills throughout the state has
been considerably reduced.

It has been the policy of the department to make allowance
for idle time in the collection of the inspection fees, and as a
result of the conditions just noted the revenues have not
yielded as large a surplus over the appropriation as was the
case two years ago. A detailed monthly statement of receipts
for the biennial period ending September 30, 1910, is appended
hereto.

As required by law, the department has continued the work
of collecting statistics of manufactures, the results of which
work are presented in the tabulated statements published elsewhere in this report. The inspectors are provided with statistical blanks for this purpose and are instructed to return a
blank completely filled out covering each establishment inspected. It occurs at times, however, that the proper officer
who should give the information is not present when the inspectors call, and assurances given that the blanks will be filled
out and forwarded by mail are not always carried out. For
this and other similar reasons, the statistical tables are not as
complete as might be desired. They are of value chiefly as
indicating the nature and relative importance of the various
manufacturing industries of the state, as also supplying much
valuable information with reference to general labor and wage
conditions.

The importance of this feature of the work of the department
is fully realized, and if, as has elsewhere been recommended, au-

thority is granted for employing additional inspectors, it will be possible to give more attention thereto.'

STATEMENT OF FEES COLLECTED FROM FACTORY INSPECTION FROM SEPTEMBER 1, 1908, TO SEPTEMBER 30, 1910.

1908.		1909.		1910.	
September	$1,285	April	$790	January	$940
October	1,020	May	770	February	680
November	790	June	2,410	March	710
December	670	July	1,275	April	980
1909.		August	1,080	May	975
January	880	September	1,430	June	2,210
February	620	October	1,085	July	1,185
March	595	November	860	August	965
		December	650	September	1,225

FACTORY INSPECTION FUND, SEPTEMBER 30, 1910.

Collected in fees from September 30, 1908, to September 30, 1910.............. $24,795 00

Expenditures from September 30, 1908, to September 30, 1910................. 18,866 62

ACCIDENTS

ACCIDENTS

Public attention, in this as well as other countries, is being directed at the present time as never before to the subject of accidents in machinery-employing establishments. Involved in the interest that is being awakened in this problem is the question of providing adequate compensation for injuries sustained by wage-earners working in such establishments. The effort to remove such cases from the domain of the courts and to substitute for the awards of juries a schedule of payments classified according to the nature of the injury sustained is meeting with approval and assistance in many states.

In our own state, public interest in the question crystalized during the past summer in a convention held in the city of Tacoma, where preliminary plans looking toward the adoption of an employer's liability law, embodying the above principle, were considered. Under existing conditions, the bulk of the money annually paid out by employers as the result of damage suit cases is absorbed in lawyer's fees, court costs and similar expenses. The burden on the employer is a heavy one, and the benefits actually accruing to those who sustain the injuries are slight, often amounting to practically nothing. That the present system must undergo a radical change, and ultimately give way to some plan of reasonable and immediate compensation without lawsuits, is now generally agreed.

At the same time it is gratifying to note the fact that the number of accidents growing out of defective or unprotected machinery is constantly growing less. To determine exactly how much has been accomplished in this direction will not be possible until some method of securing complete reports of all accidents occurring in factories and other establishments where machinery is used has been adopted. Such information as is available, however, indicates that substantial progress in preventing accidents and resultant damage suits is being made. Accompanying this article there is presented a tabulated showing of reports from 51 mills, employing a total of approximately 10,000 men. The number of accidents occurring in these mills for a two-year period, from August 1, 1908, to August 1, 1910, is given, the accidents being classified as "minor," "serious" and "fatal." For the first year of the period, the number of accidents per 1,000 men employed is as follows: Minor, 105.2; serious, 6.1; fatal, 1.4. For the second year the reports show: Minor, 108.8; serious 6.5; fatal, 1.5. It will be readily recognized that this is an excellent showing, particularly as relates to the number of serious and fatal accidents. With regard to the apparently large number of minor accidents, attention is called to the fact that a large percentage of such accidents are not properly chargeable to unguarded machinery. The mill-owners make a practice of keeping a record of the smallest injuries sustained by their employees, no matter how they may be caused, this feature of the situation being well explained by the following communications:

SEATTLE, WASH., Sept. 7, 1910.

Mr. Chas. F. Hubbard, State Labor Commissioner, Olympia, Wash.:

DEAR SIR—Your letter of September 6th at hand. The writer has made a further and more minute investigation of the statement which we sent you, and it occurs to him that probably sixty to seventy per cent. of what we have listed as serious accidents would hardly be considered serious by you for the purpose of your statistics. In making up the list of serious accidents, we included in them injuries like sprained ankles, crushed fingers or toes, as well as some accidents which resulted in the loss of one finger. We thing that probably such accidents for your purpose should be rated as minor accidents. In trying to recall from memory some of the more serious accidents which have happened, we feel that they are practically altogether due to the carelessness of employes. The accident which resulted in our blacksmith getting his hand badly crushed and the loss of one finger, as well as having the bones in his hand shattered, was due to his crawling under the log deck without saying anything to any one and putting his hand on one of the arms of the kickers. He did this whilst the machinery was in motion and whilst we were pulling up logs. The man operating the kickers, not knowing he was there, kicked a log off and caught his hand.

Another accident whereby our edgerman lost two or three of his fingers was due to him putting his hand into the edger whilst it was running at full speed in order to push a fairly large-sized edging down into the conveyor below the edger. He did not use the iron bar that is provided for this purpose, and as he put his whole weight on the edging it broke and he lost his balance and fell over against one of the saws.

Another man who had three fingers cut off was a trimmerman in the dry-planing-mill. His saw became loose and he reported the matter to the foreman of the planing-mill. The latter told him not to touch it until he shut off the engine. This man, however, tried to pull the belt off with his hand while it was running full speed, with the result that he got badly mixed up with the steel pulley and the saw.

The two cases of fatal injury were not due to lack of guards on the machinery, but were due to the carelessness of the men themselves. One man was killed in the corner of our machine shop in a place where there is absolutely no machinery but a small shaft running 105 revolutions per minute. It is 14 feet from the ceiling and 18 feet from the side wall, and there is absolutely nothing to take a man up there. What purpose led this man to climb up there we do not know, but we simply found him hanging by some of his clothes after his life had been all crushed out.

The other fatal accident was due to the foreman of our sawmill walking in front of the edger. He had been instructed not to do so in the reckless way that he was in the habit of doing, and on this particular occasion, just after a flooring cant had gone through, an edging ½x2½ was hurled out from the edger through the double leather apron which protects the saws and was driven into his side.

As regards the inspection of our mill, would say that we have always found this to be very thorough, and we have always complied promptly with the recommendations of the inspectors.

The accidents included all of those not only in the mill, but also in the yard work, handling and piling lumber, and also the work in the planing-mill.

We hope this will give you the information that you need, and if there is any additional details that we can furnish we will be very glad to do so.

Yours truly,

THE SEATTLE LUMBER CO.,

By H. KIRK, *Treasurer.*

SEATTLE, WASHINGTON, Aug. 13, 1910.

Mr. C. F. Hubbard, State Labor Commissioner, Olympia, Wash.:

DEAR SIR—Answering your letter of the 10th inst.

The slight accidents are not caused by machinery, but are cases such as these: A man scratches his hand; hits his hand with his own hammer; falls off a stage. We make a note of everything, however slight, because we have seen serious results from small injuries.

Six serious accidents is a small number for so large a plant.

Your inspector, Mr. Gregg, is very careful, if not exacting, but we have never objected to his demands and have always been as desirous as he could be to protect the machinery. The insurance company has twice reduced our rates because of our carefulness and because of the great reduction in the number of accidents since Moran Bros. Co. ran the plant.

Yours very truly,
THE MORAN COMPANY,
J. V. PATTERSON, *General Manager.*

SEATTLE, August 8, 1910.

Honorable Charles F. Hubbard, Commissioner of Labor, Olympia, Washington:

DEAR SIR—Replying to your circular letter of the 1st inst., we hand you herewith report of accidents to our employes for a period of two years; as requested.

I should state that this report includes every accident reported to the office, and our men are instructed to report the slightest accidents, such as a cut or bruised finger, so that a large proportion of the number included in the report would probably not ordinarily be considered accidents at all.

Yours very truly,
SEATTLE CEDAR LUMBER MFG. CO.,
By W. H. McEWAN, *Treasurer.*

TACOMA, WASHINGTON, U. S. A., August 5, 1910.

Mr. Chas. F. Hubbard, State Commissioner of Labor, Olympia, Wash.:

DEAR SIR—* * * Our average number of employes now is about five hundred, and during the periods for which you wish a report we have had one fatal injury, which occurred during the first period mentioned, and if by "serious" is meant a loss of arms or legs or permanent disability, we have had none. If by "minor" is meant any injury sufficient to necessitate surgical attendance, there have been probably on an average of six or seven per month, a large part of which were infections resulting from scratches, slivers or other causes which could not be classified as accidents.

Yours truly,
THE WHEELER, OSGOOD CO.,
By R. H. CLARKE, *Treasurer.*

TABULATED SHOWING OF ACCIDENTS AS REPORTED BY FIFTY-ONE MILLS.

No. men employed.	No. Accidents Aug. 1, 1908, to Aug. 1, 1909.			No. men employed.	No. Accidents Aug. 1, 1909, to Aug. 1, 1910.		
	Minor.	Serious.	Fatal.		Minor.	Serious.	Fatal.
				1,477	7	2	1
700	160	12	2	750	150	6	
668	165	15		767	255	10	2
680	49			488	36		1
500	72		1	500	72		
				350	24	3	1
350	26			400	31		
300	45	1	1	300	84	2	3
300	11		3	280	6		
				800	3	1	2
240	6	1		240	23	1	
222	7	4		227	9	5	
204	6	2		230	30	4	
200	23			200	29	1	
200	2			200	4		
200				210	60		1
190				190	17	4	1
175	21			150	10	1	2
175	4	1		175	6	2	
170	27	6	1	170	35	15	1
152			1	152		1	
146	49	1	1	174	58		
144	14			166	20	3	
130	2			130			
130	48			130	42	1	1
126				184			
125	4			125	2		
125	5			125	6		
84	6			82	3		
				78	3	1	
75				75			
75	10	1		75	15		
70	3			75	4		
65		1		90			
65				65			
62	15			111	18		
60				60	1		
60	1			60	1		
50	1			55	1		
50	7			55	3	2	
50	1		1	50			
50		2		40	6	1	
50				50	1		
45	3						
45	1			45	1		
40	3			80	5		
				40	1		
30				30			
30	3						
25				25			
23	2			25	3		
18				25			
15	1			25	2		
9				12	1		
Totals, 7,688	808	47	11	10,018	1,090	66	16

NUMBER OF ACCIDENTS FOR EACH 1,000 MEN EMPLOYED.

August 1, 1908, to August 1, 1909.			August 1, 1909, to August 1, 1910.		
Minor.	Serious.	Fatal.	Minor.	Serious.	Fatal.
105.2	6.1	1.4	109.8	6.5	1.5

REPORTS OF ACCIDENTS.
Returned by Employer on Blanks Furnished by the Bureau.

Thos. Wood, Tacoma; age, 19; Aug. 20, 1908; American; single; employed as general helper; hand caught in jointer machine; lost left index finger and sustained flesh cuts on two others; machine was not guarded at time; stated that accident was due to his own carelessness.

Joe Havlick, Tacoma; Sept. 14, 1908; Austrian; married; employed at carrying edgings from edging machine to slab truck; lost his balance and was caught on revolving saw; fatally injured; machinery reported as being properly guarded and accident stated to have been unavoidable.

August Money, Tacoma; age, 48; Oct. 19, 1908; American; employed as millwright; was attempting to put belt over moving pulley and his jumper caught in the shaft; resulted fatally, his neck and back being both broken.

Jos. Charron, Seattle; age, about 45; Nov. 3, 1908; Canadian; was not employed in mill, but was seeking employment; fell on moving belt and was crushed between belt and pulley, resulting fatally; no one witnessed accident, which was unknown until body was found.

W. J. Preston, Seattle; age, 39 years; December 11, 1908; English; machinist; married; a quantity of waste in his jumper pocket came in contact with revolving shaft, his clothing caught and he was wound around the shaft, being fatally injured.

Henry Taylor, Pe Ell, Lewis county; age, about 35; Canadian; employed in sawmill as edgerman; reached into machine after sliver and lost his right hand.

John Crocker, Seattle; age, about 46; Dec. 28, 1908; Canadian; employed as teamster; was kicked by a horse, injury resulting fatally.

E. H. Hannoford, Camas, Clarke county; age, 19; Jan. 5, 1909; American; single; employed as winder on paper manufacturing machine; head and chest crushed, injury resulting fatally; was accidentally drawn between two large paper reels.

O. Lepper, Seattle; age, 30; Feb. 6, 1909; single; German; employed as edgerman; lost right arm at elbow; attempted to clean off figure board without stopping the feed rolls; was taken to hospital and given good care; machinery reported as properly guarded, and carelessness on his own part charged as the cause of the accident.

Lee Marler, Hoquiam; age, 25; Feb. 26, 1909; married; employed in lumber mill as trip man; in removing a piece of lumber, he stepped on a transfer chain and the dog on the chain drew his foot under; right foot was badly torn; machinery reported as properly guarded.

Lorenz Mackee, Tacoma; age, 32; April 19, 1909; German; single; employed as foreman of malthouse in brewery; hand and forearm crushed by being drawn into revolving gear; machinery reported as properly guarded; wages were paid during his disability.

Mike Boscovitch, Aberdeen; age, 38; April 21, 1909; Austrian; married; feeding edging grinder; attempted to clean cylinder while machine was in operation, contrary to instructions; lost thumb and first two fingers; machinery reported as properly guarded; disabled three weeks; allowed half pay.

Albert Kennedy, Aberdeen; age, 25; May 12, 1909; American; single; employed as lath trimmer; right leg sawed off three inches above ankle; was standing at machine; lost his balance and leg thrown against saw; machinery reported as being properly guarded; wages not paid during disability.

S. Sasaki, Tacoma; age, 21; July 22, 1909; Japanese; wife in Japan; employed as dogger on head carriage in saw mill; accident caused by trying to move taper stick when log was being turned; one hand badly cut, but man was not permanently disabled; wages were not paid during period of disability.

K. Inonye, Tacoma; age, 32; Japanese; Aug. 4, 1909; married; employed cutting slabs for fuel; was attempting to replace a belt on a moving pulley; was caught in the shaft and whirled around, his body being torn limb from limb; machinery reported in good condition.

Ertel Scott, Sedro-Woolley; age, 14; Aug. 16, 1909; American boy; employed at loading wood; fell in a conveyor and arm was caught in chain; no one saw him until after he was caught; injury was severe, but time of disablement not reported.

Wm. Simmons, Kalama; age, 22; No. 18, 1909; American; employed as laborer; single; body pierced by board thrown backward through edger; injury proved fatal.

Jos. Sertoft, Globe, Pacific county; age, 24; Dec. 9, 1909; Russian Pole; married; employed in lumber mill at jacking logs; fatally injured; attempted to move pinion while machine was in motion; was crushed between two gear wheels.

John Pongratz, Seattle; age, 45; Jan. 18, 1910; German; married; employed as sawmill foreman and head millwright; was struck by a piece of edging thrown from edger machine; ribs fractured and internal injuries inflicted, from which he died in about 20 hours.

John King, McKenna, Pierce county; age, 45; Feb. 26, 1910; American; single; employed as grader and trimmer in planing-mill; lost right thumb, forefinger, and one-half of middle finger; inattention to work reported as cause of accident.

W. McNeil, Seattle; age, 49; Mar. 9, 1910; married; employed as sweeper in sawmill; skull and shoulders fractured, injuries resulting fatally; supposed to have been caught while attempting to crawl through a moving belt.

J. W. Frith, Baker, Skagit county; age, 21; March 15, 1910; English; single; caught on shaft and whirled around, death resulting; there were no eye witnesses to the accident; was employed as oiler in cement factory.

J. J. Fox, Centralia; age, 29; May 21, 1910; American; married; employed as edgerman in lumber mill; hand cut off above wrist; was putting two boards, one on top of other, through edger, when his glove caught between the boards; the rollers bearing down made it impossible to get his hand out, and it was drawn against the saw.

John A. Wise, Hoquiam; age, 24; June 1, 1910; American; single; operating cut-off saw; upper side of head split open, resulting in death; no one saw accident, the exact cause of which was not determined; machinery reported as properly guarded.

J. Baegel, Arlington; June 27, 1910; married; employed as sawyer; cut his left hand; machinery reported as properly guarded; doctor's fee paid by mill.

Clarence E. Spaulding, Seattle; age, about 45; June 27, 1910; American; married; employed as millwright in flour mill; left arm and jaw broken, skull fractured, resulting fatally; died eight hours after accident; caught in machinery while engaged in examining a roll bearing; said to have proceeded contrary to instructions; machinery reported as properly guarded.

Fred Johnston, Little Falls, Lewis county; Aug. 4, 1910; Swedish; married; employed at sawing lumber for use in loading sewer-pipe cars; stood in front of saw pulling board, instead of pushing it from the rear of saw; hand came in contact with saw and four fingers lost; wages paid during disability, and was given employment as soon as able to return to work.

FENDERS ON STREET CARS.

In the last report of the bureau, the results were shown of several investigations that had been held with a view to ascertaining the effectiveness of the class of fenders generally employed by street car companies in this state. Quoting from that report: "It developed clearly that the street car companies as a whole are using fenders on their cars that are poorly constructed and far behind the standards maintained in other states. It also was made plain that the companies, owing to the expense involved, will proceed very slowly in replacing present equipment with more suitable fenders."

With the results of the investigations above mentioned in hand, the commissioner proceeded to take such measures as seemed advisable to secure the general adoption of a satisfactory

—3

class of fenders. A great deal of correspondence, together with personal conferences with the managers of the companies operating in the larger cities of the state, followed. Photographs were taken of fenders used in different cities, showing many of them to be little short of death traps, and sample devices used in other states were secured and tested.

After a final determination had been reached as to the style of fenders that would satisfactorily meet the conditions in this state, conditions that are particularly difficult to overcome, by reason of the steep grades over which many of the street car lines are operated, the next step was to secure their adoption. In the cities of Everett and Tacoma, the fenders in use were particularly poor, and hence the first efforts were directed toward securing improved conditions in those places. Notices were served on the managements of the operating companies that proper fenders must be installed, but in Tacoma, particularly, such notices were received with evasion and finally with a practical refusal of compliance.

Thereupon the commissioner, in conjunction with the prosecuting attorney of Pierce county, secured a warrant for the arrest of Manager Dimmock of the Tacoma Railway & Power Company, and plans were made to push the prosecution vigorously. Mr. Dimmock, however, requested a conference, which was held in the prosecuting attorney's office, and thereupon entered into an agreement to send east immediately for six Providence fenders and to have same installed on the cars as soon as possible. These fenders, however, did not prove adapted to hill streets.

In the meantime, the master mechanic employed in the shops of the Everett company had been experimenting with the manufacture of a fender of his own invention, in which were incorporated a number of suggestions and improvements offered by this department. An important feature of this fender is a device whereby the fender "apron" is dropped to the tracks, the release being instantaneous, and accomplished by the motorman pressing a valve with his foot, or by air-brake attachment. By this means a human body or other object of any size will be scooped up and carried along until the car is brought to a stop. Back of the fender is an upright spring cushion or buffer which receives the impact of any body taken up by the apron, greatly reducing the resultant shock. These fenders are also constructed in such a manner as not to interfere with the operation of the cars on the steepest grades, and are of sufficient width to cover the entire front of the car.

In both Everett and Tacoma fenders of the above type are being rapidly installed, and it is anticipated that their general use will soon be extended to the other cities of the state where steep grades are encountered.

The Providence drop fender, manufactured in Providence, R. I., is considered by the commissioner as the best car fender for level streets among seventy different types examined. These fenders are now in use in the cities of North Yakima, Bellingham and Aberdeen.

Another improvement suggested by the commissioner and quite widely adopted by the street car companies, notably in Seattle, is a triangular frame or guard projecting in advance of the front wheels of the cars attached to truck frame and running within a few inches of the track. The tendency of this device is to sheer a body with which it comes in contact away from the track before being reached by the wheels.

In general, it may be added that the companies are manifesting a different attitude toward the requirements of the department and are showing a far greater willingness than formerly to adopt needed safety appliances.

Cost of Living in Washington

COST OF LIVING IN WASHINGTON.

For a number of years past, it has been the custom to present in the biennial reports of this bureau a comparative statement, dealing with prices of a lengthy list of food commodities. The list includes the bulk of articles which enter into the everyday fare of the average householder, with the addition of certain commodities which might be classified as luxuries. Wholesale prices as quoted from time to time in the larger commercial centers of the state have constituted the basis for the various tabulations made, and figures have been secured, beginning with the year 1900, and for each year thereafter up to and including 1910. The same list of commodities has been used in the investigations for each succeeding year, and in cases where articles are usually sold in proprietary packages, the prices deal as nearly as possible with the same brands from year to year. Where certain brands have been altered or taken from the market, others of similar quality have been substituted. Thus, in presenting prices on wheat flour, the brands used in the tabulations for 1910 are not the same as those used for 1900, quotations no longer being made on the latter. The same quality and grade, however, are compared in all cases.

In the tables appended hereto will be found the results of the investigation of this subject as conducted during the current biennial period. Prices for 1900 are given as a base and increases or decreases in the cost of the different commodities considered are shown for a period of years terminating with 1910. For the latter year, a final comparison is presented with prices quoted in 1900.

An analysis of the tabulations supplies abundant evidence in support of the common conviction that the cost of living is advancing out of proportion to increases in compensation paid to wage-earners. Moreover, it is important to note that in the list of commodities which have advanced most rapidly are included such staples as rye, graham and wheat flour, rice, eggs, lard, beans, ham, bacon and fresh meats, the average increase in cost of the above commodities for the period mentioned being 72 per cent.

Scarcely any article has advanced more rapidly than wheat flour, which is undoubtedly our most important food commodity. In 1900 the first grade article was quoted at $3.25 per barrel, wholesale; 1901, $3.40 a barrel; 1902, $3.40 a barrel; 1903, $4 a barrel; 1904, $4 a barrel; 1905, $4.60 a barrel; 1906, $4.40 a barrel; 1907, $4.40 a barrel; 1908, $5.15 a barrel; 1909, $5 a barrel; 1910, $6.15 a barrel. It will be seen that while there have been periods of fluctuation, the inclination for the whole period has been for a steady advance, and for 1910 a barrel of flour at wholesale costs nearly double what it did in 1900, on a percentage basis, the actual increase being 89 per cent.

The commodities which show the least increase in price are various kinds of canned and dried fruits, canned vegetables, canned fish, and similar articles, which would not be classed among absolute necessaries. Taken as a group they constitute but a small portion of the ordinary household fare.

COST OF LIVING. TABLE NO. I—SHOWING WHOLESALE PRICES OF HOUSEHOLD COMMODITIES, 1900-1910.

COMMODITY.	Price 1900	Price 1905	Per cent. increase 1905 over 1904	Per cent. decrease 1905 over 1904	Price 1906	Per cent. increase 1906 over 1905	Per cent. decrease 1906 over 1905	Price 1907	Per cent. increase 1907 over 1906	Per cent. decrease 1907 over 1906	Price 1908	Per cent. increase 1908 over 1907	Per cent. decrease 1908 over 1907	Price 1909	Per cent. increase 1909 over 1908	Per cent. decrease 1909 over 1908	Price 1910	Per cent. increase 1910 over 1909	Per cent. decrease 1910 over 1909	Per cent. increase 1910 over 1900	Per cent. decrease 1910 over 1900
Baking powder, per lb	$0.462	$0.40	....	....	$0.40	....	....	$0.413	....	....	$0.413	....	....	$0.413	....	....	$0.4125	....	....	....	....
Small white beans, per lb	.0825	.0875	16	....	.04	6⅔	....	.035	....	12½	.04	14	....	.053	32½	....	.05¾	8½	....	77	....
Lima beans, per lb	.055	.05	25	....	.055	10	....	.05	....	9	.055	10	....	.05¼	....	4½	.05¼	....	....	....	4½
Cove oysters, per can	.176	.1625	1½	....	.1625	....	....	.195	20	....	.195	....	....	.19	....	2⅔	.1875	....	1⅓	6½	....
Salmon (talls, per can)	.116	.125	20	....	.133	6½	....	.105	....	20	.113	7¾	....	.12	6	....	.1125	....	6¼	....	3
Blackberries, 2½ lbs., per can	.166	.145	....	....	.16	10½	....	.16	....	....	166	....	....	.154	....	7½	.154	....	....	....	6⅔
Cherries, black, per can	.175	.137	....	....	.125	....	8⅔	.23	84	....	.22	....	4	.18	....	18	.154	....	14½	....	12
Plums, per can	.125	.113	....	....	.116	2⅔	....	.125	9	....	.125	....	....	.12	....	4	.129	7½	....	3	....
Peaches, per can	.23	.175	....	....	.19	8½	....	.195	2½	....	.195	....	....	.16⅔	....	14½	.145	....	12½	....	37
Raspberries, per can	.186	.22	....	....	.22	....	....	.195	....	11	.208	6½	....	.19	....	8⅔	.208	9½	....	12	....
Baked beans, per can	.116	.117	....	....	.117	....	....	.118	....	....	.118	....	....	.117	....	....	.117	....	....	....	....
Canned peas, per can	.125	.104	....	....	.108	4	....	.105	....	....	.121	15	....	.121	....	....	.112	....	7½	....	10⅔
Canned asparagus, per can	.305	.31	40	....	.37	20	....	.375	....	....	.354	....	6	.312	....	12	.27	....	13½	....	11½
Canned corn, per can	.095	.09⅓	....	20	.075	....	20	.075	....	....	.095	25	....	.092	....	3	.091	....	....	....	4¼
Canned succotash, per can	.135	.12	2⅔	....	.125	4	....	.125	....	....	.125	....	....	.125	....	....	.125	....	....	....	7⅓
Canned tomatoes, per can	.091	.07	....	15	.095	30⅔	....	.10	5¼	....	.095	....	5	.096	1	....	.083	....	13½	....	9
Coffee (first quality), per lb	.33	.29	....	6½	.30	3⅓	....	.30	....	....	.30	....	....	.30	....	....	.30	....	....	....	....
Coffee (second quality), per lb	.125	.153	15	....	.158	3½	....	.166	5	....	.166	....	....	.166	....	....	.151	....	9	21	....
Evaporated milk, per can	.092	.096	....	....	.094	....	2	.095	....	....	.095	....	....	.095	....	....	.08⅔	....	9	....	6
Dried apples, per lb	.11	.07	8	....	.105	50	....	.09	....	14	.125	40	....	.07	....	44	.11	57	....	....	....
Dried apricots, per lb	.17	.11	4⅔	....	.11	....	....	.18	63	....	.25	39	....	.11¾	....	58	.11¾	....	....	....	31
Dried currants, per lb	.10	.10	....	....	.095	5	....	.11	15	....	.105	....	5	.10½	....	....	.10	....	4⅔	....	....
Dried peaches, per lb	.115	.09	20	....	.10	11	....	.13	33	....	.145	....	11	.095	....	34½	.09	....	5⅓	....	21⅔
Dried [illegible], per lb	.12	.10	....	20	.11	10	....	.13	18	....	.125	....	4	.12½	....	....	.12½	....	....	4	....
Dried [illegible], per lb	.08	.09	20	....	.09	....	....	.105	16	....	.135	29	....	.135	....	....	.14	3⅔	....	75	....
Dried prunes, per lb	.07	.04	....	20	.05	25	....	.065	30	....	.07	....	8	.065	....	7	.06¼	....	6½	....	11
Dried raisins, per lb	.1225	.055	....	18½	.065	18	....	.10	55	....	.105	5	....	.08	....	23⅔	.06½	....	18¾	....	47
Oatmeal crackers, per lb	.10	.10	....	....	.10	....	....	.10	....	....	.10	....	....	.10	....	....	.10	....	....	....	....
Soda crackers, per lb	.055	.065	....	7	.075	15½	....	.07	9⅓	....	.075	7	....	.07	....	9⅓	.07½	7	....	37	....
Catsup, per pint	.18	.18	....	....	.18	....	....	.166	....	8	.166	....	....	.20	20	....	.20	....	....	11	....
Wheat flour, 1st grade, per bbl	3.25	4.60	8¼	....	4.40	....	4⅓	4.00	....	9	5.15	28¾	....	5.00	....	3	6.15	23	....	89	....
Wheat flour, 2d grade, per bbl	2.95	4.25	6¼	....	3.75	....	11¾	3.50	....	7	4.65	33	....	4.45	....	4	5.90	32⅔	....	100	....
Meal, per lb	.0325	.04	....	....	.04	....	....	.04	....	....	.042	5	....	.042	....	....	.04	....	4⅔	23	....

COST OF LIVING. TABLE NO. I.—SHOWING WHOLESALE PRICES OF HOUSEHOLD COMMODITIES, 1900-1910—Concluded.

COMMODITY.	Price 1900	Price 1905	Per cent. increase 1905 over 1904	Per cent. decrease 1905 over 1904	Price 1906	Per cent. increase 1906 over 1905	Per cent. decrease 1906 over 1905	Price 1907	Per cent. increase 1907 over 1906	Per cent. decrease 1907 over 1906	Price 1908	Per cent. increase 1908 over 1907	Per cent. decrease 1908 over 1907	Price 1909	Per cent. increase 1909 over 1908	Per cent. decrease 1909 over 1908	Price 1910	Per cent. increase 1910 over 1909	Per cent. decrease 1910 over 1909	Per cent. increase 1910 over 1900	Per cent. decrease 1910 over 1900
Meal, per lb	.016	.021	10		.022	5		.022			.024	9		.06	6		.026	4	5¾	62½	
Rolled oats, 2-lb. pkg	.104	.106	8¼		.097		7½	.097			.104	7		.10		3½	.104	4	20¾		2¾
Wheat flr, 5-lb. pkg	.237	.20			.20			.20	18		.23			.29	26	2	.23	28¾		90¾	22¼
Graham flur, 10-lb. pkg	.165	.215	4¾		.20	6	7½	.20	10		.25	25		.245		11	.315	4¾	12½	44	
Rye flour, 50-lb. sack	1.00	1.18			1.25	38		1.37	22		1.37			1.37½	4		1.44	4¾		8	
Sago, per lb	.045	.0325			.045	11		.055	7		.045		18	.04		3½	.063	4		55¼	
Honey	.135	.14			.14			.15	4		.14	6		.146			.146			8	
Rice, per lb	.045	.0675			.065			.0675			.07			.07			.07		3¾	53¼	
Soda, per lb	.0625	.0625			.0625			.0625			.0625			.0625			.0625				
Table salt, per lb	.025	.0225			.0225			.02			.0225			.0225			.0225	4¼		15	
Vinegar, per gal	.20	.16			.15	2		.19	26		.20	12½		.22	10		1.25	13½		39	
Maple syrup, per gal	.90	.90	6¾		.90			.90			.90			1.25	39		1.25			21	
Sugar, gran dry, per lb	.05	.065	6¼		.066	11		.051	9¾		.0645	6¼		.0606	9		.0606	4¾		22	
Tea, per lb	.50	.50			.50	3½		.50	14		.50			.50	3		.50	4		2¾	
Flour, per lb	.32	.32		6¼	.32			.35	3		.36			.37	45¼		.39	5		9¾	
Butter, dairy, per lb	.24	.18		18	.20			.23	40	10	.25	11		.25	74		.26	18¾		92	
Eggs, ranch, per doz	.25	.34		10¾	.35			.40	25	10	.33	10		.48	8¾		.48	30½		82¾	
Eggs, clean, per doz	.23	.26		3¾	.26			.25	22	12	.23	12		.40			.42	29½		26¾	
Cheese, full cream, per lb	.15	.14	6		.145			.13	16		.155	3		.16	6¾		.19	4	12½	94	
Lard, per lb	.0825	.09		14	.0875			.13			.115	11		.12½	81		.16	5		93	
Ham, per lb	.1275	.125		16	.125			.15	25		.135	10		.14¾	5¾		.19¾	18¾		53	
Bacon, per lb	.1175	.135		10	.225			.165	22		.145	12		.17	17½		.22	36½		87	
Beef, per lb	.08	.065	11	16¼	.06			.07	16	4¾	.0775	10¾		.07½			.12	29¾		50	
Mutton, per lb	.10	.075	6¼		.105	6¾		.10			.09		10	.09			.12	26¾		20	
Beef hogs, per lb	.08	.075			.10			.10	5		.105	6		.08½		19	.13	33½		62¾	
Hogs, dressed, per lb	.075	.085	11		.095	6¾		.106	5		.09	5		.105	6¾		.13	63		60	
Hens, dressed, per lb	.15	.15			.10			.10	5		.105			.10			.12	20		40	
Potatoes, Irish, per 100 lbs	.17	.225	33¼		.16	40		.17	20		.116			.116	19		.21	23½		60¾	40
Potatoes, sweet, per lb	1.00	1.20	50		1.00		16¾	1.20	40		1.20			1.25	4		1.10	12	12	10	
Cabbage, per lb	.025	.0175		12	.025		16¾	.035	20		.0375	35¾		.0175	50	53¾	.0225	28¾		10	
Sugar?, per lb	.01	.015			.0125			.015			.01			.01½			.01½			50	10

COST OF LIVING. TABLE II.—LIST OF COMMODITIES SHOWING INCREASE 1908 OVER 1900; ALSO LIST OF COMMODITIES SHOWING INCREASE 1910 OVER 1900.

COMMODITIES.	Percentage increase 1908 over 1900....	Percentage increase 1910 over 1900....	COMMODITIES.	Percentage increase 1908 over 1900....	Percentage increase 1910 over 1900....
Cove oysters	10¾	6½	Dressed hogs	33⅓	60
Canned raspberries	11¾	12	Chickens	6	40
Canned plums	....	3	Turkeys	30	60½
Coffee (cheap grade)	33	21	Potatoes	20	10
Dried pears	4	4	Cabbage	50	50
Dried plums	68	75	Small white beans	....	77
Soda crackers	....	37	Eggs, eastern	....	82⅔
Wheat flour, 1st grade	58½	89	Catsup, pint	....	11
Wheat flour, 2nd grade	57⅔	100	Vinegar	....	15
Oatmeal	23	23	Maple syrup	....	39
Cornmeal	37	62½	Beef	....	18¾
Graham flour	54	90⅓	Veal	....	20
Rye	37	44	Canned cherries	25	....
Honey	3¾	8	Canned asparagus	13⅔	....
Rice	32	55½	Canned tomatoes	4½	....
Granulated sugar	8⅔	21	Condensed milk	3½	....
Butter, creamery	12½	22	Dried apricots	4	....
Butter, dairy	....	8⅓	Dried apples	13½	....
Eggs, ranch	82	92	Dried currants	5	....
Cheese	3½	26⅔	Dried peaches	26	....
Lard	40	94	Oatmeal crackers	36	....
Ham	6	53	Table salt	10	....
Bacon	23	87	Sweet potatoes	50	....
Mutton	25	62½	Average	25	44

RENTS.

The relation of rentals to the cost of living is an important consideration, inasmuch as a considerable portion of the income of the average wage-earner is paid out for house rent. It is quite true that many workingmen now own their own homes or are acquiring them by the payment of monthly installments, but the great majority are still rent-payers, and probably will continue to be for many years to come. The following tabulation representing reports of individual wage-earners from a number of cities and towns may probably be considered as fairly illustrative of conditions generally throughout the state.

TABLE SHOWING PERCENTAGE OF RENT TO WAGES.

Name of City.	Wages per month.	Rent per month.	Perc'tage of rent to wages.	Trade.
Seattle	$27 66	$10 00	36	Laundry.
Seattle	106 25	25 00	23	Pressman.
Seattle	40 00	14 00	35	Waitress.
Seattle	62 50	18 00	29	Cook.
Seattle	62 50	15 00	24	Cigarmaker.
Seattle	75 00	12 50	17	Laundryman.
Seattle	133 33	25 00	19	Engraver.
Seattle	100 00	15 00	15	Pressman.
Seattle	110 83	25 00	23	Pressman.
Tacoma	62 50	15 00	24	Machinist.
Tacoma	87 50	13 00	15	Wireman.
Tacoma	91 66	20 00	22	Wireman.
Bellingham	50 00	15 00	30	Carpenter.
Bellingham	54 00	18 00	33	Pressman.
Bellingham	90 00	20 00	22	Pressman.
Bellingham	54 00	12 50	23	Wireman.
Everett	82 00	17 00	22	Electrician.
Everett	83 33	13 75	17	Electrician.
Everett	37 50	14 00	37	Mill hand.
Everett	41 66	10 00	24	Mill hand.
Olympia	125 00	15 00	12	Printer.
Tono	100 00	11 00	11	Miner.
Tono	100 00	9 00	9	Miner.
Tono	78 75	5 00	6	Miner.
Tono	100 00	9 00	9	Miner.
Cle Elum	86 66	12 00	14	Laundryman.

SUMMARY.

Number cases reported... 26
Trades represented 13
Number of cities and towns represented... 7
Average wages per month... $78 56
Average rent paid.. $15 55
Average per cent. rent to wages.. 21.5

Statistics of Organized Labor .

BREWERY ENGINEERS AND FIREMEN, SEATTLE—Organized
Oct., 1902; present membership, 60; 500 per cent. increase in
membership since organization; not incorporated; 100 per cent.
of trade organized locally; branch of Brewery Workers' International Union; national secretary, Jas. Procbstte, corner Vine
and Calhoun streets, Cincinnati, O.; membership fee, $10.00;
monthly dues, $1.00; sick benefit determined by union; strike
benefit, $7.00 per week; total amount paid out in benefits during
past year, $140.00; members are paid by the week; average
wages, $3.50 per day; number of working hours per day, 8; per
week, 56; 2 members been idle during past year; aggregate loss
of time, 52 weeks; same amount of idleness during 1909 as
1908; members are working under contract with employers
which was made May 6, 1901, and will expire April 15, 1913;
25 per cent. increase in wages during past five years; no de-.
crease in number of working hours; no established system of
apprenticeship; union been involved in no strikes during past
year; present secretary, W. E. Green, box 192, Georgetown,
Wash.

TYPOGRAPHICAL UNION, ABERDEEN, No. 573—Organized
1902; present membership, 32; 300 per cent. increase in membership since organization; not incorporated; 100 per cent. of trade
organized locally; branch of International Typographical
Union; national secretary, J. W. Hays, Indianapolis, Ind.;
membership fee, $10.00; monthly dues, 45 cents and 1½ per
cent. of earnings; strike benefit, $7.50 to $12.00 per week, paid
by International Union; funeral benefit, $75.00; no benefits paid
out during past year; members are paid by the day; average
wages, $4.50; number of working hours per day 8, per week
48; 3 members been idle during past year; aggregate loss
of time, 3 months; not as much idleness during 1909 as 1908;

union working under no contract with employers; increase in wages during past year, $1.00 per day; no decrease in number of working hours during past five years; apprentices must serve 4 years; one apprentice allowed to each five journeymen or fraction thereof; union been involved in no strikes during past year; present secretary, V. T. Evans, Aberdeen, Wash. .

ENGINEERS' UNION, EVERETT—Organized April 17, 1908; present membership, 31; increase in membership since organization, 20; not incorporated; 85 per cent. of trade organized locally; branch of I. U. of S. E.; national secretary, R. A. McKee, 606 Main street, Peoria, Ill.; membership fee, $10.00; monthly dues, 50 cents; no regular benefits; total amount paid in benefits during past year, $57.00; members are paid by the day; average wages, $3.50; number of working hours per day, 10; 12 members been idle during past year; aggregate loss of time, 24 months; not as much idleness during 1909 as 1908; union working under no contract with employers; 10 per cent. increase in wages during past five years; no decrease in working hours during past five years; no system of apprenticeship; no strikes during past year; present secretary, Donald McBain, 2005 McDougal avenue, Everett, Wash.

CARPENTERS' AND JOINERS' UNION, GEORGETOWN LOCAL No. 530—Organized June 14, 1904; present membership, 69; increase in membership since organization, 52; not incorporated; 100 per cent. of trade organized locally; branch of United Brotherhood of Carpenters and Joiners; national secretary, Frank Duffy, Indianapolis, Ind.; membership, $10.00; monthly dues, $1.00; sick benefit, $7.00 per week; accident benefit, same; funeral benefit, $100.00 to $200.00; wife's death benefit, $25.00 to $50.00; members are paid by the week; average wages, $4.50 per day; number of working hours per day except Saturday 8, Saturday 4, per week 40; all of the members been more or less idle during past year; aggregate loss of time, 30 per cent.; not as much idleness during 1909 as 1908; union is working under no contract with employers; during past five years wages increased from $4.00 per day to $5.00, then decreased to $4.50 per day; apprentices must serve 3 years, then pass a board of examiners; union been involved in no strikes during past year; present secretary, F. M. Sharp, 9003 Eighth avenue S., Seattle, Wash.

CARPENTERS' UNION, RAYMOND—Organized May 18, 1909; 60 per cent. increase in membership since organization; not incorporated; 80 per cent. of trade organized locally; branch of American Federation of Labor; national secretary, Frank Duffy, Indianapolis, Ind.; membership fee, $5.00; monthly dues, 50 cents; no benefits; average wages of members per day, $3.50; number of working hours per day 8, per week 48; 25 per cent. of members idle during past year; aggregate loss of time, 598 days; as much idleness during 1909 as 1908; increase in wages during past five years, 4½ cents per hour; decrease in number of working hours per day during past five years, 1 hour; apprentices must serve 3 years and but one apprentice allowed to 5 journeymen; 1st year receive $2.50 per day, 2nd year $2.75, 3rd year $3.00; the union is now involved in a strike, the details of which will be found under the chapter devoted to strikes; present secretary, D. S. Tannehill, Raymond, Wash.

PILE DRIVERS AND BRIDGE WORKERS, SEATTLE—Organized 1889; present membership, 250; increase since organization, 246; 65 per cent. of trade organized locally; branch of Structural Iron Workers; national secretary, J. J. MacNamara, Indianapolis, Ind.; initiation fee, $10.00; monthly dues, $1.00; funeral benefit, $100.00; total paid out in benefits during 1909, $150.00; members are paid by the day; average wages per day, $4.00; hours per day, 9; 20 per cent. of trade idle during past 12 months; about same idleness during 1909 as during 1908; union does not work under contract; increase of 50 cents per day in wages during past five years; no decrease in working hours during past five years; union has no established system of apprenticeship; union has been engaged in one strike since Jan. 1, 1909 (see chapter on strikes and lockouts); local secretary, Chas. Hixon, box 1327, Seattle.

BRIDGE AND STRUCTURAL IRON WORKERS, SEATTLE—Organized 1896; 99 per cent. of trade organized locally; branch of In-

—4 ·

ternational Ass'n Bridge and Structural Iron Workers; national
secretary, J. J. McNamara, Central Life Bldg., Indianapolis,
Ind.; membership fee, $25.00.; monthly dues, $1.15; accident
benefit, $5 per week; strike benefit determined by union; funeral
benefit, $100.00; total amount paid out jn benefits during past
year, $590.00; members are paid by the day; average wages per
day, $4.50; number of working hours per day except Saturday
8, Saturday 4, per week 44; number of members idle during past
year, 10; aggregate loss of time, three months; not as much
idleness during 1909 as 1908; union working under no contract
with employers; increase in wages during past five years, $1.75
per day; decrease in working hours per day, 2; one apprentice
is allowed to every 7 journeymen on structural work, one to
every 2 journeymen on finish work; apprentices receive $3.00 per
day, and allowed to take an examination before a board of the
union every 90 days until they can qualify as a journeymen;
union been involved in no strikes during past year; present secretary, H. W. Pohlman, Labor Temple, Seattle, Wash.

ELEVATOR CONSTRUCTORS, SEATTLE—Organized Nov. 20,
1906; present membership, 40; increase in membership since
organization, 30; not incorporated; 90 per cent. of trade organized locally; branch of International Union of Elevator Constructors; national secretary, Wm. Young, 1952 N. 19th street,
Philadelphia, Penn.; membership fee, $50.00 for mechanics and
$30.00 for helpers; monthly dues, $1.25 for mechanics and $1.00
for helpers; strike benefit, regular wages; members are paid by
the hour or day; average wages, $5.00 per day for mechanics,
$3.00 per day for helpers; number of working hours per day
except Saturday 8, Saturday 4, per week 44; 10 members been
idle during past year; aggregate loss of time, 2,860 days; not
as much idleness during 1909 as 1908; union entered contract
with employers May 1, 1910, expires May 1, 1911; no system
of apprenticeship; union was engaged in strike which began
May 1, 1909, and lasted 20 days (see chapter on strikes and
lockouts); present secretary, W. E. Montgomery, 417 James
street, Seattle, Wash.

PILE DRIVERS AND WOODEN BRIDGE WORKERS, TACOMA—Organized Dec. 30, 1907; present membership, 59; increase in membership since organized, 48; not incorporated; 90 per cent. of trade organized locally; branch of International Association Bridge and Structural Iron Workers; national secretary, J. J. McNamara, 422-424 Amer. Cent. Safe Bldg., Indianapolis, Ind.; membership fee, $100; monthly dues, $1.00; funeral benefit, $100.00; members are paid by the day; average wages, $3.50 per day; number of working hours per day 8 and 9, per week 48 and 54; few members been idle during past year; aggregate loss of time, one year; not as much idleness during 1909 as 1908; contract made with 75 per cent. of contractors for closed shop; 15 to 30 per cent. increase of wages during past five years; no system of apprenticeship; no strikes during past year; present secretary, C. O. Smith, Tacoma, Wash.

UNITED MINE WORKERS, RAVENSDALE — Organized Nov., 1903; present membership, 238; increase in membership since organization, 138; not incorporated; 90 per cent. of trade organized locally; branch of United Mine Workers; national secretary, Edwin Perry, rooms 1101 to 1106 State Life Bldg., Indianapolis, Ind.; membership fee, $10.00; monthly dues, 75 cents; funeral benefit, $600.00; strike benefit determined by local union; members are paid by piece and by day; average wages per day, $3.00; number of working hours per day 8, per week 48; not as much idleness during 1909 as 1908; union entered into contract with employers Sept. 1, 1908, which will expire Aug. 31, 1910; 10 per cent. increase in wages during past five years; 2 hours' decrease in working hours per day during past five years; no system of apprenticeship; union been involved in no strikes during past year; present secretary, Geo. W. Lish, Ravensdale, Wash.

RETAIL CLERKS, TACOMA No. 367—Organized Jan. 1, 1910; present membership, 27; increase in membership since organization, 20; 20 per cent. of trade organized locally; branch of Retail Clerks' International Protective Association; national secretary, H. J. Conway, P. O. box 1581, Denver, Col.; member-

ship fee, $3.00; monthly dues, 50 cents; sick benefit, $5.00 per
week; funeral benefit, $25.00 to $200.00; out-of-work benefit,
·dues, one-half; members are paid by the week and month; average wages per day, $2.50; number of working hours per day ex-
cept Saturday 9½ to 10, Saturday 15 to 16 hours; no members
been idle during past year; union working under no contract
with employers; wages increased very little during past five
years; apprentices usually serve one year; number of apprentices allowed stores decided by local union; present secretary,
W. R. Huggatt, 3712 So. 7th street, Tacoma, Wash.

PRINTING PRESSMAN, BELLINGHAM, No. 157—Organized
1905; present membership, 10; no increase in membership since
organization; not incorporated; 95 per cent. of trade organized
locally; branch of International Printing Pressmen and Assistants' Union; national secretary, Patrick J. McMullen, Second
National Bank Bldg., Cincinnati, O.; membership fee, $10.00;
monthly dues, $1.00; international pays benefits; strike benefit,
single men receive $5.00 per week, married men $7.00; funeral
benefit, $100.00; installing tuberculosis sanitarium and home;
no benefits paid out during past year for this union; members
are paid by week; average wages per day, $3.25; number of
working hours per day 8, per week 48; 5 members been idle
during past year; aggregate loss of time, 12 months; as much
idleness during 1909 as 1908; no increase in wages during past
five years; no decrease in number of working hours; apprentices
must serve 4 years; no strikes during past year; present secretary, Chas. S. Hall, box 481, Bellingham, Wash.

PAINTERS, DECORATORS AND PAPERHANGERS, SEATTLE LOCAL
No. 300—Organized March 7, 1901; present membership,
400; increase in membership since organization, 375; union
incorporated Dec. 7, 1904; one-half of trade organized locally;
branch of B. of P. D. and P.; national secretary, J. C. Skemp,
LaFayette, Ind.; membership fee, $25.00; monthly dues, $1.00;
sick benefit, $7.00 per week; accident benefit, per week, $7.00;
funeral benefit, $50.00 to $300.00; total amount paid out in
benefits during past year, $602.00; members are paid by the
hour and week; average wages per day, $4.50; number of

working hours per day except Saturday 8, Saturday 4, per week 44; 10 per cent. of members been idle during past year; not as much idleness during 1909 as 1908; working under no contract with employers; increase of wages during past five years, $1.00 per day; apprentices must serve 3 years; present secretary, Jas. Truto, 310 Harvard avenue N., Seattle, Wash.

SHINGLE WEAVERS' UNION, MARYSVILLE LOCAL No. 13—Organized 1901; present membership, 100; 50 per cent. increase in membership since organization; not incorporated; 100 per cent. of trade organized locally; branch of Shingle Weavers' Union of America; national secretary, W. E. Willis, 66 Maynard Bldg., Seattle, Wash.; membership fee, $5.00; monthly dues, $1.00; members work by piece, hour and day; average wages, $4.00 per day; number of working hours per day 10, per week 60; 100 members have been idle during past year; aggregate loss of time, 5 months; not as much idleness during 1909 as 1908; union working under no contract with employers; wages increased 25 per cent. during past five years; no decrease in working hours; no system of apprenticeship; union been involved in no strikes; local secretary, O. F. Chartier, Marysville, Wash.

BARTENDERS' INTERNATIONAL LEAGUE, VANCOUVER LOCAL No. 425—Organized Oct. 3, 1910; increase in membership since organization, 31; not incorporated; branch of Bartenders' International League of America; national secretary Jere L. Sullivan, Commercial-Tribune Bldg., Cincinnati, O.; membership fee, $7.00; monthly dues, $1.00; funeral benefit, $50.00; no benefits paid out during past year; members are paid by the week and month; average wages, $3.25 per day; number of working hours per day 10, per week 60; 4 members been idle during past year; aggregate loss of time, 1,252 days; as much idleness during 1909 as 1910; local secretary, Geo. H. Sanford, 410 E. Sixteenth street, Vancouver, Wash.

CARPENTERS' UNION, EVERETT LOCAL No. 562—Organized April 20, 1900; present membership, 213; increase in membership since organization, 175; not incorporated; 95 per cent. of trade organized locally; branch of United Brotherhood of Carpenters' and Joiners of America; national secretary, Frank

Duffy, Carpenters' Bldg., Indianapolis, Ind.; membership fee,
$10.00; monthly dues, 75 cents; members are paid by the day;
average wages, $4.50 per day; number of working hours per
day 8, per week 48; 30 members been idle during past year;
aggregate loss of time, 28,080 days; not as much idleness during
1909 as 1908; union not working under contract with employers; increase in wages during past five years, 90 cents per
day; apprentices must serve 3 years, first year receive $2.50
per day, second year $3.00 per day, third year $3.50; union
been involved in no strikes during past year; local secretary,
A. E. Crandell, 3227 Lombard avenue, Everett, Wash.

MOVING PICTURE AND PROJECTION MACHINE OPERATORS'
UNION, TACOMA—Organized Dec. 14, 1909; present membership, 21; increase in membership since organization, 4; not incorporated; branch of International Alliance of Theatrical
Stage Employees; national secretary, Geo. M. Hart, State
Hotel, State and Harrison streets, Chicago, Ill.; membership
fee, $25.00; monthly dues, 75 cents; members are paid by week
and hour; number of working hours per day except Saturday
6½ to 8, Saturday 1 to 2 hours longer; no system of apprenticeship; union been involved in no strikes during past year; secretary, J. C. Manning, 2506 North Puget Sound avenue, Tacoma,
Wash.

PAINTERS', DECORATORS' AND PAPERHANGERS' UNION, HO-
QUIAM—Organized Oct., 1903; present membership, 20; membership has doubled since organization; all of trade organized
locally; branch of Painters, Decorators and Paperhangers of
America; national secretary, J. C. Skemp, Lafayette; membership fee, $15.00; monthly dues, $1.00; funeral benefit, $150.00
to $400.00; members are paid by the day; average wages,
$4.00; number of working hours per day 8, per week 48;
three-fourths of members have been idle during past year;
aggregate loss of time, 20 per cent.; as much idleness during
1909 as 1910; union working under no contract with employers;
increase of $1.00 per day in wages during past five years; de-
crease in number of working hours, 2; union involved in no
strikes during past year.

BARTENDERS' INTERNATIONAL LEAGUE, WALLA WALLA—Organized in 1905; present membership, 77; increase in membership since organization, 54; 99 per cent. of trade organized locally; branch of Hotel and Restaurant Employees' International Alliance; national secretary, Jere L. Sullivan; membership fee, $20.00; monthly dues, 75 cents; sick benefit, $7.50 for 6 weeks; funeral benefit, $50.00; total amount paid out in benefits during past year, $237.00; members are paid by the month; average wages, $2.75 per day; working hours per day except Saturday 10, Saturday 9½; 6 members been idle during past year; aggregate loss of time, one-third of year; more idleness during 1909 than 1910; union working under contract with employers; increase in wages during past five years, 33 1-3 per cent.; decrease in number of working hours per day, 2; present secretary, A. H. Barnes, 112 W. Main street, Walla Walla, Wash.

HOD CARRIERS' BUILDING LABOR UNION, ABERDEEN—Organized 1901; present membership, 29; not incorporated; national secretary, Ernest Villard, Albany, N. Y.; membership fee, $10.00; monthly dues, 50 cents; funeral benefit, $100.00; members are paid by the day; average wages, $3.50 per day; number of working hours per day 8, per week 48; aggregate loss of time during past year, 12 months; not as much idleness during 1909 as 1908; union not working under contract with employers; increase in wages during past five years, 50 cents; no system of apprenticeship; present secretary; Chas. Craig, box 541, Aberdeen, Wash.

LONGSHOREMEN, EAGLE HARBOR—Organized August, 1907; present membership, 14; membership fee, $50.00; monthly dues, 75 cents; sick benefit, $5.00; total amount paid out in benefits during past year, $105.00; members are paid by the hour, receiving an average of $5.40 per day; number of working hours per day 9, per week 54; all members have been more or less idle during past year; aggregate loss of time, one-third of the year; as much idleness during past year as in 1908; increase in wages during past five years, ten cents per hour; the union is engaged at present with a strike against the Pacific Creosoting

Company; total amount of wages lost to employes during strike, so far, $100.00; present secretary, J. O. Jocobsqn, box 13, Creosote, Eagle Harbor, Wash.

STEAM FITTERS, HELPERS, SPOKANE LOCAL 464—Organized November 19, 1904; present membership, 11; membership fee, $35.00; monthly dues, $1.20; sick benefit, $5.00 per week for thirteen weeks in one year; strike benefit, $10.00 per week for 16 weeks in one year; funeral benefit, $100.00; members are paid by the day at an average of $3.00 per day; number of working hours per day 8, per week 44; received an increase of 60 cents per day in wages during past five years.

CARPENTERS' UNION, U. B. OF C. AND J. OF A., CLE ELUM— Present membership, 43; increase in membership since organization, 33; membership fee, $10.00; monthly dues, 75 cents; no benefits paid out during 1909; wages average $4.00 per day; average number of working hours per day 8, per week 48; 15 members been idle during past year; not as much idleness during 1909 as 1908; union is not working under contract with employers; one apprentice is allowed to every six carpenters; apprentice receives 30 cents per hour; union participated in no strikes during past year; present secretary, Geo. Grant, Cle Elum, Wash.

JOURNEYMEN BARBERS, BELLINGHAM—Organized November, 1902; present membership, 50; organization is not incorporated; 90 per cent. of trade organized locally; branch of Journeymen Barbers' International Union of America; national secretary, Jacob Fischer, 222 Michigan street, Indianapolis, Ind.; membership fee, $5.00; monthly dues, $1.00; sick benefit, $5.00 per week; funeral benefit, from $60.00 to $500.00; total amount paid out in benefits during past year, $5.00; members paid $16.00 per week and percentage; average working hours per day 9½, per week 54; no members idle during past year; union is under no contract with employers; no increase in wages during past five years; working hours decreased one hour per day during past five years; apprentices must serve three years before being admitted to union; present secretary, C. E. Suetterlein, 1303 Commercial street, Bellingham, Wash.

SEATTLE TYPOGRAPHICAL UNION No. 202—Organized October 11, 1882; present membership, 387 males and 4 females; organization is not incorporated; 95 per cent. of trade organized locally; branch of International Typographical Union; national secretary, J. W. Hays, Newton Claypool Bldg., Indianapolis, Ind.; membership fee, $7.00; monthly dues are collected on percentage-of-earnings system; strike benefit, $5.00 per week for single men and $7.00 for married men; funeral benefit, $75.00; have home for aged and sick members; old age pension for members 60 years old and over; members are paid by the day; wages are $4.25 to $5.00 for day work and $5.50 for night work; number of working hours per day, 7 and 8; not as much idleness during 1909 as 1908; union is working under contract with employers; have had an increase in wages of 25 cents to $1.00 per day; one-half hour decrease in working hours per day during past five years; apprentices must serve four years before being admitted to the union and must be 20 years of age; union has been involved in no strike during past year; present secretary, R. M. McCullough, room 108, Labor Temple, Seattle, Wash.

POSTOFFICE CLERKS' UNION, SEATTLE LOCAL 28—Organized May 28, 1908; present membership, 49 males and 2 females; increase in membership since organization, 20; union is not incorporated; 30 per cent. of trade organized locally; branch of National Federation Postoffice Clerks; national secretary, Geo. F. Pheiffer, 377 Albion street, Milwaukee, Wis.; membership fee, $1.00; monthly dues, 50 cents; sick benefit, $5.00 per week for 10 weeks; total amount paid out in benefits during past year, $11.00; members are paid by the year in semi-monthly installments; union has no system of apprenticeship; present secretary, Wm. D. Swarthant, 4319 4th avenue N. E., Seattle, Wash.

GLAZIERS' UNION, SEATTLE LOCAL No. 188—Organized March 7, 1905; present membership, 42; increase of 46 since organization; was incorporated Dec. 7, 1894; 90 per cent. of trade organized locally; branch of Brotherhood of Painters, A. F. of L.; national secretary, Frank Morrison, 801-809 G. street N. W., Washington, D. C.; membership fee, $15.00;

monthly dues, $1.00; benefits determined by union; total amount
paid out in benefits, $200.00.; members are paid by the day,
averaging $3.75 per day; working hours per day 8, per week
48; working hours Saturday 8, except during the months of
June, July and August, 4 hours per day; 3 members idle during
past year; members have averaged 5 months' idleness; less
idleness during 1909 than 1908; union is not under contract
with employers; wages have increased 50 cents per day during
past five years; working hours have decreased one hour per day;
one apprentice is allowed for first five journeymen, two for eight
or more journeymen; apprentices shall serve three years at
the trade before they are eligible to journeymen's wages; present secretary, J. A. LaRocque, 7810 Stroud avenue, Seattle,
Wash.

BREWERY WORKERS, LOCAL No. 28—Present membership
is 90; union is incorporated; branch of International Brewery
Workers; national secretary, A. Huebner, corner Vine and Calhoun streets, Cincinnati, Ohio; membership fee, $10.00; monthly
dues, $1.00; strike benefit, per week, $7.00; out-of-work benefit,
dues free; members are paid by the week; average wages, $4.00
per day; average of eight members idle during past year; as
much idleness during 1909 as 1908; union under contract with
employers, which will expire May, 1911; apprentices must be
18 and no more than 20 years of age; receive $14 per week the
first and $16 per week the second year; present secretary, Gott-
fried Ischi, P. O. box 899, Spokane, Wash.

MUSICIANS' UNION, OLYMPIA LOCAL No. 342 A. F. OF M.—
Organized 1908; present membership, 32 males and 7 females;
increase in membership since organization, 17; is not incorporated; branch of American Federation of Musicians; national
secretary, Owen Miller, St. Louis, Mo.; membership fee, $10.00;
monthly dues, 25 cents; members are paid by the hour at the
rate of $1.00 per hour or fraction; present secretary, E. E.
Taylor, Olympia, Wash.

PRINTING PRESSMEN'S UNION, SPOKANE, No. 81—Organized
1889; present membership, 42; increase in membership since

organization, 30; union is not incorporated; 90 per cent. of trade organized locally; branch of International Printing Pressmen *and* Assistants; national secretary, Patrick J. McMullin, Second National Bank Bldg., Cincinnati, Ohio; membership fee, $15.00; monthly dues, $1.25; strike benefit, $5.00 single men and $7.00 married men; funeral benefit, $125.00; no benefits paid out during past year; members are paid by the week; average wages, $25 per week; number of working hours per `day 8, per week 48; Saturday one-half holiday during June, July and August; two members been idle during past year; an increase of 12 per cent. in wages during past year; apprentices must serve four years under competent journeymen and must work as journeyman six months, drawing journeyman's scale, before accepted into full membership; union involved in no strikes during past year; present secretary, Wm. J. Coates, 311 Sprague avenue, Spokane, Wash.

WAITRESSES' UNION, SEATTLE LOCAL 240—Organized 1900; present membership, 375; increase in membership since organization, 335; 95 per cent. of trade organized locally; branch of Hotel and Restaurant Employees' International Alliance; national secretary, J. L. Sullivan, Commercial-Tribune Building, Cincinnati, Ohio; membership fee, $3.00; monthly dues, 75 cents; sick benefit, $4.00 per week; strike benefit, $1.00 per day; funeral benefit, local and international, each $50.00; total amount paid out in benefits during past year, $900.00; members are paid by the week; average rate, $1.60 per day; number of working hours per day 10, per week 60; all members have had steady employment during past year; union under contract with employers, which will expire June 1, 1911; present secretary, Alice M. Lord, Labor Temple, Seattle, Wash.

CARPENTERS' UNION, CENTRALIA LOCAL—Organized March, 1908; present membership, 40; increase in membership since organization, 22; not incorporated; about 50 per cent. of the trade organized locally; branch of National Federation of Labor; national secretary, Frank Morrison, 801-809 G street N. W., Washington, D. C.; membership fee, $5.00; monthly dues, 75 cents; sick benefit, $2.50 per week; funeral benefit,

$200.00; disability benefit, $100.00 to $400.00, depending on years of membership; total amount paid out in benefits during past year, $40.00; members work by day; average wages, $3.50 per day; number of working hours per day 8, per week 48; no members idle during past year; not as much idleness during 1909 as 1908; union working under no contract with employers; apprentices admitted to union and allowed to work at lower wage scale until qualified to become journeyman; union involved in no strikes during past year.

COOKS' AND ASSISTANTS' UNION, SEATTLE No. 33—Organized September, 1907; present membership, 150; increase in membership since organization, 75; not incorporated; 75 per cent. of trade organized locally; branch of Hotel and Restaurant Employees' International Alliance; national secretary, J. L. Sullivan, Commercial-Tribune Building, Cincinnati, O.; membership fee, $5.00; monthly dues, $1.00; sick benefit, $7.00 per week; strike benefit, $1.00 per day; funeral benefit, $125.00; total amount paid out in benefits during past year, $1,000.00; members work by the week; average wages, $3.00 per day; number of working hours per day 11, per week 66; about 35 members been idle during past year; as much idleness during 1909 as 1908; union working under contract with employers, which expires June 1 of each year; no system of apprenticeship; union been involved in no strikes during past year; present secretary, Jas. R. Harris, P. O. box 594, Seattle, Wash.

MINERS' LOCAL UNION, No. 2373, BURNETT—Organized July, 1907; present membership, 166; increase in membership since organization, 136; not incorporated; branch of U. M. W. of A.; national secretary, Edwin Perry, 1101-1106 State Life Bldg., Indianapolis, Ind.; membership fee, $5.00; monthly dues, 75 cents; members work by the day; average wages, $3.00 per day; number of working hours per day 8, per week 48; not as much idleness during 1909 as 1908; union working under contract with employers, which will expire September 1, 1910; increase of 40 per cent. in wages during past five years; 2 hours' decrease of working hours during past five years; present secretary, Dennis Cahill, Burnett, Wash.

COOPERS' UNION, No. 69, SPOKANE—Organized October 1, 1906; present membership, 20; increase in membership since organization, 8; not incorporated; 100 per cent. of trade organized locally; branch of Coopers' International Union of America; national secretary, Wm. R. Deal; membership fee, $5.00; monthly dues, 75 cents; strike benefit, $6.00 per week; funeral benefit, $50.00; members work by the day; average wages, $4.25 per day; number of working hours per day 8, per week 48; 6 members idle during past year; aggregate loss of time, 8 per cent.; not as much idleness during 1909 as 1908; union working under contract which will expire May 1, 1911; increase of $1.00 per day in wages during past five years; one apprentice is allowed to every ten members; must serve 3 years; no strikes during past year; present secretary, Jos. Klinkner, Hillyard, Wash.

CARPENTERS AND JOINERS, WALLA WALLA—Organized August 12, 1902; present membership, 128; not incorporated; 90 per cent. of trade organized locally; branch of United Brotherhood of Carpenters and Joiners of America; national secretary, Frank Duffy, Carpenters' Building, Indianapolis, Ind.; disability benefit, $200.00 to $400.00; funeral benefit, $100.00 to $200.00; members are paid by the piece or hour; average wages, $4.00 per day; number working hours per day 8, per week 48; about the same amount of idleness in 1909 as 1908; union under no contract with employers; increase in wages during past five years, $1.00 per day; decrease in number of working hours, 2; apprentices must serve 3 years under journeyman and then stand an examination; present secretary, C. L. Chapman, 512 E. Alder street, Walla Walla, Wash.

PLASTERERS' UNION, SEATTLE—Organized April 24, 1899; present membership, 125; increase in membership since organization, 100; not incorporated; 75 per cent. of trade organized locally; branch of Operative Plasterers' International Association; national secretary, Joseph McIlveen, 2909 Wylie avenue, Pittsburg, Penn.; membership fee, $25.00; monthly dues, 75 cents; strike benefit, $5.00 per week; funeral benefit, $50.00; total amount paid out in benefits during past year, $250.00;

members are paid by the day; average wages per day, $6.00; number of working hours except Saturday 8, Saturday 4, per week 44; 50 members been idle during past year; aggregate loss of time, about six months; not as much idleness during 1909 as 1908; union under no contract with employers; apprentices must serve 4 years and be 18 years of age or over; wages, first year $5.50 per week, second year $2.00 per day, third year $3.00 per day, fourth year $4.00 per day; present secretary, H. R. Bates, 925 Twenty-second Avenue South, Seattle, Wash.

ELECTRICAL WORKERS, SEATTLE LOCAL No. 77—Organized August 28, 1897; present membership, 300; increase in membership since organization, 285; not incorporated; 75 per cent. of trade organized locally; branch of International Brotherhood of Electrical Workers; national secretary, J. W. Murphy, Springfield, Ill., P. O. box 42; membership fee, $10.00; monthly dues, $1.60; sick benefit, $8.00 per week; funeral benefit, $100.00; total amount paid out in benefits during past year, $2,000.00; members are paid by the day and month; average wages, $4.00 per day; number of working hours per day 8, per week 48; union working under contract with employers; 10 per-cent. increase in wages during past five years; decrease of one hour per day during past five years; apprentices must work three years under journeyman; no strikes during past year; present secretary, Madden Blair, room 13, Labor Temple, Seattle, Wash.

LAUNDRY WORKERS' UNION, CLE ELUM—Organized December, 1909; small increase in membership since organization; incorporated in December, 1909; branch of Laundry International Union; national secretary, John J. Manning, Troy, New York; membership fee, male $3.00, female $2.00; monthly dues, male 75 cents, female 60 cents; members are paid by the week; males average $3.33 and females $1.15 per day; working hours per day except Saturday 10, Saturdays 5 to 7, per week 54; no members been idle during past year; union working under contract which will expire December, 1910; no established system of apprenticeship; present secretary, Mary Long, Cle Elum. Wash.

BARBERS, EVERETT LOCAL No. 446—Organized October 11, 1902; present membership, 61; increase in membership since organization, about 40; 99 per cent. of trade organized locally; branch of Journeymen Barbers of America; national secretary, Jacob Fischer, Indianapolis, Ind.; membership fee, $5.00; monthly dues, $1.00; sick benefit, $10.00 per week; funeral benefit, $75.00 to $500.00; members are paid by the week; average wages per day, $3.00; number of working hours per day except Saturday 10, Saturday 13, number of working hours per week 63; no members been idle during past year; not as much idleness during 1909 as 1908; during past five years wages changed from 60 per cent. straight to same basis with $16.00 per week guaranteed; no strikes during past year; present secretary, W. O. McAlister, 1316 Broadway, Everett, Wash.

SHINGLE WEAVERS' UNION, LITTLE ROCK—Organized May, 1903; present membership, 40; increase in membership since organization, 31; 60 per cent. of trade organized locally; branch of International Shingle Weavers' Union; national secretary, W. E. Willis, 66 Maynard Bldg., Seattle, Wash.; membership fee, $5.00; monthly dues, $1.00; members are paid by the piece, averaging $3.50 per day; number of working hours per day, 10; aggregate loss of time of idle members during past year, 8 per cent.; not as much idleness during 1909 as 1908; increase in wages during past five years, about 10 per cent.; no decrease in working hours during past five years; apprentices allowed card at half the initiation fee and dues until competent to do skilled work, when given full card and pay full dues; present secretary, F. W. Twiple, Little Rock, Wash.

BRICKLAYERS UNION No. 3, SPOKANE—Organized in 1888; present membership, 250; not incorporated; 95 per cent. of trade organized locally; branch of Bricklayers', Masons' and Plasterers' International Union of America; national secretary, Wm. Dobson, Indianapolis, Ind.; membership fee, $16.00; monthly dues, $1.00; accident benefit, $5.00 per week for 13 weeks; strike benefit, $7.00 per week for single men and $10.00 per week for married men; funeral benefit, $300.00; $150.00 for wife's funeral benefit; total amount paid out in benefits during past year, about $400.00; members work by the hour; average wages, $6.00 per day; number of working hours per day except Saturday 8, Saturday 4; about one-third of the members been idle during past year; apprentices must serve nine months a year for three years, first year receive $6.00 per week, second $9.00, and third year $12.00; present secretary, Frank Culbert, box 911, Spokane, Wash.

ORNAMENTAL IRON WORKERS, SEATTLE—Organized December, 1906; present membership, 40; no increase in membership since organization; not incorporated; 75 per cent. of trade organized locally; branch of International Association B. and S. I. W.; national secretary, J. J. McNamara, American Central Life Bldg., Indianapolis, Ind.; membership fee, $5.00; monthly dues, $1.00; funeral benefit, $50.00; death benefit, $100.00; members are paid by the week; average wages, $3.00 per day; number of working hours per day 8, per week 48; 50 per cent. of members been idle during past year; not as much idleness during 1909 as 1908; union working under no contract with employers; 25 per cent. increase in wages during past five years; one hour decrease in number of working hours; one apprentice is allowed to each mechanic; present secretary, Wm. Zurugenberg, Labor Temple, Seattle, Wash.

CIGARMAKERS' UNION, SEATTLE No. 188—Organized April 15, 1887; present membership, 74 males, 2 females; not incorporated; 98 per cent. of trade organized locally; branch of Cigarmakers' International Union of America; national secretary, G. W. Perkins, Monon Bldg., Chicago, Ill.; membership fee, $3.00; monthly dues, $1.20; sick benefit, $5.00 per week for 13 weeks during year; strike benefit, $5.00 per week; out-of-work benefit, $3.00 per week for 16 weeks during year; funeral benefit, $50.00 for two-year members, $200.00 for five-year members, $350.00 for ten-year members, and $550.00 for fifteen-year members; total amount paid out in benefits during past year, $970.00; members are paid by the piece; average wages per day, $3.50; number of working hours per day except Saturday 8, Saturday 6, per week 46; 10 members been idle during past year; not as

much idleness during 1909 as 1908; one apprentice is allowed
to two journeymen, two to ten journeymen, and three to thirty
journeymen, and no more; present secretary, Jos. Kokesh, 5603
Rainier avenue, Seattle, Wash,

ELECTRICAL WORKERS, BELLINGHAM LOCAL NO. 314—Organized December 20, 1903; present membership, 56; increase
in membership since organization, 44; 70 per cent. of trade
organized locally; branch of Independent Brotherhood of Electrical Workers; national secretary, J. W. Murphy, box 42,
Springfield, Ill.; membership fee, $10.00; monthly dues, $1.25;
sick benefit, $5.00 per week; accident benefit, $5.00 per week;
funeral benefit, $100.00; total amount paid out in benefits
during past year, $145.00; members are paid by the day and
month; average wages per day, $3.00; number of working hours
per day 8, per week 48; 15 members been idle during past year;
aggregate loss of time, 25 months; not as much idleness in 1909
as 1908; union working under contract with employers which
was made February 1, 1910, and expires February 1, 1911;
increase in wages during past five years, 25 cents per day; no decrease in number of working hours; one apprentice allowed to
four journeymen; apprentices must serve three years; present
secretary, Geo. H. Moore, Bellingham, Wash.

BAKERY AND CONFECTIONERY WORKERS' UNION, SPOKANE NO.
74—Organized October 29, 1899; present membership, 135;
increase in membership since organization, 122; not incorporated; 95 per cent. of trade organized locally; branch of B.
and C. W. I. U. of A.; national secretary, Otto E. Fischer, 212
Bush Temple, Chicago, Ill.; membership fee, $25.00; monthly
dues, $1.25; sick benefit, $6.00 per week; strike benefit, $6.00
per week; funeral benefit, $100.00 to $350.00; total amount
paid out in benefits during past year, $70.00; members are
paid by the week; average wages per day, $4.00; number of
working hours per day 8 and 9, per week 48 and 54 hours; 20
members been idle during past year; aggregate loss of time, 60
weeks; more idleness in 1909 than 1908; union is working under
contract with employers which was made May 1, 1910, and will

—5

expire May 1, 1911; increase in wages during past five years, $5.00 per week; decrease in number of working hours, 2; apprentices must serve 2 years, then take a practical examination; present secretary, Wm. Horn, P. O. box 388, Spokane, Wash.

WEB PRESSMEN'S UNION, SEATTLE No. 26—Organized January, 1908; present membership, 40; increase in membership since organization, 14; not incorporated; 100 per cent. of trade organized locally; branch of International Printing Pressmen and Assistants' Union; national secretary, P. J. McMullen, 501 Second National Bank Bldg., Cincinnati, O.; membership fee, $25.00; monthly dues, 1 1-4 per cent. of earnings; sick benefit determined by local union; strike benefit, $7.00 per week for married men, $5.00 for single men; funeral benefit, $100.00; total amount paid out in benefits during past year, $70.00; members are paid by the day; averages wages, $4.25 per day; number of working hours per day, 8; one member been idle during past year; union working under contract with employers which was made in 1909 and expires December, 1910; increase in wages during past five years, $1.00 per day; apprentices must serve 4 years; union involved in no strikes during past year; present secretary, A. B. Hoglund, 336 Twenty-ninth avenue, Seattle, Wash.

CARPENTERS' UNION, BELLINGHAM LOCAL No. 756—Organized 1902; present membership, 76; not incorporated; branch of United Brotherhood of Carpenters and Joiners; national secretary, Frank Morrison; membership fee, $20.00; monthly dues, 75 cents; sick benefit, $4.00 per week; funeral benefit, $400.00; members are paid by the hour; averages wages, $4.00 per day; number of working hours per day, 8; about one-half of members been idle during past year; more idleness during 1909 than 1908; union is working under no contract with employers; one apprentice is allowed to every four journeymen; present secretary, C. R. Henderson, 2320 Elizabeth street, Bellingham, Wash.

BOOKBINDERS' UNION, SPOKANE, No. 122—Organized June 27, 1902; present membership, 20; 100 per cent. increase in membership since organization; not incorporated; 100 per cent.

of trade organized locally; branch of International Brotherhood of Bookbinders; national secretary, James W. Dougherty, 132 Nassau street, New York; membership fee, $25.00; monthly dues, $1.00; strike benefit, $7.00 married men, $5.00 single men; out-of-work benefit determined by union; funeral benefit, $100.00; total amount paid out in benefits during past year, $200.00; members are paid by the hour; average wages per day, $4.00; number of working hours per day 8, per week 48; about the same amount of idleness during 1909 as 1908; union is working under no contract; increase in wages during past five years, $2.50 per week; no decrease in number of working hours; apprentices must be between 16 and 18 years of age and must serve five years; present secretary, William Dye, box 307, Spokane, Wash.

BEER DRIVERS' UNION, SPOKANE—Organized 1882; present membership, 31; increase in membership since organization, 15; not incorporated; branch of International Union of the United Brewery Workers; national secretary, Adam Huebner, Cincinnati, O.; membership fee, $11.00; monthly dues, 75 cents; strike benefit, $7.00 per week; no benefits paid out during past year; members are paid by the week; average wages per day, $3.50; number of working hours per day 8, per week 48; two members been idle during past year; aggregate loss of time, 30 days; as much idleness during 1909 as 1908; union is working under contract with employers which was made May 1, 1909, and will expire May 1, 1911; no increase in wages during past five years; no decrease in number of working hours; no established system of apprenticeship; present secretary, Fred R. Maddux, 203½ S. Howard street, Spokane, Wash.

WAITERS' ALLIANCE, SPOKANE No. 63—Organized September, 1901; present membership, 200; increase in membership since organization, 150; not incorporated; 90 per cent. of trade organized locally; branch of H. and R. E. A. of A.; national secretary, Jere L. Sullivan, Commercial-Tribune Bldg., Cincinnati, Ohio; membership fee, $10.00; monthy dues, $1.00; sick benefit, $7.00 per week; accident and strike benefits, same; funeral benefit, $50.00; total amount paid out in benefits during past year,

$219.00; members are paid by the day and week; average wages per day, $2.30; number of working hours per day 10, per week 70; no members been idle during past year; union working under contract with employers which expires April 30, 1911; 30 cents per day increase in wages during past five years; no decrease in number of working hours; no system of apprenticeship; union involved in one strike during past year (see chapter on strikes); present secretary, Fred Cardamone, P. O. box 510, Spokane, Wash.

MINE WORKERS, WILKESON LOCAL UNION 2634—Organized August, 1907; present membership, 485; no increase in membership since organization; 100 per cent. of trade organized locally; branch of United Mine Workers of America; national secretary, Edwin Perry, State Life Building, Indianapolis, Ind.; membership fee, $10.00; monthly dues, 75 cents; strike benefit, $5.40 to $12.00 per week; $600.00 death benefit paid in case of death from accident while at work; members are paid by the piece and by the day; average wages per day, $3.00; number of working hours per day 8, per week 48; 40 members been idle during past year; aggregate loss of time, 11,000 days; not as much idleness during 1909 as 1908; union working under contract with employers entered into July 1, 1909, will expire August 31, 1910; 20 per cent. increase in wages during past year; two hours decrease in number of working hours; no system of apprenticeship; union involved in one strike (see chapter on strikes); present secretary, August Abraham, Wilkeson, Wash.

BREWERY WORKERS' UNION, ABERDEEN—Organized 1905; present membership, 19; increase in membership since organization, 2; not incorporated; 100 per cent. of trade organized locally; branch of International U. of U. B. W. of A.; national secretary, Adam Huebner, Cincinnati, O.; membership fee, $10.00; monthly dues, $1.00; strike benefit, $7.00 per week; funeral benefit, $75.00; members are paid by the week; number of working hours per day 8, per week 48; not as much idleness during 1909 as 1908; union working under contract with employers which will expire May, 1913; apprentices must be between the ages of 18 and 20 years and must serve two years;

one apprentice is allowed to each brewery and one for each fifteen members therein; present secretary, Max Enderle, Aberdeen, Wash.

SAW MILL WORKERS, EVERETT LOCAL No. 24—Branch of International Brotherhood of W. and S. M. W.; national secretary, Alex Livingston, Lothrop, Mont.; membership fee, $2.50; monthly dues, 50 cents; no benefits except by subscription; members are paid by the hour; average wages per day, $2.25; number of working hours per day except Saturday 10, Saturday 9, per week 60; no members been idle during past year; union is working under no contract with employers; increase in wages during past five years, per day, 50 cents; no decrease in number of working hours; no system of apprenticeship; no strikes during past year; present secretary, Gorden Muertz, 1615 Hoyt, Everett, Wash.

SHEET METAL WORKERS, SPOKANE—Ninety per cent. of trade organized locally; branch of S. M. W. I. A.; national secretary, John E. Bray, 325 Nelson Bldg., Kansas City, Mo.; membership fee, $50.00; monthly dues, $1.00; funeral benefit, $100.00; no benefits paid out during past year; members are paid by the hour; average wages, $4.50 per day; number of working hours per day 8, per week 40; 10 members been idle during past year; not as much idleness during 1909 as 1908; union working under contract with employers entered into January 1, 1910, and will expire January 1, 1911; wages been increased 50 cents per day during past five years; no decrease in number of working hours; apprentices must serve four years; present secretary, Geo. T. Bond, 707½ W. Third avenue, Spokane, Wash.

SHINGLE WEAVERS' UNION, EVERETT—Organized May, 1901; present membership, 380; increase in membership since organization, 280; incorporated; 100 per cent. of trade organized locally; branch of I. S. W. U. of A.; national secretary, W. E. Willis, Room 66 Maynard Bldg., Seattle, Wash.; membership fee, $5.00; monthly dues, $1.00; strike benefit, $6.00 per week; members are paid by the piece and by the day; average wages, $4.50 per day; number of working hours per day, 10; 10 per cent. of the members been idle during past year; not as much idleness during 1909 as 1908; union working under no contract with employers; wages been increased 15 per cent. during past five years; no decrease in number of working hours; apprentices must serve one year; present secretary, Chas. Knecht, Oakes avenue, Everett, Wash.

COOKS' AND WAITERS' UNION, TACOMA LOCAL No. 61—Organized June 27, 1901; present membership, 254 males and 50 females; increase in membership since organization, 276; 85 per cent. of trade organized locally; branch of Hotel and Restaurant Employees' International Alliance; national secretary, Jere L. Sullivan, Commercial-Tribune Bldg., Cincinnati, Ohio; membership fee, male $5.00, female $3.00; monthly dues, male $1.00; female 50 cents; sick benefit, male $7.00 per week, female $5.00 per week; funeral benefit, married $120.00, single $100.00; total amount paid out in benefits during past year, $120.00; members are paid by the week; average wages per day, male $2.25, female $1.75; number of working hours per day 10, per week 60; five per cent. of the members have been idle during past year; aggregate loss of time of idle members, 4,475 days; more idleness during 1909 than 1908; union working under contract with employers; contracts run indefinitely and expire on 30 days' notice; 15 per cent. increase in wages during past five years; decrease of one hour per day; no system of apprenticeship; union involved in one strike, which lasted one month (see chapter on strikes); present secretary, Geo. Humphrey, 1137½ Commerce street, Tacoma, Wash.

TYPOGRAPHICAL UNION, OLYMPIA—Organized 1890, present membership, 15 males and 1 female; not incorporated; 90 per. cent of trade organized locally; branch of I. T. U.; national secretary, J. W. Hays, Indianapolis, Ind.; membership fee, $7.00; monthly dues, one-half of one per cent. of earnings; strike benefit, $7.00 per week; funeral benefit, $75.00; other benefits, old age pension; members are paid by the hour, but cannot receive less than one half days' pay; average wages per day, $5.00; number of working hours per day 7½, per week 45; no members been idle during past year; more idleness during 1908 than 1909; union working under contract with employers entered into January, 1908, which will expire December 31, 1910; 33 1-3 per cent. increase in wages during past five years; one-half hour decrease in number of working hours; apprentices must serve four years; union involved in no strikes during past year; present secretary, Geo. L. Levy, 410 Fifth · street, Olympia, Wash.

ELECTRICAL WORKERS, EVERETT LOCAL No. 632—Organized January 23, 1909; present membership, 16; no increase in membership since organization; 90 per cent. of trade organized locally; branch of I. B. of E. W.; national secretary, J. W. Murphy, P. O. box 42, Springfield, Ill.; membership fee, $10.00 and $15.00; monthly dues, $1.25; sick benefit, $7.00 per week; accident benefit, same; funeral benefit, $100.00; members are paid by the day and month; average wages per day, $4.00; number of working hours per day 8, per week 48; as much idleness during 1909 as 1908; union working under verbal contract with employers: 25 per cent. increase in wages during past five years; decrease in number of working hours, one; one apprentice is allowed to four journeymen; no strikes during past year; present secretary, G. Vingen, 4112 Hoyt, Everett, Wash.

ELECTRICAL WORKERS, TACOMA LOCAL No. 76—Organized 1903; present membership, 55; not incorporated; 90 per cent. of trade organized locally; branch of International Brotherhood of Electrical Workers; national secretary, J. W. Murphy, box 42, Springfield, O.; membership fee, $15.00; monthly dues, $1.25; sick benefit, $5.00 per week; strike benefit, $5.00 per week for ten weeks; funeral benefit, $100.00; members are paid by the hour; average wages of members per day, $4.00; number of working hours per day except Saturday 8, Saturday 4, per week 44; six members been idle during past year; not as much idleness during 1909 as 1908; union is working under no contract with employers; increase in wages during past five years, 50 cents per day; no decrease in number of working hours per day; apprentices must serve six months before they are allowed to join union; must serve three years and pass an examination before becoming journeymen; present secretary, C. O. Nelson, 1202 S. Nineteenth street, Tacoma, Wash.

CARPENTERS' UNION, ABERDEEN No. 883—Organized May, 1901; present membership, 150; increase in membership since organization, 115; not incorporated; 100 per cent. of trade organized locally; branch of U. B. of C. and J. of A.; national secretary, Frank Duffy, Carpenters' Bldg., Indianapolis, Ind.; membership fee, $15.00; monthly dues, 50 and 75 cents; accident benefit, $50.00 to $200.00 according to length of membership; strike benefit regulated by National Union; funeral benefit, $25.00 to $100.00; total amount paid out in benefits during past year, $300.00; members are paid by the hour; average wages per day, $3.60; number of working hours per day 8, per week 48; all members been more or less idle during past year; aggregate loss of time, 15 per cent.; same amount of idleness during 1909 as 1908; union working under no contract with employers; increase in wages during past five years, 60 cents per day; decrease in number of working hours, one; apprentices must be under 21 years of age, must serve three years and pass an examination; present secretary, F. E. Hile, 1509 W. Seventh street, Aberdeen, Wash.

LAUNDRY WORKERS, SEATTLE LOCAL No. 24—Organized January, 1910; present membership, male 13, female 20; not incorporated; 5 per cent. of trade organized locally; branch of International Laundry Workers; national secretary, Chas. F. Baily, box 11, Station 1, New York; membership fee, $1.00; monthly dues, 50 cents; members are paid by the hour and week; average wages of members per day, males $2.66, females $1.66; number of working hours per day 9, per week 54; union working under contract with employers entered into March 8, 1910, and expires March 8, 1911; no system of apprenticeship; present secretary, J. E. Flanagan, 361 Valley street, Seattle, Wash.

PAINTERS, DECORATORS AND PAPERHANGERS, SPOKANE LOCAL No. 269—Organized 1895; present membership, 233; not incorporated; 90 per cent. of trade organized locally; branch of P. P. and D. of A.; national secretary, J. C. Skemp, LaFayette, Ind.; membership fee, $25.00; monthly dues, $1.00; sick benefit,

$5.00 per week; accident, $5.00 per week; funeral benefit, $50.00 to $300.00; other benefits, wife's death and total disability benefit; total amount paid out in benefits during past year, $400.00; members are paid by the hour; average wages of members per day, $5.00; number of working hours per day except Saturday 8, Saturday 4, per week 44; 50 to 100 members been idle during past year; aggregate loss of time, 30 to 40 per cent.; not as much idleness during 1909 as 1908; union working under contract with employers entered into April 1, 1910 and will expire April 1, 1911; wages increased $1.50 per day during past five years; decrease in number of working hours, half a day on Saturday; apprentices must sign a contract to serve under same employer for three years; must be under 21 years of age; one apprentice allowed to every 6 men and one to every 10 men thereafter; union involved in no strike during past year; present secretary, G. H. Fleming, 04423 Madison street, Spokane, Wash.

AMALGAMATED SHEET METAL WORKERS, SEATTLE No. 99—Organized 1898; present membership, 135; increase in membership since organization, 100; 90 per cent. of trade organized locally; branch of Amalgamated Sheet Metal Workers' International Alliance; national secretary, J. E. Bray, 325 Nelson Bldg., Kansas City, Mo.; membership fee, $26.00; monthly dues, $1.00; funeral benefit, $100.00; other benefits by donation; total amount paid out in benefits during past year, $800.00; members are paid by the hour; average wages of members per day, $4.00; number of working hours per day except Saturday 8, Saturday 4, per week 44; 15 members idle during past year; aggregate loss of time, 450 days; not as much idleness during 1909 as 1908; union working under no contract with employers; no increase in wages during past five years; no decrease in number of working hours; present secretary, Raymond B. Morrison, 571 Harrison street, Seattle, Wash.

BARBERS' UNION, SEATTLE LOCAL No. 195—Organized 1905; present membership, 270; increase in membership since organization, 200; not incorporated; 50 per cent. of trade organized locally; branch of J. B. I. U. of A.; national secretary, Jacob

Fischer, Indianapolis, Ind.; membership fee, $10.00; monthly
dues, $1.25; sick benefit, $10.00 per week; funeral benefit, $75.00
to $500.00; total amount paid out in benefits during past year,
$600.00; members are paid by the week; average wages per day,
$3.00; number of working hours per day except Saturday 10,
Saturday 14½, per week 64½; 15 members been idle during
past year; aggregate loss of time, 634 weeks; not as much idleness during 1909 as 1908; increase in wages during past five
years, $4.00 per week; decrease in number of working hours
per day, 2; apprentices must serve three years with practical
barber; present secretary, Adolph A. Gierch, 417 Arcade Annex,
Seattle, Wash.

PHOTO-ENGRAVING UNION, SEATTLE—Organized April 10,
1903; present membership, 40; increase in membership since
organization, 33; 100 per cent. of trade organized locally;
branch of International Photo-Engravers' Union; national secretary, L. A. Schwarz, 228 Apsley street, Philadelphia, Penn.;
membership fee, $25.00; dues, $16.00 per year; strike benefit,
$10.00 per week for married members and $7.00 per week for
single members; funeral benefit, $75.00 from international and
$25.00 from local; members usually paid by the week; average
wages, $4.50 per day; number of working hours per day except
Saturday 8, Saturday 8 and 4½; three members idle during
past year; aggregate loss of time, 4 or 5 months; not as much
idleness during 1909 as 1908; members working under contract
with employers made April, 1909, and expires April, 1912;
increase in wages during past five years, $6.00 per week; one
hour per day decrease in number of working hours since organization; one apprentice allowed to four journeymen and two to
seven; apprentices must register with both local and international union and are supposed to work in the one shop until becoming journeymen; union determines the scale of wages; no
strikes during past year; present secretary, Geo. M. Handley,
P. O. box 865, Seattle, Wash.

MINE WORKERS' UNION, FRANKLIN—Organized May, 1907;
present membership, 54; organization is incorporated; branch
of United Mine Workers of America; national secretary, Edwin

Perry, Indianapolis, Ind.; membership fee, $10.00; monthly dues, 75 cents; accident benefit, $1.00 per day; strike benefit, $4.50 per week; funeral benefit, if killed in mine, $600.00; members are paid by piece and by the day; average wages, $4.00 per day; number of working hours per day 8, per week 48; 25 members been idle during past year; aggregate loss of time, three months; more idleness during 1909 than 1908; members working under contract with employers made September 1, 1908, and expires September 1, 1910; 20 per cent. increase in wages during past five years; decrease in number of working hours per day, 2 to 4; no system of apprenticeship; union been involved in no strikes during past year; present secretary, S. B. Potts, Franklin, Wash.

SHINGLE WEAVERS' UNION, BELLINGHAM LOCAL NO. 8—Organized March 28, 1904; present membership, 150; increase in membership since organization, 143; not incorporated; 50 per cent. of trade organized locally; branch of S. W. U. of A.; national secretary, W. E. Willis, 66 Maynard Bldg., Seattle, Wash.; membership fee, $5.00; monthly dues, $1.00; strike benefit, $5.00 per week for single members and $7.00 per week for married members; total amount paid out in benefits during past year, $200.00; members work by day or piece; average wages, $4.00 per day; number of working hours per day 10, per week 60; 100 members idle during past year; about same amount of idleness during 1909 as 1908; 1½ per cent. increase in wages during past five years; no decrease in number of working hours; apprentices must serve two years before being admitted to union; present secretary, Frank Allen, South Bellingham, Wash.

BEER DRIVERS', HELPERS' AND STABLEMEN'S UNION, SEATTLE —Organized 1901; present membership, 93; increase in membership since organization, 63; not incorporated; 100 per cent. of trade organized locally; branch of United Brewery Workers; national secretary, Louis Kemper; membership fee, $10.00; monthly dues, $1.00; strike benefit, $7.00 per week; out-of-work benefit, exemption of dues; other benefits subscribed by members; members are paid by week; average wages, $21.50 per week; number of working hours per day 9, per week 54; 10 members idle during past year; aggregate loss of time, 2 1-4 months; not as much idleness during 1909 as 1908; members working under contract with employers made May 1, 1910, expires April 15, 1918; increase in wages during past five years, $4.50; no decrease in number of working hours; present secretary, Geo. Botly, box 34, Georgetown, Wash.

TYPOGRAPHICAL UNION, TACOMA No. 170—Organized October, 1883; present membership, 139 males, 4 females; not incorporated; 100 per cent. of trade organized locally; branch of International Typographical Union; national secretary, John W. Hays, Indianapolis, Ind.; benefits determined by union; funeral benefit, $75.00; total amount paid out in benefits during past year, $250.00; members are paid by the day; average wages per day, $4.55; number of working hours per day 8, per week 48; five members been idle during past year; aggregate loss of time, 930 days; not as much idleness during 1909 as 1908; increase in wages during past five years, 72 cents per day; have an established system of apprenticeship; no strikes during past year; present secretary, E. J. Leavelle, 208 National Bank of Commerce Bldg., Tacoma, Wash.

PRESS FEEDERS' UNION, TACOMA No. 68—Organized April, 1908; present membership, 17; increase in membership since organization, 5; not incorporated; 75 per cent. of trade organized locally; branch of American Federation of Labor; national secretary, Patrick J. McMullen, Lyric Theatre Bldg., Cincinnati, O.; membership fee, $10.00; monthly dues, $1.00; strike benefit, married members $7.50 per week, single members $5.00 per week; funeral benefit, $100.00; no benefits paid out during past year; members are paid by the hour; average wages, $2.50 per day; number of working hours per day 8, per week 48; one member been idle during past year; not as much idleness during 1909 as 1908; union is not working under contract with employers; increase in wages during past five years, $1.50 per week; apprentices must serve from 2 to 2½ years; one apprentice allowed to every four journeymen or fraction thereof; present secretary, Carl C. Bell, 3122 South Ninth street, Tacoma, Wash.

LUMBER HANDLERS' UNION, BELLINGHAM LOCAL No. 38—Organized March 3, 1902; present membership, 45; increase in membership since organization, 20; not incorporated; 100 per cent. of trade organized locally; branch of International Longshoremen's Association; national secretary, J. J. Joyce, Mutual Life Bldg., Buffalo, N. Y.; membership fee, $50.00; monthly dues, 50 cents; funeral benefit, $75.00; other benefits by special assessments; total amount paid out in benefits during past year, $397.45; members are paid by the hour; average wages, 50 cents per hour; number of working hours per day 9, per week 54; 90 per cent. of members been idle during past year; more idleness during 1909 than 1908; union working under no contract with employers; 10 cents per hour increase in wages during past five years; an apprentice must be a competent lumber stower before being admitted to. union; present secretary, Sidney R. Lines, 1309 Easton avenue, South Bellingham, Wash.

CARPENTERS AND JOINERS, TACOMA LOCAL No. 470—Organized 1900; present membership, 468; increase in membership since organization, 443; not incorporated; 55 per cent. of trade organized locally; branch of United Brotherhood of Carpenters and Joiners; national secretary, Frank Duffy, Carpenters' Bldg., Indianapolis, Ind.; membership fee, $7.50; monthly dues, $1.00; sick benefit, $3.50 per week; total disability benefit, $400.00; strike benefit, 33 1-3 per cent. of wages; funeral benefit, $200.00; total amount paid out in benefits during past year, $685.00; members are paid by the hour; average wages per day, $4.00; number of working hours per day except Saturday 8, Saturday 4, per week 44; from 10 to 40 per cent. of members idle during past year; not as much idleness during 1909 as 1908; wages have increased 40 cents per day during past five years; apprentices receive the first year two-fifths of scale, second year three-fifths, third year four-fifths; present secretary, F. H. Roblee, P. O. box 1204, Tacoma, Wash.

STAGE EMPLOYEES, TACOMA LOCAL No. 81—Organized January 15, 1901; present membership, 26; increase in membership since organization, 11; not incorporated; 100 per cent. of trade organized locally; branch of the Theatre Stage Employees' International Alliance of United States and Canada; national secretary, Lee M. Hart, State Hotel, Chicago, Ill.; membership fee, $25.00; monthly dues, 75 cents; members are usually paid by the week; average wages, $20.00 to $27.50 per week; number of working hours per day, 8; no members been idle during past year; not as much idleness during 1909 as 1908; union working under contract with employers made September 11, 1909, and expires September 1, 1910; wages increased in the past five years 15 per cent.; present secretary, H. A. Sullivan, Grand Theatre, Tacoma, Wash.

COOKS AND KITCHEN HELPERS, SPOKANE LOCAL NO. 450—Organized October 6, 1902; present membership, 438; increase in membership since organization, 375; not incorporated; branch of Hotel and Restaurant Employees' International Association; national secretary, J. L. Sullivan, Cincinnati, O.; membership fee, $10.00; monthly dues, $1.00; sick benefit, $7.00 per week; strike benefit, $7.00 per week; funeral benefit, $100.00; members are paid by the week and month; average wages, $3.25 per day; number of working hours per day 10 and 12, per week 70 to 84; one-third of the members been more or less idle during past year; not as much idleness during 1909 as 1908; union working under contract with employers made May 11, 1910, and expires May 1, 1911; 15 per cent. increase in wages during past five years; 1 hour decrease in number of working hours; no system of apprenticeship; union involved in one strike during past year (for details see chapter on strikes); present secretary, Gus Palmer, 108½ Howard street, Spokane, Wash.

FISHERMEN'S UNION, SEATTLE—Organized 1902; present membership, 300; not incorporated; branch of International Seamen's Union of America; national secretary, Wm. H. Frazier, 1½ A Lewis street, Boston, Mass.; membership fee, $5.00; dues, $5.00 per year; funeral benefit, $75.00; shipwreck benefit, $30.00; members are paid by the piece and by the month; average wages, $1.66; union works under contract which is made at the beginning of every fishing season; union never had a strike; agent, Fred Swanson, box 42, Seattle, Wash.

MOULDERS' UNION, SEATTLE, No. 158—Organized 1886; present membership, 100; not incorporated; branch of I. M. U. of N. A.; national secretary, Victor Kleiber, box 699, Cincinnati, O.; membership fee, $5.00; dues, 40 cents per week; sick benefit, $5.40 per week; accident benefit, same; strike benefit, $7.00 per week; out-of-work benefit, dues for 13 weeks; funeral benefit, $100.00 to $175.00; members are paid by the day; wages, from $3.56 to $4.00 per day; number of working hours per day 8 and 9, per week 48 and 54; not as much idleness during 1909 as 1908; union working under no contract with employers; 10 per cent. increase in wages during past five years; one apprentice allowed to five journeymen; union involved in one strike during past year (for details see chapter on strikes); present secretary, J. H. Blankley, 122 Twentieth avenue, Seattle, Wash.

SAILORS' UNION OF THE PACIFIC, SEATTLE—Organized March 6, 1885; present membership, 5,000; not incorporated; branch of International Seamen's Union of America; national secretary, W. H. Frazier, 1½ Lewis street, Boston, Mass.; membership fee, $5.00; monthly dues, 75 cents; shipwreck benefit, $50.00; strike benefit, $5.00 per week; funeral benefit, $75.00; members are paid by the month; average wages of members, $1.66; number of working hours per day 9, per week 54; about the same amount of idleness during 1909 as 1908; members working under contract with employers; increase in wages during past five years, $5.00 per month; no decrease in number of working hours; have no system of apprenticeship, but members making an effort to establish one; union been engaged in no strikes during past year; present secretary, A. Furuseth, San Francisco, Cal.

ELECTRICAL WORKERS, EVERETT, No. 191—Organized July 8, 1901; present membership, 88; increase in membership since organization, 80; not incorporated; 100 per cent. of trade organized locally; branch of International Brotherhood of Electrical Workers; national secretary, J. W. Murphy, Springfield, Ill.; membership fee, $10.00; monthly dues, $1.50; sick benefit, $7.00 per week; accident benefit, $7.00 per week; funeral benefit, $100.00; total amount paid out in benefits during past year, $217.00; members are paid by the day; average wages, $3.80;

number of working hours per day 8, per week 48; same amount of idleness during 1909 as 1908; union working under contract with· employers which expires February 1, 1911; increase in wages during past five years, 75 cents per day; apprentices must serve three years under competent journeyman; must then pass an examination; one apprentice is allowed to four journeymen; union involved in one strike during past year (for details see chapter on strikes); present secretary, R. J. Olinger, Everett, Wash.

SHINGLE WEAVERS' UNION, MONTESANO—Organized April, 1909; present membership, 35; increase in membership since organization, 10; not incorporated; 99 per cent. of trade organized locally; branch of International S. W. U.; national secretary, W. E. Willis, 66 Maynard Bldg., Seattle, Wash.; membership fee, $5.00; monthly dues, $1.00; members are paid by piece and by the day; average wages per day $4.00; number of working hours per·day, 10; 50 per cent. of members been idle during past year; more idleness during 1909 than 1908; members are working under no contract with employers; 12½ per cent. increase in wages during past five years; apprentices admitted to local union upon payment of one-half membership fee and one-half of monthly dues, and local union pays one-half per capita tax on them; present secretary, O. B. Shiane, Montesano, Wash.

STEREOTYPERS' AND ELECTROTYPERS' UNION, SEATTLE—Organized February 17, 1903; present membership, 25; increase in membership since organization, 16; incorporated January, 1902; 100 per cent. of trade organized locally; branch of International S. and E. U.; national secretary, Geo. W. Williams, 29 Globe Bldg., Boston, Mass.; membership fee, $10.00; monthly dues, 40 cents per capita and 1 per cent. of wages; strike benefit, $5.00 per week for single members and $7.00 per week for married members; funeral benefit, $65.00 from international union and $50.00 from local; no benefits paid during past year; members are paid by the week; average wages per day, $4.50; number of working hours per day 8, per week 48; no members idle during past year; union working under contract with employers entered into October, 1909, and expires October, 1910; increase in wages during past five years, $2.00 per day; apprentices must be 21 years of age and must serve five years under competent journeyman; wages per day for first year $1.50, second year $2.00, third year $2.50, fourth year $3.00, and fifth year $3.50; union involved in no strikes during past year; present secretary, L. A. Miller, 4112 Eastern avenue, Seattle, Wash.

MACHINISTS' UNION, SPOKANE—Organized 1900; present membership, 165; 99 per cent. of trade organized locally; branch of International Association of Machinists; national secretary, Geo. Preston, McGill Bldg., Washington D. C.; membership fee, $15.00; monthly dues, $1.75; $8.00 per week from international plus amount determined by local union; out-of-work benefit, $1.75 per week and meal ticket; funeral benefit, $200.00 from international plus amount determined by local union; total amount paid out in benefits during past year, $100.00; members are paid by hour; average wages per day, $3.70; number of working hours per day 9, per week 54; 10 members have been idle during past year; aggregate loss of time, 25,920 hours; not as much idleness during 1909 as 1908; 3½ cents per hour increase in wages during past five years; no decrease in number of working hours; an apprentice must not be under 16 nor over 21 years of age and must serve four years; union involved in one strike during past year (see chapter on strikes); present secretary, N. M. Davis, E. 1515 Joseph avenue, Spokane, Wash.

POLE-RAISERS AND ELECTRICAL ASSISTANTS, SEATTLE—Organized 1907; present membership, 96; increase in membership since organization, 60; branch of A. F. of L.; national secretary, Frank Morrison, Washington, D. C.; membership fee, $1.00, monthly dues, 50 cents; funeral benefit, $1.00 per member; total amount paid out in benefits during past year, $60.00; members are paid by the day; average wages per day, $2.75; number of working hours per day 8, per week 48; very few members been idle during past year; not as much idleness during 1909 as

—6

1908; union is working under no contract with employers; 75· cents per day increase in wages during past five years; one hour decrease in number of working hours; no established system of apprenticeship; no strikes during past year; present secretary, J. H. Frost, 1722 Boren avenue, Seattle, Wash.

SUGGESTIONS FROM WAGE-EARNERS.

The following suggestions and comments relating to labor conditions have been prepared for publication in this report by members of various trades organizations. They are presented without comment, it being the purpose to give free scope to the various writers for the expression of their respective views.

MACHINIST, TACOMA—" I would like to see all wage-earners. get an eight-hour day."

PRINTER, OLYMPIA—"Sanitary and pleasant surroundings for those whose work requires them to work within doors."

MILL HAND, EVERETT—"An eight-hour work day is enough for any common or mechanical workman."

BREWER, ABERDEEN—"Employers should be responsible for any injury received during working hours."

ENGINEER, SEATTLE—"More justice in personal injury cases, less abuse of the injunction process."

LINEMAN, SEATTLE—"The most important question confronting the wage-earner today is to increase the purchasing power of his wages."

PRESSMAN, SEATTLE—"Crush monopoly rule and politics in the state. Equal rights to the laborer as well as to the unemployed rich. Cut out all middlemen's profits."

CARPENTER, BELLINGHAM—"Times are very quiet in Bellingham. Two-thirds of our members have left the city to find. work, and the few that are here work only half the time."

CARPENTER, GEORGETOWN—"A workingman not working steady cannot save money at four dollars and fifty cents per day. If a few more trusts were formed, a workingman could not save on a six-dollar scale."

WIREMAN, TACOMA—"Equal pay for equal labor for women and girls. Eight-hour law for all laboring men and women. Weekly pay in cash instead of by check, so that it will not be necessary to cash checks at saloons."

WIREMAN, TACOMA—"Direct election of senators and judges by the people, with the initiative and recall. National and state eight-hour law. Attention to employers' liability law."

WAITRESS, SEATTLE—"I am of the opinion that eight hours should constitute a day for women wage-earners, as a woman always has household duties to perform after her day's labors are over."

CARPENTER, TACOMA—"1909 was a good year for myself. In 1908 I lost four months straight. 1910 has been good so far. As a general rule I get in ten or eleven months a year."

CARPENTER, ABERDEEN—"Tradesmen who do not work for a factory get higher wages than those in the factory, but lose at least fifteen per cent. of the time on account of bad weather or between jobs."

MILL HAND, EVERETT—"Some mills here run ten or eleven months per year, while others run five or six. They average about eight months. If the mills would run on an eight-hour day and run more steadily, it would be better for all concerned."

LAUNDRY WORKER, SEATTLE—"Our Laundry Workers' International Union has a membership of about fifty, and expect and hope to have it doubled before long. Working girls are slow to join, but I think they will soon see where it will be a great benefit to them and we will get them all."

LINEMAN, SEATTLE—"The greatest problem confronting the wage-earners of today is the perfecting of a system whereby the wage-earners who are the consumers can purchase their supplies direct from the producer, thereby increasing the purchasing power of their wages."

CARPENTER, EVERETT—"The federal government should cut off all immigration from foreign countries and furnish employment for unemployed American citizens. By confiscation or taxation the amount of idle land should be reduced and furnished to any *bona fide* occupant at no cost but improvements."

PRINTER, OLYMPIA—"The proper sanitation both of workshops and of houses that are rented is neglected. I presume that the state has authority over the shops, but there should be an inspection of houses. I think the state should maintain employment offices. In trades with strong unions it is unnecessary, but for men not organized it would help."

SALESMAN, TACOMA—"Salespeople in the Pacific Northwest are very poorly paid. The hours are bad and holidays are few and far between. The larger part of the stores keep open so late Saturday night that it makes two days' work instead of one. The ordinary salesman spends the most of what he earns."

TEAMSTER, RAVENSDALE—"The company store is a great drawback here to the employees. Most of them cannot purchase elsewhere on account of being in debt to the store. The company can charge any price they see fit, as the employees have not money to purchase anywhere else. I would suggest that all company stores be abolished."

CIGARMAKER, SEATTLE—"Only the abolition of wage slavery can benefit the human beings called 'wage-earners.' This can be done through a revolutionary organization based upon solidarity. And when the wage-earners once understand that it is they who produce all the necessary and luxurious articles in existence, then they will come to the conclusion that all these things should belong to the workers. They will take possession through a general strike. That means stop working for their exploiters and establish perfect freedom for the human race."

STRIKES AND LOCKOUTS.

STRIKES AND LOCKOUTS.

Cooks and Waiters, Tacoma.

On February 18, 1910, a strike was declared by the above union, involving 15 employees and one restaurant. The strike originated as a result of an effort on the part of the management of the restaurant to establish the open shop principle. At the expiration of thirty days, a change occurred in the management of the restaurant and an agreement satisfactory to the union was drawn up and signed. No request for outside assistance was made on behalf of those engaged in the strike and none was received. The union officers estimate a total loss in wages during the progress of the strike amounting to $600.00.

Pile Drivers and Bridge Workers, Seattle.

On the 6th day of May, 1910, a strike was declared by the above unions, involving 230 men and 10 employing firms. The demand of the union was for a decrease of one hour in the working day without any reduction in wages. The companies refused to grant the demands and at once proceeded to employ strikebreakers in the places of their former employees. The latter being unable to maintain a prolonged struggle, returned to work at the expiration of 17 days on the old basis. No outside assistance was received in conducting this strike, and the union officers estimate that the total loss in wages exceeded $15.000.00.

Elevator Constructors' Union, Seattle.

On May 1st, 1909, a strike was declared by the above union, involving 35 men and 5 employing firms. The strike resulted from an unsuccessful effort to secure the adoption and signing of a working agreement between the employers and the men. The strike continued for a period of three weeks, being settled by an agreement satisfactory to both sides. No outside assistance was received in the conduct of this strike and the amount lost in wages to employees is estimated at $2,500.00.

United Mine Workers, Wilkeson.

On November 9th, 1907, a strike was declared by the above organization against the Wilkeson Coal & Coke Company. The cause of the strike was a demand on the part of the union for an eight-hour day and recognition of the union. The strike continued until August 25th, 1909, when it was called off by the organization. On June 12, 1910, the company formally recognized the jurisdiction of the United Mine Workers of America. There were 325 men involved in the strike, and it is estimated by the union that the loss to employees in wages amounted to $250,000.00. Assistance from the organization was rendered during the progress of the strike to the extent of $85,000.00.

Longshoremen's Union, Eagle Harbor.

On the 21st day of May, 1910, a strike was declared by the Longshoremen's Union at Eagle Harbor against the Pacific Creosoting Company. The strike resulted from an effort on the part of the employers to establish an open-shop system. A total of 14 men were involved in the strike, which has not yet been settled. No outside assistance has been received in conducting this strike.

Cooks and Waiters, Spokane.

On May 11, 1910, a strike was declared by the Cooks', Waiters' and Waitresses' Unions of Spokane, involving 700 persons and 105 restaurants. This strike was the result of a demand on the part of the unions for one day's rest out of each week at the same wages previously allowed for seven full days' work. The unions state that a system had been formulated whereby sufficient help could be supplied to all restaurants and still admit of every employee having one day off each week. The employers declined to accede to the above demand, and the strike which followed had not been settled up to September 1st, 1910, although some employers granted demands. No outside assistance was received by the union, and it is estimated that the money loss to employees has totalled $8,000.00.

Iron Moulders, Seattle.

The strike of iron moulders at Seattle, which was begun May 1st, 1907, was declared off in January, 1909. This prolonged struggle was undertaken for the purpose of establishing an eight-hour day. The unions state that about fifty per cent. of the firms involved, of which there was a total of fifteen, have granted an eight-hour day. A total of 217 men were involved in the strike.

Machinists' Union, Spokane.

On June 29th, 1910, a strike was declared by the Machinists' Union of Spokane, involving about 60 men and 5 employing firms. The cause of the strike was a demand for an eight-hour day for the same compensation previously paid for nine hours. Up to September 1, 1910, no settlement of the strike had been made

COMPULSORY ARBITRATION.

COMPULSORY ARBITRATION.

Consideration is again asked of the legislature for proper legislation upon the above subject. It has long since been established as a fact that the greatest sufferer from all labor disturbances is the innocent public. An entire city may be discommoded and practically every inhabitant made to suffer substantial financial loss through a tie-up of transportation facilities or some other difficulty originating in differences between employers and employees. Irrespective of the merits of such disputes, it is coming more and more to be recognized that the public welfare should not be permitted to suffer therefrom

To secure needed protection for the public's interest in such disturbances, it is essential that the state's authority be exercised, in-so-far as may be done without undue interference with individual and corporate rights. There is no doubt that such authority can be extended at least to an investigation of the merits of important labor disputes, and a determination as to the justice of the contentions of the respective parties involved. An opinion of this character, given by a board of unbiased arbitrators, formed under legislative enactment, though it might lack the force of a judicial decision, would exercise an important influence in securing terms of settlement, fair and reasonable to all parties concerned. Supported by a public sentiment which undoubtedly would be created as the result of their investigations and deliberations, such a board as is above suggested would be instrumental in securing a peaceful settlement of a large percentage of all labor disputes.

Moreover, general conditions in the industrial world seem favorable to the adoption of some such plan of arbitration as above outlined. Labor and capital alike are coming to realize and appreciate their mutual dependence upon each other. Employers as a whole are treating their wage earners with more

consideration.   They are taking more interest in providing
healthful and sanitary surroundings in their work shops and
in supplying rest and recreation rooms for the use of employees
during their leisure hours.   It is also noticeable that wage-earners as a class are manifesting a disposition to be more conservative in their demands and to select men of judgment and
reason as their leaders.   In fact, there is reason for belief that
both sides to the labor question are becoming more and more
seriously interested in ways and means of maintaining industrial
peace.

That a state arbitration board such as is herein proposed
would exert an important influence in the same direction is not
to be doubted.   In most cases it should act as a preventive
of strikes and similar difficulties, and in case of their actual occurrence would provide the public with an authoritative and
unprejudiced opinion as to all matters at issue.

In the Dominion of Canada and elsewhere this method of arbitration has been found to work out very satisfactorily and
the adoption of the same system in this state would place Washington in line with other commonwealths which are in the lead
in the matter of advanced labor legislation.

Eight-Hour Law for Public Works.

EIGHT-HOUR LAW FOR PUBLIC WORKS.

Perhaps no labor law now on the statutes of this state is subject to more frequent violation than the above. Several causes may be assigned in explanation of this condition, but it is chiefly due to the following: First, to the small minimum fine permitted to be assessed under the law, and, second, to the fact that in a great many communities in the state public sentiment is against the enforcement of the law, and it becomes a matter of extreme difficulty to secure a jury which will bring in a conviction when cases are brought to trial, and contractors desire to increase their profits.

During the summer of 1910, so many contractors employed at public work throughout the state were found to be violating the law that it became necessary to institute a number of prosecutions in order to prevent the law becoming a dead letter. At the same time a general notice was circulated through the press as follows:

OFFICE OF STATE LABOR COMMISSIONER.

OLYMPIA, WASHINGTON, August 19, 1910.

I desire to announce through the press that inasmuch as there is a constant violation of the state eight-hour law on public work by county, state and city contractors throughout the state, hereafter no previous notice will be given contractors to cease this violation, but that prosecution will follow every case of this kind reported to this office with sufficient evidence.

This is a Federal law, and also the law in nearly all states throughout this country, and will be enforced in this state.

CHARLES F. HUBBARD,
State Labor Commissioner.

This law has been thoroughly tried out in the courts and every technicality has been resorted to, to evade and overcome its provisions, but it has stood the test and is firmly established as a part of the public policy of the state. The prospects of increased profits leads to the violation of the law in some cases,

—7

but with a heavier penalty fixed for such infractions, the number
would be greatly reduced.

In addition to the violations of the law herein reported, several
cases were pending at the time of the completion of this report.

Seattle.

On March 17, 1909, a complaint was received charging violation of eight-hour law in connection with the construction of
the new Cedar river pipe line supplying water for the city of
Seattle. The matter was taken up with the board of public
works of Seattle and immediate compliance with the law was
secured.

On march 25, 1909, a complaint was received charging violation of the eight-hour law in connection with state contract
work at the A.-Y.-P. Exposition in Seattle. The matter was
taken up with the state commissioners and the work completed
on the eight-hour basis.

Bellingham.

During the month of September, 1909, a complaint was received charging violation of the eight-hour law in connection
with street work in the city of Bellingham. The case was investigated and settled without prosecution, the contractor signing
an agreement to comply with the law.

Wenatchee.

On October 6, 1909, a complaint was filed charging violation
of the eight-hour law in connection with certain street improvement work then being carried on in the city of Wenatchee. The
charges appearing to be well founded, the commissioner visited
Wenatchee and conferred with the contractors and the city
officials. As a result of this conference, the contractors agreed
to complete the work under the eight-hour basis. This agreement was carried out, but a reduction was made in the wages
paid to correspond with the decrease in the number of working
hours. The men declined to accept the reduction and a strike
was declared. After a few days of idleness, the contractors
agreed to restore the former wage scale for an eight-hour day,
and the work was completed on that basis.

Vancouver.

On January 10, 1910, a complaint was received charging violation of the eight-hour law in connection with certain street-paving work then in progress in the city of Vancouver. The evidence in the case being weak and the prosecuting attorney not being desirous of proceeding on same, no prosecution followed. Later on a complaint was again filed from Vancouver alleging a similar violation of the law. Difficulty was again experienced in securing sufficient evidence, and on the agreement of the contractor to comply strictly with the law in the future, no further proceedings were taken.

Tacoma.

On February 25, 1910, a complaint was received charging violation of the eight-hour law in the street-cleaning department in the city of Tacoma. Inasmuch as a doubt seemed to exist as to whether the law covered this class of work, the matter was submitted to the attorney general for an opinion, as set forth, in the following correspondence:

OLYMPIA, WASHINGTON, March 22, 1910.

Hon. W. P. Bell, Attorney General, Olympia, Washington:

DEAR SIR—I desire your written decision on the "State Eight-Hour Law."

Does the present law include all employees employed in any capacity by the state, county and cities in this state?

The question in view is to ascertain if laborers employed by the city of Tacoma in cleaning streets come within the meaning of the eight-hour day, the complaint having come to me that these laborers are being worked to exceed eight hours a calendar day.

Respectfully,

CHARLES F. HUBBARD,

State Labor Commissioner.

OLYMPIA, WASH., April 26, 1910.

Hon. C. F. Hubbard, Labor Commissioner, Olympia, Washington:

DEAR SIR—Yours of the 22d inst. received, which reads as follows:

"I desire your written decision on the 'State Eight-Hour Law.'

"Does the present law include all employees employed in any capacity by the state, counties and cities in this state?

"The question in view is to ascertain if laborers employed by the city of Tacoma in cleaning streets come within the meaning of the eight-hour day, the complaint having come to me that these laborers are being worked to exceed eight hours a calendar day."

Sec. 5978g of Pierce's Code reads in part as follows:

"That it is a part of the public policy of the state of Washington that all work 'by contract or day labor done' for it or any political subdivision created by its laws shall be performed in work days of not more than eight hours each, except in cases of extraordinary emergency. * * * "

There is no room for construction in the law above quoted, unless it be the words "or day labor done." This might be construed that it was the intention of the legislature to limit a day's work to eight hours where the party was employed and paid by the day; and some courts have given similar expressions such a construction, and have made a distinction in such matters between persons who were paid by the month and those paid by the day, but in construing this law, in connection with the other provisions concerning the employment of labor, I believe that the distinction as to the time of making payment for the labor is too technical, and that in any work done for the public, as designated in said section, eight hours should be counted as a day's work, whether the person was employed on a contract or in general work for the state or political subdivision thereof.

Yours very respectfully,

W. P. Bell,
Attorney General.

In compliance with the foregoing opinion, notice was given that the law would be strictly enforced in the street departments of all the cities of the state, since which time no complaints of the above character have been received.

On April 30, 1910, a complaint was received charging violation of the eight-hour law in connection with the construction of the stadium building at Tacoma. The case was taken up with the prosecuting attorney, and after a conference with the contractor in charge of the work prosecution was dropped on the agreement of the contractor to complete the work on the eight-hour basis.

Monroe.

On May 20, 1910, a complaint was received charging violation of the eight-hour law in connection with the construction of a school building at Monroe. The case was reported by this office to the prosecuting attorney, who secured compliance with the law without prosecution.

Coupeville.

On June 16, 1910, a complaint was received charging violation of the eight-hour law in connection with the construction of a safe in the court house at Coupeville. On advice from this office, the contractor was arrested and brought to trial, but by reason of public sentiment being against the enforcement of the law, an acquittal resulted. A second charge was brought against the same party but before a hearing was reached he left the town and the case against him is still pending.

Chehalis.

On June 25, 1910, a complaint was filed charging violation of the eight-hour law in connection with the construction of a school building then under construction in the city of Chehalis. The case was taken up with the prosecuting attorney, and on the 30th of the month the contractor established the eight-hour day on the work. Prosecution was thereupon dropped.

Seattle.

On June 25, 1910, a complaint was received charging violation of the eight-hour law in connection with certain street work then in progress in the city of Seattle. The matter was referred to the board of public works of Seattle for adjustment.

Anacortes.

On July 9th, 1910, a complaint was received charging violation of the eight-hour law in connection with street work then in progress in the city of Anacortes. The matter was taken up with the prosecuting attorney, and compliance with the law secured without resort to prosecution.

Bothell.

On July 25, 1910, a complaint was received charging violation of the eight-hour law at Bothell, in King county. The commissioner took the matter up with the mayor of the town, but on investigation no evidence was forthcoming to substantiate the charges and the case was dropped.

State Road Work.

On August 10, 1910, a complaint was received charging violation of the eight-hour law in connection with the construction of a state road near Seattle. Owing to insufficiency of the evidence, the case was not carried to a prosecution.

Hoquiam.

On August 20, 1910, a complaint was received charging violation of the eight-hour law in connection with the construction of a state road near Hoquiam. Investigation showed that the charges were well grounded, and a warrant for the contractor in charge of the work was secured. The case came to trial on September 1, and a conviction and fine of $25 and costs was secured.

Bellingham.

On August 29, 1910, a complaint was received charging violation of the eight-hour law at Bellingham in connection with a street-paving contract. The commissioner went to Bellingham on September 1st and a conference was held with the mayor, the prosecuting attorney, and the offending contractor also present. An agreement was reached whereby the contractor agreed to comply with the law and the case was dropped. Another case was reported at the same time, but no evidence in support of the charges was secured.

Silver Lake.

On September 8, 1910, a complaint was received charging violation of the eight-hour law at Silver Lake in connection with a state road contract. The case was taken up with the prosecuting attorney, but, as no evidence sufficient to secure a conviction was forthcoming, no arrests were made.

Tacoma.

On September 21, 1910, a complaint was received charging violation of the eight-hour law in connection with certain bridge construction work then in progress in the city of Tacoma. The evidence in the case being conclusive, a warrant was issued for the arrest of the foreman in charge of the work. The trial occurred in the justice's court and a conviction and fine of $25.00 and costs secured.

Raymond.

On September 27, 1910, a complaint was filed charging violation of the eight-hour law in connection with the construction of a school house in the town of Raymond, in Pacific county. Investigation of the case having shown that the charges were well grounded, prosecution followed and a conviction and fine secured.

Ventilation of Printing Offices.

VENTILATION OF PRINTING OFFICES.

During the summer of 1908 the attention of the department was called to certain unhealthy conditions which prevailed generally in the mechanical departments of the large newspaper offices of the state. Such conditions arose from the operation of linotype machines, which are an important part of the equipment of all the daily papers. Each of these machines is provided with a melting pot in which a quantity of metal, composed chiefly of lead, antimony and tin, is maintained constantly in a molten state, a gas flame usually being used for that purpose. The fumes arising therefrom are not only exceedingly annoying to the operators and others employed about the machines, but unhealthy as well, especially in poorly ventilated rooms.

The above facts having been ascertained through personal inspection of the different establishments, a remedy for the conditions complained of was sought. It was found that the objectionable fumes could be carried off by means of flues leading from the melting pots through the roof or side of the building, and the various newspaper proprietors were requested to provide their linotype rooms with the necessary equipment for this purpose. After some delays the newspapers in the cities of Seattle, Spokane, Bellingham and Everett complied with the requirements of the department, and both employers and employees have since expressed their general satisfaction with the apparatus installed.

The Typographical Union extended a vote of thanks to the commissioner for his efforts in the above connection.

Complaints of Wage-Earners.

COMPLAINTS OF WAGE-EARNERS.

In addition to the regular duties required by law to be performed by this department, and which, under appropriate headings, are discussed at length in this report, numerous requests are received for the adjustment of difficulties arising between individual wage-earners and their employers. Such complaints arise from a number of different causes, an enumeration of the more important of which will be helpful as a means of informing the public with reference to some of the abuses to which laboring men, particularly those who do not belong to the organized crafts, are subjected at the hands of unscrupulous employers.

A frequent cause of complaint is found in excessive charges for hospital fees, with no adequate accommodations provided when the men become sick or injured. The fees are held out of the wages on pay day and where a large number of men are employed amount to a considerable sum, yet cases arise where practically no hospital provisions of any nature are made.

Another abuse is a charge often assessed against employees for the use of springs and mattresses in sleeping quarters. The beds may be of the cheapest kind and have stood the wear and tear of long service, yet a charge of $2.50 to $4.50 will be made for their use, even though the employee has used them but a fraction of a month and furnished his own blankets. In this way the original cost may be returned to the employer several times over, in the course of a single year.

Discrimination against wage-earners on account of their membership in labor unions is by no means infrequent, although this is one of the most difficult kinds of abuse to prove.

Unnecessary delay and inconvenience in securing wages due when men leave their employment or are discharged gives rise to numberless complaints, many employers and foremen taking this means of "getting even" with men who have earned their ill-will.

The food provided in camps where the men are forced to take their meals at the company boarding-house is often of the poorest quality and wretchedly cooked. Charges are invariably made sufficient to enable the employer to furnish substantial meals properly prepared, yet in their greed for a little extra profit it often occurs that the food served is almost unfit for human consumption. Complaints of the above nature come most frequently from railroad and state road camps.

Various other grievances brought to the attention of the department include requirement on the part of employers for a full seven-day week, Sunday being regarded as any other work day; also frequent disagreements as to the rate of pay, employers refusing to give the amounts guaranteed by the employment agencies. Hiring men for one class of work and putting them at something more arduous is of common occurrence, as is also the custom of holding the blankets and clothing of men until employment agencies' fees and transportation are worked out, often at a less rate of pay than was originally agreed upon.

The foregoing and other complaints, some of which have been referred to elsewhere, will afford a fair idea of the disadvantages which confront the man who is seeking a job and is unfortunate enough to fall into the hands of an unscrupulous employer or employing agent. Fortunately, the number of men who are willing to take such unfair advantages is relatively small. Most employers treat their men fairly, and it is a very small minority only that practice the abuses brought out in this article. Many of such abuses cannot be brought within the reach of existing laws, but whenever complaints are reported it is the policy of this department to investigate and secure the best possible adjustment. With the adoption of somewhat more stringent legislation, as is elsewhere recommended in this report, the number of such complaints would doubtless be greatly lessened.

EMPLOYMENT OF WOMEN.

EMPLOYMENT OF WOMEN.

The commissioner of labor shall appoint one female as assistant commissioner of labor, and such female assistant shall have charge, under the direction of the commissioner of labor, of the enforcement of all laws relating to the health, sanitary conditions, surroundings, hours of labor and all other laws affecting the employment of female wage-earners. She shall receive a salary of twelve hundred dollars per annum, and shall be allowed her actual and necessary expenses in the performance of her duties as such assistant. Such salary and expenses to be paid in the same manner as other expenses of the office of commissioner of labor. (Laws of Wash. 1909, Ch. 227).

In accordance with the above law, Mrs. B. H. Mason, of Seattle was appointed to the position, assuming her duties in June, 1909. A report of her work is as follows:

OLYMPIA, October 1, 1910.

Hon. C. F. Hubbard, State Commissioner of Labor, Olympia, Wash.:

SIR—In compliance with your request, I submit the following brief summary of work as your assistant in the new department for women and children in the Labor bureau of this state.

Beginning work in June of last year, I have at present writing visited all the principal cities of the state and many of the smaller ones. Fourteen counties are represented in the statistical report which follows. As the department was a new one, my work has assumed more of the constructive and educational than the aggressive. It has seemed wise to act on the premise that in cases where state laws affecting women and children were not observed, it was in large measure a matter of ignorance of the laws and not of wilful intent to violate. In consequence, my first inspections have involved the notification of all employers of female and child labor of the state laws relating to such classes of labor, and advising them that hereafter a most careful supervision and enforcement of the laws affecting them would occur. It is gratifying to report that I have been met with courtesy and the information sought has been freely supplied. Suggestions and corrections offered have been kindly received and in numerous cases acted upon at once.

The health officers of the cities visited have co-operated and lent their aid in every possible way, many times accompanying me, and thus correcting immediately some damp or unwholesome workshop or filthy toilet accommodation.

—8

No state provision is yet made for separate toilets, wash or dressing rooms for women employees, and no cities save Seattle, Spokane and North Yakima were provided with such local ordinances.

A report was, therefore, made to all health officers of places visited that were without these sanitary conveniences for the women employees, with the result that Tacoma, Bellingham, and Hoquiam have sent in copies of such local ordinances passed during the year.

It has been observed by your assistant that the long 10-hour day is inflicting an injury on the working women of the state. Since there is no minimum of hours stipulated by the law for a week's work, many of them work 70 hours, and are therefore, deprived of that leisure which is an essential element of healthy living, self-help and self-education.

The girls employed in drug stores, confectionery, and ice cream parlors and in many restaurants work the seven full days. In places where shorter working hours are observed it is usually accomplished through organization of the workers themselves, thus proving conclusively that as men through organization secure for themselves shorter hours, better wages and improved sanitary conditions, so women workers must use the same weapon to accomplish like results.

The physical structure of woman and her special functions make the protection of her health a matter for public concern, and justifies the special legislation which is designed to compensate for some of the burdens which rest upon her.

This department most earnestly recommends an eight-hour day, and a six-day week for all women wage-earners.

CHILD LABOR.

The new labor law providing that no girl under 16 be employed without special permit by a superior court judge is becoming generally known and observed. We trust the educational limit will be raised to that age, and thus the school life of both boys, and girls be prolonged. The two years between 14 and 16, while almost useless for industrial purposes, are most valuable for educational purposes and assures them of greater industrial efficiency in the future.

This department would also urge the re-enactment of the "Messenger Service Law," which for two years successfully restricted employment of young boys in messenger and telegraph service. No provision is made for these boys in the idle hours, and loafing, tobacco and cigarette habits, together with irregular meals and hours, so soon cause them to deteriorate in health and morals as to make their future a subject of deep concern to all public-spirited citizens, and legislation in their interest an imperative necessity.

The attention of this department has been called to the large number of young lads of 7 to 10 years engaged in street traffic in the larger cities of the state. The authority of this department does not extend to these children as they are recognized by the courts as "street merchants," and require special ordinance or legislation. New

York, Boston, Cincinnati and Milwaukee have passed ordinances regulating the work of children in the street trades. These laws forbid boys under 12 and girls under 16 from engaging in any street trade, while boys between 12 and 16 must secure permits and wear badges. We recommend to the larger cities of the state similar laws for the protection of these children.

In conclusion, I wish to acknowledge the aid extended by the chief of this department in the effort made to serve the best interests of the working-women and children of the state, a class of laborers to whom any government must stand peculiarly related.

Respectfully submitted,

BLANCHE H. MASON,

Assistant State Labor Commissioner.

The accompanying tables will indicate the different cities in which this inspection work has been carried on, the various classes of establishments investigated and some insight into the conditions found in each. The results of the reinspection work will not be available for use in the present report. The following tables are made from reports of each place inspected.

TABLE NO. 1—STATISTICS OF ESTABLISHMENTS EMPLOYING FEMALE LABOR.

CHEHALIS COUNTY.

Town or City	Kind of Establishment	Number females empolyed	Hours per day	Wages per day	Sanitary conditions
Aberdeen	General merchandise	6	9	$1 75	Fair
Aberdeen	General merchandise	4	9	1 75	Very good
Aberdeen	General merchandise	1	8	1 00	Fair
Aberdeen	General merchandise	2	9	1 00	Very poor
Aberdeen	General merchandise	1	9	2 50	Fair
Aberdeen	General merchandise	22	9	2 00	Very poor
Aberdeen	General merchandise	6	9	1 50	Very good
Aberdeen	General merchandise	2	9	1 50	Fair
Aberdeen	General merchandise	16	9	2 00	Very good
Hoquiam	General merchandise	2	9	1 42	Very poor
Hoquiam	General merchandise	3	9	1 50	Very poor
Hoquiam	General merchandise	1	9	85	Very good
Hoquiam	General merchandise	1	9	1 50	Fair
Hoquiam	General merchandise	3	9	2 25	Very poor
Aberdeen	Laundry	20	9	1 60	Fair
Aberdeen	Laundry	6	9	1 75	Very poor
Aberdeen	Laundry	21	10	1 50	Fair
Hoquiam	Laundry	22	10	1 60	Very good
Hoquiam	Laundry	15	10	1 65	Very poor
Hoquiam	Factory (box)	35	10	1 50	Very poor
Aberdeen	Lumber	1	8½	3 33½	Fair
Aberdeen	Lumber	1	8	2 75	Very good
Aberdeen	Hairdressing, etc.	1	9	2 33½	Very good
Aberdeen	Tailor	2	9	1 50	Very good
Aberdeen	Confectionery	1	9	83½	Fair
Aberdeen	Confectionery	1	9	2 00	Fair
Aberdeen	Confectionery	1	9	1 66½	Fair
Aberdeen	Confectionery	2	9	1 50	Very poor
Hoquiam	Confectionery	1	9	1 58	Fair
Aberdeen	Telephone	15	8	1 15	Fair
Aberdeen	Telegraph	1	9	1 35	Fair
Hoquiam	Telephone	6	8	1 25	Very good
Aberdeen	Printers	2	8	2 50	Very good
Aberdeen	Printers	2	8	2 50	Very good
Aberdeen	Meat company	1	9	2 00	Fair
Aberdeen	Real estate	1	8	1 60	Fair
Aberdeen	Bankers	1	8	3 00	Fair
Aberdeen	Restaurant	16	10	1 50	Very good
Hoquiam	Restaurant	7	10	1 25	Very good
Aberdeen	Dye works	5	9	1 75	Very good
Aberdeen	Cigar factory	3	8	1 66½	Very poor
Aberdeen	Cannery	15	8	1 75	Fair

CHELAN COUNTY.

Town or City	Kind of Establishment	Number females empolyed	Hours per day	Wages per day	Sanitary conditions
Wenatchee	General merchandise	1	10	$2 50	Very poor
Wenatchee	General merchandise	5	9	3 00	Fair
Wenatchee	General merchandise	1	9	1 88	Very poor
Wenatchee	General merchandise	2		3 00	Very good
Wenatchee	General merchandise	1	9	1 65	Very poor
Wenatchee	General merchandise	10	9	2 00	Very poor
Wenatchee	General merchandise	2	9	1 50	Very poor
Wenatchee	General merchandise	2	9	2 00	Very poor
Wenatchee	General merchandise	10	9	1 75	Fair
Wenatchee	General merchandise	2	9	1 50	Very poor
Wenatchee	General merchandise	2	8	2 25	Very poor
Wenatchee	Confectionery	1	10	2 00	Very poor
Wenatchee	Confectionery	3	10	1 16	Fair
Wenatchee	Confectionery	3	9	1 50	Very good
Wenatchee	Bakery	1	10	1 15	Fair
Wenatchee	County treasurer	5	8	2 45	Very good
Wenatchee	County auditor	2	8	2 25	Very good
Wenatchee	Abstract company	4	8	2 35	Fair

TABLE NO. 1—Continued.

CHELAN COUNTY—Continued.

Town or City	Kind of Establishment	Number females employed	Hours per day	Wages per day	Sanitary conditions
Wenatchee	Abstract company..........	2	8	1 87	Fair
Wenatchee	Real estate company........	1	8	2 00	Very poor
Wenatchee	Real estate company........	1	8	1 34	Fair
Wenatchee	Real estate company........	1	9	1 92	Fair
Wenatchee	Dentist....................	1	8	1 00	Fair
Wenatchee	Dentist....................	1	8	1 66	Fair
Wenatchee	Dentist....................	1	9	1 00	Very good
Wenatchee	Hairdresser	4	....	2 00	Fair
Wenatchee	Hotel......................	9	8	1 50	Very good
Wenatchee	Laundry	16	10	1 65	Very poor
Wenatchee	Printing...................	1	8	1 83	Very poor
Wenatchee	Telephone..................	10	10	1 50	Very good
Wenatchee	Nursery company...........	1	8	1 50	Fair
Wenatchee	Lumber	2	8	2 25	Fair

CLARKE COUNTY.

Town or City	Kind of Establishment	Number females employed	Hours per day	Wages per day	Sanitary conditions
Vancouver	General merchandise........	1	9	$0 83½	Very good
Vancouver	General merchandise........	2	9	1 12½	Fair
Vancouver	General merchandise........	6	9	1 50	Fair
Vancouver	General merchandise........	10	9	1 10	Fair
Vancouver	General merchandise........	2	9	1 50	Fair
Vancouver	General merchandise........	7	9	1 00	Fair
Vancouver	General merchandise........	4	9	1 00	Very poor
Vancouver	General merchandise........	11	9	1 50	Very good
Vancouver	General merchandise........	4	9	1 15	Very good
Vancouver	Laundry	8	....	1 25	Very poor
Vancouver	Laundry	15	10	1 25	Very good
Vancouver	Laundry	18	10	1 50	Fair
Vancouver	County treasurer	3	7½	2 50	Very poor
Vancouver	County clerk...............	1	8	1 53	Very poor
Vancouver	County auditor.............	3	8	2 00	Very poor
Vancouver	Printing office.............	2	8	1 50	Fair
Vancouver	Printing office.............	2	8	2 00	Fair
Vancouver	Photography	2	9	1 75	Fair
Vancouver	Telephone	14	8½	1 25	Very good
Vancouver	Confectionery.............	10	9	1 25	Very poor
Vancouver	Meat......................	1	9	2 50	Very poor
Vancouver	Hotel......................	7	10	1 25	Very good
Camas	Paper manufacturing.......	20	10	1 10	Very poor

KING COUNTY.

Town or City	Kind of Establishment	Number females employed	Hours per day	Wages per day	Sanitary conditions
Auburn	General merchandise........	3	9	$1 61	Very poor
Auburn	General merchandise........	3	9	1 33	Very poor
Auburn	General merchandise........	1	8½	1 33	Fair
Kent	General merchandise........	2	9	1 16	Very poor
Kent	General merchandise........	2	9	1 92	Very poor
Kent	General merchandise........	1	9	3 33	Very good
Kent	General merchandise........	1	9	1 66	Very poor
Kent	General merchandise........	1	9	1 25	Very poor
Seattle	General merchandise........	3	9	1 66	Fair
Seattle	General merchandise........	2	9	1 00	Fair
Seattle	General merchandise........	5	9	1 58	Very good
Seattle	General merchandise........	2	9	1 16	Very poor
Seattle	General merchandise........	10	8½	1 33	Very good
Seattle	General merchandise........	9	9	1 50	Very poor
Seattle	General merchandise........	33	10	1 54	Fair
Seattle	General merchandise........	125	10	1 40	Fair
Seattle	General merchandise........	20	10	1 63	Fair
Seattle	General merchandise........	200	10	1 42	Very good
Seattle	General merchandise........	6	8½	2 53	Very good
Seattle	General merchandise........	7	8½	2 15	Very good
Seattle	General merchandise........	10	9	2 33	Very good
Seattle	General merchandise........	30	9	90	Fair
Seattle	General merchandise........	9	8½	2 50	Fair

TABLE NO. 1—Continued.

KING COUNTY—Continued.

Town or City	Kind of Establishment	Number females empolyed	Hours per day	Wages per day	Sanitary conditions
Seattle	General merchandise	25	9	2 08	Very poor
Seattle	General merchandise	20	9	2 66	Very poor
Seattle	General merchandise	41			Very poor
Seattle	General merchandise	20	10	1 66	Very poor
Seattle	General merchandise	50	9	1 43	Fair
Seattle	General merchandise	100	9	1 00	Fair
Seattle	General merchandise	7	8½	1 33	Fair
Seattle	General merchandise	75		2 00	Fair
Seattle	General merchandise	25	9½	1 75	Fair
Seattle	General merchandise	75	8½	2 33	Very good
Seattle	General merchandise	50	8½	2 66	Very good
Seattle	General merchandise	15	8½	2 33	Very poor
Seattle	General merchandise	6		2 56	Very poor
Seattle	General merchandise	250	8½		Very good
Seattle	General merchandise	500	8½		Very good
Seattle	General merchandise	40	9	1 33	Very good
Auburn	Condensed milk mfg	25	6	Pce w'k	Very good
Kent	Condensed milk mfg	100	10	1 41	Very good
Seattle	Apron mfg	3	8	1 00	Very good
Seattle	Paper box mfg	10	9	1 16	Fair
Seattle	Men's boots and shoes mfg	40	11	1 66	Very good
Seattle	Knitting mfg	18	9	1 46	Very good
Seattle	Glove mfg	10	9	1 46	
Seattle	Women's apparel mfg	10	9	1 44	Fair
Seattle	Knitting mfg	26	9	1 63	Very good
Seattle	Glove mfg	3	8	2 25	Fair
Seattle	Paper box mfg	25	9	1 16	Fair
Seattle	Bag mfg	35	9	Pce w'k	Very good
Seattle	Canned fruits	50		1 43	Fair
Seattle	Chewing gum	12	9	1 62	Fair
Seattle	Flour and rolled oats	15	8½	1 50	Very good
Seattle	Overall mfg	65	8	2 12	Very good
Seattle	Baking powder, spices	26	8	1 61	Fair
Seattle	Tent and awning mfg	20	8½	2 12	Fair
Seattle	Shirt mfg	40	8½	1 91	Fair
Seattle	Tent and awning mfg	2	8	2 00	Fair
Seattle	Tent and awning mfg	6	8	2 16	Very poor
Seattle	Tent and awning mfg	14	8½	1 75	Fair
Seattle	Tent and awning mfg	4	8	2 25	Very poor
Seattle	Oiled clothing mfg	12	9	1 50	Very good
Seattle	Candy mfg	50	10	1 31	Very poor
Seattle	Candy and cracker mfg	45	10	1 72	Fair
Seattle	Candy mfg	4	8½	1 50	Very poor
Seattle	Candy and cracker mfg	50	10	1 40	Fair
Seattle	Candy mfg	6	9	1 50	Very poor
Seattle	Macaroni mfg	4	9	1 16	Very good
Seattle	Laundry	125	10	1 50	Fair
Seattle	Laundry	3		1 75	Very poor
Seattle	Laundry	8	10	1 25	Very good
Seattle	Laundry	75	10½	1 75	Very good
Seattle	Laundry	75	10	2 00	Fair
Seattle	Laundry	35	10	1 80	Fair
Seattle	Laundry	28	10	1 85	Fair
Seattle	Laundry	12	10	1 83	Fair
Seattle	Laundry	80	10	1 90	Very poor
Seattle	Laundry	8	10	1 75	Fair
Seattle	Laundry	15	10	1 66	Very poor
Seattle	Laundry	125	10	2 00	Very good
Seattle	Laundry	2	9	2 00	Fair
Seattle	Laundry	25	10	2 00	Fair
Seattle	Laundry	8	10	2 00	Fair
Seattle	Laundry	50	10	1 80	Fair
Seattle	Laundry	70	10	1 74	Very good
Seattle	Laundry	20	10		Fair
Seattle	Laundry	50	10	1 75	Fair
Seattle	Laundry	6			
Seattle	Laundry	6	10	1 50	Fair
Seattle	Laundry	30	10	1 85	Fair
Seattle	Laundry	16	10	1 66	Fair

TABLE NO. 1—Continued.
KING COUNTY—Continued.

Town or City	Kind of Establishment	Number females employed	Hours per day	Wages per day	Sanitary conditions
Seattle	Laundry	10	10	1 73	Very good
Seattle	Laundry	8	9	2 00	Fair
Kent	Laundry	7	9	1 55	Very poor
Seattle	Restaurant	3	10	1 83	Very good
Seattle	Restaurant	3	10	1 50	Very good
Seattle	Restaurant	3	10	1 90	Fair
Seattle	Restaurant	4	10	1 25	Fair
Seattle	Restaurant	4	10	1 66	Fair
Seattle	Restaurant	20	10	1 87	Fair
Seattle	Restaurant	20	10	1 87	Very poor
Seattle	Restaurant	4	10	1 66	Very good
Seattle	Restaurant	10	9	1 75	Very good
Seattle	Restaurant	10	10	1 66	Very good
Seattle	Restaurant	15	10	1 75	Very good
Seattle	Restaurant	9	10	1 58	Very good
Seattle	Restaurant	10	10	1 66	Very good
Seattle	Restaurant	13	10	1 66	Very good
Seattle	Restaurant	3	11	1 28	Fair
Seattle	Restaurant	12	10	1 66	Very good
Seattle	Restaurant	4	10	1 25	Fair
Seattle	Restaurant	4	10	1 83	Fair
Auburn	Restaurant	2	10	1 16	Very good
Auburn	Restaurant	1	....	83 and b'd	Very poor
Auburn	Restaurant	2	....	66 b.a'dr.	Very poor
Seattle	Hotel	6	8	1 15	Very good
Seattle	Hotel	2	8	66 r.a'db.	Very good
Seattle	Hotel	12	9	1 15	Very good
Seattle	Hotel	9	8	1 15	Very good
Seattle	Hotel	5	9	1 15	Very good
Seattle	Hotel	8	8	1 33	Very good
Seattle	Hotel	5	8	1 33	Very good
Seattle	Hotel	10	9	66 r.a'db.	Very good
Seattle	Hotel	5	8	1 15	Very good
Auburn	Hotel	2	9	83 r.a'db.	Fair
Auburn	Printing office	1	9	1 33	Very poor
Kent	Printing office	3	8	1 33	Very poor
Seattle	Printing and binding	1	9	1 66	Fair
Seattle	Printing and binding	8	8	1 33	Fair
Seattle	Printing and binding	25	8	1 75	Very good
Seattle	Printing and binding	3	8	1 58	Fair
Seattle	Printing and binding	6	8	1 75	Very poor
Seattle	Printing and binding	25	8	1 88	Fair
Seattle	Printing and binding	5	8	1 75	Very poor
Seattle	Printing and binding	8	8	1 75	Fair
Seattle	Printing and binding	12	8	1 91	Fair
Auburn	Bank	1	7	2 00	Very good
Kent	Bank	1	7½	1 66	Very good
Kent	Bank	1	7	66⅔	Very good
Auburn	Law office	1	6	1 00	Very good
Kent	Law office	1	7	66⅔	Very good
Seattle	Tailors	12	9	2 00	Fair
Seattle	Tailors	3	9	2 75	Fair
Seattle	Tailors	1	9	1 50	Very good
Seattle	Tailors	5	9	2 16	Very good
Seattle	Dye works	25	9½	2 28	Very good
Auburn	Telephone	2	7	2 00	Very poor
Kent	Telephone	2	7	87½	Very poor
Kent	Telephone	3	10	79	Very good
Seattle	Telephone	220	8	1 73	Very good
Seattle	Telephone	13	8	1 61	Very good
Seattle	Hair-dressing parlors	50	10	2 37	Very poor
Seattle	Bottling works	12	8	1 50	Fair
Seattle	Drug store	15	8	1 98	Fair

Bureau of Labor

TABLE NO. 1—Continued.

KITTITAS COUNTY.

Town or City	Kind of Establishment	Number females employed	Hours per day	Wages per day	Sanitary conditions
Ellensburg	General merchandise.........	4	9	$2 25	Very good
Ellensburg	General merchandise.........	3	9	2 50	Very poor
Ellensburg	General merchandise.........	2	9	1 33	Very good
Ellensburg	General merchandise.........	2	9	1 90	Very good
Ellensburg	General merchandise.........	2	9	1 75	Very poor
Ellensburg	General merchandise.........	2	9	1 50	Fair
Ellensburg	General merchandise.........	1	8	1 50	Very pcor
Ellensburg	General merchandise.........	2	9	1 90	Very poor
Ellensburg	Hotel and restaurant........	4	10	1 50	Very good
Ellensburg	Hotel and restaurant........	2	10	1 50	....
Ellensburg	Hotel and restaurant........	2	10	1 50	Very poor
Ellensburg	Hotel and restaurant........	2	10	1 50	Very pocr
Ellensburg	Hotel and restaurant........	1	10	1 50	Very good
Ellensburg	City clerk's office..........	1	8	1 90	Very poor
Ellensburg	County auditor's office......	1	8	3 00	Very good
Ellensburg	County clerk's office........	1	8	3 00	Very good
Ellensburg	Confectionery..............	8	....	83	Very good
Ellensburg	Laundry	11	10	1 50	Very good
Ellensburg	Laundry	15	10	1 50	Very poor
Ellensburg	Printing office	1	9	2 00	Very poor
Ellensburg	Dye works.................	1	9	1 50	Very good
Ellensburg	Meat	1	9	2 25	Very poor
Ellensburg	Telephone	7	8	1 25	Fair
Ellensburg	Hair-dressing	1	9	85	Very good

LEWIS COUNTY.

Town or City	Kind of Establishment	Number females employed	Hours per day	Wages per day	Sanitary conditions
Centralia	General merchandise.........	2	9	$1 00	Fair
Centralia	General merchandise.........	2	9	84	Very poor
Centralia	General merchandise.........	3	9	1 42	Very good
Centralia	General merchandise.........	1	8½	2 15	Very good
Centralia	General merchandise.........	10	9	1 66	Fair
Centralia	General merchandise.........	1	8	1 00	Very good
Centralia	General merchandise.........	1	9½	1 00	Very poor
Centralia	General merchandise.........	6	9	2 44	Very good
Centralia	General merchandise.........	4	9	2 25	Very good
Chehalis	General merchandise.........	10	9½	1 50	Very poor
Chehalis	General merchanidse.........	8	9	1 75	Very good
Chehalis	General merchandise.........	1	8	2 14	Very good
Chehalis	General merchandise.........	1	9½	1 42	Fair
Chehalis	General merchandise.........	1	9½	1 00	Very poor
Chehalis	General merchandise.........	4	9	1 17	Fair
Chehalis	General merchandise.........	3	9½	1 25	Fair
Chehalis	General merchandise.........	1	7	1 50	Very poor
Centralia	Restaurant.................	4	....	92 and b'd	Very good
Centralia	Restaurant.................	3	10	1 16 and b'd	Fair
Centralia	Hotel.....................	6	10	83 and b'd	Very good
Chehalis	Hotel.....................	6	10	1 00	Very good
Chehalis	Hotel.....................	5	10	90	Very good
Chehalis	Hotel.....................	3	10	2 00	Very good
Centralia	Printing office	1	9	1 50	Very good
Centralia	Printing office	2	8	1 50	Very poor
Chehalis	Printing office	2	8	1 50	Very good
Chehalis	Printing office	2	9	1 58½	Very poor
Centralia	Laundry	14	9	1 27	Very poor
Centralia	Laundry	10	9	1 30	Very poor
Chehalis	Laundry	10	10	1 35	Very poor
Chehalis	Court house	1	8	2 40	Very good
Chehalis	Court house	4	8	2 04	Very good
Chehalis	Electric Co................	1	9	2 00	Very poor
Centralia	Telephone	10	8	1 14	Very good
Chehalis	Telephone	5	8	1 00	Very good
Centralia	Glove factory..............	14	8½	1 46	Very good
Chehalis	Milk factory	6	9	1 50	Very poor
Chehalis	Meat	1	9	2 08	Very poor

TABLE NO. 1—Continued.

LEWIS COUNTY—Continued.

Town or City	Kind of Establishment	Number females employed	Hours per day	Wages per day	Sanitary conditions
Centralia	Bank	1	8½	2 50	Very good
Centralia	Stenographer	1	8	2 00	Very good
Centralia	Law office	1	8	1 66	Very good

PIERCE COUNTY.

Town or City	Kind of Establishment	Number females employed	Hours per day	Wages per day	Sanitary conditions
Puyallup	General merchandise	4	9	$1 08	Fair
Puyallup	General merchandise	4	9	1 08	Fair
Tacoma	General merchandise	40	9	1 29	Very good
Tacoma	General merchandise	175	9	2 56	Very good
Tacoma	General merchandise	50	8½	2 15	Fair
Tacoma	General merchandise	4	9	1 59	Very poor
Tacoma	General merchandise	65	....	1 66	Very good
Tacoma	General merchandise	25	....	....	Very good
Tacoma	General merchandise	175	9	1 25	Very good
Tacoma	General merchandise	150		1 83	Very good
Tacoma	General merchandise	15	9	1 50	Fair
Tacoma	General merchandise	20	9	3 16	Very good
Tacoma	General merchandise	6	8½	1 59	Very good
Tacoma	General merchandise	4	9	1 59	Fair
Tacoma	General merchandise	30	9	1 75	Very good
Tacoma	General merchandise	9	9	1 05	Very poor
Tacoma	General merchandise	2	....	....	Very good
Tacoma	General merchandise	2	....	2 00	Very good
Tacoma	General merchandise	4	9	1 70	Fair
Tacoma	General merchandise	3	....	2 00	Very good
Tacoma	General merchandise	2	9	92	Fair
Tacoma	General merchandise	2	9	2 06	Very poor
Tacoma	General merchandise	1	9	1 33½	Very good
Tacoma	General merchandise	5	9	1 12½	Very poor
Sumner	General merchandise	2	9	1 50	Very poor
Sumner	General merchandise	1	9	1 00	Very poor
Puyallup	Fruit cannery	50	10	1 62	Very good
Puyallup	Fruit cannery	40	10	1 50	Fair
Puyallup	Box factory	12	10	1 25	Very poor
Tacoma	Cigar mfg	8	8	2 54	Very good
Tacoma	Cigar mfg	1	8	1 00	Very poor
Tacoma	Cigar mfg	1	....	1 33	Very poor
Tacoma	Cigar mfg	10	8	1 33	Very poor
Tacoma	Cigar box mfg	8	9	1 39	Very poor
Tacoma	Box mfg	30	....	....	Very poor
Tacoma	Candy and cracker mfg	75	....	1 75	Very good
Tacoma	Candy and cracker mfg	15	10	1 70	Very poor
Tacoma	Candy and cracker mfg	5	9	1 20	Very poor
Tacoma	Potato chips mfg	1	8	1 16	Very good
Tacoma	Lumber mfg	2	8	2 42	Very poor
Tacoma	Lumber mfg	1	....	1 26	Fair
Tacoma	Mattress mfg	9	9	1 62	Very good
Tacoma	Macaroni mfg	9	....	1 12½	Very poor
Tacoma	Overall mfg	60	8	2 22	Very good
Tacoma	Shoe mfg	12	10	1 62	Very good
Tacoma	Meat packing mfg	10	10	1 85	Very good
Tacoma	Catsup, etc., mfg	20	10	1 50	Very good
Tacoma	Shirt mfg	4	9	1 61	Fair
Tacoma	Tent and awning mfg	1	9	1 66	Very good
Tacoma	Tinware mfg	2	10	1 21	Fair
Tacoma	Coffee and spices mfg	5	8½	1 50	Very good
Sumner	Fruit cannery	90	10	1 50	Very good
Puyallup	Printing office	1	8	1 50	Very poor
Tacoma	Bindery and printing office	15	8	1 16	Very good
Tacoma	Bindery and printing office	5	8	1 38	Very poor
Tacoma	Bindery and printing office	10	8	1 16	Very poor
Puyallup	Laundry	5	10	1 75	Very poor
Tacoma	Laundry	....	10	1 62½	Very poor
Tacoma	Laundry	45	....	1 62½	Very poor
Tacoma	Laundry	75	10	1 62½	Very good
Tacoma	Laundry	8	10	1 35	Very poor
Tacoma	Laundry	45	10	....	Very poor

TABLE NO. 1—Continued.

PIERCE COUNTY—Continued.

Town or City	Kind of Establishment	Number females employed	Hours per day	Wages per day	Sanitary conditions
Tacoma	Laundry	8	10	1 30	Very poor
Tacoma	Laundry	20	9½	1 33½	Very poor
Tacoma	Laundry	8	10	1 25	Fair
Tacoma	Laundry	35	10	1 07	Fair
Tacoma	Laundry		10	1 37	Very good
Tacoma	Laundry	8	10	1 75	Fair
Tacoma	Laundry	10	10	1 00	Fair
Sumner	Laundry	3	10	1 25	Very poor
Puyallup	Telephone	4	8	66	Very good
Puyallup	Telephone	3	7	76	Fair
Tacoma	Telephone	85	8	2 00	Very good
Tacoma	Telephone	8	8	1 33	Very good
Sumner	Telephone	3	9	1 99	Very poor
Tacoma	Confectionery parlor	7	9	1 40	Very good
Tacoma	Confectionery parlor	7	9½	1 42	Fair
Tacoma	Dye works	8	9	1 54	Fair
Tacoma	Dye works	3	9	1 75	....
Tacoma	Hairdresser	8	......	78	Very good
Tacoma	Doctor's office	1	......	2 50	Very good
Tacoma	Pharmacist's	7	9	2 56	Very good
Sumner	Office (tel. operator)	1	8	2 65	Very poor
Tacoma	Restaurant	5	......	1 25	Very good
Tacoma	Restaurant	7	10	......	Very good
Tacoma	Restaurant	14	......	2 15 and b'd	Fair
Tacoma	Restaurant	15	8	96 and b'd	Fair
Tacoma	Restaurant	2	10	2 00	Very poor
Tacoma	Restaurant	4	......	1 00 and b'd	Fair
Tacoma	Restaurant	8	10	1 66	Very poor
Tacoma	Restaurant	8	8	1 46 and b'd	Very good
Tacoma	Restaurant	8	10	1 71 and b'd	Very poor
Tacoma	Restaurant	3	10	1 50	Very good
Tacoma	Restaurant	4	10	1 00	Very good
Tacoma	Restaurant	10	6	1 00 and b'd	Very good
Tacoma	Hotel	4	......	79 bd, r'm	Very good
Tacoma	Hotel	3	......	92 bd, r'm	Very good
Tacoma	Hotel	3	......	94 bd, r'm	Very good
Tacoma	Hotel	4	9	66 bd, r'm	Very good
Tacoma	Hotel	11	9	1 15	Very good
Tacoma	Hotel	6	9	1 15	Very good
Tacoma	Tailor	2	9	1 08	Very good

SKAGIT COUNTY.

Anacortes	General merchandise	6	9	$1 41⅜	Very good
Anacortes	General merchandise	2	9	1 46	Very good
Anacortes	General merchandise	3	9	2 00	Very good
Anacortes	General merchandise	1	9	1 66	Very good
Anacortes	General merchandise	1	9	1 66	Very poor
Mt. Vernon	General merchandise	4	8½	......	Very good
Mt. Vernon	General merchandise	5	9	......	Very poor
Anacortes	Cannery	25	10	2 00	Fair
Anacortes	Cannery	40	10	2 00	Fair
Anacortes	Cannery	50	10	1 65	Very poor
Anacortes	Cannery	7	10	2 75	Very good
Anacortes	Cannery	60	10	2 00	Very poor
Fidalgo	Cannery	40	11	2 00	....
Fidalgo	Cannery	150	......	......	Very poor

TABLE NO. 1—Continued.

SKAGIT COUNTY—Continued.

Town or City	Kind of Establishment	Number females employed	Hours per day	Wages per day	Sanitary conditions
Mt. Vernon	Cannery	20	10	1 25	Very poor
Mt. Vernon	Cannery	12	8½	1 50	Very good
Mt. Vernon	Cannery	4	7	1 25	Very poor
Anacortes	Printing office	1	9	1 33	Very good
Anacortes	Printing office	1	9	1 25	Very good
Mt. Vernon	Printing office	2	9	1 16⅔	Fair
Anacortes	Telephone	8	9	1 00	Very good
Mt. Vernon	Telephone	3	8	....	Very poor
Mt. Vernon	Telephone	9	8	1 06½	Very good
Anacortes	Laundry	12	10	1 62	Very good
Mt. Vernon	Laundry	4	10	....	Very poor
Mt. Vernon	Laundry	8	10	1 50	....
Mt. Vernon	County treasurer	1	8	2 33	Very good
Mt. Vernon	County auditor	3	8	2 33	Very good

SNOHOMISH COUNTY.

Town or City	Kind of Establishment	Number females employed	Hours per day	Wages per day	Sanitary conditions
Everett	General merchandise	7	9	$2 92	Very poor
Everett	General merchandise	25	9	....	Very good
Everett	General merchandise	5	9	3 33½	Very good
Everett	General merchandise	4	9	....	Very good
Everett	General merchandise	2	9	1 33½	Fair
Everett	General merchandise	2	8	1 33½	Fair
Everett	General merchandise	9	9	92	Very poor
Everett	General merchandise	20	8½	2 42	Very good
Everett	General merchandise	15	9	1 56	Very poor
Everett	General merchandise	18	8½	2 12	Fair
Everett	General merchandise	4	9	1 71	Fair
Everett	General merchandise	16	9	1 68	Very poor
Snohomish	General merchandise	3	9	2 17	Very poor
Snohomish	General merchandise	4	9	2 08	Fair
Snohomish	General merchandise	8	9	2 30	Very good
Snohomish	General merchandise	7	9	1 55	Very poor
Snohomish	General merchandise	2	9	....	Fair
Edmonds	Veneer and box factory	3	10	1 50	Very poor
Everett	Tent factory	3	8	1 50	Very poor
Everett	Casket factory	4	8	1 33½	Very good
Lowell	Paper factory	35	10	1 47	Very good
Snohomish	Glove factory	6	9	1 44	Very poor
Everett	Restaurant	6	10	1 35	Very good
Everett	Restaurant	4	10	66⅔ and b'd	Very good
Everett	Restaurant	5	....	1 92	Very poor
Everett	Restaurant	2	10	1 50 and b'd	Very good
Everett	Restaurant	2	10	1 66 and b'd	Very good
Everett	Hotel	9	10	1 08 and b'd	Very good
Snohomish	Hotel	4	10	1 52 and b'd	Very good
Everett	Laundry	18	10	1 60	Very good
Everett	Laundry	18	10	1 65	Fair
Everett	Laundry	25	10	1 52	Very poor
Everett	Laundry	4	10	1 70	Very poor
Everett	Laundry	16	10	1 59	Very good
Snohomish	Laundry	6	9	1 25	Very poor
Edmonds	Telephone	2	9	1 25	Very good
Everett	Telephone	30	8	90	Very good
Everett	Telephone	32	8	1 15	Very good
Snohomish	Telephone	4	10	92	Very poor
Snohomish	Telephone	6	8	83¾	Very poor
Everett	Cigar mfg	6	8	1 62	Fair
Everett	Confectionery	2	9	1 43	Very good
Edmonds	Printing office	1	8	2 00	Very good
Snohomish	Printing office	2	8	1 37	Very poor
Everett	Tailor	8	9	2 46	Very poor

TABLE NO. 1—Continued.

SPOKANE COUNTY.

Town or City	Kind of Establishment	Number females employed	Hours per day	Wages per day	Sanitary conditions
Spokane	General merchandise	125	9	....	Very good
Spokane	General merchandise	75	9	$1 40	Very poor
Spokane	General merchandise	85	9	2 00	Very good
Spokane	General merchandise	100	9	2 00	Very good
Spokane	General merchandise	2	9	2 00	Very poor
Spokane	General merchandise	25	9	2 25	Very poor
Spokane	General merchandise	20	9	1 85	Fair
Spokane	General merchandise	75	9	1 50	Very poor
Spokane	General merchandise	20	9	2 00	Very good
Spokane	General merchandise	30	9	1 65	Fair
Spokane	General merchandise	15	9	2 25	Fair
Spokane	General merchandise	45	9	1 50	Fair
Spokane	General merchandise	2	9	1 75	Very poor
Spokane	General merchandise	50	9	1 75	Very good
Spokane	General merchandise	4	9	2 00	Very good
Spokane	General merchandise	30	9	2 00	Fair
Spokane	General merchandise	12	9	2 25	Fair
Spokane	General merchandise	12	9	2 25	Fair
Spokane	General merchandise	10	9	1 25	Fair
Spokane	General merchandise	15	9	2 75	Fair
Spokane	General merchandise	200	9	2 00	Very good
Spokane	General merchandise	12	9	2 00	Very good
Spokane	General merchandise	27	9	2 75	Fair
Spokane	General merchandise	8	9	2 25	Fair
Spokane	General merchandise	8	9	1 50	Very poor
Spokane	General merchandise	8	9	1 75	Very good
Spokane	General merchandise	7	9	1 75	Very poor
Spokane	General merchandise	13	9	2 00	Fair
Spokane	General merchandise	150	9	1 66⅔	Fair
Spokane	Laundry	25	10	1 47	Fair
Spokane	Laundry	110	9	1 50	Very good
Spokane	Laundry	60	10	1 50	Fair
Spokane	Laundry	....	10	1 50	Very poor
Spokane	Laundry	25	10	1 75	Fair
Spokane	Laundry	15	10	1 60	Fair
Spokane	Laundry	6	10	1 35	Very poor
Spokane	Laundry	45	10	1 75	Very good
Spokane	Laundry	30	10	1 50	Very good
Spokane	Laundry	35	10	1 75	Very good
Spokane	Hotel	1	8	1 50	Very good
Spokane	Hotel	4	8	1 40	Very good
Spokane	Hotel	10	8	1 25	Very good
Spokane	Hotel	6	9	1 50	Very good
Spokane	Hotel	5	8	1 50	Very good
Spokane	Hotel	7	9	1 50	Very good
Spokane	Hotel	9	10	1 75	Very good
Spokane	Restaurant	4	10	1 50	Very poor
Spokane	Restaurant	9	10	1 50	Very good
Spokane	Restaurant	12	10	1 50	Very good
Spokane	Restaurant	16	10	1 50	Very good
Spokane	Restaurant	1	10	1 50	Very poor
Spokane	Restaurant	4	10	1 50	Very poor
Spokane	Mfg. mattresses, etc	4	8	2 00	Fair
Spokane	Mfg. garments	15	9	1 25	Very poor
Spokane	Mfg. garments	6	9	1 75	Very poor
Spokane	Mfg. tents and awnings	14	9	2 00	Very poor
Spokane	Mfg. garments	2	8½	1 00	Very poor
Spokane	Mfg. garments	100	8	2 08	Very good
Spokane	Bindery and printing	20	....	1 50	Very good
Spokane	Printing office	2	8¼	2 25	Fair
Spokane	Printing office	10	8	1 30	Very poor
Spokane	Printing office	1	8	3 00	Fair
Spokane	Printing office	12	8	1 25	Very poor
Spokane	Lithographing	4	8	1 50	Very poor
Spokane	Printing	2	8	1 50	Very poor
Spokane	Cracker and candy company	75	9	....	Fair
Spokane	Cracker and candy company	75	10	1 25	Very good
Spokane	Confectionery	7	9½	1 25	Very poor
Spokane	Confectionery	25	9½	1 85	Very good

TABLE NO. 1—Continued.

SPOKANE COUNTY—Continued.

Town or City	Kind of Establishment	Number females employed	Hours per day	Wages per day	Sanitary conditions
Spokane	Confectionery	8	10	1 82	Very poor
Spokane	Confectionery	3	9½	1 33	Very poor
Spokane	Bakery	2	7	2 50	Very good
Spokane	Dye works	7	9	1 75	Fair
Spokane	Florist	8	9	2 25	Fair
Spokane	Telephone	175	8	1 80	Very good
Spokane	Hair-dressing	18	9	1 50	Very poor
Spokane	Pharmacy	10	9	2 00	Fair
Spokane	Cigar factory	1	8	83½	Very poor

THURSTON COUNTY.

Town or City	Kind of Establishment	Number females employed	Hours per day	Wages per day	Sanitary conditions
Olympia	General merchandise	2	9	$1 50	Very good
Olympia	General merchandise	10	9	1 66	Very good
Olympia	General merchandise	5	9	75	Very good
Olympia	General merchandise	3	9	1 00	Very poor
Olympia	General merchandise	9	9	1 66	Very good
Olympia	General merchandise	2	9	2 00	Fair
Olympia	General merchandise	8	9	2 00	Very good
Olympia	Knitting mills	15	9	1 00	Fair
Olympia	Spices	1	7½	1 66	Fair
Olympia	Laundry	12	10	1 25	Very poor
Olympia	Laundry	12	10	1 25	Fair
Olympia	Printing	9	8	1 00	Fair
Olympia	Dye works	2	9	1 50	Fair
Olympia	Telephone	10	8	1 15	Very good
Olympia	Hotel	6	10	1 00 r.a'db.	Very good

WALLA WALLA COUNTY.

Town or City	Kind of Establishment	Number females employed	Hours per day	Wages per day	Sanitary conditions
Walla Walla	General merchandise	4	9	$1 50	Very poor
Walla Walla	General merchandise	8	9	1 75	Very good
Walla Walla	General merchandise	8	9	60	Fair
Walla Walla	General merchandise	1	9	1 50	Very poor
Walla Walla	General merchandise	2	9	1 12½	Very good
Walla Walla	General merchandise	1	9	2 50	Fair
Walla Walla	General merchandise	2	9	1 90	Very poor
Walla Walla	General merchandise	3	9	2 25	Fair
Walla Walla	General merchandise	....	8½	2 00	Very good
Walla Walla	General merchandise	2	9	1 00	Fair
Walla Walla	General merchandise	5	9	2 50	Very poor
Walla Walla	General merchandise	4	8½	2 00	Fair
Walla Walla	General merchandise	12	9	1 75	Very poor
Walla Walla	General merchandise	2	9	85	Very poor
Walla Walla	General merchandise	1	8½	2 88	....
Walla Walla	General merchandise	1	7	2 80	Fair
Walla Walla	General merchandise	2	9	2 25	Very good
Walla Walla	General merchandise	5	9	1 65	Very poor
Walla Walla	General merchandise	5	9	1 50	Fair
Walla Walla	General merchandise	11	9	2 50	Very good
Walla Walla	General merchandise	5	9	2 00	Fair
Walla Walla	General merchandise	1	8	1 90	Very good
Walla Walla	General merchandise	6	9	2 00	Very good
Walla Walla	General merchandise	27	9	1 95	Very good
Walla Walla	General merchandise	10	9	2 00	Very good
Walla Walla	Confectionery	3	8	1 17	Very good
Walla Walla	Confectionery	3	10	1 25	Very poor
Walla Walla	Confectionery	2	9	1 50	Fair
Walla Walla	Confectionery	9	9	1 50	Fair
Walla Walla	Confectionery	3	9	1 25	Very poor
Walla Walla	Laundry	20	10	1 35	Very poor
Walla Walla	Laundry	15	10	1 35	Fair
Walla Walla	Laundry	36	10	1 50	Very poor
Walla Walla	Restaurant	2	9	1 80	Very poor
Walla Walla	Restaurant	3	9	83	Very good
Walla Walla	County clerk	1	8	2 30	Very good

TABLE NO. 1—Continued.

WALLA WALLA COUNTY—Continued.

Town or City	Kind of Establishment	Number females employed	Hours per day	Wages per day	Sanitary conditions
Walla Walla	County assessor	1	8	3 00	Very good
Walla Walla	Telephone	40	8	1 50	Very good
Walla Walla	Postoffice	1	8½	2 50	Very good
Walla Walla	Dye works	1	8	3 00	Fair
Walla Walla	Printing office	4	8	1 50	Very poor

WHATCOM COUNTY.

Town or City	Kind of Establishment	Number females employed	Hours per day	Wages per day	Sanitary conditions
Bellingham	General merchandise	30	9	$2 58	Fair
Bellingham	General merchandise	45	9	1 25	Very good
Bellingham	General merchandise	5	9	1 25	Very good
Bellingham	General merchandise	12	9	2 08	Very good
Bellingham	General merchandise	30	9	1 25	Very good
Bellingham	General merchandise	6	9	2 66	Very good
Bellingham	General merchandise	6	9	....	Very good
Bellingham	General merchandise	3	9	1 25	Very good
Bellingham	General merchandise	3	....	1 70	Very poor
Bellingham	General merchandise	25	9	1 50	Very good
Bellingham	General merchandise	5	9	1 50	Very good
Bellingham	General merchandise	10	9	1 33	Very good
Bellingham	General merchandise	1	8½	1 66	Very poor
Bellingham	General merchandise	15	9	71	Very poor
Blaine	General merchandise	3	9	92	Very good
Blaine	General merchandise	3	9	83	Very poor
Bellingham	Confectionery	3	....	95	Very poor
Bellingham	Confectionery	3	....	1 04	Very good
Bellingham	Confectionery	20	9	....	Fair
Bellingham	Confectionery	2	10	83⅓	Very poor
Bellingham	Confectionery	1	9	....	Very poor
Blaine	Confectionery	1	8	1 33	Very good
Bellingham	Cannery	400	10	....	Very good
Bellingham	Cannery	50	10	....	Very poor
Bellingham	Cannery	15	....	....	Very poor
Blaine	Cannery	40	....	Pce w'k	Very poor
Blaine	Cannery	75	....	Pce w'k	Very poor
Blaine	Cannery	70	....	....	Very good
Blaine	Cannery	50	....	....	Very poor
Chuckanut	Cannery	35	....	....	Very good
Bellingham	Telephone	30	8	1 24	Very good
Bellingham	Telephone	3	8½	1 50	Very good
Blaine	Telephone	3	8	1 00	Very poor
Blaine	Telephone	2	10	92	Very good
Bellingham	Laundry	33	10	1 42½	Fair
Bellingham	Laundry	12	10	1 41	Fair
Bellingham	Laundry	12	10	1 37½	Very good
Bellingham	Laundry	5	10	1 57	Very good
Bellingham	Laundry	4	10	1 42	Very good
Blaine	Laundry	5	10	1 25	Very poor
Bellingham	Hotel and restaurant	3	....	1 16⅔	Very poor
Bellingham	Hotel and restaurant	3	10	1 25	Very good
Bellingham	Hotel and restaurant	12	....	....	Very good
Bellingham	Hotel and restaurant	15	....	....	Very good
Bellingham	Hotel and restaurant	5	....	....	Very good
Bellingham	Hotel and restaurant	2	10	1 16	Very good
Bellingham	Hotel and restaurant	5	....	1 50	Very good
Bellingham	Hotel and restaurant	4	10	1 50	Very poor
Bellingham	Hotel and restaurant	6	10	1 25	Very poor
Blaine	Hotel and restaurant	2	7	86	Very good
Blaine	Hotel and restaurant	1	9	1 00	Very good
Bellingham	Dye works	4	8	1 62½	Very poor
Bellingham	Bakery	1	10	1 00	Very good
Bellingham	Glove factory	8	8	1 00	Very good
Bellingham	Cigar factory	2	8	2 16	Very poor
Bellingham	Sewing machines	1	10	66⅔	Very poor
Bellingham	Hair-dressing	5	8½	1 92	Very good
Bellingham	Pharmacy	3	10	1 16	Very good
Bellingham	Tailor	1	10	1 00	Fair

TABLE NO. 1—Continued.

YAKIMA COUNTY.

Town or City	Kind of Establishment	Number females employed	Hours per day	Wages per day	Sanitary conditions
North Yakima	General merchandise	2	9	$2 35	Very good
North Yakima	General merchandise	4	9	2 50	Fair
North Yakima	General merchandise	6	9	2 50	Very good
North Yakima	General merchandise	31	9	2 00	Very good
North Yakima	General merchandise	1	9	1 33	Very poor
North Yakima	General merchandise	10	9	2 00	Very poor
North Yakima	General merchandise	5	9	1 10	Very good
North Yakima	General merchandise	8	9.	2 00	Very poor
North Yakima	General merchandise	4	10	1 50	Very poor
North Yakima	General merchandise	2	9	1 50	....
North Yakima	General merchandise	21	9	2 00	Very poor
North Yakima	General merchandise	4	10	75	Fair
North Yakima	General merchandise	2	8	2 50	Very good
North Yakima	General merchandise	2	9	2 50	Very poor
North Yakima	General merchandise	2	9	1 58	Very poor
North Yakima	General merchandise	7	9	2 50	Very good
North Yakima	General merchandise	20	9	2 00	....
North Yakima	Confectionery	2	9	1 75	Very poor
North Yakima	Confectionery	5	9	1 37	Very good
North Yakima	Confectionery	7	10	1 50	Very poor
North Yakima	Confectionery	4	9	1 29	Fair
North Yakima	Court house	5	8	2 50	Very good
North Yakima	County clerk's office	2	8	2 59	Fair
North Yakima	County assessor's office	3	8	2 35	Fair
North Yakima	Title and abstract company	4	8	3 00	Very poor
North Yakima	Printing office	3	8	2 25	Fair
North Yakima	Printing office	1	8	3 50	Very poor
North Yakima	Bindery	5	8	1 25	....
North Yakima	Laundry	35	10	1 60	Very poor
North Yakima	Laundry	45	10	1 60	Very poor
North Yakima	Bank	2	7	1 34	Very good
North Yakima	Storage company	2	10	1 50	Fair
North Yakima	Dye works	1	9	2 50	Very poor
North Yakima	Telephone company	21	8	1 00	Very good
North Yakima	Light and water company	3	9	2 25	Fair
North Yakima	Hotel and restaurant	5	10	1 50	Very good
North Yakima	Pharmacy	1	10	1 42	Very poor

TABLE NO. 2—STATISTICS OF ESTABLISHMENTS EMPLOYING FEMALE LABOR.
Summary by Counties and Industries for All Establishments Reported.

CHEHALIS COUNTY.

Kind of establishment	Total No. establishments inspected	Total number females employed	Average hours per day	Average wages per day	Very good	Fair	Very poor
General merchandise	14	70	9	$1 61	4	5	5
Laundry	5	84	10	1 62	1	2	2
Lumber	2	2	8	3 04	1	1	
Confectionery	5	6	9	1 52		4	1
Telephone	3	22	8	1 25	1	2	
Printing	2	4	8	2 50	2		
Restaurant	2	23	10	1 38	2		
Miscellaneous	9	64	9	1 68	3	4	2
Totals and averages	42	275	9	$1 83	14	18	10

CHELAN COUNTY.

Kind of establishment	Total No.	Total females	Hours	Wages	Very good	Fair	Very poor
General merchandise	11	38	9	$2 04	1	2	8
Confectionery	4	10	10	1 54	1	2	1
Dentist	3	3	8	1 22	1	2	
Real estate	3	3	8	1 75		2	1
Miscellaneous	12	47	8	1 86	4	5	3
Totals and averages	33	101	8	$1 68	7	13	13

CLARKE COUNTY.

Kind of establishment	Total No.	Total females	Hours	Wages	Very good	Fair	Very poor
General merchandise	9	47	9	$1 19	3	5	1
Laundry	3	41	10	1 33	1	1	1
Printing	2	4	8	1 75		2	
Miscellaneous	9	61	9	1 68	1	2	6
Totals and averages	23	153	9	$1 49	5	10	8

KING COUNTY.

Kind of establishment	Total No.	Total females	Hours	Wages	Very good	Fair	Very poor
General merchandise	39	1,778	9	$1 76	12	13	14
Factory	30	730	9	1 61	11	13	5
Laundry	26	797	10	1 80	5	16	4
Restaurant	21	156	10	1 54	11	7	3
Hotel	10	64	8	1 06	9	1	
Tailor	4	21	9	2 10	2	2	
Telephone	5	265	8	1 40	3		2
Printing	11	97	8	1 64	1	6	4
Miscellaneous	9	107	9	1 56	6	2	1
Totals and averages	155	4,015	9	$1 61	60	60	33

KITTITAS COUNTY.

Kind of establishment	Total No.	Total females	Hours	Wages	Very good	Fair	Very poor
General merchandise	8	18	9	$1 85	3	1	4
Hotels and restaurants	5	11	10		2		2
Laundry	2	26	10	1 50	1		1
Miscellaneous	9	22	9	1 84	5	1	3
Totals and averages	24	77	10	$1 73	11	2	10

TABLE NO. 2—Continued.

LEWIS COUNTY.

Kind of establishment	Total No. establishments inspected	Total number females employed	Average hours per day	Average wages per day	Very good	Fair	Very poor
General merchandise	17	59	9	$1 49	7	5	5
Restaurant	2	7	10	1 04	1	1	......
Hotel	4	20	10	1 18	4	......	......
Printing	4	7	9	1 52	1	......	3
Laundry	3	34	9	1 31	......	......	3
Telephone	2	15	8	1 07	2	......	......
Factory	2	20	9	1 48	1	......	1
Miscellaneous	7	10	8	2 10	5	......	2
Totals and averages	41	172	8	$1 40	21	6	14

PIERCE COUNTY.

Kind of establishment	Total No. establishments inspected	Total number females employed	Average hours per day	Average wages per day	Very good	Fair	Very poor
General merchandise	26	801	9	$1 62	13	7	6
Telephone	5	108	8	1 15	3	1	1
Confectionery	2	14	9	1 41	1	1	......
Dye works	2	11	9	1 65	......	1	......
Factory	26	481	9	1 56	12	4	10
Printing	4	31	8	1 30	2	......	2
Laundry	14	270	10	1 41	2	4	8
Restaurant	12	88	9	1 43	6	3	3
Hotel	6	31	9	94	6	......	......
Miscellaneous	5	19	9	1 91	4	......	1
Totals and averages	102	1,849	9	$1 44	49	21	.31

SKAGIT COUNTY.

Kind of establishment	Total No. establishments inspected	Total number females employed	Average hours per day	Average wages per day	Very good	Fair	Very poor
General merchandise	7	22	9	$1 64	5	......	2
Cannery	10	408	10	1 82	2	2	5
Printing	3	4	9	1 25	2	1	......
Telephone	3	20	8	1 04	2	......	1
Laundry	3	24	10	1 56	1	......	1
Miscellaneous	2	4	8	2 33	2	......	......
Totals and averages	28	482	9	$1 61	14	3	9

SNOHOMISH COUNTY.

Kind of establishment	Total No. establishments inspected	Total number females employed	Average hours per day	Average wages per day	Very good	Fair	Very poor
General merchandise	17	146	9	$1 96	5	6	6
Factory	5	51	9	1 45	2	......	3
Restaurant	5	19	10	142	5	......	......
Hotel	2	13	10	1 30	2	......	......
Laundry	6	87	10	1 55	2	1	3
Telephone	5	74	8	1 01	3	......	2
Printing	2	3	8	1 12	1	......	1
Miscellaneous	3	16	9	1 83	1	1	1
Totals and averages	45	409	9	$1 46	21	8	16

SPOKANE COUNTY.

Kind of establishment	Total No. establishments inspected	Total number females employed	Average hours per day	Average wages per day	Very good	Fair	Very poor
General merchandise	29	1,185	9	$1 86	9	13	7
Laundry	10	351	10	1 56	4	4	2
Hotel	7	42	8	1 48	7	......	......
Restaurant	6	46	10	1 50	3	......	3
Factory	6	141	9	1 68	2	1	3
Printing	7	51	8	1 75	1	2	4
Confectionery	6	198	9	1 40	2	1	3
Miscellaneous	7	216	9	1 73	2	3	2
Totals and averages	78	2,225	9	$1 62	30	24	24

—9

TABLE NO. 2—Continued.
THURSTON COUNTY.

Kind of establishment	Total No. establishments inspected	Total number females employed	Average hours per day	Average wages per day	Sanitary condit'ns		
					Very good	Fair	Very poor
General merchandise	7	39	9	$1 51	5	1	1
Factory	2	16	8	1 38	......	2	......
Laundry	2	24	10	1 25	......	1	1
Miscellaneous	4	27	9	1 16	2	2	......
Totals and averages........	15	106	9	$1 31	7	6	2

WALLA WALLA COUNTY.

Kind of establishment	Total No. establishments inspected	Total number females employed	Average hours per day	Average wages per day	Very good	Fair	Very poor
General merchandise	25	128	9	$1 87	9	8	7
Confectionery	5	20	9	1 83	1	2	2
Laundry	3	71	10	1 40	......	1	2
Restaurant	2	5	9	1 82	1	......	1
Miscellaneous	6	48	8	2 30	4	1	1
Totals and averages........	41	272	9	$1 64	15	12	13

WHATCOM COUNTY.

Kind of establishment	Total No. establishments inspected	Total number females employed	Average hours per day	Average wages per day	Very good	Fair	Very poor
General merchandise	16	202	9	$1 50	11	1	4
Confectionery	6	30	9	1 04	2	1	3
Cannery	8	735	10	....	3	......	5
Telephone	4	38	8	1 17	3	......	1
Laundry	6	76	10	1 41	3	2	1
Hotel and restaurant.............	11	58	10	21	3	......	3
Cigar factory	2	10	8	58	1	......	1
Miscellaneous	6	15	10	23	3	1	2
Totals and averages........	59	1,164	9	$1 30	34	5	20

YAKIMA COUNTY.

Kind of establishment	Total No. establishments inspected	Total number females employed	Average hours per day	Average wages per day	Very good	Fair	Very poor
General merchandise	17	131	9	$1 92	6	2	7
Confectionery	4	18	9	1 48	1	1	2
Printing	3	9	8	2 32	......	1	1
Laundry	2	80	10	1 60	......	......	2
Miscellaneous	11	49	9	2 00	4	4	3
Totals and averages........	37	287	9	$1 86	11	8	15

TABLE NO. 3—STATISTICS OF ESTABLISHMENTS EMPLOYING FEMALE LABOR.
Summary for the State by Counties.

COUNTY.	Total No. establishments inspected	Total number females employed	Average hours per day	Average wages per day	Sanitary condit'ns Very good	Fair	Very poor
Chehalis	42	275	9	$1 83	14	18	10
Chelan	33	101	8	1 68	7	13	13
Clarke	23	153	9	1 49	5	10	8
King	155	4,015	9	1 61	60	60	33
Kittitas	24	77	10	1 73	11	2	10
Lewis	41	172	8	1 40	21	6	14
Pierce	102	1,849	9	1 44	49	21	31
Skagit	28	482	9	1 61	14	3	9
Snohomish	45	409	9	1 46	21	8	16
Spokane	78	2,225	9	1 62	30	24	24
Thurston	15	106	9	1 31	7	6	2
Walla Walla	41	272	9	1 64	15	12	13
Whatcom	59	1,164	9	1 30	34	5	20
Yakima	37	287	9	1 86	11	8	15
Grand totals and averages...	723	12,587	9	$1 57	299	196	218

NOTE: In the foregoing tables, sanitary conditions are reported as found at time of original inspection. Changes and improvements have been required wherever necessary to meet the terms of the law.

STEAMBOAT INSPECTION

STEAMBOAT INSPECTION.

ANNUAL REPORT OF STEAMBOAT INSPECTION LAW

From October 28, 1908 to December 31, 1909, showing amount of fees collected, number of certificates and licenses issued, together with amount expended in carrying on inspection.

SHOWING LICENSES ISSUED FOR ABOVE PERIOD AS FOLLOWS:

1908 Dec.	U. S. Brannian............	Engineer	Steam	Whatcom Lake
1909 April	J. W. Gale................	M., P., and engineer ..	Gasoline..	Kachess Lake
"	L. C. Jenkins.............	M., P., and engineer ..	Gasoline..	Whatcom Lake
May	S. E. Winkler.............	Engineer	Steam	Whatcom Lake
"	Carl V. Nelson...........	M., P., and engineer ..	Steam	Whatcom Lake
"	Lee Pitman	M., P., and engineer ..	Steam	Whatcom Lake
"	Roy M. Barton...........	Engineer	Steam	Chelan Lake
"	Roy M. Barton...........	Master and pilot	Steam	Chelan Lake
"	J. C. Enlow..............	Engineer	Steam	Chelan Lake
"	Chas. Wolverton	Engineer	Steam	Chelan Lake
"	Ben F. Little.............	Master and pilot	Steam	Chelan Lake
"	C. W. Van Meter.........	Engineer	Steam	Chelan Lake
"	C. W. Van Meter.........	Master and pilot	Steam	Chelan Lake
"	E. E. Shotwell...........	Master and pilot	Steam	Chelan Lake
"	W. A. Hawley............	M., P., and engineer ..	Gasoline..	Chelan Lake
"	Ralph Hawley	M., P., and engineer ..	Gasoline..	Chelan Lake
"	A. H. Post...............	M., P., and engineer ..	Gasoline..	Chelan Lake
June	F. E. Kallock............	M., P., and engineer ..	Gasoline..	Crescent Lake
"	F. R. Eacrett............	M., P., and engineer ..	Gasoline..	Crescent Lake
"	O. C. Deiffenbach.........	M., P., and engineer ..	Gasoline..	Crescent Lake
"	Geo. H. Ladd.............	M., P., and engineer ..	Gasoline..	Crescent Lake
"	Chas. Maxwell	Engineer	Steam	Whatcom Lake
"	Chas. E. Otly............	Master and pilot	Steam	Whatcom Lake
"	Geo. L. Sly..............	M., P., and engineer ..	Gasoline..	Union Lake
"	John Campbell	M., P. and engineer ..	Gasoline..	Union Lake
"	Carl Gebbes	M., P. and engineer ..	Gasoline..	Newman Lake
"	Sam Sutton	M., P. and engineer ..	Gasoline..	Newman Lake
"	A. S. Carey..............	M., P. and engineer ..	Gasoline..	Newman Lake
"	Albert Reed	M., P., and engineer ..	Gasoline..	Newman Lake
"	Berton Rinnear	M., P., and engineer ..	Gasoline..	Newman Lake
"	Carl Young	M., P., and engineer ..	Steam	Newman Lake
"	Wm. Kipp	M., P., and engineer ..	Gasoline..	Liberty Lake
"	Evan Morgan	M., P., and engineer ..	Steam	Loon Lake
"	Edgar Becker	M., P., and engineer ..	Steam	Loon Lake
"	Hugh P. Glasgon.........	M., P., and engineer ..	Gasoline..	Medical Lake
"	A. Hubbard	M., P., and engineer ..	Gasoline..	Medical Lake
"	H. J. Lubbin.............	M., P., and engineer ..	Gasoline..	Medical Lake
"	G. F. Davis..............	M., P., and engineer ..	Gasoline..	Medical Lake
"	W. E. Thomas...........	M., P., and engineer ..	Gasoline..	Medical Lake
"	Theo. Halin	M., P., and engineer ..	Gasoline..	Liberty Lake
"	M. J. Kalez..............	M., P., and engineer ..	Gasoline..	Liberty Lake
"	C. W. Castleman.........	M., P., and engineer ..	Gasoline..	Liberty Lake
"	Chas. Ellis	M., P., and engineer ..	Gasoline..	Liberty Lake
"	Pete Stinger	M., P., and engineer ..	Gasoline..	Liberty Lake
"	H. G. Brown.............	M., P., and engineer ..	Gasoline..	Liberty Lake
"	P. Ferguson	M., P., and engineer ..	Gasoline..	Liberty Lake
"	W. D. Nickson...........	M., P., and engineer ..	Gasoline..	Liberty Lake
"	Ralph Williams	M., P., and engineer ..	Gasoline..	Liberty Lake
"	Geo. A. Jenkins..........	M., P., and engineer ..	Gasoline..	Whatcom Lake
"	Arnold Bern	M., P., and engineer ..	Gasoline..	Union Lake

LICENSES ISSUED FROM OCT. 28, 1908, TO DEC. 31, 1909—Concluded.

June	Sidney D. Finch	M., P., and engineer	Gasoline	Cushman Lake
"	J. Beck	M., P., and engineer	Steam	Medical Lake
"	Carl Shaler	M., P., and engineer	Gasoline	Medical Lake
"	Fred Tuttle	M., P., and engineer	Gasoline	Chelan Lake
"	B. J. Tuttle	M., P., and engineer	Gasoline	Chelan Lake
"	Oscar Pasley	M. P., and engineer	Gasoline	Chelan Lake
"	Geo. E. Cottrell	M., P., and engineer	Gasoline	Chelan Lake
July	C. D. Gillett	M., P., and engineer	Gasoline	Newman Lake
"	Geo. S. Helms	M., P., and engineer	Gasoline	Any lake in state
"	L. Knuppenburg	Master and pilot	Steam	Whatcom Lake
"	Gus G. Breseman	M., P., and engineer	Gasoline	American Lake
Aug.	E. A. McGoldrick	M., P., and engineer	Gasoline	Liberty Lake
"	Harold Watson	M., P., and engineer	Gasoline	Chelan Lake
"	D. M. Sterling	M., P., and engineer	Gasoline	Liberty Lake
"	H. J. Fuller	M., P., and engineer	Gasoline	Liberty Lake
"	Geo. T. Miller	M., P., and engineer	Gasoline	American Lake
"	Uri Ackerman	M., P., and engineer	Gasoline	Cle Elum Lake
"	W. H. Martin, Jr	M., P., and engineer	Gasoline	American Lake
"	John Olsen	M., P., and engineer	Gasoline	Crescent Lake
Sept.	Jas. P. Boland	M., P., and engineer	Gasoline	Lake Chelan
"	F. A. Ott	M., P., and engineer	Gasoline	Wenatchee Lake
Oct.	Geo. W. Douglas	M ster and pilot	Steam	Whatcom Lake
"	H. A. Wright	M., P., and engineer	Gasoline	Crescent Lake
"	Sam Louden	M., P., and engineer	Steam	Union Lake
"	W. F. Jacobs	M., P., and engineer	Gasoline	Crescent Lake
Nov.	A. A. Macy	M., P., and engineer	Gasoline	Chelan Lake
"	Norman W. Austin	M., P., and engineer	Gasoline	Crescent Lake

Total.. 77

SHOWING CERTIFICATES ISSUED TO THE FOLLOWING NAMED VESSELS FOR 1909.

1909	NAME	OWNER	POWER	CITY
April	Miami	J. W. Gale	Gasoline	Easton
May	Marguerite	Nelson & Pitman	Steam	Bellingham
"	Geneva	G. A. Jenkins	Gasoline	Geneva
"	Elsinore	Nelson & Pitman	Steam	Silver Beach
"	Tourist	Amos Edmonds	Steam	Lakeside
"	Lady of the Lake	Lake Chelan Navigation Co.	Steam	Lakeside
"	Cupid	A. H. Post	Gasoline	Chelan
"	G. M. T.	W. A. Hawley	Gasoline	Chelan
"	Boss	W. A. Hawley	Gasoline	Chelan
June	Olympus	F. R. Eacrett	Gasoline	Piedmont
"	Crescent	M. Earle	Steam	Piedmont
"	Susie E. Day	Elmer E. Day	Gasoline	Lake Crescent
"	Adelaide	Otly & Maxwell	Steam	Bellingham
"	Hulda	Arnold Bern	Gasoline	Seattle
"	Harold	Arnold Bern	Gasoline	Seattle
"	Esther S	Campbell Bros.	Gasoline	Seattle
"	Rainbow	Bert Ringer	Gasoline	Newman Lake
"	Kathryn	A. S. Carey	Gasoline	Newman Lake
"	Gypsy	Sam Sutton	Gasoline	Newman Lake
"	Flink	Twin Cedar Club	Steam	Newman Lake
"	Zephyr	Chas. Thrager	Gasoline	Liberty Lake
"	Gwen	Evan Morgan	Steam	Loon Lake
"	Teddy	Jas. Glasgon	Gasoline	Medical Lake
"	Iva J	G. F. Davis	Gasoline	Medical Lake
"	Georgia B	G. F. Davis	Gasoline	Medical Lake
"	Ferryette	G. F. Davis	Gasoline	Medical Lake (Sold)
"	Ferry	G. F. Davis	Gasoline	Medical Lake
"	O. K.	G. F. Davis	Gasoline	Medical Lake
"	Shamrock	G. N. Farron	Gasoline	Liberty Lake
"	Helen	W. D. Nickson	Gasoline	Liberty Lake
"	Virginia	M. J. Kale	Gasoline	Liberty Lake
"	Lotus	Chas. Ellis	Gasoline	Liberty Lake
"	Narcissus	O. H. Wolfe	Gasoline	Liberty Lake
"	Princess May	A. O. Olsen	Gasoline	Spokane
"	Iola	Theo Halin	Gasoline	Liberty Lake
"	Ramona	Geo. A. Jenkins	Gasoline	Bellingham
"	Billy Hicks	Sidney Finch	Gasoline	Hoodsport
"	Mary	Lake Chelan B. Co	Gasoline	Lakeside
"	Hyak	Lake Chelan B. Co	Gasoline	Lakeside
July	Gillett	C. D. Gillett	Gasoline	Moab
"	Northside	W. H. Martin	Gasoline	Tacoma
"	Frolic	Gus G. Breseman	Gasoline	Tacoma
Aug.	Rex	W. A. Mackenzie	Gasoline	Spokane Bridge
"	Mary Lucille	E. A. McGoldrick	Gasoline	Spokane
"	Haverine	Mrs. J. H. Watson	Gasoline	Lakeside
"	Flirt	H. J. Fuller	Gasoline	Spokane
"	Ferry	Geo. T. Miller	Gasoline	South Tacoma
"	Standard	R. P. Lumsden	Gasoline	Roslyn
Sept.	Nina	Lake Chelan B. Co	Gasoline	Lakeside
"	Clara D	F. A. Ott	Gasoline	Telma
Oct.	Helen K	O. C. Kallock	Gasoline	Seattle
"	Maude	Brace & Hergert	Steam	Seattle
	Total			52

ANNUAL REPORT OF STEAMBOAT INSPECTION LAW

From January 1, 1910 to September 30, 1910, showing amount of fees collected, number of certificates and licenses issued, together with amount expended in carrying on inspection.

LICENSES ISSUED DURING ABOVE PERIOD AS FOLLOWS:

1910				
Jan.	U. S. Brannian............	Engineer	Steam	Whatcom Lake
May	L. C. Jenkins.............	M., P., and engineer ..	Gasoline..	Whatcom Lake
"	Geo. Lombard	M., P., and engineer ..	Gasoline..	Whatcom Lake
"	Lee Pitman	M., P., and engineer ..	Steam	Whatcom Lake
June	F. E. Kalloch.............	M., P., and engineer ..	Gasoline..	Crescent Lake
"	O. C. Dieffenbach.........	M., P., and engineer ..	Gasoline..	Crescent Lake
"	Geo. A. Jenkins...........	M., P., and engineer ..	Gasoline..	Whatcom Lake
"	W. A. Hawley.............	M., P., and engineer ..	Gasoline..	Chelan Lake
"	Ralph Hawley	M., P., and engineer ..	Gasoline..	Chelan Lake
"	Thos. Johnson	M., P., and engineer ..	Gasoline..	Chelan Lake
"	Robt. R. Green............	M., P., and engineer ..	Gasoline..	Spanaway Lake
"	C. W. Van Meter..........	Engineer	Steam	Chelan Lake
"	C. W. Van Meter..........	Master and pilot	Steam	Chelan Lake
"	E. E. Shotwell............	M., P., and engineer ..	Steam	Chelan Lake
"	Ben F. Little..............	M., P., and engineer ..	Steam	Chelan Lake
"	Roy M. Barton............	Engineer	Steam	Chelan Lake
"	Roy M. Barton............	Master and pilot	Steam	Chelan Lake
"	J. C. Enlow...............	Engineer	Steam	Chelan Lake
"	J. W. Gale................	M., P., and engineer ..	Gasoline..	Kachess Lake
"	A. H. Post................	M., P., and engineer ..	Gasoline..	Chelan Lake
"	E. J. Ovington............	M., P., and engineer ..	Gasoline..	Crescent Lake
"	Victor Harris	M., P., and engineer ..	Gasoline..	Newman Lake
"	Sam Sutton	M., P., and engineer ..	Gasoline..	Newman Lake
"	C. D. Gillett..............	M., P., and engineer ..	Gasoline..	Newman Lake
"	Frank W. Porritt..........	M., P., and engineer ..	Gasoline..	Newman Lake
"	B. C. Rinear..............	M., P., and engineer ..	Gasoline..	Newman Lake
"	W. D. Nickson............	M., P., and engineer ..	Gasoline..	Liberty Lake
"	Ed. Bland	M., P., and engineer ..	Gasoline..	Liberty Lake
"	C. E. Ernst...............	M., P., and engineer ..	Gasoline..	Liberty Lake
"	D. C. Coakley.............	M., P., and engineer ..	Gasoline..	Liberty Lake
"	Robt. Skinner	M., P., and engineer ..	Gasoline..	Liberty Lake
"	Evan Morgan	M., P., and engineer ..	Steam	Loon Lake
"	Arthur Chase	M., P., and engineer ..	Steam	Loon Lake
"	M. T. McGoldrick.........	M., P., and engineer ..	Gasoline..	Liberty Lake
"	Cecil W. Cooper..........	M., P., and engineer ..	Gasoline..	Liberty Lake
"	J. R. Harvey..............	M., P., and engineer ..	Gasoline..	Chelan Lake
July	Charlie Maxwell	Engineer	Steam	Whatcom Lake
"	Oscar Oleson	Engineer	Steam	Whatcom Lake
"	C. E. Otley...............	Master and pilot	Steam	Whatcom Lake
"	Earl W. Howard...,......	M., P., and engineer ..	Gasoline..	Chelan Lake
"	Wm. H. Martin, Jr.......	M., P., and engineer ..	Gasoline..	American Lake
"	Jas. Stanley	M., P., and engineer ..	Gasoline..	American Lake
"	Sam Louden	M., P., and engineer ..	Steam	Lake Union
"	J. W. Stares..............	M., P., and engineer ..	Gasoline..	Lake Samamish
"	J. O. Sunderhauf..........	M., P., and engineer ..	Gasoline..	Lake Samamish
"	Fred King	M., P., and engineer ..	Gasoline..	Lake Samamish
Aug.	H. A. Pardee..............	M., P., and engineer ..	Gasoline..	Lake Keechelus
"	F. A. Ott.................	M., P., and engineer ..	Gasoline..	Lake Wenatchee
"	H. W. Higgins.............	M., P., and engineer ..	Gasoline..	Chelan Lake
"	W. N. Caswell............	M., P., and engineer ..	Gasoline..	Chelan Lake
"	Geo. E. Cottrell..........	M., P., and engineer ..	Gasoline..	Chelan Lake
"	B. J. Tuttle..............	M., P., and engineer ..	Gasoline..	Chelan Lake
"	W. T. Pasley.............	M., P., and engineer ..	Gasoline..	Chelan Lake
"	O. R. Pasley..............	M., P., and engineer ..	Gasoline..	Chelan Lake
"	F. J. Tuttle..............	M., P., and engineer ..	Gasoline..	Chelan Lake
"	J. A. Robbins.............	M., P., and engineer ..	Gasoline..	Liberty Lake
"	C. E. Kilbourn............	M., P., and engineer ..	Gasoline..	Silver Lake
"	C. Phalis	M., P., and engineer ..	Gasoline..	Silver Lake
"	E. A. McGoldrick..........	M., P., and engineer ..	Gasoline..	Liberty Lake
"	Raymond Sholer	M., P., and engineer ..	Gasoline..	Medical Lake
"	Clyde Jerne	M., P., and engineer ..	Gasoline..	Medical Lake
"	G. F. Davis	M., P., and engineer ..	Gasoline..	Medical Lake
Sept.	M. J. Kalez...............	M., P., and engineer ..	Gasoline..	Liberty Lake
"	Karle Hoffman	M., P., and engineer ..	Gasoline..	Liberty Lake
"	D. J. Strait..............	M., P., and engineer ..	Gasoline..	Silver Lake

Total.. 65

CERTIFICATES ISSUED TO THE FOLLOWING NAMED VESSELS, 1910.

1910	NAME	OWNER	POWER	CITY
May	Ramona............	Geo. A. Jenkins................	Gasoline..	Bellingham
"	Geneva............	Geo. A. Jenkins................	Gasoline..	Bellingham
"	Eva L............	Geo. Lombard	Gasoline..	Silver Beach
"	Elsinore...........	Douglas & Pitman.............	Steam	Bellingham
"	Marguerite........	Douglas & Pitman.............	Steam	Bellingham
June	Olympus........	Mitchell-Christofer-Kalloch	Gasoline..	Piedmont
"	Susie E. Day......	Elmer E. Day.................	Gasoline..	Lake Crescent
"	Gem...............	W. A. Hawley...............	Gasoline..	Chelan
"	G. M. T...........	W. A. Hawley...............	Gasoline..	Chelan
"	Frolic............	G. G. Breseman.............	Gasoline..	Tacoma
"	Lady of the Lake..	L. C. Navigation Co...........	Gasoline..	Lakeside
"	Tourist...........	Amos Edmonds	Steam	Lakeside
"	Miami............	J. W. Gale..................	Gasoline..	Easton
"	Cupid............	A. H. Post..................	Gasoline..	Chelan
"	Emily............	E. J. Ovington...............	Gasoline..	Piedmont
"	Gypsy............	Sam Sutton	Gasoline..	Newman Lake
"	Gillett............	C. D. Gillett................	Gasoline..	Moab
"	Kathryn...........	F. W. Porritt................	Gasoline..	Moab
"	Helen II..........	W. D. Nickson...............	Gasoline..	Liberty Lake
"	Helen............	E. E. Ernst.................	Gasoline..	Liberty Lake
"	Dreamwood.......	E. E. Ernst.................	Gasoline..	Liberty Lake
"	Liberty Belle......	D. C. Coakley................	Gasoline..	Liberty Lake
"	Gwen............	Evan Morgan	Steam	Loon Lake
"	Nymph...........	Cecil W. Cooper.............	Gasoline..	Hillyard
"	Opine.............	J. R. Harvey................	Gasoline..	Chelan
July	Joy...............	Thos. Johnson	Gasoline..	Chelan
"	Comet............	Otly & Maxwell..............	Steam	Bellingham
"	Northside.........	Wm. Martin	Gasoline..	Tacoma
"	Garryowen........	James Stanley	Gasoline..	Tacoma
"	Maude............	Brace & Hergert Mill Co........	Steam	Seattle
"	Imp..............	W. J. Stares.................	Gasoline..	Inglewood
"	Monohon..........	M. B. & Canoe Co.............	Gasoline..	Monohon
"	Grace............	Fred King ,...................	Gasoline..	Monohon
Aug.	Cascadia..........	P. Flanagan	Gasoline..	Easton
"	Clara D...........	F. A. Ott...................	Gasoline..	Telma
"	Hattie............	W. N. Caswell...............	Gasoline..	Lake Chelan
"	Rena.............	L. C. Boat Co...............	Gasoline..	Lakeside
"	Comet............	L. C. Boat Co...............	Gasoline..	Lakeside
"	Ruth.............	L. C. Boat Co...............	Gasoline..	Lakeside
"	Nina.............	L. C. Boat Co...............	Gasoline..	Lakeside
"	Wawawega........	F. W. Porritt................	Gasoline..	Newman Lake
"	Silver Queen.......	Lindberg & Kilbourn...........	Gasoline..	Silver Lake
"	Gipsy............	D. J. Strait.................	Gasoline..	Bothell
"	Mary Lucille......	E. A. McGoldrick.............	Gasoline..	Spokane
"	O. K.............	G. F. Davis.................	Steam	Medical Lake
"	Ferry............	G. F. Davis.................	Gasoline..	Medical Lake
"	Ferry II..........	G. F. Davis.................	Gasoline..	Medical Lake
"	Joy Ride.........	G. F. Davis.................	Gasoline..	Medical Lake
Sept.	Crescent..........	Soliduck Hot Springs Co......	Gasoline..	Seattle
"	Virginia..........	M. J. Kalez.................	Gasoline..	Liberty Lake
"	Islander..........	D. J. Strait.................	Gasoline..	Bothell S. L
"	Fairholme........	C. C. Dieffenbach............	Gasoline..	Lake Crescent
"	Hazel............	S. French	Gasoline..	Lake Cushman
	Total..........	....		58

STEAMBOAT INSPECTION FUND, SEPTEMBER 30, 1910.

RECEIPTS.		DISBURSEMENTS.	
Collected for licenses and certificates from Sept. 30, 1908, to Sept. 30, 1910.................	$1,600 00	Expenditures from Sept. 30, 1908 to Sept. 30, 1910..............	$2,255 73
Appropriation for two years....	1,000 00		
Total......................	$2,600 00	Total........................	$2,255 73

FARM LABOR

FARM LABOR.

As in previous years, an effort has been made to secure for this report reliable information relating to the conditions surrounding farm labor in this state. For this purpose blank forms of inquiry were sent out to a number of employing farmers, nearly all of the important agricultural counties in the state being represented in the list. This subject is one of growing interest and importance owing to the great increase in farming activity in Washington and the large number of persons who are annually turning from the cities to seek a livlihood in some form of agricultural industry. There is a marked tendency in this state in the direction of reducing the average farm acreage and proportionately increasing the number of families engaging in farming as a gainful occupation. This condition adds materially to the value of the information supplied by the practical farmers to whom the blanks above mentioned were sent. From their replies it may be said that farm labor on the whole is scarce and that competent help is difficult to secure. The wages paid are undoubtedly better then farm hands receive in most farming sections of the country and very few employing farmers report any special difficulty in keeping their help. In answer to the question, "Can you offer any suggestions that might make farm work more attractive to the average laborer?" the following replies were secured:

Clarkston.—"Better accommodations should be provided."

Clarkston.—"Treat them as brethern, as one of the family."

Davenport.—"Give the men better board and lodging. In short make them feel at home."

Davenport.—"A better place should be provided for farm workmen to sleep then the average farmers have."

North Yakima.—"Better rooming conveniences but do not think that would overcome the weakness for liquor."

Ritzville.—"I treat my men as I like to be treated when I worked out. I have two men that have been working with me four years."

Sunnyside.—"My men have less hours to work then I do and as nearly as possible they are treated as members of the family."

North Yakima.—"We have one or two men most of the time but for harvest time we need many. Farmers as a rule should give their men better treatment."

Outlook.—"I keep men by the year and they work better when the work and pay are steady. The men want a vacation the same as I do and work better for it."

Elberton.—"As a rule the hired man is used more like a slave then a man. Use him more as though he were one of the family and you will have no trouble in keeping him."

Mt. Vernon.—"There are many ways in which farm work could be made more attractive. However, to furnish those attractions the farmer must make concessions which would be detrimental and unprofitable to him."

Mt. Vernon.—"As a rule it is hard to suggest what is best, as we have so many different classes to contend with. I think if saloons were eliminated we should have better results as the men would save more money."

Pullman.—"The average farm laborer is of the traveling class and will not work very long at any one place. They only want work where wages are highest and all conveniences are furnished. As a rule farm laborers are treated well."

Cashmere.—"Make things more homelike for the men. Where you need help nearly the year round hire married men, and furnish them cottages. They should also have a garden plot and a chance to attend church and seek amusements."

Sunnyside.—"Farmers cannot afford to pay higher wages or to work their men less then ten hours. A comfortable room and good reading should be provided. The men should receive kind treatment and have as few chores as possible to do after six."

Colfax.—"Wipe out the saloons and gamblers who fleece the laborers when they go to town. The working man who can resist the saloons and is willing to work will soon become an employer himself. The well-to-do farmers of this country mostly started as farm laborers."

Ellensburg.—"Make the hours of labor to compare with the improved machinery and adopt as much of this kind of machinery as is necessary to do the work with shorter hours in the field. Always treat your employees as you would like to be treated in the same position."

Mt. Vernon.—"In my thirty two years of farming on the Sound I find that the best plan is to show yourself interested in the comfort of the man that works for you. Give him plenty to eat at the same table with yourself and always speak to him as though you were not above him.

Mt. Vernon.—"Employees on the farm should be treated more like members of the family. They should be furnished with beds and bedding and also have their washing done by the people they work for. This would make them feel very differently and they would enjoy the farm much more."

Starbuck.—"In this locality the land is largely owned by men of capital living in Seattle or elsewhere in western Washington. As a rule they have no buildings on their farms fit for man or beast to occupy. It would be a nice thing if they could be induced to erect good houses to live in and barns for stock. This would make farm life far more attractive to the laboring class."

Cashmere.—"I have always contended that a fair wage both winter and summer is the best plan. I hire at least one man that way and will keep more all the year through as soon as I can afford it. Most of our fruit growers here turn the men off in the fall and then they must look up other work or live up all their summer's earnings. That system does not encourage the best labor to remain on the farm."

North Yakima.—"The better the wages paid and the better the board, the harder it is to get good labor. All labor seems

—10

to be daffy about amusements. The men would rather work in town for fifty cents a day where they can have a glass of beer after supper and see a ten cent show. Jobs are too plentiful now for labor to stick. They know if they get broke they can soon get work, so they do not try to save."

FARM LABOR—TABLE NO. 1.

Principal Crops Raised.	Number of men employed	Wages per month (board included)	Wages per day (board included)	Wages paid man and team	Hours worked per day	Months worked per year	Wages paid harvest hands	Number of acres in farm
Adams County—								
Wheat	1	$40 00	$1 50	......	10	9	$2 50 to 3 00	600
Wheat	4	35 00	1 85	$2 50	10 and 12	9	2 00 to 3 00	1,200
Wheat and oats......	18	45 00	2 50 to 3 00	4 00	9	12	...... 3 00	1,000
Wheat	2 to 14	35 00	1 35	2 35	9 and 10	9	2 50 to 5 00	1,290
Asotin County—								
Wheat, hay and oats.	4	60 00 without board	2 00 to 2 25	4 00 to 4 50	10	12	......	900
Hay, grain and fruit.	1 to 7	without board 30 00	2 00	......	8 and 9	12	2 00 to 6 00	1,120
Chelan County—								
Hay and apples......	2	35 00	2 00	......	10	6 and 12	2 00 to 2 50	1,120
Apples	1	45 00 and 50 00	2 00 to 2 50	6 00 to 8 00	10	9 and 10	2 50 to 3 00	10
Fruit	3 to 20	40 00	1 50 to 2 50	5 00 to 7 00	10	9	2 50	65
Fruit	2	40 00	2 50	6 00	10	7	2 50	40
Columbia County—								
Wheat and barley.....	3	35 00	......	......	8 and 10	6	2 50 to 8 00	1,440
Wheat	2	35 00	1 50	5 00	10	8	2 50 to 4 00	500
Kittitas County—								
Hay	2	40 00	1 75 to 8 00	......	10	8	2 00 to 3 00	195
Hay and grain.......	1	40 00	1 50	......	10	12	2 00	200
Fruit, potatoes and alfalfa.	4	......	2 25 without b'rd	5 00	10	8	2 25	100
Klickitat County—								
Wheat	3	......	without b'rd	......	9	......	8 50 to 7 00	1,040
Lincoln County—								
Wheat and barley.....	6	35 00	1 85	4 00	10	10	2 00 to 5 00	2,000
Wheat and oats......	......	35 00	1 35	......	10 and 12	......	2 00 to 4 00	500
San Juan County—								
Hay and grain.......	2	40 00	1 50	4 00	10	12	1 50 to 2 00	160
Hay and grain.......	......	35 00 and 40 00	1 50 to 2 00	5 00	10	......	2 00	300
Skagit County—								
Oat and hay.........	3	30 00	1 50 to 2 00	5 00	10	12	2 00	200
Oats and hay........	5	37 50	1 50	4 00	10	12	2 25	320
Oats, hay and milk..	6	75 00	2 50	......	10	12	2 00 to 5 00	140
Oats and hay........	2	30 00	1 75	......	10	......	......	250

FARM LABOR—TABLE NO. 1—Concluded.

Principal Crops Raised.	Number of men employed	Wages per month (board included)	Wages per day (board included)	Wages paid man and team	Hours worked per day	Months worked per year	Wages paid harvest hands	Number of acres in farm
Whitman County—								
Wheat, oats and barley	6	40 00	1 50	4 50	10	12	2 50 to 3 00	640
Grain	5	35 00	1 50	3 00	10	9	3 00 to 3 00	1,220
Grain	1	50 00		3 50 to 5 00	10 and 11	2	2 50 to 3 00	
		40 00		4 00	10	9	3 00 to 5 00	
Yakima County—								
Fruit and alfalfa	2	40 00	2 00	4 00	10	10	2 50	200
Apples and peaches	5		2 75 to 3 00 without b'rd	5 50	10	4, 6, 12		100
Fruit			2 00 to 2 50	5 00	10			75
Fruit and hay	25	40 00	1 50	5 00	10	12	2 50 to 3 50	400
Grain and potatoes	3	30 00 to 40 00	2 00	4 50	8 and 10	8 and 12	2 00	500
Alfalfa	1	50 00	2 50	4 00	10	12		80
Alfalfa	2	40 00	2 00	4 25	10	8	2 50	82
Fruit	30	40 00		4 50 to 5 00	10	8		400
Wheat	25	35 00	1 50		10	10	4 00	1,380

FARM LABOR—TABLE NO. 2—SUMMARY.

Total number of farms reported 36
Number of men employed 217
Average wages per day with board $1 86
Average wages per month with board $42 68
Average wages per day for man and team $4 44

Average hours per day 10
Average months per year 8½
Average wages paid harvest hands $3 00
Average number of acres per farm 563

FREE EMPLOYMENT OFFICES.

FREE EMPLOYMENT OFFICES.

Free employment offices are maintained by the local authorities in the cities of Seattle, Tacoma, Spokane and Everett. These offices are all performing an important work in their respective communities and through them, many of the evils that formerly flourished in connection with the private employment agencies have been checked. Proprietors of the latter class of establishments knowing that they must meet the competition of the public agency are less inclined to misuse and take unfair advantages of the persons who apply to them for positions. Thousands of positions are annually secured for wage-earners through the free offices, and while most of them are hampered by lack of sufficient funds to carry on their work in the most satisfactory and effective manner, nevertheless the results as shown by their reports indicate beyond question that these institutions are an exceedingly helpful influence among the wage-earners of their respective cities.

Reports have been secured from all the offices mentioned above and are published herewith.

STATISTICAL REPORT OF THE PUBLIC EMPLOYMENT OFFICE OF THE CITY OF SEATTLE.

SUMMARY OF POSITIONS FURNISHED DURING 1909.—MALE.

	Jan.	Feb.	March	April	May	June	July	Aug.	Sept.	Oct.	Nov.	Dec.
Laborers	968	1,021	2,006	2,777	2,440	2,680	2,636	4,300	4,059	3,177	2,301	1,391
Carpenters	48	55	139	139	98	65	32	50	80	66	80	27
Housemen	58	58	95	140	180	180	105	87	112	159	133	94
Cooks	7	5	7	9	12	19	25	24	25	12	2	4
Farmers	16	31	70	50	37	48	56	35	25	42	19	12
Kitchen help	11	18	37	98	65	89	109	103	102	96	27	35
Teamsters	17	19	30	44	27	24	68	105	102	44	52	16
Railroad men	12		88	56	85	77	112	53	98	66	55	5
Wood cutters	18	22	25	18	9	30	14	21	68	40	28	33
Coal men	10	51	37		41	22		12	68	25	32	51
Boys	4	10	20	23	34	51	13	16	44	18	12	6
Solicitors	2	1	1	6	5	11	11	4	12	7	1	4
Waiters	6	6	10	10	7	6	19	24	26	15	13	6
Blacksmiths	8	8	3	3	2	7	2	6	2	1		3
Painters	7	8	21	64	28	20	13	4	14	13	9	5
Lathers	4	1	11	1	10	4	11	7	6	5	1	5
Janitors	2	1	5	4	6	9	1	6	4	4	1	1
Engineers	1	4	3	2	3		1	1		1	3	
Bakers	2		1	1	1	1	1	3	3	2	1	3
Plumbers		3	1	2	6	3	2	3	1	4		9
Shinglers		1	16	7	1	4	2	3	2	8	9	4
Masons	2		6	5	1	1	8	1		2	3	3
Watchmen	1		1		2	8	6	1				
Miners	1		4			1	1					
Machinists		6	6									2
Electricians		3	1									4
Firemen			2	4	3	2	3	3	1	5	4	
Tallymen			1	2		1						
Lumbermen			9	2	2		4	6	1	1	1	
Chainmen			4		1				2			
Gardeners			1	3		1	10	15				
Loggers			3	1			1		1	1		
Printers				1					1	2		
Shoemakers				1					1			
Barn men					2		1		2		1	
Butchers										3		
Sailors										1	1	
Helpers	7		2	5	5	9	10	7	7		1	4
Totals	1,226	1,825	2,664	3,428	3,113	3,823	3,280	4,869	4,813	3,764	2,776	1,726

Total number of positions furnished, 39,382.

SUMMARY OF POSITIONS FURNISHED DURING 1909, SEATTLE—FEMALE.

	Jan.	Feb.	March	April	May	June	July	Aug.	Sept.	Oct.	Nov.	Dec.
Housework	53	48	98	90	88	77	78	73	68	60	46	42
Day work	55	30	92	108	85	110	84	104	79	61	39	26
Chambermaids	3	..	7	8	4	11	21	14	13	4	6	4
Cooks	3	4	21	23	5	23	6	17	20	15	14	5
Second girl	6	7	22	8	17	23	23	18	14	10	8	6
Girls	12	10	15	11	7	12	7	11	14	12	8	9
Nurses	6	3	5	6	2	8	7	5	3	1	..	1
Waitresses	5	6	6	5	18	16	35	30	18	15	2	4
Laundresses	6	2	2	6	..	2	5	..	..	1	..	..
Factory	1	3	..	1	..	..	1	..	..	..	..	..
Clerical wrk	1	..	5	2	..	1	..	1	1	8	1	3
Seamstresses	1	1	1	3	2	..	1	2	..	4	..	..
Maids	..	..	1	2	..	..	1	1	1	3	1	..
Janitresses	..	..	..	..	..	..	2	2	2	3	..	..
Solicitors	..	..	..	..	..	..	..	1	..	..	..	..
Totals	154	114	270	272	228	278	280	276	227	191	124	100

Total number of positions furnished, 2,514.

POSITIONS FURNISHED BY PUBLIC EMPLOYMENT OFFICE, SEATTLE, WASH., YEARS 1894-1909.

Year.	Jan.	Feb.	March	April	May	June	July	August	Sept.	Oct.	Nov.	Dec.	Total
1894	180	223	257	134	201	221	244	510	600	396	256	271	2,823
1895	162	319	347	280	311	325	429	488	264	388	298	190	8,729
1896	319	221	533	240	254	318	373	250	196	291	205	318	3,403
1897	917	1,285	1,098	600	521	558	941	1,076	1,048	842	848	1,229	8,736
1898	827	726	2,015	2,231	1,516	1,960	2,965	2,427	2,714	2,108	1,128	1,128	21,948
1899	1,195	1,144	1,250	2,402	1,642	1,591	2,331	2,712	3,177	2,499	1,285	988	26,320
1900	857	784	1,306	1,497	3,129	2,682	3,873	2,869	2,882	2,025	1,162	989	20,164
1901	1,099	654	1,787	1,641	1,770	2,701	3,982	8,884	3,110	2,475	1,419	1,204	25,096
1902	1,123	1,265	1,047	2,056	1,931	1,946	3,213	2,751	3,409	3,264	1,725	1,065	24,429
1903	1,743	672	1,060	1,578	2,665	3,219	3,798	3,923	3,803	2,716	1,481	842	28,841
1904	713	707	2,342	1,208	1,490	1,531	2,644	3,081	2,820	1,838	1,207	973	19,453
1905	1,022	1,144	3,254	3,317	1,585	2,128	3,182	2,498	2,872	2,566	1,489	1,910	20,965
1906	1,888	2,272	1,304	3,230	3,366	3,261	4,603	4,689	4,218	3,138	2,043	940	35,344
1907	867	983	2,954	1,526	3,667	2,652	3,302	3,246	3,294	2,088	1,231	1,556	31,074
1908	1,380	1,439		3,095	1,496	1,611	2,231	8,008	3,186	2,541	1,926	1,826	22,295
1909					3,341	3,601	3,560	5,175	5,040	3,965	2,900		38,846

CLASSIFICATION OF POSITIONS FILLED THROUGH THE SEATTLE PUBLIC
EMPLOYMENT OFFICE, YEARS 1894-1909.

Year	Total male help supplied	Total female help supplied	Total hop pickers	Grand total	Average by month	Total expense	Cost of each position
1894	1,580	1,243	1,144	3,967	441	$909 65	22.93c
1895	1,831	1,898	2,050	5,779	482	1,120 00	19.38c
1896	1,647	1,756	135	3,403	284	727 50	21.38c
1897	6,163	2,573	2,890	11,626	969	724 08	6.24c
1898	18,154	3,794	2,235	24,183	2,015	1,877 13	5.69c
1899	20,852	5,463	1,285	27,650	2,300	1,239 41	4.49c
1900	16,082	4,082	2,682	22,846	1,904	1,132 61	4.96c
1901	19,411	5,684	1,465	26,560	2,214	1,276 69	4.8 c
1902	19,242	5,188	1,480	25,905	2,159	1,320 91	5.1 c
1903	23,302	5,689	1,465	30,305	2,525	1,479 70	4.88c
1904	15,666	3,787	1,105	20,558	1,713	1,308 36	6.36c
1905	17,763	3,202	802	21,767	1,814	1,314 19	6.08c
1906	31,792	3,552	2,490	37,834	3,153	1,526 11	4.06c
1907	28,769	2,305	280	31,074	2,589	1,549 30	4.98c
1908	20,123	2,060	....	22,183	1,848	1,321 70	5.95c
1909	36,332	2,514	....	38,846	3,237	1,623 05	4.18c

Supplemental Report of the Public Employment Office of Seattle.

September 8, 1910.

Hon. Charles F. Hubbard, State Labor Commissioner, Olympia, Wash.:

DEAR SIR—Answering your favor of the 6th inst., I beg to submit
below a statement of the result of the work of the Public Employment
Office of this city for the first eight months of the present year. The
figures represent the number of persons called for by employers, male
and female respectively.

	Men	Women
January	1,345	109
February	1,500	108
March	2,386	194
April	3,377	195
May	3,505	183
June	3,408	109
July	3,018	167
August	3,028	171
Totals	21,567	1,236

This makes a total of help called for and furnished of 22,803 for
the first eight months of this year. Our orders for help are almost invariably filled promptly.

We regret to state that our work for women is not increasing. This
is due to the persistent policy of the authorities to reduce to the lowest
possible limit the cost of operation notwithstanding our repeated requests for additional help in the ladies department. Our work for men
continues at a satisfactory rate although the results are slightly less
than those for the year 1909, which was the banner year for the office.

Yours respectfully,

A. H. GROUT,

Labor Commissioner, City of Seattle.

REPORT OF THE FREE EMPLOYMENT BUREAU OF THE CITY OF TACOMA FOR THE YEAR BEGINNING SEPTEMBER 1, 1909, AND ENDING AUGUST 30, 1910.—MALE HELP.

	Sept.	Oct.	Nov.	Dec.	Jan.	Feb.	March	April	May	June	July	Aug.
Laborers	713	540	565	771	414	272	433	497	370	482	696	776
Lumbermen	54	60	96	17	15	47	116	125	49	115	198	99
Farmers	4	14	2	3	3	9	4	5	11	8	4	8
Teamsters	4	12	7	5		5	3	7	5	9	11	7
Housemen	47	56	54	43	45	44	34	39	47	52	38	52
Kitchen help	8	10	4	15	15	8	5	8	18	14	19	12
Carpenters	2	12	8	4	4	6	3	4	6	16	11	14
Deck hands	26	12	40	4	4	9	18	11	15	13	25	15
Railroad laborers	21	23	3	13	7	8	18	16	27	22	18	17
Engineers		2		1	1	1	2	8		1	1	1
Firemen	3	6		9	7	7	7	8	5	12	4	12
Cooks			4	8	2	5	3	4	6	6	5	8
Sailors			2			4		8	10	23	12	34
Porters				11	3	2	13	7	8	4	3	6
Totals	883	747	779	887	520	427	654	742	572	777	1,045	1,061

REPORT OF THE FREE EMPLOYMENT BUREAU OF THE CITY OF TACOMA.—FEMALE HELP.

	Sept.	Oct.	Nov.	Dec.	Jan.	Feb.	March	April	May	June	July	Aug.
Maids	13	11	17	9	6	5	3	8	10	10	10	6
Day workers	56	47	49	43	47	39	56	58	69	50	69	38
Chambermaids	13	8	5	7	5	4	11	11	11	7	11	10
Waitresses	11	7	8	1	9	4	3	8	8	5	8	6
Kitchen	2	2	8	3	4	12	2	4	9	4	9	10
Nurses		3	1	1	2	2		2		3		3
Cooks	3	2	1	2	3	4		1	5	1	5	4
Totals	98	80	84	66	76	70	75	87	111	80	112	77

REPORT OF THE FREE EMPLOYMENT BUREAU OF EVERETT.

SUMMARY OF POSITIONS FURNISHED DURING 1909.—MALE.

	Jan.	Feb.	March	April	May	June	July	Aug.	Sept.	Oct.	Nov.	Dec.
Mill labrs	37	82	137	242	458	341	494	389	531	857	298	92
Mill men	3	17	27	47	42	19	61	13	8	30	18	
... men	2	1	5		9	5	14	3	5			
... flrs	3											
Bit ...	7									8		
... trs	4											
Loggers		2	10	2			6		22	26	6	
Farm ... sits		7	7	11	7	8	7	4			1	
Oks		1	5		9	1	4					
Kitchen help		1	15	11	3	3	7		2			5
... hlrs		2	2	7								
...s		4										
Solicitors		2	2	1	1	1	1	1	1	1		
Firemen			2			5	1		1			
... hlrs												
Waiters		5		5	4		4					
Waid ...				5					1			
Engineers			1		2	1		1	1			
Miscellaneous		3		8	4		2				3	
Totals	56	127	214	339	534	384	601	411	572	423	391	97

Total number of positions furnished—male, 4,079.

SUMMARY OF POSITIONS FURNISHED DURING 1909.—FEMALE.

	March	April	Sept.	Oct.
Cooks			1	
...				1
Pressers				
Chambermaids			11	17
Housework				
...				
Solicitors				
Day work			4	3
Housekeeper				
Hotel				
... lpus				

SUMMARY OF POSITIONS FURNISHED DURING EIGHT MONTHS OF 1910,
EVERETT—MALE.

	Jan.	Feb.	March	April	May	June	July	Aug.
Laborers	143	150	373	455	415	486	241	236
Loggers	2	1						
Teamsters		5	4	4	5	4	8	5
Dishwashers		2		9	6	3	4	
Carpenters	5	5	12	6	2	2		5
Janitors		2	3			1		
Painters		2						
Shoemakers	1		1				1	
Ranch hands		9	19	18	8	11	18	18
Cooks			4	4	4		4	1
Flunkeys			10	9	4	5	7	9
Donkey firemen			4		2		4	
Boys			5	4	6	6	1	
Engineers			2		1	2		
Firemen			5	5	6	11	8	8
Skidroad men			8	3	4	3	13	23
Shingle weavers			3	1			3	3
Tie makers			2					
Bolt cutters			5	17	13	7	10	10
Concrete men						40	30	17
Buckers				2	3	1	3	6
Swampers				2	8	2	3	17
Railroad laborers							42	20
Blacksmiths					3		1	
Millwrights					1		1	
Wood cutters				3	9	11		5
Cut-off sawyers					7	6		6
Miscellaneous				4	4	14	14	27
Totals	151	156	460	550	507	615	416	411

Total number of positions furnished, male, 3,266.

SUMMARY OF POSITIONS FURNISHED DURING EIGHT MONTHS OF 1910.
EVERETT—FEMALE.

	Jan.	Feb.	March	April	May	June	July	Aug.
Cooks	3	1	5	5	3	1	7	7
Waitresses	2	3	5	2	3	8	3	7
Housework	10	8	7	9	6	7	5	7
Chambermaids		2			1	3	5	
Nurses		3				1		
Housekeepers		4		1	1	1	1	2
Day work		4	2	7	8	3	8	8
Dishwashers			2	3	4		3	
Clerks			1			1	2	
Kitchen help				2	6	8	2	3
Totals	15	25	22	29	32	33	36	34

Total number of positions furnished, female, 226.

Grand total for eight months of 1910, 3,492.

REPORT OF THE FREE PUBLIC EMPLOYMENT BUREAU OF THE CITY OF SPOKANE.

	1908	1909	1910
September	377	519	· 730
October	414	618	....
November	847	725	....
December	271	400	....
January	....	287	298
February	....	888	277
March	....	227	883
April	....	875	804
May	....	497	905
June	....	296	705
July	....	363	514
August	....	585	701

LABOR CONDITIONS

LABOR CONDITIONS.

Generally speaking, labor conditions in the state during the past year have been very good. There has been a vast amount of construction and improvement work, both of a private and public nature in progress and wage earners have been well employed. This applies to both skilled and unskilled labor and for both classes, the volume of work seems to have been fairly up to the labor supply.

The increase in the cost of living expenses, however, has been felt severely and this is particularly true of our wage earning population. The price of a day's work has not advanced with the price of a sack of flour, and until the inequality involved in this condition is adjusted, the man who has nothing to sell but his time will have just cause for complaint.

To what extent this situation can be relieved through legislation may be doubtful, but in any event laws can be enacted for the improvement of the conditions under which the wage earners of the state are called upon to work.

Additional legislation, requiring employers to provide necessary comforts and conveniences for the use of their employees is urgently needed. Close contact with hundreds of industrial establishments, through the Factory Inspection work has developed the fact that the average employer gives but very little thought or attention to the physical welfare of his subordinates. Lunch rooms and rest rooms are seldom provided and toilet facilities are often unsanitary and inadequate. Those concerns which do make suitable provision for such conveniences find themselves more than repaid for the expenditure involved, through the spirit of loyalty that is awakened among their employees and in the fact that they experience little difficulty in keeping a steady and desirable class of help. Both wage earners and em-

—11

ployers alike would eventually benefit from reasonable legislative requirements along the above lines which are rapidly being adopted in the older states.

In this connection, it is desired to call particular attention to the excellent treatment accorded the men employed in the Union Mill located near Lacey in Thurston county. The mill itself is a model in every respect, utilizing electric power and fitted with the most modern machinery. A fine blower system keeps the mill free from dust, modern toilet facilities are provided and drinking faucets are installed in convenient places. The boiler room is located in a brick building apart from the main buildings.

The boarding house is also conducted with a view to securing the greatest possible comfort to the employees. The kitchen and bake room are modern and sanitary in every respect and the food is well cooked, wholesome and nicely served. Porcelain wash basins with running hot and cold water are provided, shower baths are an added attraction and there is a large reading room with comfortable chairs for the use of the men during their leisure hours. By no means the least advantage are the pleasant sleeping quarters where good beds are provided and the same system of healthful-cleanliness maintained. Board and room costs the men one dollar per day, an extremely reasonable charge considering all the comforts and conveniences provided.

The Puget Mill Co. at Port Gamble provides similar accommodations for its men, although on a much larger scale and the same excellent conditions will be found at the plant of the McGoldrick Lumber Co. at Spokane. Both of the above mills were referred to at some length in the last report of this department.

Among other establishments employing labor on a large scale, and who provide conveniences for their employes, is the mercantile store of Frederick & Nelson Co., Seattle, who are especially to be commended in this particular, as is set forth in the following letter:

OLYMPIA, WASH., Sept. 7, 1910.

Frederick & Nelson, Inc., Seattle, Wash.:

DEAR SIRS—I desire to commend you on the liberal and humane manner in which you conduct your large establishment in relation to your employes.. Mrs. Mason, deputy inspector for this department of state reports the conditions for your women employes as "ideal"; short hours and early closing, seats provided; also dining and rest rooms, cloak rooms, etc. In fact everything modern and up to date.

I consider your large store a model in every respect and I mean to give space in my forthcoming report of this Bureau to commend and call attention to your store in these particulars. One principal object of this department, in connection with factory inspection, is to better the sanitary and working conditions of the laboring class, as well as safeguarding machinery for the protection of life and limbs of employes. To say much has been accomplished in our great and growing state along this line by this department would be stating the facts midly, and with an establishment such as you conduct in Seattle much is done to assist in establishing a standard in this new state such as the older states in the East have done.

I believe employers like you are doing more towards adjusting the unpleasant differences existing between the employer and the employe in this state than any other one thing. May the time be near when there will be more such employers of labor in this state.

Yours very truly,

C. F. HUBBARD,
State Labor Commissioner.

A general adoption among employers of the policy followed by the above named establishments would prove a practical and effective step in the direction of securing permanent industrial peace in this state.

STATISTICS OF WAGE-EARNERS

STATISTICS OF WAGE EARNERS.—Wages Paid in Various Trades as Compiled from Reports of Individual Wage Earners.

Occupation	Name of City	Age	Native or foreign	Married or single	No. of children	Total No. to support	Hours per day	Days per mo.	Months per year	Own home or rent	M'thly rental	Board per week	Wages per day	Total income per year	Total disb'sements per year	Savings per year
Brewer	Aberdeen	43	Foreign	Single			8	26	10			$8 00	$4 00	$900	$900	$150
Carpenter	Aberdeen	31	Native	Married	4	6	8	26	12	Owns			3 60	900	900	Nothing
Carpenter	Tacoma	25	Native	Single			8	24	12	Owns		7 00	4 50	980	776	$125
Carpenter	Georgetown	35	Foreign	Married	2	4	8	26	12	Rent.	$15 00		4 50	1,400	750	650
Carpenter	Bellingham	64	Native	Married	8	6	8	20	8	Owns			4 00	600	600	Nothing
Carpenter	Everett	43	Native	Married	4	6	8	26	12	Owns			4 50	1,356	1,356	$400
Carpenter	Tacoma	35	Foreign	Married	8	8	8	24	10	Owns			5 00	1,400	1,400	Nothing
Carpenter	Walla Walla	48	Native	Married	2	5	8	20	8	Owns			4 00	1,000	900	$100
Carpenter	Walla Walla	43	Native	Married	3	3	8	24	8	Rent.	15 00		4 00	800	800	Nothing
Cigar maker	Seattle	34	Native	Married	1	3	8	24	6			5 50	2 50	396	396	Nothing
Cigar maker	Seattle	31	Native	Single		3	11	26		Rent.	18 00		2 75	750		Nothing
Cook	Seattle	28	Native	Married		8	8	26	12	Rent.	17 00		3 00	984	984	Nothing
Electrician	Everett	38	Native	Single		2	8	30	12	Rent.	18 75		3 10	1,000	1,000	Nothing
Electrician	Everett	39	Native	Married	2	2	8	28	12	Owns			4 00	1,090	1,080	$50
Electric hoist	Ravensdale	29	Native	Married	2	2	8	30	12	Owns			3 00	1,200	1,150	Nothing
Engineer	Seattle	34	Foreign	Married	1	3	9	26	12	Rent.	12 50	10 00	4 00	986		Nothing
Laundry worker	Seattle	31	Native	Single		4	10	26	12				3 00	832		
Laundry worker	Ole Elum	18	Native	Single			9	26	12				1 35			
Lineman	Seattle	30	Foreign	Single		2	8	28	12	Rent.	10 00	8 00	3 50	1,092	1,092	Nothing
Lineman	Seattle	46	Native	Married	2	4	8	28	12	Owns	30 00	7 00	3 50	1,092	1,092	Nothing
Lineman	Bellingham	40	Native	Married	8	5	9	22	9	Owns			3 50	700	650	$50
Machinist	Tacoma	30	Foreign	Married	2	4	8	26	12	Rent.	15 00		3 00	750	850	
Mill hand	Everett	21	Native	Married	1	3	10	26	8	Rent.	14 00	8 00	2 25	450	870	80
Mill hand	Everett	22	Native	Married	1	1	10	26	8	Rent.	10 00		2 88	500	325	175
Miner	Tono	68	Foreign	Married	2	4	8	12	12	Bent.	9 00		4 00			
Miner	Tono	25	Foreign	Single			8	12	12			5 00	4 00			
Miner	Tono	19	Foreign	Married	4	5	8	12	12	Rent.	9 00		4 00	1,600	1,400	700
Photo engraver	Seattle	30	Foreign	Single			8	26	12	Rent.	25 00		5 00	600	600	252
Pressman	Tacoma	29	Native	Single			8	26	12			6 00	2 84	882		250
Pressman	Tacoma	21	Native	Single			8	28	11	Owns	25 00		2 50	780		Nothing
Pressman	Seattle	19	Native	Married	2	2	8	28	12	Rent.	15 00	6 00	4 25	1,200	1,200	Nothing
Pressman	Seattle	35	Native	Single		4	8	23	12	Owns			4 00	1,056	900	$150

WAGES PAID IN VARIOUS TRADES—Concluded.

Occupation	Name of City	Age	Native or foreign	Married or single	No. of children	Total No. to support	Hours per day	Days per mo.	Months per year	Own home or rent	M'thly rental	Board per week	Wages per day	Total income per year	Total disb'sements per year	Savings per year
Pm	Bellingham	35	Native	Married	3	5	8	26	12	Rent	18 00	......	8 00	648	648	Nothing
Pm	Bellingham	37	Native	Married	2	4	8	26	12	Rent	20 00	......	3 46	1,060	960	$100
Pressman	Seattle	38	Foreign	Married	6	8	8	26	12	Rent	25 00	......	4 25	1,330	1,400	100
Pressman	Olympia	44	Native	Married	3	5	7½	26	12	Rent	15 00	......	5 00	1,500	1,200	300
Pm	Olympia	38	Native	Married	1	8	7½	26	12	Owns	......	......	5 00	1,500	......	300
Sal eman	Tacoma	24	Native	Single	......	......	10	26	12	......	......	6 00	2 88	900	600	100
	Tacoma	21	Native	Single	......	......	10	26	12	......	......	6 00	1 92	600	500	
fir	Seattle	38	Native	Married	5	7	9	26	12	Owns	......	......	3 85	1,196	......	Nothing
fir	Seattle	29	Native	Married	2	4	9	26	12	Owns	......	......	3 32	600	......	Nothing
fir	Ravensdale	24	Native	Single	......	......	8	30	12	Rent	6 50	......	2 66	970	970	Nothing
Waitress	Seattle	26	Native	Single	......	3	10	26	12	Rent	14 00	......	1 60	490	......	Nothing
War	Cle Elum	23	Native	Married	2	4	10	20	9	Rent	12 00	......	3 33	1,040	......	
Wireman	Bellingham	22	Native	Single	1	8	8	24	11	Rent	12 50	5 50	3 50	650	500	$150
Wireman	Tacoma	29	Native	Married	......	8	8	24	12	Rent	13 00	......	8 00	1,050	800	250
Wireman	Tacoma	23	Native	Married	......	2	8	24	12	Rent	20 00	......	4 00	1,100	......	150

SUMMARY.

Number of wage earners	50
Average age	31.6
Average number of hours per day	8.4
Average number of days per month	24.3

Average months per year	11.2
Average rent	$15 58
Average board per week	6 88
Average wage per day	3 52

STATISTICS OF WAGE EARNERS—MERCANTILE HOUSES.

Note.—Each section of the following tables represents the reports of one firm.

DRY GOODS.

DEPARTMENTS	SEATTLE No. of em-pl'y'd	No. days per mo.	Wages per month	No. hours per day	SEATTLE No. of em-pl'y'd	No. days per mo.	Wages per month	No. hours per day	SEATTLE No. of em-pl'y'd	No. days per mo.	Wages per day	No. hours per day	SEATTLE No. of em-pl'y'd	No. days per mo.	Wages per month	No. hours per day
...es	3	26-27	$90 00	9⅜	1	26	$100 00	9	17	26	$2 75	8	1	25	$90 00	9⅜
	12	26-27	83 00	9⅜	2	26	40 to 100	8⅜	11	26	1 35	8	3	25	36 00	8
Flr walkers	2	26-27	87 50	9⅜	1	26	100 00	9	16	26	3 50	8	2	25	100 00	8⅜
Clerks	15	26-27	73 00		3	26	30 to 60	8⅜	60	26	2 00	8	10	25	100 00	8⅜
...an	66	26-27	45 00	9⅜	8	26	70 to 175	9	57	26	9 50	8	20	25	48 00	8
	6	26-27	40 00		4	26	60 to 90	8⅜	175	26	1 75	8⅜				
Shippers	1	26-27	108 00	9⅜	1	26	40 00	9	9	26	2 75	8	1	25	160 00	8⅜
	16	26-27	11 20 wk						6	26	2 00	8	1	25	60 00	8
Milliners	1		65 00	9⅜	2	26	30 to 75	8⅜	5	26	3 25	8				
	2	26-27	45 00		1	26	40 00	8⅜	10	26	2 75	8				
Flr ...s									11	26	2 25	8⅜				
	1	26-27	75 00	9⅜	2	26	60 00	9	8	26	1 40	8⅜				
Drivers	4	26-27	60 00	9⅜					3	26	2 25	12				
...t ...an					1	26	100 00	9	20	26	2 50	8				
Tai' ...y ...	4		9 00 wk		1	26	50 00	9	5	30	2 50	8				
	1	26-27	52 00		2	26	25 00	9								
Clks	2	26-27	30 00						19	26	1 00	8				
Cooks'					1	26	85 00	9	2	26	3 75	8				
...g man	11		37 50						12	26	2 00	8				
Or ...	27		55 00		18	26	71 00	9	412	26	1 95	8				
...s ...t. (suits)	11		20 00													
Engine- ...	1		100 00													

STATISTICS OF WAGE EARNERS—MERCANTILE HOUSES—Continued.

DRY GOODS.

DEPARTMENTS.	TACOMA. No. of em-pl'y'd	No. days per mo.	Wages per month	No. hours per day	TACOMA. No. of em-pl'y'd	No. days per mo.	Wages per month	No. hours per day	TACOMA. No. of em-pl'y'd	No. days per mo.	Wages per day	No. hours per day	TACOMA. No. of em-pl'y'd	No. days per mo.	Wages per day	No. hours per day
Bookkeepers	2	28	$111 00	8½	2	30	$183 00	10	10	26	$4 00	9	15	28	$1 53	
	2	28	72 00	8½	2	30	60 00	10	3	26	1 50	9	8	28	1 17	
	4	28	56 66⅔	8½					7	26	75	9				
	1	28	166 66⅔	8½	3	30	210 00	10	4	26	4 00	9	1	28	5 00	
	18	28	852 00	8½	8		120 00	10					7	28	1 76	
Sal men	1	28	100 00	8½	18		1,300 00	10	35	26	2 50	9	38	28	8 01	
Saleswomen	17	28	752 00	8½	22	30	600 00	10	57	26	1 75	9	89	28	1 61	
	1	28	20 00	8½	1	30	50 00	10	2	26	3 00	9	1	28	2 88	
					2	30	100 00	10	4	26	75	9	4	28	2 38	
	1	28	130 00	8½	2		175 00	10	2	26	3 00	9	4	28	2 75	
	1	28	100 00	8½					22	26	2 00	9	5	28	1 87	
	1	28	55 00		2	30	65 00	10	2	26	2 00	9	1	28	2 17	
Elevator									1	26	1 00	9	2	28	2 08	
					1	30	66 00	10	8	26	2 00	9	1	28	1 87	
									1	26	2 75	9	7	26	1 70	
Bakers					1	30	45 00	10	1	26	3 00	9	2	28	2 00	
Bakers'									1	26	3 50	9	1	28	2 58	
men									15	26	2 50	9	2	28	2 00	
									1	26	3 00	9				
													11	28	1 07	
													2	28	1 67	
													4	28	74	
	6	28	214 00	8½	1	30	160 00	10	2	26	2 00	9	40	28	1 95	

Female and male, 8½ hours, Monday, Tuesday, Wednesday, Thursday and Friday. Satur-days—Female, 10 hours; male, 11½ hours.

STATISTICS OF WAGE EARNERS—MERCANTILE HOUSES—Continued.

DRY GOODS.

DEPARTMENTS.	SPOKANE.				SPOKANE.				SPOKANE.				TACOMA.			
	No. of em-pl'y'd	No. days per mo.	Wages per month	No. hours per day	No. of em-pl'y'd	No. days per mo.	Wages per month	No. hours per day	No. of em-pl'y'd	No. days per week	Wages per month	No. hours per day	No. of em-pl'y'd	No. days per mo.	Wages per month	No. hours per day
Bookkeepers	7	26	$1,013 26	8½	7	26	$76 50	9	•6	5½	$927 33	9½	6	26	$450 00	8½
Cashiers	8	26	307 66	8½	3	26	117 00	9					4	25	138 00	8½
Cash boys																
Floor walkers	4	26	491 30	8½	1	26	110 50	9					3	25	60 00	8½
Clerks	8	26	456 52	8½	7	26	66 50	9	10	5½	576 26	8½	1	25	150 00	
Salesmen	4	26	394 77	8½	34	26	90 00	9	30	5½	3,213 13	8½	26	25	2,540 00	8½
Salesmen	37	26	4,659 63	8½	10	26	39 00	9					54	25	2,178 00	8½
Saleswomen	102	26	5,553 93	8½	5	26	58 50	9					2	25	255 00	8½
Shippers	5	26	282 10	8½	2	26	31 00	9	8	5½	481 83	8½				
Stock boys					1	26	153 50	9	1	5½	35 00	8½				
Window dressers	3	26	227 93	8½									2	25	195 00	8½
Milliners	14	26	583 00	8½	4	26	49 50	9	8	5½	470 17	8½	6	25	490 00	8½
Stenographers	4	26	260 00	8½	1	26	32 50	9	1	5½	39 00	8½	1	25	70 00	8½
Elevator tenders	3	26	104 00	8½	1	26	78 00	9								
Collectors					8	26	54 00	9					2	25	125 00	8½
Drivers					1	26	66 00	9	2	5½	140 00	8½	2	25	144 00	8½
Watchmen	1		78 00	8½					65	5½	2,377 88	8½				
Operators in mfg. dept.					2	26	26 00	9								
Cashiers					61	26	74 75	9								
Other employees	4	26	125 66										4	25	285 00	8½
Delivery boys	31	26	680 33	8½												
Inspectors	3	26	285 02	8½												
Engineers	8	26	327 17	8½					2	5½	182 17	8½				
Porters	6	26		8½												
Tailors and dressmakers	36	26	2,758 50	8½									2	25	190 00	8½

STATISTICS OF WAGE EARNERS—MERCANTILE HOUSES—Continued.

DRY GOODS.

DEPARTMENTS.	EVERETT.				EVERETT.				ABERDEEN.				BELLINGHAM.			
	No. of em-pl'y'd	No. days per mo.	Wages per week	No. pr dy	No. of em-pl'y'd	No. days per mo.	Wages per day	No. hours per day	No. of em-pl'y'd	No. days per mo.	Wages per month	No. hours per day	No. of em-pl'y'd	No. days per mo.	Wages per month	No. hours per day
	1	26	$15 00	8½	2	26	$1 to $2		1	26	$75 00	9	1	24	$65 00	9
	2	26	8 00	8½	4	26	2 to 5						1	24	48 00	9
	2	26	17 50	8½	10	26	1 to 3		2	26	80 to 110	9	2	24	24 to 85	9
	9	26	8 50	8½									26	24	16 to 5750	9
					1	26	1 00		1	26	80 00		1	24	60 00	9
	1	26	25 00	8½	1	26	3 00						1	24	75 00	9
Milliners													2	24	16 to 48	9
									1	26	70 00		1	24	20 00	9
Drivers	1	26	8 00	8½	3	26	1 25 to 2						2	24	36 to 60	9
	1	26	18 00	8½									1	24	48 00	9
boys													2	24	10 to 20	9
									1	26	125 00	9	2	24	125 00	9

STATISTICS OF WAGE EARNERS—MERCANTILE HOUSES—Continued.

FURNITURE.

DEPARTMENTS.	SPOKANE.				SEATTLE.				TACOMA.				TACOMA.			
	No. of em-pl'y'd	No. days per mo.	Wages per month	No. hours per day	No. of em-pl'y'd	No. days per mo.	Wages per month	No. hours per day	No. of em-pl'y'd	No. days per mo.	Wages per month	No. hours per day	No. of em-pl'y'd	No. days per mo.	Wages per month	No. hours per day
	2	24	$125 00	9	1	30	$60 00		1	26	$75 00	9	2		$100 to $110	10
	1	24	65 00	9	1	30	75 00		1	26	200 00	9				
	1	24	130 00	9												
	1	24	100 00	9	2	30	50 00		4	26	100 00	9	7		65 to 150	10
	2	24	40 00	9	7	30	120 00		1	26	45 00	9	4		65 to 90	10
	15	24	100 00	9				10	1	26	70 00	9	1		50 00	10
	2	24	50 00	9	5	26	2 25, 2 50da	10								
	3	24	85 00	9	1	26	2 00 da						1		50 00	10
	3	24	80 00	9									1		60 00	10
	1	24	130 00	9	1	30	60 00	10	1	26	30 00	9	1		75 00	10
	2	24	85 00	9	2	26	1 50 da						8		100 00	10
	2	24	80 00	9												
Drivers	3	24	40 00	9	3	26	2 50, 2 75da	10	2	29	65 00	10				
	8	24	80 00	9												
	1	2f	65 00	9												
y sewers.	2	24	75 00	9												
Upfitters	6	24	40 00	9												
	2	24	65 00	9												
	4	24	80 00	9												
	1	24	80 00	9												
	1	24	75 00	9												
	2	24	80 00	9												
	1	24	100 00	9												
	3	24	120 00	9												
managers	4	24	85 00	9												
			160 00		9	26	2 00, 4 00da	10	10	26	50 00	9	7		8 00 da	10

STATISTICS OF WAGE EARNERS—MERCANTILE HOUSES—Continued.

DEPARTMENTS	FURNITURE — TACOMA				TACOMA				STATIONERY — SEATTLE				GROCERY — SEATTLE			
	No. of em-pl'y'd	No. days per mo.	Wages per day	No. hours per day	No. of em-pl'y'd	No. days per mo.	Wages per month	No. hours per day	No. of em-pl'y'd	No. days per mo.	Wages per month	No. hours per day	No. of em-pl'y'd	No. days per mo.	Wages per month	No. hours per day
Bookkeepers	1	26	$6 75	9	1	26	$80 00	10	2	27	$75 00	9	16	26	$75 00	10
Cashiers	1	26	3 00	9	1	26	135 00	10					3	26	50 00	10
Cash boys									4	27	20 00		1	26		
Floor walker	1	26	3 00	9										26	100 00	10
Clerks	10	26	3 to 6 65	9	9	26	125 00	10	5	27	100 00	9	25	26	100 00	10
Salesmen				10	7	26	90 00	10	1		60 00	9	4	26	70 00	8
Saleswomen	14	26	2 to 4 16		1	26	65 00	10					50	26	60 00	10
Shippers					4	26	25 00	10					10	26	30 00	10
Stock boys													3	26	100 00	10
Bakers	1	26	2 50	9									7	26	50 00	10
Baker's helpers	1	26	2 00	9									2	26		
Stenographers	1	26	2 50	9	4	28	60 00		1		60 00	9			60 00	10
Elevator tenders															85 00	10
Collectors	1	26	2 50	10									1	26	65 00	10
Drivers	1	26	4 00	10	1	26	65 00	10					23	26	50 00	10
Watchmen	2	30	5 00	9	1	30	60 00	12					2	26		
Carpet layers	1	26	4 16	9												
Shade	1	26	3 00	9												
Finisher	1	26	2 75	10	4	28	45 00	10					12	26	60 00	10
Seamstress	1	26	1 75	10												
Upholsterer	1	26	8 50	9												

STATISTICS OF WAGE EARNERS—MERCANTILE HOUSES—Continued.

HARDWARE.

DEPARTMENTS.	SEATTLE.				ABERDEEN.				BELLINGHAM.					NORTH YAKIMA.			
	No. of em-pl'y'd	No. days per mo.	Wages per month	No. hours per day	No. of em-pl'y'd	No. days per mo.	Wages per month	No. hours per day	No. of em-pl'y'd	No. days per mo.	Wages per month	No. hours per day	No. of em-pl'y'd	No. days per mo.	Wages per month	No. hours per day
Clerks	1	26	$100 00	9	1	26	$75 00	8	2	25	$125 00	9	2		$100 00	
	1	26	70 00	9					1	25	40 00	9	1		40 00	
	3	26	75 00	9	1	26	70 00	10	5	25	90 00	9	14		90 00	
	2	26	80 00	9	1	26	75 00	10	10	25	75 00	10				
	3	26	125 00	9												
Shippers	1	26	100 00	9	1	26	40 00	10	1	25	100 00	10	1		75 00	
	1	26	50 00	8									3		60 00	
	2	26	70 00	9	1	26¾	25 00	4	1	25	50 00	9				
	1	26	50 00													
Collectors	1	26	60 00										1		100 00	
													2		60 00	
Watchman	1	26	60 00	10	2	26	90 and 125	10	3	25	60 00	10				
Tin and plumbers					1	26	200 00	10					18		3 50 to 5 da	
	8	26	4 00 da.	8					7	25	50 00	10				
Tile	8	26	8 50 da.	8												
File	4	26	5 50 da.	8												
	4	26	8 25 da.	8												
	5	26	2 50 da.	9												

STATISTICS OF WAGE EARNERS—MERCANTILE HOUSES—Continued.

DEPARTMENTS.	HARDWARE. TACOMA.				RESTAURANT. TACOMA.				RESTAURANT. SPOKANE.				RESTAURANT. SEATTLE.			
	No. of em-pl'y'd	No. days per mo.	Wages per month	No. hours per day	No. of em-pl'y'd	No. days per week	Wages per week	No. hours per day	No. of em-ply'd	No. days per mo.	Wages per day	No. hours per day	No. of em-pl'y'd	No. days per mo.	Wages per week	No. hours per day
Bookkeepers	1	26	$70 00	10					1	30	$2 75	9½				
Cashiers																
Clerks	2	26	65 00	10												
Salesmen	2	26	75 and 100	10												
Shipper	1	26	65 00	10												
Driver	1	26	40 00	10												
Bakers					1	6	$10 50 brd.	10	1	30	4 00	8	4	24	82 00	10
Bkrs' helpers									1	30	2 00	9	1	24	14 00	10
Wts, men					4	6	6 00 brd.	10	24	30	3 00	8½	13	24	176 50	10
Wts, women					1	6	10 00 brd.	10	3	30	2 25	10				
Cooks									5	30	3 75	10	4	30	106 25	10
Cooks' helpers									1	30	2 25	10	2	30	26 00	10
Cashiers									16	30	2 00	9				
Clr									1	30		10				
Chef					1	6	3 00 brd.	4	1	30	7 00	10	6	30	60 00	12
By					1	6	3 00 brd.	4								
Porter					1	6	6 00 brd.	10								
Dhr																

STATISTICS OF WAGE EARNERS—Continued.

CONFECTIONERY STORES.

DEPARTMENTS.	SEATTLE.				SEATTLE.				TACOMA.			
	No. of em'pl'y'd	No. days per mo.	Wages per day	No. hours per day	No. of em'pl'y'd	No. days per mo.	Wages per month	No. hours per day	No. of em'pl'y'd	No. days per mo.	Wages per month	No. hours per day
Bookkeeper					1	26	$3 00 da.	9				
Cashiers					4	26	1 50 da.	9	12	24	$416 00	9
Saleswomen	10	28	$1 56	9	4	26	1 50 da.	9				
Shipper					1	26	80 00	9				
Stock boy					1	26	3 00 da.	9				
Factory girls	8	26	1 30	9								
Drivers	1	26	1 50	9	8	26	2 50 da.	9				
Candy makers	2	26	4 75	9	2	26	100 00 da.	9	2	24	172 00	9
Waiters, men	5	26	1 80	9	2	26	2 00 da.	9	2	24	76 00	9
Dishwasher	1	26	1 88	9	10	30	1 42 da.	8				
Cooks' helpers	2	26	1 85	10	1	26	100 00	8				
Ice cream mkr	1	26	3 00	9	2	30	75 00	8				
Soda men	8	26	3 42	9					2	24	136 00	9
Porters	4	26	1 70	10								
Managers					2	28	150 00	10				

STATISTICS OF WAGE EARNERS.

HOTELS.

DEPARTMENTS.	SEATTLE.				SEATTLE.				SEATTLE.				SEATTLE.			
	No. of em-pl'y'd	No. days per mo.	Wages per month	No. hours per day	No. of em-pl'y'd	No. days per mo.	Wages per month	No. hours per day	No. of em-pl'y'd	No. days per mo.	Wages per month	No. hours per day	No. of em-pl'y'd	No. days per mo.	Wages per month	No. hours per day
Bookkeepers	1	30	$125 00	8	2	30	$100 00	9	1	26	$75 00	8	1	30	$150 00	8
Clerks	2	30	35 00	8	2	30	45 00	9	2	30	85 00	10	1	30	40 00	8
Salesmen	3	30	125 00	8	3	30	100 00	9	3	30	85 00	10	2	30	75 00	8
Saleswomen					4	30	100 00	9								
Stock boys	2	30	50 00	8	2	30	60 00	9								
Bar tenders	1	30	60 00	10	2	30	50 00	9	2	30	35 00	10	3	30	35 00	8
Laundry workers	8	30	30 00	8	3	30	30 00	9					4	30	50 00	8
Drivers					2	30	60 00	9					1	30	100 00	10
Watchmen	2	30	90 00		2	30	90 00	9	1	30	35 00	10	2	30	40 00	8
Bakers	1	30	90 00	10	1	30	40 00	9						30	90 00	8
Bakers' helpers	1	30	40 00	10	20	30	40 00	9					10	30	45 00	8
Waiters, men	10	30	45 00	9												
Waiters, men	1	30	35 00	9												
Cooks	4	30	200 00	9	4	30	100 00	9	2	30	35 00		2	30	150 00	8
Cooks' helpers	9	30	125 00	9	3	30	45 00	9					3	30	60 00	8
Bell boys	8	30	100 00	9	10	30	20 00	9	2	30	35 00	10	6	30	35 00	8
Porters	5	30	60 00	10	12	30	35 00	10					2	30	40 00	8
Kitchen help			35 00		20	30	40 00									
Chambermaids	9	30	21 00	8	8	30	35 00	9	4	30	38 00	10	7	30	35 00	8
Housekeepers	2	30	40 00	9					1	30	90 00					
Bar tenders	3	28	25 00	10	2	30	35 00	8					2	30	75 00	8
Telephone operators	2	30	25 00 wk.	8												
			40 00													

—12

STATISTICS OF WAGE EARNERS—Continued.

HOTELS.

DEPARTMENTS.	NORTH YAKIMA.				EVERETT.				ABERDEEN.				TACOMA.			
	No. of em-pl'y'd	No. days per mo.	Wages per month	No. hours per day	No. of em-pl'y'd	No. days per mo.	Wages per month	No. hours per day	N. of m-pl'y'd	No. days per mo.	Wages per month	No. hours per day	No. of em-pl'y'd	No. days per mo.	Wages per month	No. hours per day
Bookkeepers	1	30	$100 00	8	1	30	$70 00	9	1	30	$95 00	10-12	1	30	$100 00	9
Cashiers	1	30	50 00	8					1	30	20 00	11	2		40 00	
Cash boys																
Head	1	30	90 00	8		30	50 00	10	3	30	60, 50, 30	10	8		95 00	
Clerks	2	30	85 00	12		30	30 00	9					2			
Saleswomen	1	30	60 00	10		30	20 00	9					2		48 00	
Stock boys						30	60 00	9							42 50	
tor tenders					2								1		55 00	
Drivers													1		100 00	
Men													1		50 00	
Bakers	1	30	35 00	7		30	35 00	8	8	30	30 00	8	26		37 00	
Bakers' helpers	7	30		7		30	90, 50	9	3	30	110, 60, 70	10				
men	3	30	100 00	10		30	35 00	9	5	30	215 00		5		100 00	
Cks, men	5	30	40 00	12		30	40 00	8					23		50 00	
Cooks' helpers																
Cashiers									4	30	25 00	10	58		50 00	
Gr pies													4		90 00	9
ids	8	30	30 00	8	2	30	25 00	8								
Bartenders	3	30	100 00	8	2	30	75, 50	9								
Housekeepers	1	30	40 00	10	1	30	30 00	12								
Houseman	1	30	30 00	10					2	30	35, 40	10				
Porters	3	30	40 00	12	2	30	40 00	10	1	30	20 00	11				
Bell boys	1	30	15 00	12	1	30	32 50	12	1	30	55 00	10				
Engineers					1			8								
fry men					3	30	25, 70	8								

STATISTICS OF MANUFACTURES

STATISTICS OF MANUFACTURES.

TABLE NO. 1.—Compiled from statistical blanks collected by the Deputy Factory Inspectors. Each line in the following tables represents the report of one firm. Capacity and daily output of lumber mills are reported in terms of feet, board measure; shingle mills in terms of pieces.

Town or City	Goods Manufactured or Handled	Date when est'b'lished	Capital invested in plant	Daily capacity	Daily output	Males employed Skil'd	Males employed Un-skil'd	Females em-ply'd	Hours per day Males	Hours per day Females	Days per mo. males	Mos. per year	Days per mo. females	Wages Males Skilled	Wages Males Un-skilled	Wages females	Kind of power used
ADAMS COUNTY.																	
Ritzville	Flour and feed	1896	$100,000	500 bbls.	......	4	......	......	10	......	26	12	......	$3 00	$2 50	......	Electric
Lind	Flour and feed	1905	40,000	300 bbls.	300 bbls.	2	10	8	10	......	26	9	......	4 00	2 50	......	Electric
ASOTIN COUNTY.																	
Anatone	Flour and feed	1906	$17,500	100 bbls.	56 bbls.	4	1	......	12	......	26	3	......	$3 00	$2 50	......	Steam
Anatone	Flour and feed	1905	15,000	100 bbls.	90 bbls.	5	1	......	12	......	26	8	......	3 50	2 50	......	Water'
Asotin	Flour and feed	1895	10,000	50 bbls.	50 bbls.	1	3	......	12	......	26	12	......	3 50	2 25	......	Steam
Asotin	Lumber	1901	100,000	30,000ft.	25,000ft.	5	15	......	10	......	26	......	......	......	......	......	
BENTON COUNTY.																	
Prosser	Elec. and water	1903	$100,000	$125 val.	$42 val.	2	......	......	12	......	30	12	......	$3 00	......	......	Steam
Kennewick	Laundry	1909	15,000	......	......	2	2	10	10	10	26	12	24	3 00	$1 50	$1 60	S. and E.
Kennewick	Laundry	1909	12,000	......	......	2	1	10	10	10	26	12	20	2 75	1 50	1 50	Electric
Prosser	Laundry	1907	4,000	......	......	2	2	4	10	10	26	12	20	......	2 50	1 50	Water
Prosser	Flour	1887	15,000	100 bbls.	100 bbls.	2	3	......	12	......	24	12	......	3 75	2 50	......	
CHEHALIS COUNTY.																	
Hoquiam	Shingles	1906	$250,000	700,000	700,000	18	13	......	10	......	26	12	......	$3 75	$2 25	......	Steam
Hoquiam	Shingles	1882	150,000	225,000	50,000	15	......	......	10	......	23	12	......	4 10	2 60	......	Steam
Aberdeen	Shingles	1909	70,000	75,000	75,000	15	50	......	10	......	25	11	......	3 50	2 25	......	Steam
Elma	Shingles	1907	60,000	100,000	90,000	10	8	......	10	......	20	8	......	3 75	2 75	......	Steam
Hoquiam	Shingles	1907	50,000	350,000	300,000	30	20	......	10	......	24	12	......	4 00	2 50	......	Steam

Place	Product	Year	Capital													Power
Aloha	Shingles	1905	50,000	275,000	250,000		15	12		10		95	10		8 75	2 50	Steam
Moclips	Shingles	1906	50,000	00,000	200,000		12	10		10		90	10		8 75	2 25	Steam
Hoquiam	Shingles	1902	47,000	250,000	250,000		18	14		10		28	10		4 50	2 25	Steam
Aberdeen		1904	30,000	120,000	120,000		11	4		10		23	10		4 25	2 25	Steam
Aberdeen		1905	30,000		120,000		12	4		10		24	10		3 00		Steam
		1907	30,000	200,000	160,000		13	4		10		22	10		4 00	2 50	Steam
		1906	25,000	200,000			14	7		9		24	10		5 00	2 75	
Summit	Shingles	1904	24,000	200,000	175,000		14	10		11		24	10		4 75	2 50	Steam
	Shingles	1907	23,000	175,000	175,000		15	9		8		24	10		5 00	2 75	Steam
	Shingles	1909	20,000	200,000	150,000		14	3		9			10				
		1910	16,000	70,000	70,000		7			12		25	10		4 25	2 50	Steam
		1904	15,000	120,000	120,000		13	8		10		30	10		4 00	2 50	
Aberdeen		1907	10,000	120,000	125,000		20	6		12		30	10		4 00	2 50	
Elma		1906	9,000	125,000	120,000		8	5		7		22	10		4 00	2 68	
		1907	7,000	120,000	100,000		10	5		12		20	10		4 50	2 90	
Elma	Shingles	1910	6,500	100,000	65,000		9	5		12			10		6 62	2 25	
Elma	Shingles	1909	5,000	65,000	90,000		9	10		12		20	10		4 00	2 25	
Hoquiam		1908	5,000	90,000	35,000		6	19		12			10		4 00	2 10	
		1907		1800			88	3		13		25	10		4 10	2 25	
Aberdeen	Lumber	1897	300,000	140,000	140,000		18	70		13		26	10		4 22	2 25	Steam
		1905	250,000	100,000ft.	100,000ft.		90	95		12		23	10		4 00	2 68	
	Lumber	1896	50,000	150,000ft.	150,000ft.		91	46		12		30	10		4 45	2 15	
		1905	243,000	200,000ft.	200,000ft.		94	280		11		25	10		8 75	2 25	
	Lumber	1905	202,000	275,000ft.	300,000ft.		15	100		12		28	10		3 15	2 25	
Junction City	Lumber	1905	104,000	125,000ft.	125,000ft.		40	50		12		23	10		8 75	2 00	Steam
Hoquiam		1905	90,000	150,000ft.	150,000ft.		50	90		12		98	10		8 50	8 00	Steam
	Lumber	1902	90,000	130,000ft.	160,000ft.		24	183		12		28	10		5 00	2 00	
Aberdeen		1909	150,000	95,000ft.	100,000ft.		20	60		11		25	10		5 00	2 95	
		1903	100,000	100,000ft.	150,000ft.		90	75		11		22	10		4 00	2 00	Steam
		1908	100,000	125,000ft.	125,000ft.		90	90		12		25	10		8 76	2 40	Steam
Aberdeen	Lumber	1902	100,000	65,000ft.	100,000ft.			60		10		25	10		8 85	2 50	Steam
As	Lumber	1905	60,000	20,000ft.	50,000ft.		17	45		11		25	10		8 25	2 00	
Aberdeen		1905	60,000	80,000ft.	80,000ft.		15	13		12		26	10		8 75	2 25	
Moclips	Lumber	1904	29,000	80,000ft.	80,000ft.		18	80		11		30	10		2 90	2 00	
		1903	25,000	35,000ft.	35,000ft.		5	10		10		24	10		3 75	1 75	
	Wood products	1909	100,000	30,000ft.	30,000ft.		88	21		12			10		4 00	2 50	Steam
		1909	40,000				40	18		9		25	10		4 62	2 00	Electric
		1908	40,000	360 boards	80 boards		90	90		12		88	10		2 80	1 75	
		1906	40,000	$60 val	$60 val		90	90		12		25	8		2 76	2 50	
		1905	10,000				5	5		12			9		4 50	2 50	
		1907	10,000				7	7		12			8		3 00	2 00	Electric
	Wood products	1909	5,000	400 boards	400 boards	400 boards	20	25		12			10		2 75	2 15	Electric

CHEHALIS COUNTY—Continued.

Town or City	Goods Manufactured or Handled	Date when est'b'lished	Capital invested in plant	Daily capacity	Daily output	Males employed Skil'd	Males Un-skil'd	Fe-males em-pl'y'd	Hours per day Males	Hours per day Fe-males	Days per mo. males	Mos. per year	Days per mo. fe-males	Wages, Males Skilled	Wages, Males Un-skilled	Wages fe-males	Kind of power used
	W od s	1907	$45,000			12	4		10		26	12		$3 00	$3 00		Steam
		1904	30,000			7	3		9		26	12		3 00	2 50		Electric
		1897	25,000			12	9		9		26	12		3 75	2 00		Electric
		1897	10,000			8	3		9		26	12		3 50	2 40		Electric
		1905	4,500			3			8		26	12		3 50			Electric
																	Electric
	Tanks	1902	25,000	$85 val.	$90 val.	8		25	10	10	26	12	25	$3 00		$2 00	Steam
Elma		1909	7,000	$125 val.	$75 val.	5		4	10	10	25	12	26	4 00		1 80	Steam
Hoquiam		1906	5,000	$70 val.		2		18	10	9	26	12	26	2 75		1 38	Steam
		1906	5,000			4		17	9	9	24	12	22	3 25		1 60	Steam
		1907	4,000	60 bbls.	50 bbls.	2	2	14	10	10	26	12	26	3 50	2 50	1 75	Steam
	r d s, ice	1902	100,000	8 tons ice		16			8		26	12		3 50			Steam
		1904	100,000	300c clams								4½					
	Canned mon.	1904	36,000	800 cases	400 cases	30	50	30	10	8	26	3	25	2 50	2 50		Steam
	d th.	1904	50,000	800 cases	400 cases	50	30		10		30*	3		3 00	2 00		Steam
	t, d goods	1906		33,600 kwh	11,000 kwh	10	13		9		30	12		4 00	2 25		Steam
	Electricity, grain	1910	246,000	8 tons	2 tons	2		1	8	8½	26	12	26	3 00		3 80	Steam

CHELAN COUNTY.

Town or City	Goods Manufactured or Handled	Date when est'b'lished	Capital invested in plant	Daily capacity	Daily output	Males employed Skil'd	Males Un-skil'd	Fe-males em-pl'y'd	Hours per day Males	Hours per day Fe-males	Days per mo. males	Mos. per year	Days per mo. fe-males	Wages, Males Skilled	Wages, Males Un-skilled	Wages fe-males	Kind of power used
Wenatchee	r d d	1907	$75,000	400 bbls.	200 bbls.	2	10		10		26	10		$4 00	$2 50		Electric
Chelan Falls	r d d.	1897	15,000	150 bbls.	150 bbls.	3	5		10		26	10		4 00	2 50		Water
Wenatchee	t, d goods	1908	75,000	12 tons ice	7 tons ice												S. and E.
Wenatchee		1902	12,000	10 gal. fruit	10 gal. fruit	4	10		10		26	11		4 50	2 50	$1 40	Electric
Leavenworth	r	1903	360,000	$125 val.	$75 val.	2	2	15	10	10	25	12	22	3 00	1 50		Steam
Leavenworth	Lumber	1903		125,000ft.	125,000ft.	12	15		10		25	9		3 00	2 25		S. and E.
Chelan	d	1902	8,000	100,000ft.	100,000ft.	20	90		10		26	9		3 00	2 00		
						8	1		10			10		3 50	2 50		

OLALLAM COUNTY.

Town or City	Goods Manufactured or Handled	Date when est'b'lished	Capital invested in plant	Daily capacity	Daily output	Males employed Skil'd	Males Un-skil'd	Fe-males em-pl'y'd	Hours per day Males	Hours per day Fe-males	Days per mo. males	Mos. per year	Days per mo. fe-males	Wages, Males Skilled	Wages, Males Un-skilled	Wages fe-males	Kind of power used
Port Angeles	Shingles	1903	$10,000	120,000	190,000	12	5		10		22	9		$3 75	$2 50		Steam
Port Williams	Shingles	1908	8,000	60,000	60,000	5	4		10		25	6		4 80	2 50		Steam

Location	Product	Year	Capital	Value	Output															Power
Port [nlles]	Shingles	1910	5,000	60,000	60,000		6	8			10		20	8		4 80	2 25			team
Port [Gant.]	Shingles	1910	5,000	90,000	90,000		12	6			10		25			5 00	2 75			steam
Port Angeles	Shingles	904	4,500	40,000	40,000		3	2			10		22	7		4 20	2 85			steam
Port Angeles	Shingles	908	4,000	35,000	35,000		3	2			10		24	8		4 00	3 00			steam
Port Angeles	Shingles	906	4,000	50,000	40,000		5	2			10		24			4 00	2 25			team
Port Angeles	Shles	906	4,000	20,000	45,000		4	1			10		20	8		3 50	2 25			team
Port Angeles	Shingles	802	4,000	45,000	45,000		3	2			10		20			3 50	2 50			team
Port Angeles	Shles	1910	3,000	40,000	40,000		4	2			10		20	8		3 50	2 25			team
Port Angeles	Shingles	900	2,500	30,000	30,000		3	1			10			9		4 25	2 00			team
Port Angeles	Shingles	900	2,000	60,000	60,000		4	4			10		25	9		4 00	2 50			team
Port Angeles	Shingles	907	2,000	50,000	50,000		5		1		10	10	20	8	30	3 00	2 50	$1 75		team
Port Angeles	Shingles	908	1,500	60,000	60,000		9	15			10		22	6		4 00	2 25			team
Port Angeles	Lumber	906	24,000	20,000 t.	20,000 t.		3	20	10		10		18		20	4 00	2 50	2 50		team
	refined salmon			cases	50 cases								30							steam

CLARKE COUNTY.

Location	Product	Year	Capital	Value	Output															Power
Vancouver	lber	895	$300,000	65, oft.	65,000ft.	35	95	2		10	9		25	10	25	$3 50	$2 25	$2 50		Steam
Hall	u fber	907	160,000	50,000ft.	80,000ft.	5	13			10			30	9		4 50	2 38			steam
Etna	lber	906	70,000	80,000ft.	80,000ft.	70	32			10	11		26	10		4 25	2 50			team
Vancouver	lber	906	80,000	50,000ft.	50,000ft.	10	29			10			25	11		4 00	2 25			steam
Heisson	lber	1909	20,000	50,000ft.	50,000ft.	6	20			10						3 00	2 25			steam
Amboy	lber	907	20,000	75, oft.	60,000ft.	4	12			10			26			5 00	2 95			team
Lucia	lber	907	10,000	40, oft.	25,000ft.	4	10			10	11		25	11		3 50	2 65			steam
Bush Prairie	Lumber		9,000	35, oft.	20,000ft.	1	44		3	10	12		22	12	30	4 00	2 75	1 00		steam
La otter	Lumber	901	8,000	40,000ft.	40,030 ft.	4	12			10	8		20	11		3 50	2 25			steam
Vancouver	lber	904	5,000	25,000ft.		3	10			10	8		20	8		3 00	3 00			steam
La Cner	u lber	906	5,000	30,000ft.	30,000ft.	5	9			10	8		17	8		4 00	2 00			steam
Vancouver	Lumber	1907	3,000	5,000ft.		1	1			10	8		20	10		2 50	2 00			steam
Ridgefield	u lber	908	4,000	20,000ft.	20,000ft.	4	10			12	10		23	9		8 50	2 00			steam
Bush Prairie	Lumber	908	4,000	25,000ft.	25,000ft.	3	20			10	9		25	12		3 00	2 50			team
Camas	Lumber	903		30,000ft.	30,000ft.	2	10			12	12		25	12		2 75	2 00			team
Vancouver	Gen'l mill cwrk.	907	20,000	$200 val.		6	4			10	12		26	12		4 00	2 25			Electric
Vancouver	Machinery	1910	7,000			4			7				26	12		4 00	2 00			steam
Vancouver	Beer	1869	300,000			35	2		18	9	10		25	12		4 00	2 75			steam
Vancouver	Brick	1876	4,000	36,000 b.	16,000 b.	3	2		15	8	8		25	6		3 25	2 00			team
as	Carriage repair	906	4,000			3	2		18	9	10		26	12		3 25	2 00			Electric
	Wood lp, per	1906		25t's paper 30 t's pulp	10t's paper 10 t's pulp															
Camas	Paper, aper bags	906	10,000	75t's aper	60t's aper	8	39	7		12	12		28	12	26	2 50	1 85	1 10		team
Vancouver	Laundry	908	10,000	$100 val.	$75 val.	30	70	18	10	12	10		28	12	26	2 75	1 85	1 25		team
Vancouver	laiy	909				6		15	8	12	8		24	12	24	2 50		1 40	E. and S.
mer	Laundry	909				6		18	10	10	10		26	12	26	2 75		1 40	steam

COLUMBIA COUNTY.

Town or City	Goods or mill	Date when est'b'lished	Capital invested in plant	Daily capacity	Daily output	Males employed Skil'd	Males employed Un-skil'd	Females em-ploy'd	Hours per day Males	Hours per day Females	Days per mo., men	Mos. per year	Days per mo., fe-males	Wages, Males Skilled	Wages, Males Un-skilled	Wages fe-males	Kind of power used
Dayton	Flour and feed	.....	$40,000	250 bbls.	250 bbls.	5	7	...	10		26	12		$3 00	$2 50	...	Water
Dayton	Flour and feed	1892	40,000	250 bbls.	250 bbls.	8	...		10		26	10		3 00	...	...	Water
Huntsville	Flour and mill	1892	25,000	60 bbls.	50 bbls.	2	1		10		26	10		3 00	2 50		Water
Dayton	Wagons	1909	10,000			2	2		10		26	12		3 50	2 50		Electric
Dayton	Lumber	1883	35,000			2	1		10		25	10		5 00	2 00		Steam

COWLITZ COUNTY.

Town or City	Goods or mill	Date when est'b'lished	Capital invested in plant	Daily capacity	Daily output	Males employed Skil'd	Males employed Un-skil'd	Females em-ploy'd	Hours per day Males	Hours per day Females	Days per mo., men	Mos. per year	Days per mo., fe-males	Wages, Males Skilled	Wages, Males Un-skilled	Wages fe-males	Kind of power used
alna	Lumber	909	$30,000	85, 000ft.	85,000ft.	20	30		10		22	12		$3 25	$1 12½		Steam
Lexington	Lumber	905	42,000	35, 000	30,000ft.	6	14		10		25	12		3 12	2 25		Steam
Lexington	Lumber	906	41,000	40, 000	30,000ft.	7	22		10		22	11		3 75	2 25		Steam
Kelso	Lumber	909	40,000	10, 000ft.	6,000ft.	3	5		10		24	10		4 00	2 25		Steam
Oak Point	lumber	904	36,000	40,000ft.	30,000ft.	6	14		10		24	10		3 50	2 50		Steam
Oak Point	lumber	893	30,000	22, 000ft.	22,000ft.	4	8		10		20	8		3 50	2 25		Steam
Kelso	lumber	908	20,000	25, 00ft.		6	12		10								Steam
West Kelso	lumber	906	35,000	35,000ft.	40,000ft.	7	23		10		22	4		3 50	2 00		Steam
Oak Point	lumber	904	20,000	40,000ft.	25,000ft.	7	13		10		24	11		3 00	2 00		Steam
Kelso Lake	lumber	894	15,000	25, 00ft.	25,000ft.	6	5		10		22	10		3 00	2 50		Steam
Yan	Lumber	907	12,500	30,000ft.	25,000ft.	2	10		10		25	11		4 00	2 50		Steam
Kelso	lumber	907	11,000	25,000ft.	25,000ft.		30		10		25	10			2 75		Steam
Silver Lake	lumber	890	10,000	35,000ft.	20,000ft.	6	8		10		25	8		3 50	2 50		Steam
Castle Rock	lumber	1910	7,500	10,000ft.	10,000ft.	2	5		10		25			4 00	2 75		Steam
Castle Rock	lumber	1910	4,000	25,000ft.	20,000ft.	6	8		10		25			3 50	2 50		Steam
Kalama	lumber	908	4,000	50,000ft.	50,000ft.	4	30		10		26				2 50		lam Steam
Kelso	Shingles	1894	100,000	400,000	400,000	35	20		10		24	12		4 00	2 25		Steam
Castleville	Shingles	1907	25,000	20000		13	7		10		25	12		5 00	3 00		Steam
Castle Rock	Shingles	893	20,000	130,000	130,000	11	8		10		25	10		3 75	2 50		team
Castle Rock	Shingles	899	15,000	130,000	130,000	11	7		10		25	10		4 50	2 40		Steam
Castle Rock	Shingles	1907	15,000	130,000	130,000	11	6		10		24	10		4 50	2 25		Steam
Kelso	Shingles	1894	12,500	60,000	60,000	6	5		10		22	8		4 00	2 50		Steam
Kelso	Shingles	1910	12,000	110,000	100,000	8	5		10		26	10		4 70	2 50		Steam
Kelso	Shingles	901	12,000	120,000	110,000	14	10		10		20	12		4 50	2 85		Steam
Castle Rock	Shingles	907	10,000	140,000	140,000	11	7		10		26	7		4 50	2 50		Steam
Kelso	Shingles		10,000	130,000	110,000	11	8		10		20	9		3 75	2 65		Steam
Kelso	Shingles	890	7,500	65,000	55,000	6	5		10		25	7		3 50	2 50		team
Kelso	Shingles	908	3,000	60,000	60,000	9	3		10			8		4 00	2 50		team
Kelso	Shingles			125,000	125,000	13	7		10		22	6		4 00	2 25		Steam

DOUGLAS COUNTY.

Place	Product	Year	Capital	Output	Output									Wages	Wages		Power
Bridgeport	Flour and feed	1895	$30,000	250 lb.	125 bbls.		8	3	12		28	10		$3 00	$2 50		Steam
Waterville	Flour and feed	1908	15,000	100 bbls.	100 bbls.		6	2	10		26	12		3 50	2 50		Electric
Bridgeport	Lumber	1908	6,000	12,000ft.	12,000ft.		10	4	10		26	5		3 50	2 50		Steam

FERRY COUNTY.

Place	Product	Year	Capital	Output	Output									Wages	Wages		Power
Karamin	Lumber	1906	$15,000	45,000.	40,000ft.		12	10	10		25	10		$4 00	$2 50		Steam
Danville	Lumber	1905	10,000	25,000.	25,000ft.		18	7	10		24	7		3 57	2 77		Steam
Karamin	Lumber	1909	8,000	40,000.	30,000ft.		8	4	10		25	10		3 00	2 50		Electric
Rockcut	Lumber	1907	8,000	65,000.	25,000ft.		6	3	10		26	9		3 50	2 50		Steam
Barston	Lumber	1909	6,000	22,000.	22,000ft.		13	3	10		20	8		3 00	2 50		Steam
Barston	Lumber	1909	4,500	15,000ft.	15,000ft.		5	3	10		20	8		3 00	2 50		Steam

FRANKLIN COUNTY.

Place	Product	Year	Capital	Output										Wages	Wages		Power
Pasco	Laundry	1907	$10,500	$400 val.		12	8	2	10	10	25	12	25	$2 50	$1 66	$1 50	Steam

GARFIELD COUNTY.

Place	Product	Year	Capital	Output	Output									Wages	Wages		Power
Pomeroy	Flour and feed	1905	$20,000	125 bbls.	100 bbls.		2	3	10		20	8		$4 00	$3 00		Water

GRANT COUNTY.

Place	Product	Year	Capital	Output	Output									Wages	Wages		Power
Hartline	Flour, feed, grain		$100,000	500 bbls.			13	2	10		25	10		$4 00	$2 50		Steam

JEFFERSON COUNTY.

Place	Product	Year	Capital	Output	Output									Wages	Wages		Power
Port Townsend	Shingles	1909	$10,000	60,000	80,000		8	5	10		26	10		$4 00	$2 50		Steam
Center	Shingles	1908	10,000	80,000	,000		8	9	10		24	11		4 10	2 40		Steam
Quilcene	Shingles	1909	4,200	75,000			2	9	10		22	12		4 00	2 50		Steam
Quilcene	Shingles	1908	4,000	50,000	6000		3	6	10		26	10		4 00			Steam
Port Discovery	Shingles		4,000	65,000	60000		2	9	10		23	8		4 00	2 75		Steam
Center	Shingles	1909	2,000	60,000			1	8	10		24	10		4 10	2 50		Steam
Quilcene	Shingles	1902	1,200	100,000	00000		7	10	10		25	11			2 00		Steam
Quilcene	Shingles	1908		100,000			5	10	10		26	12		4 35	2 00		Steam

JEFFERSON COUNTY—Continued.

Town or City	Class or allied	Date when est'b-lished	Capital invested in plant	Daily capacity	a'ly 'tput	Males employed Skil'd	Un-skil'd	Fe-males em-pl'y'd	Hours per day Males	Fe-males	Days per mo. males	Mos. per year	Days per mo. fe-males	Wages, Males Skilled	Un-skilled	Wages fe-males	Kind of power used
Port Townsend	...ber	1890	$7,000	30,000ft.	15,000ft.	6	14		10		20	12		$4 25	$2 25		Steam
Port Ludlow	...ber	1875	1,000,000	160,000ft.	125,000ft.		308		10		26	12			2 27		S. and E.
Irondale	Iron and steel	1910		150 tons	100 tons	130	315	1	11	9	24	11		4 62	2 75	1 80	Steam
Port Townsend	...er	1905	25,000	50 bbls.	15 bbls.	2	3		9		26	12		4 50	3 00		Steam
Port Townsend	...ty	1906	30,000	140 kw	115 kw	9	1		10		28	12		2 33			Steam
Port Townsend	...ary		12,000		$75 val.	3	4	18	10	10	24	12	24			$1 50	Steam

...D COUNTY.

Coupeville	Shingles	1909	$6,000	100,000	100,000	8	6		10		20	12		$3 50	$2 50		Steam
	Shingles	1909	5,000	25,000	25,000	4			10					8 50			Steam
	Lumber	1883	4,000	10,000ft.	...ft.	3	2		9		20	12		8 50	2 50		Steam

...NG ...UY.

Kerriston	...gles	1907	$18,300	200,000	200,000	6	54		10		24	10		$4 75	$2 00		Steam
...le	...gles	1905	100,000	25,000	20,000	10	10		10		22	12		2 75	2 25		6in
...th	...gles	1882	80,000	160,000	100,000	16	11		10		25	11		4 00	2 25		te6in
...le	...gles	1889	80,000	500,000	500,000	10	68		10		24	11		8 75	2 10		6in
...le	...gles	1899	75,000	180,000	150,000	15	7		10		26	12		3 40	2 25		Steam
...er	...gles	1901	67,500	125,000	60,000	4	36		10		23	9		4 00	2 60		Steam
...hore	...gles	1906	50,000	225,000	225,000	17	11		10		25	10		4 65	2 15		6in
...dle	...gles	1903	50,000	225,000	225,000	10	30		10		25	11		4 20	3 04		6in
...n	...gles	1905	50,000	200,000	200,000		61		10		25	11			3 25		4th
...le	...gles		38,000	140,000	140,000	5	18		10		24	8		8 27	3 04		1th
...n	...gles	1899	35,000	220,000	220,000	20	9		10		25	10		4 50	2 00		e6th
Inglewood	...gles	1908	25,000	200,000	200,000	20	9		9		24	12		4 50	2 75		e5in
Riverside	...gles	1900	25,000	20,000		3			10		26	10		4 00			Electric
Seattle	...gles	1907	25,000	200,000	200,000	23	3		10		23	10		4 00			6in
...le	...gles	1903	22,000	140,000	140,000	21	6		10		25	10		4 50	2 75		Steam
...th	...gles	1898	15,000	210,000	210,000	19	11		10		22	9		3 75	2 65		t e6in
May Creek	...gles	1904	15,000	200,000	175,000	16	5							3 60	2 50		Steam
...l	...gles	1905	15,000	175,000	175,000	17	4		10		25	10		4 00	2 50		Steam

Place	Product	Year	Capital	Value 1	Value 2	Power
?le	Shingles	1906	14,000	176,000	200,000	Steam
Preston	Shingles	1906	12,000	150,000	150,000	Steam
Baring	Shingles	1903	12,000	50,000	60,000	Steam
?lish	Shingles	1905	11,000	200,000	240,000	Steam
Yesler	Shingles	1908	10,200	90,000	100,000	Steam
?	Shingles	1909	10,000	125,000	125,000	Steam
Lester	Shingles	1899	10,000	100,000	110,000	Steam
Samamish	Shingles	1902	10,000	100,000	100,000	Steam
Algona	Shingles	1900	8,000	50,000	120,000	Steam
?le	Shingles	1905	8,000	100,000	100,000	Steam
Sherwood	Shingles	1908	7,500	85,000	90,000	Steam
lack ?er	Shingles	1907	7,000		20,000	Steam
Bo Lake	Shingles	1910	6,000	60,000	230,000	Steam
Seattle	Shingles	1904	5,000	60,000	60,000	Steam
Seattle	Shingles	1903	4,200	40,000	50,000	Steam
Seattle	Shingles	1900	4,000		40,000	Steam
Seattle	Shingles	1910	900	17,000	25,000	Steam
Redmond	bar	1896	300,000	650,000	700,000	S. and E.
?in	ber	1896	186,400	75,000ft.	75,000ft.	Steam
Seattle	Mr	1907	180,000	60,000ft.	97,540ft.	Steam
Seattle	bar	1906	170,000	35,000ft.	60,000ft.	Steam
Seattle	Mr	1906	150,000	70,000ft.	60,000ft.	Steam
Seattle	ber	1889	137,000	40,000ft.	50,000ft.	Steam
Seattle	Mr	1906	125,000	40,000ft.	40,600ft.	Steam
Preston	ber	1906	118,000	70,000ft.	70,000ft.	Steam
Bryn Mawr	bar	1897	100,000	100,000ft.	100,000ft.	S. ...E.
?er	bar	1900	100,000	40,000ft.	40,000ft.	Steam
?ey	Mr	1907	100,000	200,000ft.	200,000ft.	Steam
Seattle	ber	1874	100,000	35,000ft.	35,000ft.	Steam
Seattle	Mr	1905	93,000	60,000ft.	60,000ft.	Steam
Seattle	bar	1894	90,000	70,000ft.	70,000ft.	Steam
Seattle	bar	1897	90,000	20,000ft.	35,000ft.	Steam
?	bar	1892	75,000	75,000ft.	75,000ft.	Steam
Seattle	bar	1889	67,500	75,000ft.	75,000ft.	Steam
Seattle	bar	1907	60,000	50,000ft.	50,000ft.	Steam
Seattle	bar	1906	60,000	40,000ft.	40,000ft.	Steam
Seattle	bar	1886	50,000	70,000ft.	70,000ft.	Steam
Seattle	bar	1905	50,000	115,000ft.	115,000ft.	Steam
?	bar	1906	50,000	75,000ft.	75,000ft.	Steam
Enumclaw	bar	1897	50,000			Steam

KING COUNTY—Continued.

Town or City	Goods Manufactured or Handled	Date when est'b'lished	Capital invested in plant	Daily capacity	Daily output	Males employed Skill'd	Males employed Un-skill'd	Fe-males em-pl'y'd	Hours per day Males	Hours per day Fe-males	Days per mo., males	Mos. per year	Days per mo., fe-males	Wages, Males Skilled	Wages, Males Un-skilled	Wages fe-males	Kind of power used
Gr too Siding	Lumber	1906	$42,000	60,000ft.	60,000ft.	9	30		10		25	10		$4 17	$2 25		Steam
dále	Lumber	1889	40,000	50,000ft.	35,000ft.	38	14		10		25	12		2 96	2 25		Steam
Orilla	Lumber	1906	40,000	25,000ft.	20,000ft.	10	40		10		23	11		4 00	2 25		Steam
dále Valley	Lumber	1907	40,000	40,000ft.	35,000ft.	30	40		10		26	12		3 25	2 25		Steam
Seattle	Lumber	1908	40,000	75,000ft.	30,000ft.	9	28		10		22	12		3 50	2 00		Steam
dále	Lumber	1907	25,000	25,000ft.	20,000ft.	10	20	1	10	8	25	11		3 00	2 35		Steam
Preston	Lumber	1900	40,000	60,000ft.	45,000ft.	10	25		10		24	11		4 25	2 25		Steam
Wilburton	Lumber	1905	38,000	65,000ft.	66,000ft.	12	57		10		25	11		3 29	2 25		Steam
North and	Lumber	1906	30,000	75,000ft.		40	40		10		24	11		3 00	2 35		Steam
dáth end	Lmer	1906	30,000	75,000ft.	75,000ft.	15	70		10		24	9		4 25	2 50		Steam
th	Lmer	1900	39,000	75,000ft.	63,000ft.	8	24		10		26	12		3 88	2 66		Electric
dále	Lumber	1907	27,700	26,000ft.		11	12		10		25	12		2 97	2 00		Steam
dále	Lumber	1907	25,000	30,000ft.	25,000ft.	10	15		10		24	11		4 00	1 85		Steam
Barneston	Lumber	1896	20,000	60,000ft.	50,000ft.	10	24		10		26	12		2 75	2 00		Steam
Kent	Lumber	1900	20,000	25,000ft.	25,000ft.	8	50		10		26	12		3 00	2 50		Steam
dále	Lumber	1906	20,000	40,000ft.	50,000ft.	20	5		10		26	12		2 75	1 75		Steam
Algona	Lumber	1909	20,000	50,000ft.	25,000ft.	25	18		10		20	12		3 50	2 30		Steam
Skykomish	Lumber	1901	15,000	30,000ft.	50,000ft.	7	8		10		25	10		2 40	2 25		Steam
Grotto Spur	Lumber	1906	12,000	25,000ft.	25,000ft.	9	8		10		24	12		2 70	2 23		Steam
dále	Lumber	1909	10,000	20,000ft.	15,000ft.	5	7		10		25	10		3 00	2 25		Steam
dále	Lumber	1899	10,000	20,000ft.	15,000ft.	7	7		10		24	12		2 87	2 00		Steam
Kent	Lumber	1900	10,000	15,000ft.		5	2		10		20	12		3 00	2 00		Steam
Covington	Lumber	1900	7,000	15,000ft.	15,000ft.	4	13	1	10	10	25	12	30	3 00	2 50	$1 16	Steam
Milton	Lumber	1908	5,000	15,000ft.	8,000ft.	5	15		10		26	12		3 25	2 25		Steam
dále	Lumber	1907		30,000ft.	30,000ft.	4	7		10		25	12		3 00	2 00		Steam
Barneston	Lumber	1899		50,000ft.	40,000ft.	20	40		10		26	12		3 00	2 00		Steam
dále	Lumber	1899		60,000ft.	60,000ft.	10	15	6	10	8	25	12		3 50	2 25		S. and E.
dále	Lumber			75,000ft.	50,000ft.	35	85		10		26	12		2 75	2 00		S. and E.
Seattle	W'od products	1884	150,000			46	22		14		26	12	26	3 25	2 25		Steam
dále	W'd products	1901	97,000			35	7	1	10	9	26	12		3 75	2 75	3 00	E. & C. A.
dále	W'd products	1884	60,000	$450 val.	$450 val.	37	40		10		25	12		3 50	2 25		Steam
dále	W'd products	1906	50,000	$1,000 val.	$750 val.	45	15		9		26	12	25	3 30	2 25	2 25	Electric
dále	W'd products	1903	50,000	$200 val.		30	10		10		25	12		4 00	1 50		Elc
dále	W'd products	1905	40,000			7	15		9		26	12		8 00	2 00		Elc
Setle	W'd products	1906	30,000			8	14		9		26	12		2 25	2 25		Elc

Location		Product	Year	Capital												Power
Seattle		W od products	1902	25,000					20	2			10		12	22	Electric
Seattle		Wd products	1909	25,000		$200 xl.	$200 xl.		20	10			9		12	23	Steam
Seattle		W od parts	1905	25,000		1000 kgs.	$50 pkgs	26	23	1		9		12	22	Steam
Seattle		W od products	1888	20,000		8,000ft.	400 pkgs		14	2	2	10		11	24	Gas
Seattle		Wd parts	1906	20,000		5,000ft.	4,000ft.		8	17		9		10	24	Steam
Seattle		W od parts	1906	20,000			8,000ft.		20	15		9		12	24	Mac
Seattle		W od parts	1907	15,000					20	5		9		12	25	Steam
Seattle		W od products	1907	15,000		$80 xl.	$200 xl.		6			9		12	25	l Gas
Seattle		W od r parts	1908	15,000		100 bales	50 bales		2	6		9		12	25	team
Seattle		Wd products		12,000	500		500 bars		6	2		9		12	26	Mac
Seattle		W od products	1906	10,000		$500 xl.	$300 xl.		23	1		9		12	26	Mac
Seattle		Wd products	1909	10,000		$100 xl.	$30 xl.		13			10		12	26	Electric
Seattle		W od products	1903	10,000					14			9		12	24	Mac
Seattle		W od products	1901	10,000		100 pkgs	400 pkgs		16	3		9		12	26	Mac
Seattle		Wd products	1909	6,000		$100 xl.	$80 xl.		9	3		10		10	23	Electric
Seattle		W od products	1905	5,500		$60 xl.	$100 xl.		5			8		12	28	Electric
Seattle		Wd products	1908	5,000		$250 xl.	$25 xl.		12	2		8		12	24	Electric
Seattle		W od products	1910	5,000		$200 xl.	$50 xl.		5			10		12	26	Electric
Seattle		W od products	1908	2,500		$100 xl.	$350 xl.		3			8		11	28	Steam
Seattle		W od products	1891	2,500		$250 xl.			25			8		10	24	Mac
Seattle		W od products	1902	2,500		$25 val.	$25 val.		5	3	2	10		12	26	Electric
Seattle		W od parts	1907	1,200					4	4		9		12	26	Steam
Seattle		Machl nry	1906	2,868,000	$7,000 val.	$3,200 val.		2	12	12		9		12	26	Electric
Seattle		Mry	1881	500,000	1 1 line	1 engine		230	290		8	2	12	26	
Seattle		Mry	1882	500,000	$3,000 xl.	$3 000 val.		100	100		9		12	29	Electric
Seattle		Mry	1887	100,000	$300 xl.	$500 xl.		85	114		9		13	26	
Seattle		Mry	1908	150,000	2 mach's,w'k	Average 30 mach's,y'r		21	32		8		12	26	l
Seattle		Machinery	1900	100,000	20 ons	12 tons		20	5		9		12	28	Electric
Seattle		Mry	1889	100,000				30	35		9		12	25	
Seattle		Machinery	1908	75,000	$300 val.	$300 val.		34	10		9		12	26	Electric
Seattle		Machinery	1906	60,000				20	8		9		12	26	Electric
Seattle		Mry	908	60,000	20 tons	10 tons		10	5		10		12	28	
Seattle		Mry	1899	50,000				8	5		9		12	28	Electric
Sale		Mry	180	40,000	$400 val.	$200 val.		14	4		8		12	25	
Sale		Mry	908	40,000	$1,000 val.	$300 val.		5	2		9		13	26	Electric
Sale		Mry	1901	40,000	$150 val.	$125 val.		4	8		10		12	25	Electric
Seattle		Mry	1880	35,000	25 tons	3 tons		10	3		8		12	25	Gas
Seattle		Mry	1900	15,000				10	8		9		12	26	Electric
Seattle		Machinery	1887	15,000	$500 val.	$225 val.		9	5		10		12	26	l Gas
Seattle		Mry	1900	15,000	$250 val.	$150 val.		14	2		10		12	26	Mac
Seattle		Mry	900	10,000	$200 val.	$100 val.		9	8		9		12		Mac
Seattle		Mry	900	10,000	$50 val.	$25 val.		4	4		8		12		Mac
Seattle		Mry	1907	10,000				4	4		8		12		Mac

KING COUNTY—Continued.

Town or City	Goods Manufactured or Handled	Date when est'b'lished	Capital invested in plant	Daily capacity	Daily output	Males employed Skil'd	Males employed Un-skil'd	Fe-males em-pl'y'd	Hours per day Males	Hours per day Fe-males	Days per mo. males	Mos. per year	Days per mo. fe-males	Wages, Males Skilled	Wages, Males Un-skilled	Wages fe-males	Kind of power used
Seattle	Machinery	1909	$5,000		$35 val.	8	2		9		26	12		$4 50	$1 75		Electric
Seattle	Machinery	1905	4,000	$100 val.		4	1		9		26	12		4 50	1 00		Electric
Seattle	Machinery	1888	2,500		$20 val.	8	3		9		26	12		4 00	2 35		Electric
Seattle	Machinery	1906	2,000	$75 val.		2	1	1	8	8	26	12	26	4 50	1 00	$2 00	Electric
Seattle	Machinery	1909	1,800	$50 val.	$35 val.	4	6		8		24	12		3 75	2 50		Electric
Seattle	Machinery	1898	1,000		$40 val.	4	1		9		25	12		3 80	2 25		Electric
Seattle	Machinery	1888	300	$40 val.		5	1		9		26	12		4 00	2 50		Electric
Seattle	Machinery	1907				8	2		9		26	12					Electric
Seattle	Flour and feed	1902	400,000	2000 bls. fl'r 70 tons f'd	881 bls. fl'r 29 tons f'c	25	7				26	12		8 75	2 50		Electric
Seattle	Flour, cereals, f'd	1889	300,000	400 bbls.	400 bbls	25	75	10	10	8	26	12	26	4 00	2 50		Electric
Seattle	Flour	1897	200,000	1,250 bbls.	925 bbls.	8	34		10		26	11		6 20	2 76		Electric
Seattle	Flour, cereals, f'd	1905	120,000	100 tons f'd 250 bls. c'ls	100 tons f'd 250 bls. c'ls	20	60	10	9	9	25	12	25	4 00	2 75	1 50	Steam
Seattle	Hay and grain	1908	50,000	350 bbls.	250 bbls.	80			10		26	12		2 75			Electric
Seattle	Flour and feed	1892	75,000	1000 sks. f'd	30 tons	5	11		10		26	12		3 50	2 75		Electric
Seattle	Flour and feed	1907	20,000	20 tons f'd	20 tons f'd	2	5		10		25	12		3 00	2 50		Electric
Seattle	Feed	1889	8,000	80 tons	30 tons	8	8		10		26	12		2 75	2 25		Electric
Benton	Brick, clay prod's	1902	2,500	100,000 b.	100,000 b.	4	75		10		25	10		8 00	2 25		S. and E.
Taylor	Brick, clay prod's	1901	286,000	30,000 b.	30,000 b.	25	30		10		30	12		3 25	2 25		Steam
Seattle	Brick, clay prod's	1906	185,000	75 tons	66 tons	15	70		10		28	12		2 75	2 00		Steam
Auburn	Brick	1888	158,000			10	12		9		28	12		8 00	2 00		Electric
Seattle	Brick, lay pr'g	1906	100,000	25,000	20,000	30	18	1	10	8	30	12		3 50	2 85		Steam
Seattle	Brick, clay prod's	1906	50,000	30,000	28,000	6	19		10		26	12		3 00	2 65		Electric
Seattle	Brick, clay	1906	30,000	25,000	25,000	10	20		9		25	12		4 00	2 50		Steam
Seattle	Laundry	1908	25,000			5	75	75	10	9	30	12	26	3 75	2 50	2 00	Steam
Seattle	Laundry	1904	250,000	$400 val.	$100 val.	10	20	80	10	10	28	12	30	3 75	3 00	1 66	Steam
Seattle	Laundry	1890	60,000	$400 val.	$400 val.	16	4	60	10	10	30	12	30	3 00			Steam
Seattle	Laundry	1905	60,000	$900 val.	$600 val.		38	84	10	10	28	12		3 00			Steam
Seattle	L'undry	1899	32,000	$250 val.	$150 val.	11		45	10	10	26	12	26	3 00	1 50	1 50	Steam
Seattle	Laundry	1908	18,000	$150 val.	$185 val.	2	40	10	10	10	30	12	30	3 00	2 00	1 50	F. and S.
Seattle	Laundry	1902	15,000	$200 val.	$100 val.	3	1	11	10	10	28	12	28	3 00	1 50	2 00	Steam
Seattle	Laundry	1910	15,000	$200 val.	$105 val.	10	2	12	10	10	28	12	20	2 50	1 15	1 35	Steam
Seattle	Lat dry	1907	10,000	$200 val.	$175 val.	10	1	28	10	10	25	12	26	3 00	2 00	2 00	Electric
Seattle	Laundry	1908	10,000	$100 val.	$75 val.	1	30	4	10	10	26	12		2 75	1 00	1 00	Steam
Seattle	Laundry	1906	8,000						10			12					Steam

City	Product	Year	Capital	Output	Output 2	1	2	3	4	5	6	7	8	Wage	Wage	Wage	Power
Seattle	Laundry	1906	3,800			2	3	12	10	10	30	12	18	3 00	2 50	1 50	Stm team
Seattle	Laundry	1880				15	150	40	10	10	28	12	28	3 00	8 68	2 00	Electric
Seattle	Beer	1908	2,000,000	500 bbls	750 bbls				10	10	30	12		4 00			E. and S.
Seattle	Beer	1902	150,000	150 bbls	150 bbls	34	150		8	8	28	12		3 68	8 68		E. and S.
Seattle	Ice	1890	104,500	100 bbls	90 bbls				9	8	26	12		4 00			E. and S.
Seattle	Ice, steam heat	1909	200,000	35 tons	35 tons	22		11	8	8	26	12		3 68			E. and S.
Seattle			15,000	30 tons	750 hp heat												
Seattle	Crackers, candy	1905	150,000	$200 val.		3	31	66	10	8	30	12	23	3 25	2 15	1 19	E. and S.
Seattle	Crackers, candy	1888	100,000	750 bbls		15	15	65	7	10	23	12	20	3 97	2 10	1 25	Steam
Seattle	Pack'gh'se prod's	1904	100,000	150 bbls		10	180	11	9	10	20	12	26	4 00	2 00	1 50	S. and E.
Seattle	Pack'gh'se prod's	1885	1,500	90 bbls		85	2		9	10	26	12		3 25			
Seattle	Printing	1900	60,000	35 tons		3		30	8	8	25	12	25	3 83	2 00	1 83	Elec
Seattle	Printing	1899	50,000	30 tons		15	10	6	8	8	25	12	25	3 35		1 35	Elec
Seattle	Wool, leather	1896	50,000	35,121 p'rs		65		9	8	8	25	12	25	4 00		2 50	Elec
Seattle	Wool, leather	1905	40,000	490 lbs. w'l	800 skins	7	10		9	9	26	12	24	2 75	2 00		Steam
Seattle	Wool, leath e	1894	40,000	300 val.	$300 val.	9	2		7	9	26	12	24	2 75	2 00		Elec
Seattle	Wall plast re	1906	25,000	50 tons	25 tons	16	18	25	9	10	26	12	28	3 00	2 50		Elec
Seattle	Wall tar	1905	15,000	20 tons	15 tons	2	4	50	9	9	26	12	28	3 50	2 25		S. and W.
Seattle	Electric L. & P.	1899	3,500,000	12,200 kw	12,200 kw	75	5	6	8	8	24	12		3 40	2 42	2 00	Elec
Seattle	Boots and shoes	1891	250,000	1 000 p'rs	400 p'rs	50	66		8	10	27	12	24	3 00	2 50	2 50	Electric
Seattle	Fish	1900	200,000	100 tons	75 tons	50	15	28	10	8	26	12	24	4 25	2 70	2 50	Steam
Seattle	Syrups and jams	1908	188,000	$1000 val.	$1000 val.	11	70	3	8	10	26	12	28	4 00	2 00	1 75	Steam
Auburn	Condensed milk	1902	125,000	600 cases	600 ses	25	16	9	9	9	26	12	26	4 50	2 25		Elec
Sale	Bags	1904	125,000	10000 bags	35000 algs	6	55	25	8	8	26	12	26	3 50	2 80	1 75	Electric
Seattle	Shirts	1904	60,000	75 doz.	75 doz.	15	2	50	10	10	25	12	25	3 10	2 50	1 86	Elec
Seattle	Brooms	1904	50,000	100 doz.	100 doz.	12	10	55	9	8	25	12	24	3 00	1 50	1 50	Electric
Seattle	Electrical supplies	1908	50,000			10	12	6	8	10	26	12		4 00	2 00		Electric
Seattle	Tin ans	1905	36,000	900 val.	50,000 cans	10	50		10	10	25	12	26	6 00			Elec
Seattle	Paper boxes	1900	25,000	200 boxes	150 boxes	5		15	8	8	25	12	25	3 50	2 50	2 00	Elec
Seattle	Spices	1888	20,000	900 val.	$2000 val.	30	60	20	10	8	26	12	24	2 75	1 75	1 25	Elec
Seattle	Baskets	1908	15,000	200 doz.	125 dz.	14	2	35	9	8	25	12		5 50	2 50		Elec
Seattle	Kiln ice	1904	15,000			3	3		9	8	26	12		8 71			Elec
Seattle	Cloaks and suits	1902	5,700	100 garm'ts	42 garm'ts	15		30		8	26	12	26			1 65	Elec
Seattle	Bedding	1888		100 mattr's	100 mattr's		5										
Seattle				75 springs	75 springs		38										
Seattle	Wire rope	1906		3½ tons	3½ tons	20		40	10	10	26	12	26	3 50	2 50	2 00	Electric
Seattle						8								4 00	2 50		Electric

KITSAP COUNTY.

Town or City	Goods Manufactured or Handled	Date when est'b'lished	Capital invested in plant	Daily capacity	Daily output	Males employed Skil'd	Males employed Un-skil'd	Fe-males em-pl'y'd	Hours per day Males	Hours per day Fe-males	Days per mo., males	Mos. per year	Days per mo., fe-males	Wages, Males Skilled	Wages, Males Un-skilled	Wages fe-males	Kind of power used
Paulsbo	Shingles	1907	$35,000	55,000	......	2	2	....	10	..	20	8	..	$3 50	$2 50	......	Steam
Colby	Shingles	1909	15,000	60,000	......	4	10	....	10	..	20	10	..	5 00	2 25	......	Steam
Paulsbo	Shingles	1908	12,000	90,000	80,000	7	6	....	10	..	24	10	..	4 00	2 25	......	Steam
Colby	Shingles	1909	3,750	50,000	50,000	2	9	....	10	..	24	11	..	4 25	2 00	......	Steam
Eagle Harbor	Lumber	1908	300,000	75,000ft.	75,000ft.	10	20	....	10	..	30	12	..	3 50	2 50	......	Steam
Colby	Lumber	1909	15,000	25,000ft.	......	4	10	....	10	..	20	10	..	5 00	2 25	......	Steam
Colby	Lumber	1909	3,750	25,000ft.	25,000ft.	4	19	....	10	..	24	11	..	4 25	2 00	......	Steam
Port Gamble	Lumber	1853	......	200,000ft.	100,000ft.	35	160	....	10	..	26	12	..	3 75	1 78	......	Steam
Port Blakely	Lumber	1866	......	150,000ft.	150,000ft.	61	146	....	10	..	26	12	..	8 00	2 00	......	Electric
Winslow	Ship Blds, rep'r's	1902	300,000	150,000ft.	150,000ft.	125	75	1	8	8	26	12	26	4 50	2 25	$2 50	Steam

KITTITAS COUNTY.

Town or City	Goods Manufactured or Handled	Date when est'b'lished	Capital invested in plant	Daily capacity	Daily output	Males employed Skil'd	Males employed Un-skil'd	Fe-males em-pl'y'd	Hours per day Males	Hours per day Fe-males	Days per mo., males	Mos. per year	Days per mo., fe-males	Wages, Males Skilled	Wages, Males Un-skilled	Wages fe-males	Kind of power used
Roslyn	Beer	1894	$75,000	40 bbls.	25 bbls.	9	..	..	8	..	25	12	..	$3 50	$2 60	..	S. and E.
Ellensburg	Ice	1906	25,000	25 tons	15 tons	1	2	..	9	..	27	12	..	3 70	..	..	W. and S.
Ole Elum	Electricity	1903	......	20,000ft.	15,000ft.	5	..	..	8	..	30	12	..	3 20	2 37	..	S. and E.
Ole Elum	Lumber	1903	7,500	......	......	5	14	..	10	..	25	10	..	3 75	..	..	Steam
Ole Elum	Electric, st'm pl't	1910	......	20,000ft.	14,000ft.	5	9	..	8	..	30	8	..	3 20	3 00	..	S. and E.
Ellensburg	Lumber	......	10,000	13,000ft.	......	5	11	..	10	..	26	8	..	4 00	..	..	Steam
Ellensburg	Lumber	1889	10,000	100 bbls	......	2	2	..	10	..	25	8	..	4 00	2 50	..	Water
Ellensburg	Flour and feed	......	20,000	$60 val.	......	4	..	9	10	9	26	12	24	1 83	..	$1 00	Water
Ole Elum	Laundry	1906	7,000	......	......												Steam

KLICKITAT COUNTY.

Town or City	Goods Manufactured or Handled	Date when est'b'lished	Capital invested in plant	Daily capacity	Daily output	Males employed Skil'd	Males employed Un-skil'd	Fe-males em-pl'y'd	Hours per day Males	Hours per day Fe-males	Days per mo., males	Mos. per year	Days per mo., fe-males	Wages, Males Skilled	Wages, Males Un-skilled	Wages fe-males	Kind of power used
Goldendale	Flour, cereals, r'd	1904	$25,000	120 bbls.	25 bbls.	2	2	..	10	..	26	12	..	$4 00	$2 50	..	Water
Goldendale	Laundry	1904	6,000	$400 val.	$120 val.	1	..	4	10	9	26	12	20	1 50	..	$1 20	Steam
Goldendale	Lumber	1908	1,500	80,000ft.	20ft.	3	9	..	10	..	20	4	..	4 00	2 50	..	Steam
Goldendale	Lumber	1880	6,000	200,000	..	3	..	..	10	..	26	8	..	3 00	..	..	Steam

LEWIS COUNTY.

Town or City	Goods Manufactured or Handled	Date when est'b'lished	Capital invested in plant	Daily capacity	Daily output	Males employed Skil'd	Males employed Un-skil'd	Fe-males em-pl'y'd	Hours per day Males	Hours per day Fe-males	Days per mo., males	Mos. per year	Days per mo., fe-males	Wages, Males Skilled	Wages, Males Un-skilled	Wages fe-males	Kind of power used
Mineral	Shingles	1907	$80,000	200,000	200,000	13	10	..	10	..	25	10	..	$5 00	$2 50	..	Steam
Centralia	Shingles	1907	25,000	250,000	240,000	26	20	..	10	..	20	11	..	3 50	2 25	..	Steam
Dryad	Shingles	1891	14,000	200,000	500	16	9	..	10	..	25	10	..	3 50	..	..	Steam

Location	Product	Year														Power
Centralia	Shgls	904	12,075	125,000	125,000		13	5		10		23	12		4 70		t. &m
alia	Shgls	1910	12,000	120,000	100,000		10	5		10		20	10		4 00		S. eam
alane	Shingles	889	10,000	68,000			12	18		10		22	12		8 25		Sam
Dryad	ella	982	9,000	125,000	125,000		11	2		10		25	10		3 50	2 25	te&m
ella	Shingles	905	8,650	120,000	125,000		12	4		10		26	12		4 00	2 25	Sam
Flynn	Shgls	905	7,000	115,000	115,000		10	5		10		22			4 00	3 50	te&m
Chehalis	Shgls	986	7,000	60,000	70,000		6	10		10		20	10		5 00	2 50	Sam
hgls	lgs	986	5,000	75,000	175,000		9	4		10					4 45	2 00	Sam
Walville	gls	1910	5,000	90,000	900		6	5		10					4 50	2 00	te&m
allk	lhr	908	1,000,000	100,000	100,000ft.		9	4		10		22	10	$2 00	8 00	2 00	Sam
ella	lthr	985	500,000	125,000ft.	125		24	87	24	10		24	11		8 00	2 00	Sam
lle Falls	lhr	907	400,000	80,00ft.		8	6	70	15	10		20	12		8 00	2 00	te&m
alk	lhr	907	250,000	80,00ft.	100		15	85	10	10	1	23	12		8 50	2 00	tem
tall	Lumber	983	200,000	90,000ft.	100,000ft.		10	150	9	10		26	6		8 75	2 95	Sam
ll	Lumber	988	100,000	50,000ft.	100,000ft.		12	26	11	10		25	8		8 50	2 15	tm
ell	Lumber	986	100,000	90,000ft.	100,000ft.		11	24	12	10		25	11		8 50	1 75	Sam
ell	I lhr	982	80,900	80,000ft.	200ft.		30	50	30	10		26	12		8 20	2 12	Sam
tal	lhr	903	80,000	75,000ft.	100,000ft.		7	45	7	10		12	10		8 80	2 35	Sam
ella	lhr	985	78,500	84,000ft.	75,000ft.		16	80	16	10		22	12		8 75	2 00	te&m
Centralia	lhr	903	75,000	60,000ft.	100,000ft.		13	57	13	10		28	10		8 25	2 95	Sam
Dryad	lhr	985	75,000	100,000ft.	100ft.		7	60	7	10		15	12		8 00	2 00	S. and E.
Dty	lhr	1889	65,000	40,000ft.	40,000ft.		8	18	8	10		21	8		8 80	2 15	Steam
Ada	lhr	988	60,000	75	75		10	80	10	10		23	12		8 25	1 00	Sam
Pe Ell	Lumber	905	40,000	30	30		10	25	5	10		29	12		8 00	2 00	Sam
Ml	lhr	905	40,000	75	75		5	15	10	10		29	10		8 50	2 95	Sam
Ctla	lhr	1906	30,000	80	40,000ft.		10	13	6	10		24	12		8 00	2 25	tem
alne	lhr	1891	25,000	35	35ft.		5	10	7	10		29	12		8 60	2 00	te&m
Ctla	lhr	900	20,000				10	9	9	10		24	12		8 80	2 00	Sam
Centralia	lhr	905	18,000	25,000ft.	25,000ft.		8	17	6	10		29	16		8 00	2 60	Sam
Napavine	lhr	903	15,000	30,000ft.	30,000ft.		12	12	8	10		28	24		8 50	2 50	te&m
Pe Ell	lhr	904	15,000	30,000ft.	30,000ft.		12	20	5	10		28	26		8 00	2 00	tm
Chehalis	Lumber	904	12,000	60,000ft.	60,000ft.		10	40	10	10		23	20		8 25	2 00	Sm
Man.		1889	10,000	40,000ft.	40,000ft.		10	17	8	10		22	20		4 00	2 25	alc
le	Gs	908	10,000	95	95		12	10		10		24	20		8 00		Sam
Dryad	Lumber	905	7,000	45,000ft.	45,000ft.		6	40	6	10		26	20		8 00	2 50	Sm
vine	lhr	907	4,000	15,000ft.	15,000ft.		1	6	1	10		26			8 75	2 50	Sam
Mefill	Lumber	904	7,000	35,000ft.	85,000ft.		6	9	6	10		29			4 00	2 50	dm
e	Gs	900	3,500	8,000ft.	10,000ft.		3	7	3	10		20			4 00	2 00	Sun
Napavine	Lumber				10,000ft.			60							2 75		Sm
Centralia	Lumber	192		10,	10,		12	80	25	10		26	12		8 75	2 50	Steam
Chehalis	Wood products	982	77,000	800 doors	800 doors		40	95	40	10		25	12		8 00	1 95	te&m

LEWIS COUNTY—Continued.

Town or City	Gds mfd or sld	Date when est'b'lished	Capital invested in plant	Daily capacity	Daily output	Males employed Skil'd	Males employed Un-skil'd	Females em-pl'y'd	Hours per day Males	Hours per day Fe-males	Days per mo., males	Mos. per year	Days per mo., fe-males	Wages, Males Skilled	Wages, Males Un-skilled	Wages fe-males	Kind of power used
Centralia	Wd l dls	1902	$35,000			50	50		10		24	12		$2 50	$2 00		Steam
Centralia	Wd pails	1904	26,300	30,000ft.	25,000ft.	12	18		10		25	12		2 95	2 00		Steam
Little Falls	Wd dbs	1903	25,000	400 columns	400 columns	15	20		10		25	12		3 00	2 00		Steam
Little Falls	Wd products	1908	15,000	20ft.	20ft.	4	30		10		20	12		3 50	2 00		Steam
Centralia	Wd products	1902	10,000	6,000ft.	400ft.	4	1		10		20	8		3 00	2 00		Steam
Chehalis	Wd products	1902	8,000	700 posts	500 posts	3	2		10		22	8		3 50	2 00		Steam
Centralia	Wd products	1901	7,000	350 doors	200 doors	8	11		10		20	12		3 75	2 25		Steam
Wk	Wd products	1908	6,500			2	1		10		22	10		3 00	2 00		Steam
Wls	W od products	1908	5,000		5 cars, mo.	3	5		10		22	12		4 00	2 00		Steam
Chehalis	Wd products	1910	3,000		250 columns	20	15				25			2 50	2 00		Electric
Gls	Brick and tile	1906	60,000	1500 cases	900 cases	7	60	15		10	25	12	25	3 20	2 40	$1 60	Steam
Lile Falls	Sewerpipe ad tile	1901	20,000	20,000 brick	10,000 brick	4	4		9½		24	12		2 75	2 25		Steam
Centralia	Mi ry	1902	30,000	2 cars	2 cars	7	45		10		26	12		3 25	2 25		Electric
Centralia	Machinery	1908	20,000			22	6		9		26	12		4 00	2 50		Electric
Centralia	Ice	1907	15,000	8 tons	5 ns	15	5		10		26	12		4 00	2 50		Electric
Chehalis	Laundry	1906	4,500			1	2	9	10	7	26	12	20	2 75	2 00	1 05	Steam
Centralia	dry	1908	3,750	$80 val.	$55 val.	1	3	11	9½	9½	26	12	20	3 00	2 50	1 50	Electric

LINCOLN COUNTY.

Town or City	Gds mfd or sld	Date when est'b'lished	Capital invested in plant	Daily capacity	Daily output	Males employed Skil'd	Males employed Un-skil'd	Females em-pl'y'd	Hours per day Males	Hours per day Fe-males	Days per mo., males	Mos. per year	Days per mo., fe-males	Wages, Males Skilled	Wages, Males Un-skilled	Wages fe-males	Kind of power used
Beardan	Flour and feed	902	$65,000	450 bls.	450 bls.	6	10		10		26	10		$3 50	$2 50		Electric
Odessa	Flour and feed	982	50,000	350 bls.	25 bls.	6	10		10		26	9		3 50	2 50		Steam
Harrington	Flour and feed	980	50,000	300 bls.	300 bls.	4	7		10		26	9		3 75	2 25		Electric
Davenport	Flour and feed	892	50,000	300 bls.	400 bls.	10	3		10		25	9		3 00	2 00		Electric
Wilbur	Flour and feed	980	44,000	500 bls.	500 bls.	3	20		10		26	12		4 50	2 50		Steam
Sprague	Flour and feed	981	35,000	300 bls.	250 bls.	6	11		10		26	9		3 00	2 50		Electric
Oreston	Flour and feed	982	30,000	400 bls.	25 bls.	6	6		10		26	8		3 80	2 50		Steam
Sprague	Flour and feed	982	35,000	100 bls.	300 bls.	8	10		10		25	9		3 50	2 50		Electric
Ohamokane	Lumber	907	35,000	25,000ft.	25,000 sl.	5	20		10		26	4		4 00	2 50		Steam
Davenport	Laundry	908	3,500	$850 val.	$250 al.	2		6	10	10	26	12	22	3 00		$1 40	S. and E.

MASON COUNTY.

Town or City	Gds mfd or sld	Date when est'b'lished	Capital invested in plant	Daily capacity	Daily output	Males employed Skil'd	Males employed Un-skil'd	Females em-pl'y'd	Hours per day Males	Hours per day Fe-males	Days per mo., males	Mos. per year	Days per mo., fe-males	Wages, Males Skilled	Wages, Males Un-skilled	Wages fe-males	Kind of power used
Shelton	Shingles	1909	$14,000	95,000	85,000	7	8		10		25			$5 00	$2 50		Steam
Elms	Shingles	1908	12,000	140,000	110,000	10	5		10		22			4 50	2 50		Steam

Location	Product	Year	Capital														Power
Elma	Shingles	1908	7,000	60,000	60,000	8	3	10		22	11		4 50		3 00		Steam
Matlock	Shingles	1906	5,400	50,000	45,000	7	11	10		23	12		8 85		2 80		Steam
Shelton	Machine shop	1890	10,000			8	8	10		23	12		8 00		2 38		Steam
Matlock	Machine shop	1908	4,000			2	2	10		26	12		4 50		2 50		Steam

OKANOGAN COUNTY.

Location	Product	Year	Capital														Power
Molson	Lumber	1907	$5,000	20,000ft.	20,000ft.	4	12	10		22	4		$3 50		$2 50		Steam

PACIFIC COUNTY.

Location	Product	Year	Capital														Power
Raymond	Lumber	1905	$200,000	150,000	150,000ft.	15	120		10		26	12		$4 00	$2 15		Steam
South Bend	ber	1905	200,000	100,000ft.	115,000ft.	30	170		10		25	12		4 00	2 25		Steam
South Bend	ber	1905	175,000	75,000	175,000ft.	21	80		10		26	12		8 00	2 25		Steam
	ther	1902	175,000	150,000	150,000ft.	45	75		10		24	10		3 75	2 25		team
Raymond	Lumber	1906	150,000	106,000	100,000ft.	16	89		10		26	12		4 00	90		Steam
South Bend	u ber	1905	150,000	100,000	100,000ft.	15	70		10		26	12		8 50	2 3		Steam
South	eber	1900	150,000	125,000		20	100		10		24	11		4 00	2 15		team
Raymond	ther	1906	125,000	40,000ft.	85,000ft.	25	60		10		25	12		3 75	2 25		Steam
Frances	Lumber	1893	115,000	90,000ft.	90,000ft.	12	40		10		24	11		3 50	2 15		Steam
Raymond	Lumber	1906	160,000	70,000ft.	70,000ft.	15	40		10		26	12		4 00	2 25		Steam
Raymond	Lumber	1906	85,000	100,000	90,000ft.	15	50		10		25	11		4 00	2 00		Steam
Knappton	Lumber	1889	65,000	45,000ft.	45,000ft.	13	57		10		26	12		8 25	2 25		Steam
Frances	u ber	1902	40,000	65,000ft.	45,000ft.	8	22		10		22	12		8 50	2 00		team
Raymond	ber	1907	35,000	50,000ft.	60,000ft.	7	38		10		22			3 75	2 25		Steam
Lebam	Lumber	1907	15,000	35,000ft.	35,000ft.	5	18		10					8 50	2 00		team
Gl be	Lumber	1902	15,000	15,000ft.	15,000ft.	1	5		10					4 00	2 00		Steam
Lebam	ber	1903	10,000	12,000ft.	12,000ft.	1	7		10	20	22	12	25	4 00	2 25		Steam
ico	ber	1903	6,000	8,000ft.	8,000ft.	3	10		10	12			26	8 75	2 25		Sem
ed	Lumber	1905	5,000	10,000ft.	40,000ft.	5	6		10		24	10		3 00	2 00		Sem
ed	Wood products	1910	100,000	$1500 val.	$1500 val.	17	4		10		24	12		2 75	1 75		Sem
ed	plis	1908	50,000	250000 bsk.	200000 bsk.	6	30		10		25	12		3 50	2 00		Sem
ed	W?d products	1907	10,000			1	2		9		26	11		8 00	2 50		teSm
South Band	ry	1891	20,000			12	6		10		25	9		4 00	2 50		teSm
Raymond	Shingles	1908	50,000	300,000	300,000	21	9		10		26	10		5 00	2 50		Steam
	Shingles	1902	25,000	200,000	290,000	18	12		10		23			3 50	2 25		Steam
Gbe	Shingles	1909	15,000	60,000	60,000	5	7		10		26			4 00	2 00		Sem
?	?s	1910	15,000	140,000	140,000	26			10		24	10		4 00	2 75	$1 25	Sem
r?es	S?s	1910	15,000	160,000		14	7		10		22	10		4 25	2 75	1 50	Sem
South Bend	Shingles	1910	15,000	110,000	110,000	18			10		20	10		4 00	2 75		Steam
South Bend	Shingles	1890	11,000	118,000	115,000	10	8		10					4 00	2 25		Steam

PACIFIC COUNTY—Continued.

Town or City	Goods Manufactured or Handled	Date when estb'lished	Capital invested in plant	Daily capacity	Daily output	Skil'd	Un-skil'd	Fe-males em-pl'y'd	Hours per day Males	Hours per day Females	Days per mo. male	Days per mo. fe-males	Wages Males Skilled	Wages Males Un-skilled	Wages fe-males	Kind of power used
Frances	Shingles	1906	$3,000	30,000	30,000	3	3	...	10	...	25	...	$3 00	$2 25	...	Steam
Frances	Shingles	1905	1,500	30,000	30,000	2	3	...	10	...	30	...	4 50	2 50	...	Steam
Ilwaco	Canned salmon	1904	15,500	1200 cases	600 cases	23	29	3	10	...	90	7	3 00	2 25	...	Steam
South Bend	Canned salmon	...	...	400 cases	130 cases	5	2	3	10	...	94	...	4 00	2 25	...	Steam
Raymond	Electricity	1906	50,000	...	135 w	3	1	...	10	...	90	...	3 00	2 50	...	Steam
South Bend	Laundry	1908	3,000	...	...	...	1	5	10	9	90	20	3 50	2 50	$1 00	Steam

PIERCE COUNTY.

Town or City	Goods Manufactured or Handled	Date when estb'lished	Capital invested in plant	Daily capacity	Daily output	Skil'd	Un-skil'd	Fe-males em-pl'y'd	Hours per day Males	Hours per day Females	Days per mo. male	Days per mo. fe-males	Wages Males Skilled	Wages Males Un-skilled	Wages fe-males	Kind of power used
Tacoma	Lumber	1898	1,000,000	258,000ft.	200,000ft.	...	290	...	12	...	26	...	$5 25	$3 00	...	Steam
Tacoma	Lumber	1898	750,000	500,000ft.	350,000ft.	273	361	...	12	...	26	...	3 05	1 90	...	S. and E.
Tacoma	Lumber	1907	200,000	200,000ft.	100,000ft.	...	75	...	11	...	20	...	...	2 90	...	Steam
Buckley	Lumber	1900	150,000	60,000ft.	...	30	67	...	9	...	24	...	...	2 25	...	Steam
Eatonville	Lumber	1906	125,000	125,000ft.	120,000ft.	34	67	1	12	...	25	...	8 75	1 80	...	Steam
Puyallup	Lumber	1906	125,000	55,000ft.	50,000ft.	12	54	8	12	10	23	20	8 00	2 00	$1 00	Steam
S. Prairie	Lumber	...	100,000	35,000ft.	35,000ft.	10	58	...	9	...	26	...	4 00	2 25	...	Steam
Tacoma	Lumber	1905	100,000	30,000ft.	80,000ft.	8	90	...	11	...	25	...	4 35	2 25	...	Steam
Ashford	Lumber	1902	84,000	85,000ft.	85,000ft.	4	85	...	11	...	22	...	4 25	2 15	...	Steam
Kapowsin	Lumber	1906	75,000	60,000ft.	60,000ft.	15	45	...	10	...	26	...	2 75	2 25	...	S. and E.
Elbe	Lumber	1906	60,000	50,000ft.	40,000ft.	25	45	...	12	...	25	...	...	...	...	Steam
Tacoma	Lumber	1898	50,000	50,000ft.	50,000ft.	5	67	...	12	...	23	...	8 50	2 00	...	Steam
Bismark	Lumber	1908	50,000	40,000ft.	50,000ft.	20	47	...	12	...	26	...	4 50	2 15	...	Steam
Buckley	Lumber	1895	42,388	40,000ft.	85,000ft.	8	34	...	10	...	25	...	4 00	...	...	Steam
Naples	Lumber	1906	30,000	40,000ft.	30,000ft.	14	15	...	8	...	22	...	...	...	...	Steam
Kapowsin	Lumber	1907	25,000	40,000ft.	25,000ft.	4	20	...	10	...	26	...	8 00	2 75	...	Steam
Tacoma	Lumber	...	25,000	30,000ft.	40,000ft.	5	90	1	12	8	25	26	8 35	2 15	2 00	Steam
South Prairie	Lumber	1906	25,000	80,000ft.	30,000ft.	15	97	...	10	...	24	...	3 00	2 25	...	Steam
Arline	Lumber	1904	20,000	35,000ft.	30,000ft.	9	11	...	12	...	26	...	2 50	2 00	...	Steam
Milton	Lumber	1909	20,000	20,000ft.	20,000ft.	9	22	...	12	...	26	...	3 25	2 25	...	Steam
Ohop	Lumber	1906	15,000	20,000ft.	30,000ft.	14	16	...	12	...	24	...	4 00	2 25	...	Steam
Midland	Lumber	1906	12,500	20,000ft.	15,000ft.	8	6	...	12	...	25	...	3 00	2 00	...	Steam
Puyallup	Lumber	1906	10,000	15,000ft.	25,000ft.	4	10	...	12	...	26	...	8 00	2 00	...	Steam
Tacoma	Lumber	1910	10,000	85,000ft.	...	7	8	...	12	...	26	...	8 00	2 25	...	Electric

	Year	Capital	Product	Product	Hands (M)	Hands (F)								Power
Harding	Lumber	1901	10,000	20,000ft.		5	17		10			25	13	3 50	2 25	Steam
Win	Lumber	1906	7,500	40,000		6	14		10			25	11	3 50	2 25	Steam
Bay	Lumber	1904	7,530	60,000ft.		34	40		10			20	11	3 15	2 35	Steam
Gig Bay	Lumber	1910	7,000	20,000ft.		5	10		10			24	12	3 25	2 00	Steam
Gig Har.	1884	7,000	6,000ft.		2	2		10			26		2 50	2 00	Water
	Lumber	1910	3,000	3,000ft.		2	1		10					3 00	2 00	Steam
	Lumber	1909				10	2		10					3 00	1 50	Electric
	Lumber	1902	1,200			5	30		10					3 00	2 25	S. and E.
	Shingles	1906	750,000	50,000ft.	50,000ft.	136	180	1	10			24	12	3 05	1 90	S. and E.
	Shingles	1888	125,000	100,000ft.	100,000ft.	16	16		10			26	12	3 50	2 25	Steam
	Shingles	1895	50,000	200,000	460,000	10	33		10			20	11	4 50	2 15	Steam
	Shingles	1902	30,000	130,000	400,000	6	16		10			24	12	4 00	2 50	Steam
	Shingles	1902	25,000	325,000	60,000	15	10		10			25	10	4 00	2 75	Steam
	Shingles	1904	18,000	50,000	180,000	15	5		10			23	9	4 00	2 00	Steam
	Shingles	1897	15,000	180,000	250,000	30	1		10			24	12	3 25	2 25	Steam
	Shingles	1908	12,000	210,000	125,000	11	6		10			24	10	4 50	2 00	Steam
	Shin gas	1908	11,000	110,000	50,000	9	5		10			26	12	4 00	2 00	Steam
	Shingles	1907	10,000	90,000	100,000	10	5		10			24	10	4 00	2 50	Steam
	Shingles	1909	10,000	100,000	100,000	12	8		10			30	11	4 50	2 00	Steam
	Shingles	1904	7,500	125,000	250,000	8	20		10			25	10	4 00	2 35	Steam
	Shin gas	1905	7,500	100,000	90,000	6	4		10			25	11	3 15	2 25	Steam
	Shingles	1906	4,000	210,000	80,000	2	6		10			25		3 50	2 50	Steam
	Shingles	1910	5,000	65,000	100,000	11	5		10			26		3 50	2 00	Steam
	Shingles	1910	5,000	90,000	125,000	10	7		10			24		4 00		Steam
	Shingles	1910	3,000	110,000	30,000	4			10	8		22	12	3 75	2 50	Steam
				25,000	25,000	4	1	2	10			25	8	2 50	3 00	25
	Shin gas		1,000	25,000	25,000	11	7	10	10	8	10	25	8	4 00	1 85	Steam
Pittsburg				120,000	120,000	60	5	1	10	8	1	28		3 50	2 35	Steam
	W od	1889	250,000	1 60ft.	16000ft. L	1	329	2	10	9	30	18	12	1 00	2 00	Steam
	W od	1902	100,000	17000ft. p.	17000ft. p.	4	40	10	10			22	12	3 25	2 00	25
	W od	1902	52,500			13	51	1	10	8	30	19	12	3 00	2 00	Steam
	W od	1906	45,000			20	30		10			24	12	3 00	2 00	Steam
	Wd products	1889	42,500	400 doors	400 doors	30	5		10			22	10	3 25	2 00	30
	Wd products	1908	40,000	900	3000 boxes	4	30	30	10	9		25	12	3 00	2 00	Electric
	Wd	1906	40,000	800 val	$400 val	20	10		10	8	1	22	12	2 75	2 00	Electric
	Wd products	1908	30,000	$150 val	$200 val	13	5		10			25	12	3 25	2 00	Electric
	W od	1909	25,000	$150 val		5	8		10	8		25	12	3 00	2 50	Electric
	W od	1910	2,500	$120 val		7	3		9			25	12	3 75	2 00	Steam
	W od products	1888	1,000		85 wheels	2	2		9			25	12	3 35	2 10	
Machinery	1910	100,000	85 wheels	150 wheels	75	25										
Machinery	1889	76,000	8 tons iron	8 tons iron	106	68										
Machinery	1886	31,000	8t brass cast	8t brass cast												
							62	60	68		9		25	12	3 00	1 75	Steam

KING COUNTY—Continued.

Town or City	Goods Manufactured or Handled	Date when est'b'lished	Capital invested in plant	Daily capacity	Daily output	Males employed Skil'd	Un-skil'd	Females em-pl'y'd	Hours per day Males	Fe-males	Days per mo. males	Mos. per year	Days per mo. fe-males	Wages Males Skill'd	Un-skilled	Wages fe-males	Kind of power used
Seattle	M'ry	1909	$5,600	$100 val.		8	2		9		26	12		$4 50	$1 75		Electric
Seattle	M'ry	1905	4,000		$35 val.	4	1		9		26	12		4 50	1 00		Electric
t'le	Machinery	1888	2,500	$75 val.	$20 val.	8	3	1	9	8	26	12	26	4 00	85		Electric
Seattle	Machinery	1906	2,000	$50 val.	$35 val.	2	1		9		24	12		4 00	1 00		Electric
Seattle	M'ry	1909	1,800	$40 val.		4	6		8		25	12		3 75	2 50		Electric
d'le	M'ry	1888		$40 val.	$40 val.	4	1		9		26	12		3 80	2 25		Electric
Seattle	Machinery	1888	300			5	2		9		26	12		4 00	2 50		Electric
Seattle	M'ry	1907				3	7		9		26	12					Electric
Seattle	Flour and c'd	1902	400,000	2000 bls. f'r 70 tons f'c	881 bls. f'r 29 tons f'c	25			10	8	26	12	26	3 75	2 50	$2 00	Electric
Seattle	Flour, cereals, f'd	1889	300,000	400 bbls.	400 bbls.	25	75	10	10	8	26	12		4 00	2 50		Electric
Seattle	Flour, cereals, f'd	1897	200,000	1,250 bbls.	925 bbls.	8	34		10		26	11		6 20	2 75	1 50	Electric
Seattle	Flour, cereals, f'd	1906	120,000	100 tons f'd 250 bls. c'ls	100 tons f'd 250 lb. e'ls	20	60		9	9	25	12	25	4 00	2 75		Steam
Seattle	B'y nd grain	1906	50,000	360 bbls.	250 bbls.	80	11		10		26	12		8 50	2 75		Electric
Seattle	Flour nd c'd	1892	75,000	900 sks. f'd	30 tons	5	5		10		28	12		8 00	2 50		Electric
Seattle	Flour nd c'd	1907	20,000	20 tons f'd	20 tons f'c	2	8		10		28	12		8 00			Electric
Seattle	Fl'ur nd c'd	1892	8,000	30 tons	30 tons	4			10		25	12		2 75			Electric
Seattle	Feed	1899	2,500	100,000 b.	10,000 b.	25	75		10		28	12		3 00	2 25		Electric
Renton	Brick, clay prod's	1902	185,000	100,000 b.	10,000 b.	15	30		10		26	12		8 25	2 00		S. and E.
Taylor	Brick, clay prod's	1901	158,000	30,000 b.	30,000 b.	10	70		10		26	12		2 75	2 00		Steam
Seattle	Brick, clay prod's	1906	100,000	75 tons	65 tns	30	12		10		30	12		3 50	2 00		Electric
Auburn	Brick	1888	50,000	25,000	20,000	6	18	1	10	8	26	12		3 50	2 65		Electric
Seattle	Brick, clay prod's	1905	30,000	30,000	28,000	10	19		9		26	12		3 50	2 65		Steam
Seattle	Brick	1906	25,000	25,000	25,000	5	20		10		25	12		4 00	2 50		Steam
t'le	Brick, clay prod's	1906	250,000			10	75		10		30	12	26	3 75	2 50	2 00	Steam
Seattle	Laundry	1904	60,000	$400 val.	$100 val.	16	29	60	10	9	28	12	28	3 75	3 00	1 66	Steam
Seattle	Laundry	1890	60,000	$400 val.	$400 val.		4	84	10	10	28	12	28	3 00	2 00		Steam
Seattle	Laundry	1905	32,000	$600 val.	$600 val.	11	38	45	10	10	28	12	28		3 00	1 50	F. and S.
Seattle	Laundry	1899	18,000	$250 val.	$150 val.	2	40	10	10	10	30	12	30	3 00	2 00	1 50	Steam
Seattle	Laundry	1902	15,000	$150 val.	$135 val.	8	1	11	10	10	28	12	28	3 00	1 50	2 00	Steam
Seattle	Laundry	1910	15,000	$100 val.	$100 val.	10	2	12	10	10	30	12	30	2 50	1 15	1 85	Electric
Seattle	Laundry	1907	10,000	$200 val.	$105 val.	10	1	26	10	10	25	12	20	2 00	2 00	1 60	Electric
Seattle	Laundry	1908	10,000	$200 val.	$175 val.	1	30	4	10	10	25	12	28	2 50	2 00		Steam
Seattle	Laundry	1908	8,000	$100 val.	$75 val.				10	10	28	12	28	2 75	1 00		Steam

Location	Product	Year	Capital	Material	Product	1	2	3	4	5	6	7	8	Wage 1	Wage 2	Wage 3	Power
Dupont	High explosives	1906				75	80		10	8	25	12		3 50	2 25		E. and S.
Tacoma	Blk bks, gen prtg	1878				24	4		8		25	12	26	3 73	1 04	1 48	Electric
Tacoma	Ice	1900				2	3		12	9	25	12		3 50	2 50		Steam
Tacoma	Table condiments	1880	50,000	50,000 val.	$500 val.	5	25	9	10		25	12	26	4 16	2 88		Steam
Tacoma	Ore reduction	1901	520,000	450 tons ore	$11000 val.	80	70	8	8	10	30	12		3 50	2 50	1 25	E. and S.
Tacoma	Ore reduction	1906	254,000	600 tons ore	$16000 val.	40	80	2	10		26	12	24	3 00	2 35		E. and S.
Tacoma	Glue	1906	25,000	1000 lbs.	800 lbs.	1	8		10	10	26	12				1 25	Electric

SAN JUAN COUNTY.

Location	Product	Year	Capital	Material	Product	1	2	3	4	5	6	7	8	Wage 1	Wage 2	Wage 3	Power
Friday Harbor	Canned salmon	190?	$20,000	2000 cases	750 cases	6	35	35	10	5	30	5	19	$2 am		$0 90	Steam

SKAGIT COUNTY.

Location	Product	Year	Capital	Material	Product	1	2	3	4	5	6	7	8	Wage 1	Wage 2	Wage 3	Power
Anacortes	Lumber	1904	$200,000	150,000ft.	150,000ft.	39	77		12		26	12		$2 50			Steam
Anacortes	Lumber	1904	150,000	100,000ft.	95,000ft.	18	55		12		26	12		4 28	$2 11		Steam
Anacortes	Lumber	1904	100,000	120,000ft.	120,000ft.	12	24		11		26	11		2 50			Steam
Bar Lake	Lumber	1909	100,000	80,000ft.	75,000ft.	8	45		11		25	11	30	3 25	25		Steam
McMurray	Lumber	1902	92,500	75,000ft.	50,000ft.	38	32		12		26	11		4 00	1 85		Steam
Lyman	Lumber	1909	55,000	50,000ft.	50,000ft.	13	82		11		26	11		3 50	2 25		Steam
Bar Lake	Lumber	1900	52,000	75,000ft.	70,000ft.	4	34		10		25	10		3 00	2 25		Steam
Sedro-	Lumber	1906	42,500	40,000ft.	40,000ft.	1	15		11		22	11		4 00	2 25		Steam
La Bar.	Lumber	1909	30,000	35,000ft.	20,000ft.	5	25				25			3 00			Steam
Minkler	Lumber	1902	20,000	50,000ft.	40,000ft.	12	15		9		25	9		3 75	40		Steam
Mt.	Lumber	1900	18,000	20,000ft.	25,000ft.	9	22		12		24	12		3 25			Steam
Burlington	Lumber	1903	15,000	25,000ft.	15,000ft.	4	9		11		23	11		4 00	2 00		Steam
Clear Lake	Lumber	1900	15,000	15,000ft.	40,000ft.	4	16	10	12		30	12	30	2 50	2 00		Steam
Bow	Lumber	1910	15,000	40,000ft.	25,000ft.	14	20		10		26	10		4 25	2 20		Steam
Birds View	Lumber	1900	12,000	60,000ft.	60,000ft.	6	12		9		25	9		3 50	2 25		Steam
Sedro-Woolley	Lumber	1907	12,000	25,000ft.	15,000ft.	8	4		11		24	11		4 00	2 25		Steam
Belleville	Lumber	1906	10,000	15,000ft.	20,000ft.	5	9		10		25	10		2 75	2 50		Steam
Anacortes	Lumber	1902	10,000	20,000ft.	8,000ft.	3	5		9		25	9		5 00	2 50		Steam
Big Lake	Lumber	1909	8,000	8,000ft.	75,000ft.	5	11		11		26	11		3 50	2 50		Steam
Big Lake	Lumber	1900		90,000ft.	50,000ft.	10	2		12		26	12		3 50	2 50		Steam
Baker	Lumber	1900		50,000ft.	13,000ft.	2	80				26			3 50	2 00		Steam
Anacortes	Lumber	1910		16,000ft.	50,000ft.	4	12				24			8 00	2 50	$1 50	Steam
Anacortes	Lumber	1910		50,000ft.	100,000ft.	17	6				24			3 25	2 00		Steam
Baker	Lumber	1910		125,000ft.	13,000ft.	15	12				26			3 25	2 00		Steam
Anacortes	Lumber	1910		16,000ft.	100,000ft.	4	7				24			3 75	2 50		Steam
McMurray	Shingles	1902	92,500	225,000	200,000	38	23		12		26	12		3 25	1 88		Steam
Bar Lake	Shingles	1902	50,000	325,000	325,000	20	15		12		25	12		3 75	2 50		Steam
Van Horn	Shingles		40,000	200,000	200,000	11	5		10		22	10		4 00	2 50		Steam

KITSAP COUNTY.

Town or City	Goods Manufactured or Handled	Date when est'b'lished	Capital invested in plant	Daily capacity	Daily output	Males employed Skil'd	Un-skil'd	Fe-males em-pl'y'd	Hours per day Males	Fe-males	Days per mo. males	Mos. per year	Days per mo. fe-males	Wages Males Skilled	Un-skilled	Wages fe-males	Kind of power used
Paulsbo	Shingles	1907	$35,000	55,000		2	2		10		20	8		$3 50	$2 50		Steam
Colby	Shingles	1909	15,000	60,000		4	10		10		20	10		5 00	2 25		Steam
Paulsbo	Shingles	1908	12,500	90,000	80,000	7	6		10		24	10		4 00	2 25		Steam
Colby	Shingles	1909	3,750	50,000	50,000	2	9		10		24	11		4 25	2 00		Steam
Eagle Harbor	Lumber	1908	300,000	75,000ft.	75,000ft.	10	20		10		30	12		3 50	2 50		Steam
Colby	Lumber	1909	15,000	25,000ft.		4	10		10		20	10		5 00	2 25		Steam
Colby	Lumber	1909	3,750	25,000ft.	25,000ft.	4	19		10		24	11		4 25	2 00		Steam
Port Gamble	Lumber	1853		200,000ft.	100,000ft.	85	100		10		26	12		3 75	1 78		Steam
Port Blakely	Lumber	1856		150,000ft.	150,000ft.	61	146		10		26	12		3 60	2 00		Electric
Winslow	Ship Blds, rep'r's	1902	300,000			125	75	1	8	8	26	12	26	4 50	2 25	$2 50	Steam

KITTITAS COUNTY.

Town or City	Goods Manufactured or Handled	Date when est'b'lished	Capital invested in plant	Daily capacity	Daily output	Males employed Skil'd	Un-skil'd	Fe-males em-pl'y'd	Hours per day Males	Fe-males	Days per mo. males	Mos. per year	Days per mo. fe-males	Wages Males Skilled	Un-skilled	Wages fe-males	Kind of power used
Boslyn	Beer	1894	$75,000	40 bbls.	25 bbls.	9			8		25	12		$3 50			S. and E.
Ellensburg	Ice	1906	25,000	25 tons	15 tons	1	2		9		27	12		3 70	$2 60		W. and S.
Ole Elum	Electricity	1903				5			8		30	12		3 80			S. and E.
Ole Elum	lumber	1908	7,600	20,000ft.	15,000ft.	5	14		10		25	10		3 75	2 37		S. and E.
Ole Elum	fire, st'm plt	1908				5			8		30	8		3 20			Sm
Ellensburg	lumber	1910	10,000	20,000ft.	14,000ft.	5	9		10		25	8		4 00	3 00		Sm
Ellensburg	Flour and feed	1889	10,000	13,000ft.		2	11		10		25	8		4 00	2 50		Water
Ole Elum	Laundry	1906	20,000 7,000	100 bbls. $60 val.		4	2	9	10		26	12	24	1 33		$1 00	team

KLICKITAT COUNTY.

Town or City	Goods Manufactured or Handled	Date when est'b'lished	Capital invested in plant	Daily capacity	Daily output	Males employed Skil'd	Un-skil'd	Fe-males em-pl'y'd	Hours per day Males	Fe-males	Days per mo. males	Mos. per year	Days per mo. fe-males	Wages Males Skilled	Un-skilled	Wages fe-males	Kind of power used
Goldendale	Flour, cereals, Yr'd	1904	$25,000	120 bbls.	25 bls.	2	2		10		26	12		$4 00	$2 50		Water
Goldendale	Dairy	1908	6,500	$400 val.	$120 val.	1		4	10	9	26	12	20	1 50	2 50	$1 20	team
Goldendale	Lumber	1906	1,500	80,000ft.	20, 0tt.	3	9		10		20	4		3 00			Steam
Goldendale	Lumber	1880	6,000	$60 val.		3			10		26	8		3 00			team

LEWIS COUNTY.

Town or City	Goods Manufactured or Handled	Date when est'b'lished	Capital invested in plant	Daily capacity	Daily output	Males employed Skil'd	Un-skil'd	Fe-males em-pl'y'd	Hours per day Males	Fe-males	Days per mo. males	Mos. per year	Days per mo. fe-males	Wages Males Skilled	Un-skilled	Wages fe-males	Kind of power used
Mineral	Shingles	1907	$30,000	200,000	200,000	13	10		10		25	10		$5 00	$2 50		Steam
Centralia	Shingles	1907	25,000	250,000	240,000	26	20		10		20	11		3 50	2 25		team
Dryad	Shingles	1891	14,000	200,000	200,000	16	9		10		25	10		3 50			Steam

SKAMANIA COUNTY.

SNOHOMISH COUNTY.

Stevenson	Lumber	1909	$35,000	40,000ft.	35,000ft.	20	25		10		25	9		$3 00	$2 65		Steam

Monroe	Shingles	1906	$212,000	175,000	140,000	21	26		10		24	12		$8 50	$2 50		Steam
Three Lakes	Shingles	1903	200,000	450,000	200,000	37	66		10		25	10		3 00	2 25		Steam
Startup	Shingles	1901	86,000	180,000	180,000	13	6		10	8	26	11		3 98	2 50	$1 92	Steam
Everett	Shingles	1903	85,000	500,000	250,000	20	32	2	10		25	12	26	5 00	2 50		Steam
Everett	Shingles	1907	77,000	650,000		11	31		10		25	10		5 00	2 50		Steam
Everett	Shingles	1897	75,000	600,000	560,000	27	34		10		26	9		5 50	2 40		Steam

LEWIS COUNTY—Continued.

Town or City	Goods Manufactured or Handled	Date when est'b'lished	Capital invested in plant	Daily capacity	Daily output	Males employed Skil'd	Males employed Un-skil'd	Fe-males em-ply'd	Hours per day Males	Hours per day Fe-males	Days per mo., males	Mos. per year	Days per mo., fe-males	Wages, Males Skilled	Wages, Males Un-skilled	Wages fe-males	Kind of power used
Falls	Wood products	1902	$35,000	....	....	50	50	..	10	..	24	12	..	$2 50	$2 00	..	Steam
Centralia	Wood products	1904	26,300	30,000ft.	25,000ft.	12	18	..	10	..	26	12	..	2 95	2 00	..	Steam
Little Falls	Wood products	1903	25,000	400 columns	400 columns	15	20	..	10	..	25	12	..	3 00	2 00	..	Steam
Little Falls	Wood products	1903	15,000	20ft.	20ft.	4	30	..	10	..	26	12	..	3 50	2 00	..	Steam
Centralia	Wood products	1902	10,000	6,000ft.	400ft.	4	1	..	10	..	20	8	..	3 50	2 95	..	Steam
Centralia	Wood products	1902	8,000	700 posts	500 posts	3	2	..	10	..	20	12	..	3 75	2 25	..	Steam
Falls	Wood products	1901	7,000	350 doors	200 doors	3	11	..	10	..	22	10	..	3 00	2 00	..	Steam
Centralia	Wood products	1903	6,500	....	....	2	1	..	10	..	10	10	..	4 00	2 00	..	Steam
Vick	Wood products	1903	5,000	....	5 cars, mo.	3	5	..	10	..	22	12	..	2 50	2 00	..	Steam
Falls	Wood products	1910	3,000	....	250 columns	20	15	..	..	..	25	..	..	3 20	2 00	..	Electric
Falls	Condensed milk	1906	60,000	1500 cases	900 cases	7	60	15	10	10	25	12	25	2 75	2 40	$1 60	Steam
Falls	Brick and tile	1901	20,000	20,000 brick	10,000 brick	4	4	..	9½	..	24	12	..	3 25	2 25	..	Steam
Idle Falls	Sewerpipe and tile	1902	....	2 cars	2 cars	7	45	..	10	..	26	12	..	4 00	2 25	..	Electric
Centralia	dairy	1902	30,000	....	....	22	6	..	9	..	26	12	..	4 00	2 50	..	Electric
Centralia	dairy	1903	20,000	....	....	15	5	..	10	..	25	12	..	4 00	2 00	..	Steam
Centralia	Ice	1907	15,000	8 tons	5 tons	1	2	9	10	7	26	12	20	2 75	..	1 05	Steam
Falls	Laundry	1905	4,500	....	....	1	3	11	10	9½	30	12	20	3 00	2 50	1 50	Electric
Centralia	Laundry	1906	3,750	$350 val.	$55 val.	1											

LINCOLN COUNTY.

Reardan	Flour and feed	....	$65,000	450 bbls.	450 bbls.	6	10	..	10	..	28	10	..	$3 50	$2 50	..	Electric
Odessa	Flour and feed	1902	50,000	350 bls.	325 bbls.	6	10	..	10	..	26	9	..	3 00	2 25	..	Steam
Harrington	Flour and feed	1900	50,000	300 bls.	300 bbls.	4	7	..	10	..	26	9	..	3 75	2 00	..	Electric
Davenport	Flour and feed	1892	50,000	400 bbls.	400 bbls.	10	3	..	10	..	26	12	..	3 00	2 00	..	Electric
Wilbur	Flour and feed	1890	50,000	500 lbs.	500 bbls.	3	20	..	10	..	26	9	..	4 00	2 50	..	Steam
Sprague	Flour and feed	1901	44,000	300 bbls.	250 bbls.	6	11	..	10	..	28	9	..	3 00	2 50	..	Electric
Creston	Flour and feed	1902	35,000	225 bbls.	225 bbls.	6	6	..	10	..	28	8	..	3 50	2 00	..	Steam
Sprague	Flour and feed	1902	30,000	400 bls.	300 bbls.	3	10	..	10	..	25	9	..	3 50	2 50	..	Electric
Ohamokane	Lumber	1907	35,000	25,000ft.	25,000ft.	5	20	..	10	..	28	4	..	4 00	2 50	..	Steam
Davenport	Laundry	1908	3,500	$350 val.	$250 val.	2	..	6	10	10	26	12	22	8 00	..	$1 40	S. and E.

MASON COUNTY.

Shelton	Shingles	1909	$14,000	96,000	85,000	7	8	..	10	..	25	..	..	$5 00	$2 50	..	Steam
Elma	Shingles	1908	12,000	140,000	110,000	10	5	..	10	..	22	10	..	4 50	3 50	..	Steam

Place	Product	Year	Capital	Value	Value	Power
?re (?ger)	Shingles	1910	17,500	120,000	120,000	Steam
?tt	Shingles	1905	17,000	75,000	—	Steam
?tt	Shingles	1907	16,000	210,000	210,000	Steam
t ?h	Shingles	1910	15,000	140,000	140,000	Steam
Gold Basin	Shingles	1909	15,000	100,000	90,000	Steam
Everett	Shingles	1907	15,000	40,000	150,000	Steam
Index	Shingles	1902	15,000	130,000	40,000	Steam
Snohomish	Shingles	1902	15,000	130,000	130,000	t Sm
Everett	Shingles	1908	15,000	70,000	130,000	Steam
Snohomish	Shingles	1908	15,000	150,000	70,000	Steam
?ke	Shingles	1901	15,000	65,000	130,000	Steam
Index	Shingles	1910	14,000	225,000	25,000	Steam
Everett	Shingles	1908	14,000	90,000	225,000	Steam
Edmonds	Shingles	1907	14,000	125,000	90,000	Steam
Monroe	Shingles	1910	14,000	100,000	125,000	Steam
Sultan	Shingles	1910	18,000	110,000	100,000	t Sm
?tt	Shingles	1905	13,000	150,000	100,000	Steam
Edmonds	Shingles	1907	13,000	160,000	160,000	Steam
Arlington	Shingles		12,700	90,000	160,000	Steam
Startup	Shingles	1891	12,500	30,000	30,000	Steam
Everett	Shingles	1909	12,500	160,000	30,000	Steam
Snohomish	Shingles	1889	12,500	110,000	150,000	Steam
Snohomish	Shingles	1892	12,000	100,000	110,000	Steam
Everett	Shingles	1908	12,000	90,000	100,000	Steam
Machias	Shingles	1903	12,000	90,000	90,000	Steam
Machias	Shingles	1907	12,000	140,000	90,000	Steam
Machias	Shingles	1902	12,000	175,000	140,000	Steam
Edmonds	Shingles	1910	12,000	100,000	175,000	Steam
Edmonds	Shingles	1900	11,600	70,000	100,000	Steam
Arlington	Shingles	1908	11,000	180,000	70,000	Steam
Granite Falls	Shingles	1906	11,000	120,000	180,000	Steam
Granite Falls	Shingles	1906	10,000	150,000	120,000	Steam
Everett	Shingles		10,000	180,000	150,000	Steam
Glin	Shingles	1886	10,000	85,000	75,000	Steam
Snohomish	Shingles	1900	10,000	130,000	70,000	Steam
Snohomish	Shingles	1900	10,000	70,000	—	Steam
?ay	Shingles		10,000	100,000	180,000	Steam
Robe	Shingles	1902	10,000	100,000	70,000	Steam
Stimson's Cr's'g	Shingles	1909	10,000	125,000	100,000	Steam
Stanwood	Shingles	1909	10,000	120,000	125,000	Steam
Marysville	Shingles	1902	10,000	75,000	50,000	Steam
Granite ?lls	Shingles	1908	10,000	75,000	75,000	Steam
Machias	Shingles	1903	10,000			Steam
?el	Shingles	1900	10,000		75,000	Steam
Arlington	Shingles	1907	10,000	75,000	50,000	Steam
Marysville	Shingles		10,000			Steam
?tford	Shingles		10,000			Steam

PACIFIC COUNTY—Continued.

Town or City	Goods Manufactured or Handled	Date when est'b-lished	Capital invested in plant	Daily capacity	Daily output	Males employed Skill'd	Males employed Un-skill'd	Fe-males em-ply'd	Hours per day Males	Hours per day Fe-males	Days per mo. males	Mos. per year	Days per mo. fe-males	Wages, Males Skilled	Wages, Males Un-skilled	Wages fe-males	Kind of power used
Frances	Shingles	1906	$3,000	30,000	30,000	3	3		10		25	4		$3 00	$2 25		Steam
Frances	Shingles	1908	1,500	50,000	30,000	2	5		10		20	7	7	4 50	2 50		Steam
Ilwaco	Canned salmon	1904	15,300	1200 cases	600 cases	53		3	10		20	8		2 05			Steam
South Bend	Canned salmon			400 cases	120 cases	5		3	10		25	4		4 00	2 25		Steam
Raymond	Electricity	1906	50,000		135 kw	3	2		10		30	12		3 50	2 50		Steam
South Bend	Laundry	1908	3,000			1	1	5	10	9	30	12	20	3 50	2 50	$1 00	Steam

PIERCE COUNTY.

Town or City	Goods Manufactured or Handled	Date when est'b-lished	Capital invested in plant	Daily capacity	Daily output	Males employed Skill'd	Males employed Un-skill'd	Fe-males em-ply'd	Hours per day Males	Hours per day Fe-males	Days per mo. males	Mos. per year	Days per mo. fe-males	Wages, Males Skilled	Wages, Males Un-skilled	Wages fe-males	Kind of power used
	Lumber	06	1,00,000	258,000ft.	20,000ft.	273	280		10		26	12		$3 25	$2 00		Steam
	Lumber	06	750,000	80,000ft.	350,000ft.	81	31	1	10	10	26	12	26	3 05	1 80		S. ad E.
Tacoma	Lumber	1907	80,000	20,000ft.	20,000ft.	70	75		10		26	12			2 00		Steam
Buckley	Lumber	06	150,000	60,000ft.	20,000ft.	34	67		10		29	9		3 25	2 20		Steam
Eatonville	Lumber	06	25,000	25,000ft.	50,000ft.	12	60	8	10		25	12	20	3 75	2 20	$1 00	Steam
Puyallup	fiber	06	25,000	55,000ft.	35,000ft.	10	54		10		23	9		8 00	1 80		Steam
S. Prairie	Lumber	86	90,000	45,000ft.	30,000ft.	8	88		10		22	11		4 00	2 00		Steam
Tacoma	fiber	92	100,000	30,000ft.	85,000ft.	4	20		10		26	12		4 25	2 25		Steam
Tacoma	fbr	84	84,000	85,000ft.	40,000ft.	15	88		10		25	11		3 00	2 15	2 00	Steam
Ashford	Lumber	1906	75,000	80,000ft.	50,000ft.	25	86		10		22	10		2 75	2 50		S. ad E.
Eln	Lumber		60,000	50,000ft.	40,000ft.	5	45		10		25	12			2 25		Steam
Elbe	fbr	06	50,000		50,000ft.	20	45		10		23	12		3 50	2 00		Steam
	Lumber	06	50,000	50,000ft.	35,000ft.	8	67		10		26	10		4 50	2 15		Steam
Bismark	fbr	05	42,883	40,000ft.	40,000ft.	14	47		8		26	12	26	4 00			Steam
Buckley	Lumber	1907	30,000	40,000ft.	30,000ft.	4	34		10		26	12		8 00			Steam
Naples	Lumber	06	25,000	40,000ft.	25,000ft.	5	15		10		26	10		3 35	2 75		Steam
Spin	Lumber	04	25,000	30,000ft.	40,000ft.	15	20	1	10	8	24	12	26	3 00	2 25	2 00	Steam
Tacoma	Lumber	06	25,000	35,000ft.	30,000ft.	9	27		10		26	12		4 00	2 15		Steam
Sh Prairie	fiber	06	15,000	20,000ft.	30,000ft.	14	11		10		24	12		2 50	2 25		Steam
Arline	Lumber	06	20,000	20,000ft.	20,000ft.	8	22		10		24	12		3 25	2 15		Steam
Milton	Lumber	06	12,000	30,000ft.	30,000ft.	8	16		10		25			4 00	2 00		Steam
Midland	Lumber	1910	10,000	15,000ft.	15,000ft.	4	5		10		26	12		3 00	2 25		Steam
Puyallup	Lumber		10,000	35,000ft.	25,000ft.	7	10		10			12					Electric

Place	Product	Year	Capital	Product (1)	Product (2)	Men	Hands	Hrs	Days	Wage hi	Wage lo	Rate	Power
Ma	hr	1901	10,000	20,000ft.		5	17	10	25	12	3 50	2 25	Steam
Harding	hr	1906	7,500	40,000ft.		6	14	10	25	11	3 50	2 25	Steam
Kapowsin	hr	1904	7,300	60,000ft.	50,000ft.	34	40	10	20	11	3 15	2 35	Steam
Orting	hr	1910	7,000	20,000ft.	15,000ft.	5	10	10	24	12	3 25	2 25	Steam
Ice Bay	hr	1891	7,000	6,000ft.	3,000ft.	2	2	10	26		2 00	2 00	Water
Gig Harbor	hr	1910	3,000	10,000ft.	3,000ft.	2	1	10			3 00	1 50	Steam
Bd	Lumber	1909	3,000			10	2	10		12	3 00	2 00	Electric
lla	Lumber	1902	1,200	50,000ft.	50,000ft.	5	30	10	24	12	3 00	2 25	S. and E.
lla	Shingles	1906		100,000ft.	100,000ft.					11		1 90	S. and E.
Eatonville	Shingles	1888	750,000	450,000	200,000	136	180	28	24	12	3 05	2 25	Steam
	Shingles	1908	125,000		130,000	16	38	10	25	12	4 00	2 25	Steam
Bay	Shingles	1885	50,000	400,000	385,000	10	33	10	24	12	4 00	2 15	Steam
Tacoma	Shingles	1902	30,000	60,000	50,000	6	16	10	23	10	4 00	2 50	Steam
Win	Shingles	1902	25,000	180,000	180,000	15	10	10	25	10	4 00	2 75	Steam
My	Shingles	1904	18,000	180,000	180,000	15	5	10	24	9	3 25	1 75	Steam
8th Prairie	Shingles	1907	15,000	250,000	210,000	30	15	10	22	12	4 00	2 25	Steam
Sumner	Shingles	1908	12,000	125,000	110,000	11	1	10	30	10	4 00	2 00	Steam
Pittsburg	Shingles	1908	12,000	90,000	90,000	9	6	10	25	12	4 00	2 00	Steam
Kal	Shingles	1907	11,000	100,000	100,000	10	5	10	24	10	4 50		Steam
Kapowsin	Shingles	1909	10,000	125,000	125,000	12	8	10	22	8	4 00		Steam
Wog	Shingles	1904	10,000	100,000	100,000	8	5	10	24	11	4 50	2 35	Steam
Harding	Shingles	1905	7,500	250,000	210,000	16	20	10	25	10	5 15	2 25	Steam
Midland	Shingles	1906	7,500	90,000	65,000	6	4	10	25	11	5 50	2 00	Steam
Winma	Shingles	1910	4,000	80,000		2	6	10	20	11	4 00	2 50	Steam
	Shingles	1910	5,000	100,000	90,000	11	5	10	24		8 50		Steam
Pittsburg	Shingles	1910	5,000	125,000	110,000	4	7	10	22		8 00	2 60	Steam
	Shingles	1910	3,000	25,000	25,000	4	1	10	25	12	8 00	2 00	Steam
	Shingles	1910	1,000	30,000	25,000	4	5	10	25	12	4 00	1 85	Steam
	Shingles		120,000	120,000	120,000	11	899	10	25	12	8 50	2 25	Steam
Wd	1889	250,000	16000ft. L	16000ft. L	60	40	25	23	12	3 25	2 00	1 60	Steam
Wd	1902	100,000	17000ft. p.	17000ft. p.	1	51	23	10	3 60	2 00	1 00	Steam
Wd	1902	100,000			4	30	18	10	3 00	2 00	1 50	Steam
Wd	1906	52,500	400 doors	400 drs	13	9	26	10	3 25	2 00	1 00	Steam
Wd	1889	45,000	3000 boxes	3000 boxes	20	30	26	10	3 00	2 00		Steam
Wd	1903	42,000	400 doors	400 drs	30	26	24	10	3 25	2 00		Steam
Wd	1905	40,000	$400 val.	$200 val.	4	10	22	10	3 00	2 00	2 00	Steam
Wd	1906	30,000	$200 val.	$150 val.	20	5	28	10	2 75	2 00		Electric
Wood	1906	25,000			13	8	22	10	3 00	2 00		Electric
Wd	1909	10,000	$150 val.	$120 val.	5	3	25	12	3 75	2 50		Electric
Wd	1910	2,500			2	2	25	12	3 75	2 10		Electric
Mry	1888	100,000	$500 val.	85 wheels	75	25		12	3 00	1 75		Steam
Mry	1886	76,000	8 tons iron	8 tons iron	106	68						
Mry	1886	31,000	3t brass cast	3t brass cast								
T				150 wheels	150 wheels	60	62	9	25	12	3 00	1 75	Steam

PIERCE COUNTY—Continued.

Town or City	Goods Manufactured or Handled	Date when est'b'lished	Capital invested in plant	Daily capacity	Daily output	Males employed Skil'd	Males employed Un-skil'd	Females em-pl'y'd	Hours per day Males	Hours per day Fe-males	Days per mo. males	Mos. per year	Days per mo. fe-males	Wages, Males Skilled	Wages, Males Un-skilled	Wages fe-males	Kind of power used
Bismark	Machinery	1908	$30,000			40	90		9		26	12		$3 00	$2 25		E. and S.
Tacoma	M'ry	1884	80,000			100	25		9		26	12		3 75	3 25		Gasoline
S. Tacoma	M'ry	1907	25,000	25000 lb ir'n	15000 lb ir'n	10	20	1	9		25	12		4 00	1 90	$2 00	Electric
Tacoma	M'ry	1908	15,000	$300 val.		6	4		9	6	20	12	25	8 00	1 80		Electric
Tacoma	M'ry	1909	7,000		$125 val.	3	2	3	9	9	26			8 60	2 25	2 20	S. and E.
Tacoma	Machinery	1899				405	520		9		20	12		8 40	2 00		Electric
Tacoma	M'ry	1907				5		3	9	8	26	12	26	4 00		1 25	Steam
Tacoma	Flour, feed, grain	1904	350,000	2000 bbls.	200 bbls.	20	50		10		26	12		3 00	2 50	2 00	Electric
Tacoma	Hay, grain, cer'ls	1903	300,000	500 bbls.		5	25	1	10	8	26	12	26	8 50	2 30	1 50	S. and E.
Tacoma	Flour and feed	1901	290,000	4000 bbls.	1750 bbls.	12	28	4	10	8	26	12	26	3 00	2 75	2 00	Electric
Tacoma	Flr and grain	1889	160,000	2100 bbls.	10 tons	1	75	1	10	10	26	12	26		2 50	1 92	Electric
Tacoma	Cereals	1892	25,000	40 tons	10 bbls.	1	3		10	10	26	12			2 50		Electric
Tacoma	Furniture	1910	5,000	35 bbls.	$1000 val.	90	1		10		25	12		8 10	2 50		Steam
Tacoma	Furniture	1904	150,000	$2500 val.	$300 val.	5	60	4	10	9	25	12	25	2 75	2 00	1 75	Electric
Tacoma	Furniture	1904	50,000	$500 val.	18 doz ch'rs	90	30	3	10	8	25	12	25	3 00	2 00	1 25	Electric
Tacoma	Furniture	1909	15,000	20 doz ch'rs		5	11		10		25	12		2 50	2 25		Electric
Tacoma	Furniture	1908	12,000	150 beds	$600 val.	90	24	5	9	8	26	12	26	3 00	2 00	1 50	Electric
Tacoma	Laundry	1900	45,000	$500 val.	$400 val.	40	40	65	10	10	26	12	22	3 00	2 00	1 50	Steam
Tacoma	Laundry	1906	20,000	$250 val.	$200 val.	25		85	10	10	26	12	26	3 00		1 50	S. and E.
Tacoma	Laundry	1880	15,000	$300 val.	$175 val.	15	43	30	10	10	26	12	23	3 00	1	1 42	Steam
Tacoma	Laundry	1909	10,000	$100 val.	$90 val.	7		39	10	10	26	12	24	2 50		1 50	E. and S.
Tacoma	Laundry	1904	10,000	$75 val.	$65 val.	25		7	10	10	25	12	25	2 85		1 30	Electric
Tacoma	Laundry	1907	10,000	$100 val.	$100 val.	28	1	4	10	10	24	12	20	1 85	1 00	1 00	Steam
Tacoma	Laundry	1904	8,000	$40 val.	$25 val.	1		22	10	10	24	12	25	8 50	1 50	1 37	Steam
Tacoma	Laundry	1906	6,000	$80 val.	$70 val.	8		8	10	10	26	12	20	1 75		1 75	Steam
Tacoma	Laundry	1904	5,000	$75 val.	$65 val.	24	4	7	12	8	24	12	20	2 00	1 10	1 35	Steam
Tacoma	Brick	1906	50,000	35,000 brick		18	32		10		26	9		3 00	2 25	1 50	Electric
Tacoma	Crushed rock	1909	12,000	400 tons	200 tons	3	18		8		25	12		3 00	2 25		Electric
Tacoma	Beer and malt	1888	500,000	500 bbls.	400 bbls.	4	25		8		26			4 00	2 75		S. and E.
Tacoma	Fresh, sm mts h'd	1904		250 dale	175 dale	75											Electric
Tacoma	Shoes	1908	150,000	250 hogs	225 hogs	235	45	10	10	10	26	12	26	3 00	2 00	1 35	Electric
Tacoma	Wagons	1901	10,000	400 sheep	300 hogs	25	10	10	9	9	24	11	22	8 15	1 40	1 85	Electric
Tacoma	Plumbing, heat'g	1891	5,000	600 pairs	400 pairs	5	10		9		26	12		9 25	2 00		Electric
				$400 val.	$400 val.				8		26	12		3 00			Electric

Location	Product	Year	Value	Value		Men	Men							Wage	Wage		Power
Dupont	High explosives	1908		$500 val.		75	30		10		26	12		8 50	2 25	1 43	E. and S.
Tacoma	Blk bks, gen prtg	1878				24	4	10	8	8	28	12	26	3 73	1 04		Electric
Tacoma	Ice	1900	50,000	$500 val.		2	3		12		28	12		4 16	2 88		Steam
Tacoma	Table condiments	1900	520,000	450 tons ore	$11000 val.	5	25	9	8	8	30	12	26	3 25	2 50	1 25	Steam
Tacoma	Ore reduction	1890	254,000	600 tons ore	$16000 val.	90	70	8	8		30	12		3 50	2 50		E. and S.
Tacoma	Ore reduction	1901	25,000	1000 lbs.		40	80		8	10	30	12		3 00	2 50		E. and S.
Tacoma	Glue	1906		800 lbs.		1	3	2	10		26	12	24	3 00	2 35	1 25	Electric

SAN JUAN COUNTY.

Location	Product	Year	Value	Value		Men	Men							Wage			Power
Friday Harbor.	Cd salmon	190?	$20,000	2000 cases	750 cases	6	35	35	10	5	30	5	19	$2 and		$0 90	Steam

SKAGIT COUNTY.

Location	Product	Year	Capital	Output	Output	Men	Men		Hrs		Days			Wage	Wage		Power
Anacortes	Lumber	1904	$200,000	150,000ft.	150,000ft.	39	77		10		26	12		$2 50	2 11		Steam
Anacortes	Lumber	1904	150,000	100,000ft.	96,000ft.	18	55		10		26	12		4 28	$2 11		Steam
Anacortes	Lumber	1899	100,000	120,000ft.	120,000ft.	12	24		10		26	12		2 50			Steam
Big Lake	Lumber	1902	100,000	80,000ft.	75,000ft.	3	45		10		25	11		3 25	2 25		Steam
Big Lake	Lumber	1902	92,500	75,000ft.	50,000ft.	38	22		10		26	12		3 25	1 85		Steam
Big Lake	Lumber	1909	55,000	50,000ft.	50,000ft.	8	32		10		26	11		4 00	2 50		Steam
Big Lake	Lumber	1900	52,000	75,000ft.	70,000ft.	13	34		10		25	10		3 50	2 25		Steam
Sedro-Woolley	Lumber	1906	42,500	40,000ft.	40,000ft.	4	15		10		22	10		3 50	2 25		Steam
Big Lake	Lumber	1909	30,000	40,000ft.	40,000ft.	1	15		10		25	11		3 00	2 25		Steam
La Conner	Lumber	1902	20,000	35,000ft.	20,000ft.	5	25		10		25						Steam
Montborne	Lumber	1900	18,000	50,000ft.	40,000ft.	12	15		10		24	9		3 75	2 40		Steam
Mt. Vernon	Lumber	1903	15,000	50,000ft.	25,000ft.	9	22		10		23	12					Steam
Burlington	Lumber	1910	15,000	25,000ft.	25,000ft.	4	6	1	10	10	20	11	30	3 25	2 00	$1 50	Steam
Big Lake	Lumber	1900	15,000	20,000ft.	15,000ft.	14	16		10		26	12		4 00	2 00		Steam
Bow	Lumber	1907	12,000	40,000ft.	40,000ft.	6	20		10		25	10		2 50	2 20		Steam
Birdsview	Lumber	1907	12,000	60,000ft.	60,000ft.	8	4		10		20	9		4 25	2 25		Steam
Sedro-Woolley	Lumber	1906	10,000	25,000ft.	25,000ft.	5	9		10		24	11		4 25	2 25		Steam
Mt. Vernon	Lumber	1902	10,000	15,000ft.	15,000ft.	3	5		10		25	10		4 00	2 50		Steam
Anacortes	Lumber	1909	10,000	20,000ft.	20,000ft.	5	11		10		26	9		2 75	2 30		Steam
Big Lake	Lumber	1900	8,000	8,000ft.	8,000ft.	10	2		10		26	11		5 00	2 25		Steam
Big Lake	Lumber	1900		90,000ft.	75,000ft.	2	30		10		26	12		3 50	2 00		Steam
Baker	Lumber	1910		50,000ft.	50,000ft.	4	12		10		26	12		3 50	2 00		Steam
Baker	Lumber	1910		16,000ft.	13,000ft.	17	6		10		24			3 50	2 00		Steam
Anacortes	Lumber	1910	50,000	50,000ft.	50,000ft.	15	12		10		24			3 25	2 00		Steam
Baker	Lumber	1910	125,000	125,000ft.	100,000ft.	4	7		10		26			3 25	2 00		Steam
McMurray	Lumber	1910	16,000	16,000ft.	13,000ft.	38	6		10		24	12		3 50	1 85		Steam
Big Lake	Shingles	1902	92,500	225,000	200,000	20	23		10		25	12		3 25	2 50		Steam
Van Horn	Shingles	1902	50,000	325,000	325,000	11	15		10		25	10		3 75	2 60		Steam
		1902	40,000	200,000	200,000		5		10		22			4 00			Steam

SKAGIT COUNTY—Continued.

Town or City	Goods Manufactured or Handled	Date when est'b- lished	Capital invested in plant	Daily capacity	Daily output	Males employed Skil'd	Males employed Un- skil'd	Fe- males em- pl'y'd	Hours per day Males	Hours per day Fe- males	Days per mo., males	Mos. per year	Days per mo., fe- males	Wages, Males Skilled	Wages, Males Un- skilled	Wages fe- males	Kind of power used
Sedro-Woolley	Shingles	1905	$42,500	50,000	50,000	4	15		10		22	10		$4 00	$2 25		Steam
	Shingles	1909	35,000	200,000	200,000	17	8		10		24	10		5 00	3 00		Steam
	Shingles	1909	32,000	225,000	225,000	18	9		10		24	10		4 00	2 50		Steam
aker	Shingles	1907	25,000	180,000	150,000	20			10		24	8		4 00			Steam
Baker	Shingles	1900	25,000	120,000	110,000	10	7		10		24	9		3 50	2 50		Steam
Sauk	Shingles	1906	20,000	180,000	160,000	10	10		10		25	9		4 50	2 50		Steam
Mt. Vernon	Shingles	1901	20,000	200,000	167,000	26	6		10		20	10		4 50	2 40		Steam
Ml	Shingles	1900	18,000	200,000	160,000	11	23		10		24	9		3 75	2 50		Steam
	Shingles	1900	18,000	300,000	300,000	28	10		10		25	9		5 00	2 00		Steam
	Shingles	1906	15,000	100,000	100,000	16	6		10		26	10		4 00	2 75		Steam
	Shingles	1903	15,000	120,000	118,000	9	5		10		23	12		4 00	2 75		Steam
	Shs	1901	15,000	120,000	120,000	14	6		10		24	12		4 50	2 60		Steam
Concrete	Shs	1907	15,000	140,000	110,000	9	8		10		24	8		3 75	2 30		Steam
	Shingles	1902	14,000	120,000	115,000	11	4		10		26	8		4 00	2 00		Steam
Sah Pit.	Shingles	1908	14,000	115,000	100,000	12	5		10		26	9		4 00	8 00		Steam
	Shingles	1906	14,000	100,000	120,000	12	5		10		22	12		5 00	2 50		Steam
	Shs	1905	14,000	120,000	100,000	10	4		10		24	10		5 00	2 50		Steam
Belfast	Shingles	1907	13,000	50,000	50,000	7	5		10		25	9		4 00	2 25		Steam
	Shingles	1902	13,000	75,000	70,000	11	8		10		20	7		4 50	2 00		Steam
Edison	Shingles	1903	13,000	75,000	50,000	4	3		10		20	6		3 75	2 75		Steam
Bow	Shs	1900	12,000	85,000	85,000	10	16		10		25	9		3 75	2 25		Steam
	Shs	1909	11,000	90,000	60,000	6	4		10			10		4 00	2 25		Steam
	Shs	1905	10,000	150,000	140,000	15	9		10	10	22		30	4 25	2 75		Steam
Bellville	Shingles	1902	10,000	60,000	60,000	7		1	10		25	10		4 50	2 50	$1 25	Steam
	Shingles	1902	10,000	200,000	200,000	11	23		10		20	9		3 25	2 25		Steam
Bow	Shs	1907	10,000	70,000	70,000	10	8		10		25	8		4 00	2 25		Steam
Rockport	Shs	1900	10,000	140,000	140,000	12	14		10		22	8		3 50	2 50		Steam
La ...h	Shingles	1906	10,000	80,000	74,000	11	5		10		25	10		4 00	2 30		Steam
	Shs	1907	10,000	70,000	70,000	8	14		10		20			3 50	2 20		Steam
Bow	Shingles	1898	10,000	120,000	120,000	10	4		10		24	9		4 80	2 40		Steam
Lookout	Shingles	1910	8,000	90,000	65,000	9	5		10		20	8		4 80	3 00		Steam
Rockport	Shingles	1909	6,400	65,000	65,000	6	8		10		20	8		6 00	2 75		Steam
	Shingles	1905	6,000	66,000	55,000	8	3		10		25			4 00	2 45		Steam
	Shs	1910	6,000	60,000	60,000	5			10			11		4 75	2 35		Steam
Clr ...e	Shs	1908	6,000	90,000	90,000	9	8		10		20	10		3 50	2 50		Steam
Bay ...w.	Shs	1908	6,000	90,000	90,000	8	6		10		22						Steam
	Shs	1880	7,000	50,000	45,000	6	4		10		24	10					Steam

Location	Product	Year	Capital	Output	Output											Power
Lyman	Shingles	1902	7,000	60,000	110,000	6	4		10	26	10		5 00	2 50		Steam
	Shingles	1902	7,000	120,000		11			8	20	10		4 00			Steam
Bellville	shgles	1900	5,000	50,000	50,000	8	4		10	22	10		4 25	2 10		Steam
Sedro	...	1900	5,000	50,000	50,000	6	4		10	24	10		4 25	2 00		Steam
Sedro-Woolley	...	1905	5,000	25,000	25,000	4	1		10	24	10		3 80	2 00		Steam
Concrete	Shingles	1908	8,000	50,000	58,000	8	2		10	20	10		3 50	2 00		Steam
Roel rpt	Shingles	1902	1,600	30,000	23,000	4	1		10	22	10		3 50	2 25		Steam
Bay lew	Shingles	1900		50,000	45,000	6	2		9	20	10		4 00	2 50		Steam
Big Lake	Shingles	1904		230,000	200,000	20	10		12	26	10		5 00			Steam
Sedro-Woolley	Wd products	1905	72,000	180,000	10,000ft.	18	11		12	22	10		4 00	2 50		Steam
Mt. rh	Wd products	1910	7,000	10,000ft.		35			6	25	10		3 00	2 50		Steam
Sedro-Woolley	My	1902	15,000	$36 val.	$85 val.	3	5		12	25	9		3 50			Steam
Sedro-Woolley	Machinery	1908	8,000	$100 val.	$100 val.	12	4	8	12	26	9		3 50	2 00		Steam
site	nft	1908	750,000	1800 lb.	1200 bbls.	12	110	30	12	30	12		4 00	2 20	2 50	Electric
Anacortes	nd salmon	1901	100,000	2000 cases	659 cases	40	10	30	10	33	10		8 00	2 50	2 00	Steam
site	nd salmon	1904	70,000	2500 cases	2500 cases	9	60	50		30			4 00	2 50	2 50	Steam
Anacortes	Canned nhn	1896	50,000	3000 cases		40	75		10	25	9		3 50	2 50	2 00	Steam
Anacortes	nd hmn	1904	25,000	2500 cases	2500 cases	4	12	50	10	30	10		4 00	2 75	3 00	Steam
Anacortes	Fish products	1904	100,000	10t fert'zer	7t. fert'zer	4	16		10	26	10		2 50	2 00		Steam
				1500 gal. oil	1000 gal. oil											
				150 gal. gle	100 gal. glue											
Mt.	Salt fish	1905	50,000	5 ks	2½ tons	9		8	10	26	9		2 50			Steam
			37,000	60,000 lbs.	25,000 lbs.	6	20	5	12	30	6		3 00	2 00		Steam
Acs	nnd milk	1901	10,000	120 kw	120 kw	3		12	12	25					1 25	Steam
Acs	Electric L. nd P.	1905	8,000	$50 val.	$50 val.	4	12	6	12	28	10		2 75	2 20	1 40	Steam
Mt. Vernon	Bry	1905	7,500	$75 val.	$35 val.	1	2	6	12	25	10		3 00	2 25	1 35	Steam
Mt. Vernon	Laundry	1908	5,000	$50 val.	$30 val.	1	2	6	12	28	10		3 00		1 25	Steam
Sedro-Woolley	ldry	1903	3,800	$75 val.	$40 val.	3		8	12	20	8		2 50			Steam

SKAMANIA COUNTY.

Location	Product	Year	Capital	Output	Output											Power
Stevenson	Lumber	1909	$35,000	40,000ft.	55,000ft.	20	25		10	25	9		$3 00	$2 65		Steam

SNOHOMISH COUNTY.

Location	Product	Year	Capital	Output	Output											Power
Monroe	Shingles	1906	$212,000	175,000	140,000	21	28		10	24	10		$3 50	$2 50		Steam
Three Lakes	Shingles	1903	200,000	450,000		37.	66		10	25	10		3 00	2 25		teSm
Startup	Shingles	1901	86,000	180,000	180,000	13	6	2	10	28	10		5 00	2 50		Steam
Everett	Shingles	1903	85,000	500,000	250,000	29	32		10	33		8	3 98	2 35	$1 92	teSm
Everett	Shingles	1907	77,000	650,000		11	31		10	31	10		5 50	2 50		Steam
Everett	Shingles	1907	75,000	600,000	550,000	27	34		10	26	10		5 50	2 40		Steam

SNOHOMISH COUNTY—Continued.

Town or City	Goods Manufactured or Handled	Date when est'b'lished	Capital invested in plant	Daily capacity	Daily output	Males employed Skil'd	Males employed Un-skil'd	Females em-pl'y'd	Hours per day Males	Hours per day Fe-males	Days per mo., males	Mos. per year	Days per mo., fe-males	Wages, Males Skilled	Wages, Males Un-skil'd	Wages fe-males	Kind of power used
Everett	Shingles	1907	$75,000	200,000	200,000	8	31		10		28	10		$5 00	$2 50		Stm
Everett	...gles	1895	75,000	275,000	275,000	25	37		10		25	10		3 68	2 35		Stm
Granite Falls	...les	1910	75,000	250,000	250,000	10	10		10		25	12	25	3 50	2 50	$1 60	Stm
Everett	...les	1900	70,000	450,000	300,000	21	38	1	10	8	25	11		3 80	2 85		Stm
Three Lakes	...les	1904	50,000	100,000	100,000	4	9		10		25	11		4 00	2 25		Stm
...tt	...les	1888	45,000	325,000	280,000	20	14		10		23	9		4 50	2 50		Stm
Everett	...les	1909	40,000	300,000	300,000	26	4	1	10	5	24	9	24	5 00	2 50	1 00	Steam
...tt	...les	1904	37,500	300,000	270,000	18	14		10		25	10		4 00	2 50		Steam
Everett	...les	1906	35,000	300,000	280,000	22	14	1	10		24	7	30	5 13	2 70	2 48	Steam
...nd	Shingles	1900	30,000	200,000	175,000	14	9		10		25	8		6 00	3 00		Stm
...k	...les	1906	30,000	240,000	200,000	10	40		10		25	11		5 00	2 75		Stm
Grace	Shingles	1897	30,000	180,000	180,000	12	10		10		25	11		4 50	2 50		Steam
Everett	...les	1907	30,000	670,000	550,000	32	8		10		26	6		4 00	2 50		Stm
Darrington	...les	1907	30,000	120,000	110,000	25	29		10		25	10		4 50	2 50		Steam
Grace	...les	1897	30,000	140,000	140,000	14	5		10		25	11		4 00	2 75		Stm
...tt	...les	1888	28,500	260,000	260,000	18	6		10		24	10		5 40	2 65		Steam
...tt	...les	1898	28,500	280,000	230,000	18	14		10		25	9		5 50	2 55		Steam
...tt	...les	1900	28,000	250,000	230,000	19	11		10		25	9					Steam
Snohomish	...les	1907	25,000	190,000	190,000	21	10		10		20	9		3 25	2 50		Steam
Everett	...les		25,000	120,000	120,000	10	4		10		24	8		4 50	2 85		Stm
...lls	...les	1909	25,000	80,000	80,000	8	7		10		26	9		3 50	3 00		Stm
...lle	...les	1906	25,000	130,000	130,000	10	3		10		20	10		4 00	2 25		Stm
...rd	...les	1907	23,500	240,000	240,000	17	6		10		25	9		5 00	2 75		Stm
Granite Falls	...les	1902	22,000	175,000	150,000	12	17		10		24	8		5 00	2 50		Stm
...nda	...les	1908	22,000	90,000	90,000	9	15		10		25	9		4 00	2 85		Stm
...e	...les	1908	21,000	175,000	125,000	8	4		10		25	10		4 00	2 50		Steam
...th	...les	1905	20,000	225,000	225,000	18	13		10		20	9		3 00	2 50		Stm
Granite ...lls	...les	1909	20,000	200,000	200,000	25	12		10		24	8		4 00	2 00		Steam
Robe	...les	1902	20,000	150,000	150,000	15	2		10		24	9		4 00	3 00		Steam
Lakewood	...les	1906	20,000	180,000	160,000	10	18		10		25	10		5 00	2 75		Steam
...by	...les	1908	20,000	175,000	175,000	14	9		10		25	5		4 35	2 50		Stm
Machias	...les	1910	20,000	60,000	60,000	6	8		10		26	10		4 25	2 50		Stm
...nd	Shingles	1909	20,000	150,000	90,000	8	4		10					3 50	2 50		Stm
...er	...les	1910	20,000	90,000	90,000	8	10		10		22	11		5 00	2 50		Steam
Snohomish	...les	1908	17,500	175,000	175,000	6	8		10		26	12		3 00	2 00		Stm
Fortson	...les	1905	17,500	100,000	100,000	2	10		10		25	10		5 00	2 25		Stm

[illegible]	Shingles		1910	17,500	120,000	120,000	15			10		26	10		2 50			Steam
Everett	Shingles		1905	17,000	75,000		10	4		10		28	10		4 00	2 50		Steam
[illegible]	Shingles		1907	16,000	210,000	210,000	17	10		10		25	9		4 50	2 50		Steam
[illegible]	Shingles		1910	15,000	140,000	140,000	10	8		10		26	9		4 50	2 50		Steam
[illegible] Basin	Shingles		1909	15,000	100,000	80,000	13	6		10		23			3 50	2 65		Steam
[illegible]	Shingles		1907	15,000	150,000	150,000	18	5		10		25	10		3 50	2 50		Steam
[illegible]	Shingles		1902	15,000	40,000	40,000	6	13		10		23	10		3 00	2 50		Steam
[illegible]	Shingles		1902	15,000	130,000	130,000	10	14		10		26	8		3 00	2 00		Steam
[illegible]	Shingles		1908	15,000	130,000	130,000	14	5		10		22	12		5 00	2 35		Steam
[illegible]	Shingles		1908	15,000	70,000	70,000	6	10	1	10	10	24	9	26	4 00	2 50	2 00	Steam
Monroe	Shingles		1901	15,000	150,000	130,000	18	4		10		25	10		4 00	2 25		Steam
[illegible]	Shingles		1910	15,000	65,000	25,000	2	7		10								Steam
[illegible]	Shingles		1908	14,000	225,000	225,000	25	3		10		26	12		4 00	2 50		Steam
[illegible]	Shingles		1907	14,000	90,000	90,000	8	4		10		25	8		4 25	2 50		Steam
Monroe	Shingles		1910	14,000	125,000	125,000	12	5		10					4 20	2 00		Steam
[illegible]	Shingles		1910	14,000	100,000	100,000	10			10		20			4 50	2 75		Steam
[illegible]	Shingles		1905	13,000	100,000	100,000	10	8		10		22	9		4 25	2 50		Steam
[illegible]	Shingles		1907	13,000	110,000	100,000	8	5		10		26	6		3 75	2 50		Steam
[illegible]	Shingles			13,000	160,000	160,000	15	9		10		25	12		5 00	2 50		Steam
Startup	Shingles			12,700	150,000		20	2		10		25	10		4 50	2 25		Steam
[illegible]	Shingles		1891	12,500	160,000	150,000	5	8	2	10		25	7	30	5 00	2 50	1 50	Steam
[illegible]	Shingles		1909	12,500	30,000	30,000	2	4		10		25	12		4 00	2 25		Steam
[illegible]	Shingles		1889	12,500	30,000	30,000	3	8		10		20	11		3 00	2 30		Steam
[illegible]	Shingles		1892	12,500	160,000	150,000	7	8	2	10		24	10	30	5 00	2 25	1 12½	Steam
[illegible]	Shingles		1903	12,000	110,000	110,000	14	2		10		25	8		4 00	2 50		Steam
[illegible]	Shingles		1903	12,000	100,000	100,000	14	2		10		25	8		4 00	2 50		Steam
[illegible]	Shingles		1903	12,000	100,000	100,000	14	2		10		25	8		4 00	2 50		Steam
[illegible]	Shingles		1907	12,000	90,000	75,000	8	4		10		24	8		4 50	2 75		Steam
[illegible]	Shingles		1902	12,000	90,000	90,000	12	4		10		25	10		3 50	2 25		Steam
[illegible]	Shingles		1910	11,600	140,000	140,000	13	4		10		25	12		5 00	2 50		Steam
Granite Falls	Shingles		1900	11,000	175,000	175,000	13	8		10		25	9		4 25	6 25		Steam
Granite Falls	Shingles		1907	11,000	100,000	100,000	8	4		10		26	8		4 50	2 75		Steam
[illegible]	Shingles		1908	10,000	70,000	70,000	7	5		10		22	9		4 50	2 50		Steam
[illegible]	Shingles		1906	10,000	180,000	170,000	14	5		10		26	5		4 50	2 40		Steam
[illegible]	Shingles		1900	10,000	120,000	120,000	14	6		10		20	9		4 20	2 15		Steam
[illegible]	Shingles		1900	10,000	150,000	150,000	14	8		10		22	9		3 75	2 25		Steam
[illegible]	Shingles		1898	10,000	120,000	75,000	7	5		10		22	9		4 00	2 75		Steam
Robe	Shingles			10,000	180,000	180,000	14	10		10		20	9		5 00	2 50		Steam
[illegible] Cr's'g	Shingles			10,000	75,000	70,000	7	5	1	10	10	25	9	30	4 00	2 50	1 16	Steam
[illegible]	Shingles		1902	10,000	85,000		7	6		10		24			4 65	2 50		Steam
[illegible]	Shingles		1909	10,000	130,000	130,000	8	1		10		24	4		3 75	2 25		Steam
[illegible] Falls	Shingles		1909	10,000	70,000	70,000	6	4		10		25	6		4 00	2 75		Steam
[illegible]	Shingles		1902	10,000	100,000	100,000	12	2		10		25	8		4 00	2 25		Steam
Hazel	Shingles		1903	10,000	125,000	125,000	13	7		10		25	10					Steam
[illegible]	Shingles		1903	10,000	120,000	50,000	7	3		10		24	9		4 50	2 50		Steam
[illegible]	Shingles		1900	10,000	75,000	75,000	8	4		10		25	10		4 50	2 50		Steam
[illegible]tford	Shingles		1907	10,000	75,000	50,000	5	6		10		18	8		3 50	3 00		Steam

SNOHOMISH COUNTY—Continued.

Town or City	Goods Manufactured or Handled	Date when est'b'lished	Capital invested in plant	Daily capacity	Daily output	Males employed Skil'd	Males employed Un-skil'd	Fe-males em-ply'd	Hours per day Males	Hours per day Fe-males	Days per mo., males	Mos. per year	Days per mo., fe-males	Wages, Males Skill'd	Wages, Males Un-skilled	Wages fe-males	Kind of power used
Granite Falls	Shingles	1908	$10,000	220,000	99,000	8	5		10		28	10		$4 50	$2 50		Steam
Oso	Shingles	1910	10,000	100,000	100,000	22			10		26	10		8 25			Steam
Startup	Shingles	1907	9,339	145,000	145,000	18	10		10		28	10		4 50	2 50		Steam
Machias	Shingles	1909	9,000	150,000	150,000	14	6		10		22	9		4 75	2 25		Steam
Snohomish	Shingles	1908	9,000	90,000	90,000				10		25	10		3 75			Steam
Granite Falls	Shingles	1906	8,300	60,000	60,000	6	4		10					4 00	2 25		Steam
Stanwood	Shingles	1900	8,000	120,000	120,000	9	7		10		20	8		8 75	3 00		Steam
Sisco	Shingles	1910	8,000	100,000	100,000	9	5		10					4 25	2 50		Steam
Stanwood	Shingles	1901	8,000	100,000	90,000	10	6		10		28	10		4 65	2 85		Steam
Stanwood	Shingles	1910	8,000	125,000	80,000	9	4		10					4 00	2 00		Steam
Falls	Shingles	1907	8,000	70,000	70,000	9	2		10		24	7		4 00	3 00		Steam
Hazel	Shingles	1906	8,000	75,000	90,000	11	5	1	10		26	9		3 95	2 25		Steam
Edmonds	Shingles	1900	8,000	85,000	75,000	8	4		10		29	11		4 25	2 90		Steam
Hartford	Shingles	1906	8,000	70,000	85,000	10	5		10		29	8		4 40	2 25		Steam
Snohomish	Shingles	1902	7,500	125,000	70,000	6	11		10		28	11		4 00	2 25		Steam
Marysville	Shingles	1909	7,500	90,000	120,000	10	1		10		26	8		4 00	2 90		Steam
Florence	Shingles	1897	7,000	75,000	30,000	2	6		10		24			4 50	4 00		Steam
Everett	Shingles	1907	7,000	90,000	75,000	8	4		10		25	10		2 50	2 95		Steam
Granite Falls	Shingles	1906	6,500	70,000	70,000	7	6		10		22	8		4 00	2 00		Steam
Snohomish	Shingles	1907	6,000	90,000	90,000	16	5		10		20	9		4 00	2 95		Steam
Sisco	Shingles	1900	6,000	60,000		8	6		10		29	9		4 50	3 00		Steam
Stanwood	Shingles	1909	6,000	90,000	80,000	6	5	1	10	10	25	9		4 25	2 00		Steam
Stanwood	Shingles	1902	6,000	55,000		6	2		10		20	9		8 95	2 50		Steam
Marysville	Shingles	1904	6,000	60,000	40,000	6	3		10		20			8 60	2 75		Steam
Silvania	Shingles	1896	5,500	60,000	60,000	8	4		10		24	8		4 50	2 50		Steam
Norman	Shingles	1900	5,500	70,000		6	5		10		22	6		5 00	2 50		Steam
Snohomish	Shingles	1910	5,500	90,000	70,000	7	3		10		10	8		4 50	2 25		Steam
Arlington	Shingles	1907	5,000	100,000	95,000	8	9		10		29	9		8 75	2 50		Steam
Hartford	Shingles	1900	5,000	60,000	68,000	3	2		10					3 00			Steam
Edmonds	Shingles	1897	5,000	70,000	50,000	6	4		10		22	9		4 25	2 30		Steam
Marysville	Shingles	1900	5,000	70,000	70,000	6	4		10		29	8		4 25	2 25		Steam
Marysville	Shingles	1905	5,000	55,000	55,000	8	4		10		22	7		4 50	2 25	$1 25	Steam
Marysville	Shingles	1905	5,000	99,000	99,000	6	5		10		28	11		4 25	2 90		Steam

Place	Product	Year	Capital	Value	Value	Men	Men		Hours		Days				Wage	Wage		Power
Silvana	Shingles	1901	5,000	60,000	60,000	8	2		10		24	8			4 00	2 50		Steam
Ste	Shingles	1907	5,000	135,000	135,000	14	5		10		20	10			4 00	2 30		Steam
Marysville	Shingles	1908	5,000	75,000	75,000	9	3		10		20	9			4 25	2 50		Steam
Everett	Shingles	1902	5,000	75,000		4	4		10		21	9			3 50	2 25		Steam
Edgecomb	Shingles	1908	5,000	30,000	40,000	5	3		10		25	7			3 00	2 25		Steam
Snohomish	Shingles	1907	5,000	50,000	60,000	8	2		10		20	10			3 00	2 50		Steam
Snohomish	Shingles	1908	5,000	60,000	60,000	6	4		10						3 00	2 50		Steam
Sultan	Shingles	1900	5,000	60,000	60,000	9	4		10		20	11			3 85	2 75		Steam
Ste	Shingles	1899	5,000	65,000	65,000	8	5		10	30	25	10			3 75	2 30		Steam
Lochsloy	Shingles	1909	5,000	50,000	50,000	9	2		10		25	10			4 25	2 90		Steam
Hartford	Shingles	1904	4,500	60,000	60,000	6	4		10		20	9			4 00	8 00		Steam
Marysville	Shingles	1909	4,000	50,000	50,000	6	4		10		24	9			4 25	2 25		Steam
Hartford	Shingles	1900	4,000	70,000	65,000		3		10						4 00	2 25		Steam
Marysville	Shingles		4,000	70,000	65,000			1	10			10			4 25	3 00		Steam
Hartford	Shingles	1889	4,000	65,000	50,000	6	5		10		10	10			4 25	2 10		Steam
Oso	Shingles	1906	4,000	50,000	40,000	5	4		10		25	9			4 00	2 75		Steam
Arlington	Shingles	1909	3,000	40,000	90,000	9	8		10		25	9			4 50	2 90		Steam
Arlington	Shingles	1907	3,000	90,000	35,000	3	7		10		30	9			4 75	2 00		Steam
Lakewood	Shingles	1900	3,000	85,000	60,000	9	8		10		20	8			4 00	2 75		Steam
Summit	Shingles	1907	3,000	70,000	50,000	4	4		10		23	8			4 25	2 90		Steam
Lakewood	Shingles	1901	2,000	50,000	100,000	4	4		10		25	12			4 50	2 00		Steam
Robe	Shingles	1906	1,450	100,000	100,000	8	11		9		24	5			4 00	2 75		Steam
Granite Falls	Shingles			90,000		10	10	10	10	30	25	20		1	3 50	2 50	1 83	Steam
Stanwood	Shingles			100,000	100,000	10			9		24	9			6 50	2 50		Steam
Mite Falls	Shingles	1886	250,000	100,000	100,000	12	8		10		25	6			4 00	2 00		Steam
Getchell	Shingles	1905	212,500	120,000	120,000	2	6		10		24	9			4 00	2 25		Steam
Maltby	Shingles		200,000	125,000	125,000		9		10		23	8		3	3 25	2 16		Steam
Marysville	Shingles		150,000	30,000	25,000		3		10		25				3 80	2 50		Steam
Edgecomb	Shingles		115,000	25,000	25,000	10	6		10	25	25	10	8	2	8 50	2 70		Steam
Hartford	Shingles	1906	112,000	100,000	100,000	7	9		10	25	26	12	8		5 50	2 30		Steam
Everett	Lumber	1907	100,000	55,000	55,000	30	64		10		25	10			8 98	2 90		Steam
Monroe	Lumber	1906	85,000	200,000ft.	200,000ft.	44	54		10		24	10			8 00	2 50		Steam
Hee Lakes	Lumber	1903	77,500	125,000ft.	125,000ft.	18	134		10		25	11			8 63	2 35		Steam
Old Bar	Lumber	1899	75,000	100,000ft.	100,000ft.	40	100		10		25	11	8	1	3 80	2 25	1 75	Steam
Everett	Lumber	1906	75,000	85,000ft.	65,000ft.	8	42		10		25	11			5 00	2 15		Steam
Everett	Lumber	1902	75,000	125,000ft.	125,000ft.	24	85		10		23	12			4 90	2 70		Steam
Ever et	Lumber	1908	70,000	60,000ft.	60,000ft.	41	66		10		29	12			8 00	2 80		Steam
Everett	Lumber	1907	70,000	100,000ft.	100,000ft.	24	62		10		25	10			8 90	2 90		Steam
Granite Fils	Lumber	1910	70,000	100,000ft.	100,000ft.	20	52		10		25				8 00	2 50		Steam
Everett	Lumber	1886	65,000	60,000ft.	60,000ft.	17	78		10		25				3 63	2 35		Steam
Everett	Lumber	1907	50,000	100,000ft.	17,500ft.	44	64	8	10	25	25	10	8	1	8 80	2 10	1 60	Steam
Everett	Lumber	1900		50,000ft.		8	67		10		24	10			8 50	2 50		Steam
Stanwood	Lumber	1900		100,000ft.	50,000ft.	20	10		10		24	10			4 99	2 25		Steam
Robe	Lumber	1900			100,000ft.	8	12		10		25	11			4 00	2 25		Steam
Three Lakes	Lumber	1904																Steam

SNOHOMISH COUNTY—Continued.

Town or City	Gas fed or Wd	Date when est'b lished	Capital invested in plant	Daily capacity	Daily output	Males employed Skill'd	Males employed Un-skill'd	Fe-males em-ply'd	Hours per day Males	Hours per day Fe-males	Days per mo., males	Mos. per year	Days per mo., fe-males	Wages, Males Skilled	Wages, Males Un-skilled	Wages fe-males	Kind of power used
Est	lbr	1901	$50,000	50,000ft.	50,000ft.	8	26	1	10	8	24	11	25	$2 00	$2 00	$2 85	Steam
Est	lbr	1901	50,000	50,000ft.	65,000ft.	29	19		10		23	12		2 80	2 30		Steam
Sap	lbr		44,462	65,000ft.	66,000ft.	26	14		10		26	11		3 50	2 00		Steam
Sap	lbr		42,000	60,000ft.		4	36		10		25	11		3 25	2 00		Steam
Est	lbr	1907	40,000	75,000ft.	75,000ft.	29	26		10		25	12		3 15	2 25		Steam
Est	lbr	1909	38,500	60,000ft.	34,000ft.	7	21		10		25	10		3	2 35		Steam
Sultan	lbr	1905	35,000	60,000ft.	40,000ft.	5	7		10		22			4 00	2 50		Steam
Old Bar.	lbr	1889	35,000	50,000ft.	60,000ft.	15	10		10					3 50	2 10		Steam
Me	lbr	1906	30,000	40,000ft.	30,000ft.	5	15		10		25	11			2 00		Steam
The hl es	lbr	1904	30,000	50,000ft.	40,000ft.	10	10		10		24	12		2 50	2 00		Steam
Pilchuck	lbr	1902	27,000	60,000ft.	55,000ft.	11	6		10		25	11		3 00	2 00		Steam
Sap	lbr		26,743	40,000ft.	60,000ft.	12	9		10		26	12		2 50	1 85		Steam
Sap	lbr		25,468		20,000ft.	6	7		10		3A	11		3 00	2 00		S. and W.
Me	lbr		25,000	25,000ft.	20,000ft.	5	20		10		24			3 25	2 25		Steam
Stanwood	lbr	1907	25,000	50,000ft.	30,000ft.	10	24		10		25	12		4 00	2 50		Steam
Snohomish	lbr	1903	25,000	25,000ft.	25,000ft.	10	19		10		23	9		4 20	2 35		Steam
lbr	lbr	1880	25,000	25,000ft.	25,000ft.	5	25		10		23	11		3 85	2 50		Steam
Sad	lbr	1906	23,000	40,000ft.	40,000ft.	17	15		10			11		3 25	2 60		Steam
Rbe	lbr	1908	22,000	20,000ft.	20,000ft.	6	27		10		24	10		4 00	2 00		Steam
lbh	lbr	1903	22,000	38,000ft.		7	13	2	10		26	12	30	3 50	2 50	1 12	Steam
Ms	lbr	1908	20,000	70,000ft.	70,000ft.	5	20		10					3 50	2 50		S. and W.
Est	lbr	1907	20,000		12,000ft.		17		10			10			2 00		Steam
Marysville	lbr	1910	20,000	15,000ft.	12,000ft.	12	17		10		26	12		3 00	2 75		Steam
	lbr	1910	20,000	60,000ft.	40,000ft.	5	22		10		25	10		5 00			Steam
Fortson	Lumber	1910	17,500	25,000ft.	25,000ft.	30			10		25	10		2 50	2 50		Steam
Be	lbr	1905	17,500	40,000ft.	40,000ft.	14	27		10		23	10		3 00	2 60		Steam
lbr	lbr	1910	15,000	20,000ft.	10,000ft.	5	15		10		20			3 50			Steam
Gr te ills.	lbr	1902	15,000	50,000ft.	40,000ft.	6	14		10								Steam
Index	lbr	1906	15,000	40,000ft.	30,000ft.	27	9		10		23	12		3 50	2 65		Steam
Old Basin	Lumber	1910	15,000	25,000ft.	25,000ft.	5	18		10		25	10		4 00	2 25		Steam
Snohomish	lbr	1908	12,500	25,000ft.	15,000ft.	7	18		10		24	11		5 00	2 25		Steam
Est	lbr	1892	12,500	28,000ft.	22,000ft.	7	4		10		20	4		8 75	2 30		S. and W.
nlish	u lbr	1889	12,500	22,000ft.	10,000ft.	8	6		10		24	6		3 00	2 00		Steam
Me	lbr	1909	10,000	10,000ft.	20,000ft.	5	90		10.		90	12		3 00	2 25		Lumber
Gr se	Lumber	1906	8,000	35,000ft.		5					25						Steam

	907	8,000	30,000ft.	30,000ft.	8	27		10		29	12			3 00	8 00	2 25	Sam
	990	7,500	23,000ft.	23,000ft.	5	10		10		24	11			4 00	2 25		
	907	7,500	20,000ft.	20,000ft.	2	3		10		20				3 50	2 25		
	95	6,500	20,000ft.	12,000ft.	4	2		10		22				3 30	2 50		
Lumber	1907	5,000	25,000ft.	25,000ft.	7	3		10						3 00	2 25		
Lumber	1907	4,000	20,000ft.	20,000ft.	7	4		9		20	10						
	98	4,000			2	1		10						4 00	2 50		
	907	1,450			2			10			11			4 00	2 00		
	91				17			10			10			3 30	2 25		
Lumber			8,000ft.	10,000ft.	2	24	7	10	12	10	12	26	1 25	4 00	2 50	tSm
	98	18,500	50,000ft.	50,000ft.	20	3	10	10	27	25	8	20	1 50	2 75	2 00	Steam
	91	16,000	10,000ft.	10,000ft.	4	14	8	10	14	20	8	28	1	8 50	2 25	Sam
	996	10,000	25,000ft.	15,000ft.	50	25	9	10	6	25	10	19	1 65	2 75	2 50	
	90	6,500	60,000ft.	40,000ft.	5	30	9	10	3	28	12	22	1 26	3 00	2 00	
		1,800	180,000ft.	60,000ft.	30	90	10	10	6	28	12	26	1 75	8 23	2 00	
Laundry	1904		$0 ml	180,000ft.	7	1	9	10	1	26	12		1 66	3 00		Sam
Laundry	95	90,000	$10 val	$250 val	62			9		28	12		2 25	2 60		tth
		15,000	$0 ml	$150 val	8			10		25	12			4 00	4 00		ttm
	996	10,000	$2 ml	$100 val	10			8		25	12			3 75			tm
	90	15,000	$5 val	$45 val	6			9		28	12	8½		4 00			tn
	92	12,000		$25 val	10	5	7	9		25	12			4 00			Steam
Laundry	92	10,000	$2, 00 ml	$2,000 val	162			9	1		12	7	1 00	4 00	2 00	S. and ml
					2	68		9			12						
					1	2		9		28	12			8 50	2 50		
Machinery	1908	8,000			4	8		10		25	12			8 00	2 75		
	92		$85 val	$85 val	76	8	8	10	1	28	10	8		8 07	2 00		Steam
	92		$75 val	$75 val	15	8	9	10	2	24	12	9	2 00	3 50	2 50	
	90				3	63		10		25	11			2 70	2 25		Electric
Wd products	191	50,000	50,000ft.	50,000ft.	18	1		10		28	12			8 00			
Wd	91	50,000	$300 val	$300 val	13	11		10		28	6			3 00	2 60		
Wd	192	40,000	3,000ft.	10,000ft.	6	70		8		24	12		8 10	2 75			
Wd	96	18,000		$50 val	4	26		8		28	6			2 75			Sam
	990	85,000	750 bbls	750 bbls.	3	2				20	5			8 60			
	91	25,000		25 t's feed	6					30	12						
Mc			2 tons	5 tons	4	20											
Water sd ice	197	15,000	8 tons ice	250 tons	3	8		10	30	29	12			4 00	2 00	2 00	
			800grs water	8 tons ice	3	2		10		22	12			2 50	2 00		
Paper	91	30,000	4¼ tons	800grs water	168	6	10	8		24	12		1 35	3 00			
			51,000 lbs.	6 tons													
				55,000 lbs.													

SPOKANE COUNTY.

Town or City	Goods Manufactured or Handled	Date when est'b- lished	Capital Invested in plant	Daily capacity	Daily output	Males Skil'd	Males Un-skil'd	Females em- pl'y'd	Hours Males	Hours Fe- males	Days per mo., males	Mos. per year	Days per mo., fe- males	Wages Skilled	Wages Un- skilled	Wages fe- males	Kind of power used
Milan	Lumber	1900	$120,000	50,000ft.	50,000ft.	30	45		10		26	10		$2 75	$2 00		S. and W.
Spokane	Lumber	1905	100,000	150,000ft.	130,000ft.	28	30		10		26	9		4 00	2 25		Steam
Spokane	Lumber	1898	100,000	55,000ft.	55,000ft.	62	19		10		26	12		5 00	2 50		S. and W.
Spokane	Lumber	1905	78,000	150,000ft.	150,000ft.	15	85		10		26	10		5 00	2 50		Steam
Elk	Lumber	1901	50,000	100,000ft.	100,000ft.	8	35		10		26	10		3 00	2 25		Steam
Spokane	Lumber	1905	40,000	200,000ft.	60,000ft.	8	12		10		25	11		2 50	2 25		Steam
Elk	Lumber	1901	40,000	100,000ft.	100,000ft.	10	50		10		26	12		3 00	2 00		Electric
Spokane	Lumber	1908	40,000		150,000ft.	5	15		10		26	10		4 00	2 50		Steam
Spokane	Lumber	1905	35,000	200,000ft.		17	3		10		26	9		5 00	2 50		Steam
Buckeye	Lumber	1902	35,000	50,000ft.		6	16		10		28	12		4 00	2 00		Steam
Spokane	Lumber	1907	30,000			21	19		10		28	12		2 75	2 50		Steam
Spokane	Lumber	1903	24,000	50,000ft.	30,000ft.	5	30		10		22	10		3 75	2 50		Steam
Deer Park	Lumber	1902	20,000	40,000ft.	40,000ft.	10	30		10		25	11		3 50	2 50		Steam
Deer Park	Lumber	1905	20,000	40,000ft.	40,000ft.	9	18		10		26	11		3 00	2 50		Steam
Spokane	Lumber	1906	20,000			10	17		10		26	12		3 50	2 50		Steam
Spokane	Lumber	1902	17,000	30,000ft.	30,000ft.	45	20		10		24	11		3 25	2 60		Steam
Buckeye	Lumber	1902	17,000	50,000ft.	25,000ft.	3	15		10		25	5		4 00	2 30		Steam
Westbranch	Lumber	1896	8,000	30,000ft.		5	10		10		28			3 75	2 35		Electric
Spokane	Lumber	1910	8,000	20,000ft.	20,000ft.	4	5		10		25	9		3 50	2 50		Water
Spokane	Lumber	1880	5,000			3	12		10		26	4		3 50	2 60		Steam
Spokane	Lumber	1908	5,000	35,000ft.	35,000ft.	5	20		10		22	9		3 50	2 50		Steam
Mead	Lumber	1910	4,000	30,000ft.	20,000ft.	4	8		10		26	6		3 50	2 50		Steam
Hillyard	Lumber	1904	4,000	20,000ft.	20,000ft.	4	8		10		26	12		3 50	1 50		Electric
Spokane	Lumber	1906	2,000	25,000ft.	15,000ft.	1	3		9		26	8		3 00	2 25		Steam
Spokane	Lumber	1910	2,000			2	4		10		25	11					S. and E.
Spokane	Shingles	1905	25,000	25,000	25,000	4	4		10		24	11					Steam
Spokane	Shingles	1906	8,000	50,000	50,000	6	2		10		24	11					Electric
Spokane	Shingles	1902	5,000	50,000	50,000	2	1		10		28	10		4 00	2 75		Steam
Spokane	Shingles	1908	4,500	40,000	40,000	4	1		10		24	10		4 00	2 50		Steam
Spokane	Shingles	1902	4,000	40,000	40,000	5	2		10		26	10		4 00	2 00		Steam
Spokane	Shingles	1903	4,000	40,000	40,000	5	2		10		26	10		3 50	2 50		Steam
Spokane	Shingles	1897	4,000	50,000	45,000	6	3		10		26	10		3 75	2 50		Electric
Spokane	Shingles	1908	3,500	40,000	40,000	4	2		9		24	12		3 50	2 25		S. and E.
Spokane	Wood products	1892	125,000	50,000ft.	50,000ft.	128	101		9		24	12			2 25		S. and E.
Spokane	Wood products	1908	60,000			60	25		10		24	12		3 50	2 30		Steam
Spokane	Wood products	1908	50,000			15	40		10		25	12		3 25	2 25		Steam

City	Product	Year	Capital	Output	Output	No.	No.	No.	No.	No.	No.	No.	No.	Rate	Rate	Rate	Power
Spokane	Wood products	1909	35,000	3000 boxes	3000 boxes	9	7		9		26	12		3 50	2 00		Electric
County	Wood products	1908	35,000			1	3		10		20	8			2 50		Steam
Spokane	Wood products	1896	25,000			50	25		8		26	12		3 25	2 00		Steam
Spokane	Wood products	1907	25,000			22	8		10		26	12		3 25	2 00		Electric
Spokane	Wood products	1908	14,000			20	4		10		25	12		4 00	2 25		Electric
Spokane	Wood products	1908	14,000			25	5		10		26	12		3 75	2 25		Electric
Spokane	Wood products	1909	14,000			12	3		9		26	12		2 75	1 75		Electric
Spokane	Wood products	1905	10,000			8	4		10		26			2 50			Electric
1 Word	Wood products	1909	7,000		2500 boxes	2			9		26	12		2 75	2 35		Electric
Spokane	Wood products	1905	6,000			7			10		26	12		2 50			Electric
Spokane	Wood products	1909	5,000			2	2		9		26			3 50			Electric
Spokane	Wood products	1909	5,000			5	1		9		26			4 25	2 25		Electric
Spokane	Wood products	1909	5,000			10			10		26	12		3 50	2 50		Electric
Spokane	Wood products	1909	4,000			8			9		25	12		3 25	2 50		Electric
Spokane	Wood products	1909	600	600 bbls	500 bbls	1	15		10		29	11		4 00	2 50		Electric
Spokane	Flr and feed	1904	150,000	600 bbls	500 bbls	9	6	2	10	8	26	12	26	4 00	2 75	2 75	Wer
Spokane	Flr and feed	1905	150,000	150 bls.	450 bbls	8	8	125	8	10	26	12	24	4 25	3 00	1 75	Wer
Oheney	Flr and feed	1901	50,000			4	3	62	10	8	26	12	20	3 50	2 50	1 35	Electric
Spokane	Flr and feed	1907	15,000	150 bls.		2	10	33	8	10	25	11	24	2 75	2 50	1 85	Electric
Spokane	Flr and feed	1900	3,500				4	29	10	10	29	12	24	3 50	2 75	1 50	Electric
1886	Hay and feed	1886	3,000	20ms	15 tons	1	30	36	10	10	26	12	23	2 75	3 00	1 50	Electric
Spokane	Flat and produce					2	20	20	8	10	26	12	21	3 25	2 35	1 85	Electric
Spokane	Dairy	1905	98,000	$700 val	$900 val	12	20	38	10	10	26	12	28	3 25	3 00	1 45	Steam
Spokane	Dairy	1880	50,000	$500 val	$350 val	4	8	30	8	10	26	12	26	3 50	3 85	1 40	Steam
Spokane	Dairy	1909	30,000	$200 val	$250 val	14	6	28	10	10	26	12	29	3 25	3 00	1 75	Electric
Spokane	Dairy	1890	26,000	$125 val	$150 val	4	8	6	10	10	26	12	26	3 50	3 00	1 50	Steam
Spokane	Dairy	1908	25,000	$225 val	$125 val	6	6	45	10	10	26	12	40	3 00	3 06	1 45	Steam
Spokane	Dairy	1908	20,000	$750	$80 val	5	9	20	10	10	26	12	29	3 50	2 75	1 75	Steam
Spokane	Laundry	1889	20,000	$350 gal.	$150 val	3	9	22	10	10	26	12	26	3 00	3 50	1 50	Electric
Spokane	Dairy	1880	20,000	$150 gal.	$275 val	4	13	18	10	10	26	12	25	3 25	2 75	1 50	Electric
Spokane	Dairy	1902	15,000	$75 val	$75 val	9		17	10	10	26	12	28	3 50	3 25	1 50	Steam
Spokane	Dairy	1909	10,000	$150 val	$125 val	6	7	4	10	10	26	12	26	3 00	3 00	1 40	S. and E.
Spokane	Dairy	1901	10,000	$100 val	$100 val	5	6	4	10	10	26	12	24	3 75	2 75		Steam
Spokane	Laundry	1907	7,000			3	1	70	10	10	26	12	20	3 50	3 25		S. and E.
Spokane	Dairy	1908	2,000	$50 val	$50 saces	2	2		10	10	26	3		2 50	2 25		Electric
1 kane	Dairy	1908	1,500	$75 val		5	15		10		26	11		2 25			Electric
Spokane	Feed ogds	1905	25,000	900 cases	500 saces	60	100		8		26			3 00	2 50		Steam
Freem'n, Clayt'n	Bck, extra cota	1889	300,000	18000 brick	1900 brick							11		3 00	2 60		Steam
Chester	Brick and tiling	1905	40,000	2900 brick	2900 brick	8	9		10		26	5			2 25		S. and E.
Word	Brick	1909	38,000	$150 val. tg	$150 val. tg	5	30		10		26	11		3 75	225		Steam
Mad	Brick	1902	25,000	18000 brick	990 brick	60	100		10		26	12					S. and E.
Ohester	Sewer pipe, etc.	1905	25,000	750 bbls.	160 bls.		18		8		26	12		4 00			S.
Spokane	Beer	1903	500,000	150 bbls. br	100 bls.	12	4										Electric
Chester	Beer and ice	1905	450,000	80 tons ice		25			8		24	12		400	3 50		S. and E.

SPOKANE COUNTY—Continued.

Town or City	Goods Manufactured or Handled	Date when est'b'lished	Capital invested in plant	Daily capacity	Daily output	Males employed Skil'd	Males employed Un-skil'd	Females em-pl'y'd	Hours per day Males	Hours per day Females	Days per mo., males	Mos. per year	Days per mo., females	Wages, Males Skilled	Wages, Males Un-skilled	Wages females	Kind of power used
Spokane	Beer	1902	$340,000	200 bbls.	200 bbls.	35	12	...	8	...	26	12	...	$4 00	$3 50	...	E. and S.
Spokene	Ice	1906	46,000	25 tons	25 tons	8	2	...	8	...	26	12	...	4 00	2 75	...	E. and S.
Spokane	Ice	1905	25,000	35 tons	15 tons	4	4	...	10	...	25	6	...	3 00	2 25	...	Electric
Spokane	Cold storage	1898	...	...	...	2	25	...	10	...	26	12	...	4 00	3 60	...	Electric
Spokane	Paint	1892	30,000	...	...	4	6	1	10	10	26	12	26	4 00	2 75	$1 50	Electric
Waverly	Sugar	1899	500,000	500 t. beets	1000 sks sg	10	150	...	12	...	30	2	...	3 50	2 50	...	Steam
Spokane	Dairy products	1892	111,000	...	...	25	41	9	10	8	30	12	26	3 00	2 50	2 00	S. and E.
Spokane	Dairy products	1880	400,000	6000 lbs.	6000 lbs.	20	47	10	9	8	30	26	26	4 16	2 33	2 30	Electric
Spokane	Crackers, candy	1892	50,000	...	...	10	45	75	9	9	26	12	26	3 00	2 00	1 00	Steam
Spokane	1 real iron	1900	31,500	...	...	10	6	...	9	...	26	12	...	3 10	1 88	...	Electric
Spokane	Ice	1906	1,800	...	...	18	1	...	9	...	26	10	...	3 00	...	...	Electric
Spokane	Brooms	1908	25,000	60 doz.	40 doz.	7	5	3	9	9	26	12	26	3 00	1 50	1 50	Electric
Spokane	Extracts, spec.	1900	40,000	...	...	6	8	4	8½	8	25	12	25	3 80	...	1 25	Electric
Clayton	Earthenware	1904	20,000	2000 gals.	2000 gals.	18	1	...	10	...	24	8	...	4 00	2 35	...	Steam
Spokane	Ice fixtures	1909	10,000	...	...	12	1	...	9	...	26	12	...	3 25	2 25	...	Electric
Spokane	Office fixtures	1908	9,500	...	...	3	2	...	9	...	26	12	...	3 50	2 50	...	Electric
Spokane	Saw ...	1906	5,000	...	...	...	...	...	8	...	26	12	...	3 50	3 00	...	Electric
Snohane	Show cas., fixt's	1908	4,500	50 doz gar.	50 doz gar.	3	1	75	8	8	26	12	26	3 25	2 50	2 00	Electric
Spokane	Clothing	1909	50,000	...	...	5	35	8	10	9	26	12	26	3 00	2 25	2 00	Electric
Spokane	Mattresses, sprgs	1904	15,000	...	...	15	7	3	10	9	26	12	26	3 50	2 25	...	Electric
Spokane	Plate glass	1897	2,000	...	...	8	2	...	10	...	26	12	...	3 00	2 00	...	Electric
Spokane	...	1908	41,000	...	...	12	4	4	10	9	26	12	6	3 00	2 00	1 50	Electric
Spokane	Caskets	1905	1,000	5 caskets	5 caskets	3	1	1	10	8	26	12	26	2 60	2 00	1 25	Electric
Spokane	Smoked mets, etc	1905	600,000	$6000 val.	$6000 val.	45	12	5	10	10	30	12	...	3 00	1 00	...	Electric
Helen	Beef, sheep, m't'n	1906	1,000,000	20000 h. p.	2000 kw	30	5	...	8	...	26	12	...	...	1 50	...	Water
Spokane	Electricity	1908	40,000	$700 val.	$500 val.	15	60	10	8	8	26	12	26	3 00	2 00	1 40	Electric
Spokane	Printing	1880	500,000	...	...	44	20	...	9	...	26	11	...	3 60	2 80	...	Electric
Spokane	Machinery	1900	150,000	...	...	40	90	...	9	...	26	12	...	3 75	2 75	...	Electric
Spokane	Machinery	1901	100,000	...	...	20	100	...	9	...	25	12	...	4 00	2 50	...	Electric
Spokane	... lnry	1886	75,000	...	...	100	25	...	9	...	26	12	...	3 20	2 25	...	Electric
Spokane	... lnry	1887	65,000	...	...	25	20	...	9	...	26	12	...	3 75	2 13	...	Electric
Spokane	... lry	1908	45,000	...	...	14	4	...	9	...	25	12	...	4 00	2 50	...	Electric
Spokane	Machinery	1908	40,000	...	...	10	75	...	8	...	26	12	...	4 00	2 50	...	Electric
Spokane	Machinery	1900	18,000	...	...	52	9	...	9	...	26	12	...	4 25	2 50	...	Electric
Spokane	e ... lry	1886	18,000	...	...	4	1	...	9	...	26	12	...	3 00	2 25	...	E. and S.

Location	Product	Year													Power
Spokane	Mry	1908	15,000			3	1	9		28	12		8 60	1 00	Electric
Spokane	Machinery	1902	12,000			5	2	9		28	12		4 00	3 00	Electric
Spokane	c Mry	1909	7,000			16	4	9		28	12		3 25	2 50	Electric
Spokane	Mry	1908	3,000			6	6	9		28	12		3 75	2 50	Electric
Hillyard	c Mry	1885				95	158	9		28	12		3 68	2 12	Electric

STEVENS COUNTY.

Location	Product	Year													Power
ne	ber	1910	$200,000	150,000ft.	150,000ft.	25	100	10		28	12		$5 00	$2 50	Electric
a	ber	1908	60,000	60,000ft.	45,000ft.	29	17	10		28	7		3 50	2 50	Steam
Orin	ber	1900	36,000	50,000ft.	40,000ft.	10	25	10		29	8		3 75	2 50	team
rt	ber	1908	35,000	50,000ft.	75,000ft.	6	15	10		25	4		3 00	2 75	Steam
Orin	ber	1900	20,000	100,000ft.	140,000ft.	12	23	10		26	10		8 60	2 50	6am
yon	ber	1910	20,000	0ft.	0ft.	8	3	10		24	12		8 50	2 50	Steam
ly	ber	1902	18,000	25,000ft.	25,000ft.	9	17	10		28	6		8 25	2 25	Steam
ho	ber	1909	16,000	50,000ft.	50,000ft.	14	32	10		24			4 75	2 25	team
ho	ber	1905	15,000	50,000ft.	50,000ft.	8	47	10	3	28	8	30	4 50	2 50	6am
h	ber	1908	15,000	30,000ft.	30,000ft.	7	22	10		26			8 50	2 25	6am
e	ber	1908	12,000	25,000ft.	25,000ft.	9	12	10		26	10		4 50	2 35	Steam
Marcus	Lumber	1907	11,000	25,000ft.	25,000ft.	6	16	10		26	8		3 50	2 50	Steam
dale	ber	1897	10,000	40,000ft.	35,000ft.	6	9	10		30	8		8 75	2 50	am
Colville	ber	1908	9,000	38,000ft.	37,000ft.	7	14	10		26	4		8 00	2 50	Steam
Colville	ber	1900	8,000	35,000ft.	30,000ft.	6	18	10		28	5		3 75	2 40	6am
ohn Lake	ber	1900	8,000	35,000ft.	30,000ft.	2	31	10		24	9		8 50	2 50	6am
Newport	u ber	1908	8,000	30,000ft.	0ft.	5	9	10		23	7		8 00	2 50	6am
Blue Creek	Lumber	1909	7,000	20,000ft.	18,000ft.	4	11	10		26	3		4 25	2 25	Steam
e	ber	1902	6,000	25,000ft.	0ft.	7	5	10		25	4		2 45	2 60	Steam
ly	ber	1902	6,000	25,000ft.	25,000ft.	6	18	10		21	8		4 00	2 50	team
Ryan	u ber	1907	6,000	50,000ft.	30,000ft.	4	20	10		30	7		8 25	2 50	6am
rs Falls	ber	1908	6,000	15,000ft.	15,000ft.	2	2	10		30	5		3 00	2 50	Steam
Fam	Lumber	1909	5,000	30,000ft.	25,000ft.	3	10	10		26	8		8 50	2 50	6am
ke	ber	1901	5,000	30,000ft.	26,000ft.	5	18	10		29	9		3 50	2 25	6am
Colville	h	1908	4,500	20,000ft.	20,000ft.	3	9	10		26	7		8 25	2 25	6am
ta	ber	1901	3,500	25,000ft.	18,000ft.	3	7	10		26			8 75	2 50	te6am
Colville	u ber	1909	3,000	25,000ft.	25,000ft.	1	13	10		26	6		8 00	2 50	6er
ke	ber	1905	2,500	20,000ft.	20,000ft.	2	4	10		26	3		8 25	2 50	6am
ke	ber	1909	2,300	25,000ft.	25,000ft.	2	3	10		26	4		8 25	2 25	6am
Blue Creek	ber	1909	2,000	25,000ft.	18,000ft.	4	6	10		29	8		8 25	2 25	6am
n	ck, terra cotta	1888	400,000	95 tons	70 tons	70	75	10		29	12		8 50	2 25	S. and E.

THURSTON COUNTY.

Location	Product	Year													Power
Olympia	ces	1908	3,000	250,000	200,000	22	8	10		25	10		4 00	2 00	Steam
Lacey	Shingles	1902	10,000	80,000	75,000	7	9	10					4 00	2 00	Steam
Little Rock	Shingles	1905	10,000	00	115,000	11	5	10		22	10		4 00	2 75	Steam

THURSTON COUNTY—Continued.

Town or City	Goods Manufactured or Handled	Date when est'blished	Capital invested in plant	Daily capacity	Daily output	Males Skil'd	Males Un-skil'd	Females em-pl'y'd	Hours per day Males	Hours per day Fe-males	Days per mo., males	Mos. per year	Days per mo., fe-males	Wages, Males Skilled	Wages, Males Un-skilled	Wages fe-males	Kind of power used
Lile Rck	Shingles	1894	$10,000	115,000	115,000	10	4		10		20	8		$4 00	$2 50		Steam
ditto	fles	1907	10,000	90,000	90,000	10	7		10		26	9		4 20	2 50		Steam
Lile Rck	fles	1905	7,000	115,000		18	25		10		20	9		3 00	2 50		Steam
M'osh	ber	1894	250,000	100,000ft.	70,000ft.	5	10		10		26	12		4 00	2 35		Steam
fflx	fiber	1904	75,000	70,000ft.	25,000ft.	29	10		10		24	12		3 50	2 50		Steam
Shack	fiber	1909	40,000	25,000ft.	60,000ft.	20	10		10		24	12		3 00	2 60		Steam
ffx	ber	1909	200,000	75,000ft.	250,000ft.	15	30		10		15	10		3 00	2 00		Steam
fla	fiber	1901	18,000	250,000ft.		25	6		10		23			3 85	2 00		Steam
fler	Lumber	1905	150,000	100,000ft.		15	85		10		25	12		3 00	2 25		Steam
fla	Lumber	1906	100,000	45,000ft.	45,000ft.	25	10		10		25	12		4 00	2 25		Steam
Lile Rock	Lumber	1902	50,000	80,000ft.	80,000ft.	20	50		10		24	11		4 00	2 35		Steam
ffo	fiber	1906	25,000	35,000ft.	30,000ft.	8	18		10		23	11		3 20	2 10		Steam
ffo	Lumber	1908	25,000	20,000ft.	20,000ft.	10	20		10		25	12		3 00	2 25		Steam
ffo	fiber	1907	12,000	35,000ft.	35,000ft.	5	20		10		20	11		5 00	2 50		Steam
ffe Dy Jnd	fiber	1907	10,000	40,000ft.	40,000ft.	4	34		10		24	11		4 00	2 50		Steam
Grand Jnd	fiber	1910	8,000	25,000ft.	25,000ft.	10	13		10		20	8		3 50	2 50		Steam
Rochester	fiber	1909	7,000	20,000ft.	20, 0ft.	5	4		10					3 30	2 50		Steam
Lile Rck	ber		5,000	15,000ft.	15, 00ft.	6	6		10		20	8		5 00	2 50		Steam
ffo	Stve my	1889	150,000	6 car loads	3 car loads	20	40		10		26	11		3 50	2 50		Steam
ffo	Sane my	1908	25,000	600 cu. ft.	300 cu. ft.	6	9		8		27	9		3 50	2 50		S., G., E.
Tumwater	Beer	1896	150,000	875 bbls.	350 bbls.	72	10	8	8	10	28	12	26	4 00	3 00		S. and E.
fla	Bling wks	1896	15,000	140 bbls.	140 bls.	6	20		9		25	12		3 00	2 25		Electric
fla	Mfry	1907	15,000			6	4										

WAHKIAKUM COUNTY.

Town or City	Goods Manufactured or Handled	Date when est'blished	Capital invested in plant	Daily capacity	Daily output	Males Skil'd	Males Un-skil'd	Females em-pl'y'd	Hours per day Males	Hours per day Fe-males	Days per mo., males	Mos. per year	Days per mo., fe-males	Wages, Males Skilled	Wages, Males Un-skilled	Wages fe-males	Kind of power used
Brookfield	Canned salmon	1873	$50,000	800 cases		2	30		10	10	26	7	26	$2 50	$1 00		Steam
Pillar Rock	Canned salmon	1876	40,000	700 cases		4	2	8	12		26	5		2 00 und b.	$1 50 and b.		Steam
Altoona	Canned salmon	1904	33,000	1000 cases	180 cases	1	34		3		26	4		und b.	2 00		Steam
Eagle Cliff	Canned salmon	1874		700 cases										3 00			Steam
Oathlamet	Shingles	1899					9					5					Steam
Skamokawa	Shingles	1904	15,000	250,000	230,000	23	15		10		28	8		4 00	2 50		Steam
Brookfield	Wood products	1895	7,000	6000 stv, hd					10		25	11		2 50			Steam

WALLA WALLA COUNTY.

City	Kind	No.	Capital	Output	Output											Wages			Power
Walla Walla	Lumber, millwork	905	$80,000			15	6		9		96		12				$2 50	$4 00	Elic
Walla Walla	General brk.	904	28,000			20	14		9		26		12				2 25	3 25	Elic
Walla Walla	Genl mllwk.	908	15,000			4	5		9		96		12				2 25	3 50	Electric
Walla Walla	Genl millwork	890	12,000			5	20		9		96		12				2 25	4 25	1 Elic
Walla Walla	General millwork	994	5,000			4	8		9		26		12				2 25	4 00	Electric
Walla Walla	Feed	990	80,000	300 tons	300 tons	3	11		10								2 25	5 00	Elic
Walla Walla	Flur and feed	880	50,000	350 bbls	325 bbls	5	11		10		26		12				2 25	8 80	Elic
Walla Walla	Flour and feed	184	40,000	400 bbls	400 bbls	6	10		10		25		10				2 25	3 00	W. and E.
Waitsburg	Flour and feed	865	20,000	400 bbls	400 bbls	3	12		10		26		11				2 25	8 50	Wer
Walla Walla	ad. feed	909	14,000	25 tons	18 tons	1	4		10		96		8				2 50	4 00	Wer
Prescott	Flur ad feed	884		300 bbls	300 bbls	3	7		12		96		10				2 50	8 00	Elic
Walla Walla	Beer	904	175,000	75 bbls	40 bbls	5	3		8		25		12				2 50	8 00	Wer
Walla Walla	Beer	882	100,000	60 bbls	30 bbls	6			8		96		12				3 00	8 75	S. and E.
Walla Walla	Mt.	907	150,000			19	32	2	10		96	26	12		$2 80	2 22	3 74		Elic
Walla Walla	Laundry	889	35,000	$200 val.	$200 val.	5	8	46	10	10	96	24	12		1 88	2 71	3 27		Sam
Walla Walla	Laundry	906	18,800	$90 val.	$90 val.	3	4	19	10	10	26	22	12		1 50	3 50	4 25		team
Walla Walla	Machinery		10,000			1	4	17	10	10	96	20	12		1 25	3 00	3 00		team
Walla Walla	Machinery	184	250,000	$300 val.	$300 val.	20	50	2	10	8	26	26	12		2 50	2 00	4 00		Metric
Walla Walla	Machinery	858	50,000	$125 val.	$125 val.	80	17	1	9	8	96	26	11		2 75	2 25	3 50		Metric
Walla Walla	Machinery	998	30,000				10		10		26		11			8 50			Electric
Walla Walla	Brick	905	15,000	40000 brick	20000 brick	3	2		10	8	20	26	6			2 50	3 00		Electric

WHATCOM COUNTY.

City	Product	No.	Capital	Output	Output										Wages		Power
Bellingham	Shingles	901	$250,000	300,000	300,000	110	50		10		26		12		$2 00	$3 00	team
Bellingham	Shingles	901	75,000	200,000	200,000	25	5		10		26		12		2 30	3 25	Sam
Bellingham	Shingles	1905	45,000	60,000	60,000	6	6		10						2 00	5 00	Sam
Bellingham	Shingles	1901	37,500	90,000	90,000	11	15		10		25	12			2 00	4 00	team
Deming	Shingles	908	25,000	50,000	50,000	4	8		10			11			2 25	4 50	team
Sumas	Shingles	907	25,000	125,000	125,000	14	8		10		23	9			2 75	3 00	team
Clipper	Shingles	900	25,000	90,000	90,000	8	7		10		30	8			2 50	8 00	Sam
Maple Falls	Shingles	903	20,000	50,000	50,000	12			10		24	9			2 50	8 00	team
Maple Falls	Shingles	909	20,000	100,000	100,000	10			10		25	8			2 90	4 00	team
Bellingham	Shingles	880	15,000	80,000	80,000	7			10		23	9			2 50	4 28	team
6th Ave	Shingles	896	16,000	100	120,000	12	12		10		22	8			2 90	4 20	Steam
Custer	Shingles	994	15,000	125,000	125,000	15	9		10		25	9			2 50	4 00	team
Ferndale	Shingles	908	11,000	100,000	100,000	10	7		10		20	7			2 00	4 00	Steam
Me Falls	Shingles	989	10,000	75,000	75,000	8	5		10		24	9			2 25	4 00	Steam
Custer	Shingles		10,000	50,000	50,000	5	8		10		25	8			2 00	5 00	team
Wen	Shingles	906	10,000	40,000	40,000	4	5		10	8	20	8		26	2 75	3 50	Sam
Whatcom	Shingles	982	10,000	90,000	75,000	12	4	1	10		24	9h			2 50	8 00	team
Ellm	Shingles	900	10,000	150,000	75,000	11+	8		10		25	11			2 60	3 00	team
Bellingham	Shingles	1898	10,000	100,000	80,000	4	4		10		28	10			2 50	8 00	team
Me	Shingles	905	9,000	90,000	90,000	9	4		10		22	11			2 25	4 20	team

WHATCOM COUNTY—Continued.

Town or City	Goods Manufactured or Handled	Date when est'b'lished	Capital invested in plant	Daily capacity	Daily output	Males employed Skil'd	Males employed Un-skil'd	Fe-males em-pl'y'd	Hours per day Males	Hours per day Fe-males	Days per mo., males	Mos. per year	Days per mo., fe-males	Wages, Males Skilled	Wages, Males Un-skilled	Wages fe-males	Kind of power used
Blaine	Shingles	1906	$8,000	60,000	50,000	7	3	....	10	....	26	9	....	4 00	2 75	....	Steam
Bellingham	Shingles	1905	8,000	75,000	75,000	8	0	....	10	....	24	10	....	4 00	2 75	....	Steam
Bellingham	Shingles	1901	8,000	100,000	....	8	7	....	10	....	26	8	....	4 00	2 50	....	Steam
Wickersham	Shingles	1901	8,000	90,000	90,000	6	4	....	10	....	22	9	....	4 20	2 50	....	Steam
Ouster	Shingles	1902	8,000	60,000	50,000	6	3	....	10	....	25	7	....	4 00	2 60	....	Steam
Blaine	Shies	1907	8,000	60,000	60,000	6	6	....	10	....	22	8	....	5 50	2 00	....	Steam
Goshen	Shingles	1900	7,000	60,000	50,000	6	4	....	10	....	18	8	....	4 25	2 25	....	Steam
Sile Falls	Shingles	1902	7,000	125,000	125,000	9	5	....	10	....	20	9	....	4 00	2 00	....	Steam
Deming	Shingles	1906	7,000	100,000	90,000	15	4	....	10	....	22	9	....	4 25	2 25	....	Steam
Ferndale	Shingles	1900	7,000	90,000	90,000	8	5	....	10	....	22	9	....	3 75	2 25	....	Steam
Ferndale	Shingles	1906	7,000	50,000	50,000	6	4	....	10	....	20	10	....	4 35	2 15	....	Steam
Glm	Shies	1900	7,000	70,000	70,000	7	4	....	10	....	23	8	....	4 00	2 00	....	Steam
Lynden	Shingles	1902	7,000	80,000	90,000	8	4	....	10	10	20	6½	20	4 20	2 50	....	Steam
Blaine	Shingles	1888	6,500	50,000	....	6	3	1	10	10	24	10	....	4 25	2 75	....	Steam
Rine	Shingles	1907	6,050	90,000	90,000	11	8	....	10	....	25	9	....	4 00	2 50	....	Steam
Ilßer Beach	Shingles	1907	6,000	70,000	70,000	8	4	....	10	....	22	9	....	4 25	2 25	....	Steam
Acme	Shingles	1907	6,000	60,000	60,000	6	4	....	10	....	20	9	....	4 25	2 35	....	Steam
Glm	Shingles	1907	6,000	60,000	60,000	6	4	....	10	....	20	9	....	4 25	2 25	....	Steam
Lynden	Shingles	1900	6,000	70,000	60,000	6	6	....	10	....	10	9	....	5 00	2 00	....	Steam
Rier Beach	Shingles	1906	6,000	90,000	65,000	7	2	....	10	....	23	8	....	4 00	2 25	....	Steam
Rine	Shingles	1907	6,000	50,000	50,000	11	3	....	10	....	24	12	....	4 25	2 00	....	Steam
Bellingham	Shingles	1888	6,000	90,000	....	7	4	....	10	....	25	10	....	4 00	2 75	....	Steam
Silver Beach	Shingles	1900	6,000	60,000	50,000	7	2	....	10	....	20	8	....	4 25	2 50	....	Steam
Ferndale	Shingles	1906	6,000	50,000	40,000	6	2	....	10	....	26	11	....	4 00	2 35	....	Steam
Bellingham	Shingles	1906	6,000	50,000	50,000	6	5	....	10	....	23	11	....	4 00	2 50	....	Steam
Lynden	Shingles	1908	6,000	75,000	65,000	9	4	....	10	....	20	12	....	4 25	2 50	....	Steam
Bellingham	Shies	1900	5,800	70,000	70,000	8	8	....	10	....	21	10	....	4 50	2 35	....	Steam
Kendall	Shingles	1906	5,000	50,000	44,000	5	5	....	10	....	20	6	....	4 50	2 50	....	Steam
Me Falls	Shies	1907	5,000	50,000	40,000	8	8	....	10	....	21	12	....	3 50	2 35	....	Steam
Clipper	Shingles	1897	5,000	100,000	100,000	11	5	....	10	....	28	9	....	3 50	2 75	....	Steam
Acme	Shingles	1906	5,000	60,000	50,000	6	3	....	10	....	30	8	....	4 25	2 20	....	Steam
Ame	Shies	1900	5,000	80,000	60,000	8	4	....	10	....	20	9	....	4 40	2 15	....	Steam
Deming	Shingles	1901	5,000	50,000	50,000	5	4	....	10	....	20	9	....	4 50	2 25	....	Steam
Ferndale	Shies	1900	5,000	60,000	60,000	5	3	....	10	....	20	10	....	4 25	2 95	....	Steam
Maple Falls	Shies	1909	5,000	50,000	60,000	10	4	....	10	....	24	10	....	3 50	2 95	....	Steam
Rlm	Shingles	1902	5,000	50,000	50,000	9	5	....	10	....	25	12	....	3 10	3 00	....	Steam

Location	Product	Year															Power
Lynden	Shingles	1906	5,000	60,000	50,000	6	3		10		22	8		4 25	2 50		Steam
Lawrence	Shingles	1902	5,000	90,000	90,000	6	4		10		20	9		4 00	2 25		team
Iden	Shingles	1909	5,000	75,000	70,000	8	3		10		28	10		4 50	2 50		Steam
Acme	Shingles	1908	4,500	75,000	75,000	8	5		10		25	9		4 50	2 75		Steam
Bey	Shingles	1900	4,500	40,000	40,000	5	3		10		22	9		4 00	2 20		Steam
Blaine	Shingles	1907	4,500	60,000	60,000	8	8		10		23	9		4 30	2 35		team
Bellingham	Shingles	1900	4,500	50,000	50,000	6	4		10		30	6		4 00	2 20		Steam
Ouster	Shingles	1900	4,500		60,000	5	3		10		20	9		4 00	2 20		team
Yom	Shingles	1907	4,500	50,000	60,000	5	8		10		24	10		4 30	2 20		Steam
	Shingles	1902	4,500	60,000	30,000	6	5		10		22	10		3 75	2 50		team
Elser Beach	Shingles	1900	4,000	30,000	50,000	7	8		10		25	9		4 35	2 50		Steam
Sen	Shingles	1910	4,000	50,000	30,000	6	3		10		23	9		4 50	2 25		Steam
Custer	Shingles	1900	4,000	30,000	50,000	5	8		10		22	10		4 60	2 25		Steam
Acme	Shingles	1900	4,000	50,000	60,000	6	8		10		25	10		4 00	2 50		Steam
Bellingham	Shingles		4,000	60,000	50,000	6	8		10		22	8	30	4 90	2 00		Steam
Whatcom	Shingles	1900	4,000	60,000	50,000	9	4	10	10		20	8		4 00	2 00	1 15	Steam
Kendall	Shingles	1908	4,000	50,000	75,000	5	3		10		28	9		4 25	2 50		team
Eler Bach	Shingles	1895	4,000	50,000	30,000	6	8		10		22	9		4 20	2 25		Steam
Whl	Shingles	1910	4,000	70,000	25,000	9	3		10		16	10		5 00	2 75		team
Deming	Shingles	1902	4,000	30,000	30,000	4	1		10		20	8		3 75	2 25		Steam
Lynden	Shingles	1906	3,500	25,000	30,000	2	8		10		24	9		3 50	3 00		Steam
Ferndale	Shingles	1900	3,500	30,000	60,000	5	1		10			9		3 25	2 25		team
Wickersham	Shingles	1910	3,500	30,000	45,000	6	3		10		24	7	28	4 20	2 20		Steam
Everson	Shingles	1900	3,500	40,000	40,000	7	1		10		25	7		4 50	2 00	1 00	Steam
Bellingham	Shingles	1905	8,000	35,000	40,000	9	2	9	10		25	7		4 00	2 25		Steam
Marroti	Shingles	1905	8,000	40,000	50,000	4	8		10		24	10		5 00	2 50		team
Ouster	Shingles	1907	8,000	40,000	40,000	2	2		10		23	9		3 75	2 00		Steam
Wickersham	Shingles	1905	8,000	50,000	35,000	9	8		10		25	9		3 80	2 50		Steam
Maple Falls	Shingles	1902	8,000	40,000	50,000	6	2		10		24	7		4 00	2 20		Steam
Blaine	Shingles	1903	8,000	35,000	60,000	7	8		10		23	7		3 50	2 25		team
Doran Spur	Shingles	1900	8,000	50,000	45,000	9	2		10		25	7		3 80	2 50		Steam
aple Falls	Shingles	1898	8,000	60,000	50,000	7	8		10		24	5		4 00	2 00		Steam
Bellingham	Shingles	1908	2,700	40,000	30,000	7	3		10		23	9		3 90	2 50		Steam
Wahl	Shingles	1908	2,700	45,000	40,000	7	8		10		25	9		3 50	2 00		team
Blaine	Shingles	1905	2,500	50,000	40,000	5	1		10		24	9		3 80	2 00		Steam
Blaine	Shingles	1904	2,500	45,000	40,000	5	2		10		23	7		3 00	2 00		team
	Shingles		2,000	40,000		5	8		10		26	9		3 00	2 00		Steam
Goshery	Shingles	1905	500	30,000	85,000	5	1		10		24	12		3 75	2 00		Steam
Warnick	Shingles	1907		40,000	150,000ft	10	80	10	10		28	12		3 00	2 00		team
Day	Lumber	1901	700,000	40,000	250,000ft	110	90		10		28	12		3 00	2 00		Steam
Ale Falls	Lumber	1901			100	10	75		10		26	12		3 00	2 00		Steam
Bellingham	Lumber	1909	00,300	100,000ft	0	10	80		10		28	12		3 00	2 00		Steam

WHATCOM COUNTY—Continued.

Town or City	Goods Manufactured or Handled	Date when est'b-lished	Capital invested in plant	Daily capacity	Daily output	Males employed Skil'd	Males employed Un-skil'd	Females empl'd	Hours per day Males	Hours per day Females	Days per mo. males	Mos. per year	Days per mo. females	Wages Males Skilled	Wages Males Un-skilled	Wages fe-males	Kind of power used
Bellingham	Lumber	1901	$37,500	50,000ft.	50,000ft.	24	60		10		26	12		$3 00	$2 00		Steam
	Lumber	1910	22,000	25,000ft.	25,000ft.	6	14		10		20	8		3 50	2 50		Steam
Maple Falls	Lumber	1903	20,000	25,000ft.	25,000ft.		25		10		25	10		3 00	2 75		Steam
Lynden	Lumber	1907	20,000	35,000ft.	35,000ft.	10	38		10		20	10		4 00	2 85		Steam
Lynden	Lumber	1888	20,000	30,000ft.	30,000ft.	20	30		10		25			3 50	2 25		Steam
Maple Falls	Lumber	1907	18,000	30,000ft.	25,000ft.	7	10		10		20	12		3 00	2 50		Steam
Blaine	Lumber		15,000	25,000ft.	25,000ft.	5	21		10		23			3 00	2 00		Steam
Bellingham	Lumber	1907	15,000	30,000ft.	20,000ft.	20	13		8		25	12		3 50	2 25		Steam
	Lumber	1907	12,000	25,000ft.	30,000ft.	5	16		10		26			3 75	2 50		Steam
Sumas	Lumber	1909	10,000	40,000ft.	30,000ft.	8	10		10		25	11		3 75	2 25		Steam
Sumas	Lumber	1907	10,000	20,000ft.	15,000ft.	4	12		8		22	4		3 00	2 42		Steam
Ferndale	Lumber	1909	10,000	20,000ft.	12,000ft.	5	13		10		20	9		3 50	1 75		Steam
Sumas	Lumber	1905	10,000	25,000ft.	20,000ft.	5	12		10		30	6		3 00	2 50		Steam
Deming	Lumber	1909	9,000	20,000ft.		5	9		10		24	11		3 00	2 00		Steam
Sumas	Lumber	1905	6,000	20,000ft.	5,000ft.	2	3		8		24	10		3 25	2 50		Steam
Nooksack	Lumber	1880	5,000	8,000ft.	8,000ft.	5	3		10		20			3 00	2 00		Steam
Ferndale	Lumber	1905	5,000	12,000ft.	30,000ft.	5	5		10		24			2 50	2 00		Steam
Bier Beach	Lumber	1908	4,500	30,000ft.		5	4		10		20			4 00	2 00		Steam
Blaine	Lumber	1910	4,000	7,000ft.	1,000ft.	2	3		10		25			2 75	2 50		Steam
	Lumber	1900	3,000	1,000ft.	150,000ft.	4	125		10		26	8		4 15	1 90		Steam
Bellingham	Lumber	1901	1,500	150,000ft.	20,000ft.	3	12	1	9	8	18	12	28	3 75	1 75	$1 80	Steam
	Lumber	1906		20,000ft.	6,000ft.	3	6	1	10		24	10		3 00	2 00		Steam
Everson	Lumber	1906		10,000ft.	20,000ft.	8	23		10		20	7		3 16	2 35		Steam
	Lumber	1900		25,000ft.		20	15		9		26	12		3 50	2 25		Steam
Bellingham	Machinery	1902	80,000	$75 val.	$50 val.	4	3		9		26	12		3 50	1 00		S. and E.
	Machinery	1904	27,000			8	4		9		26	12	26	3 15	1 50		Electric
Bine	Machinery	1908	10,000			2	2	1	10	8	26	12		4 00	3 00	1 25	S. and E.
Bellingham	Machinery	1902	7,500	$20 val.	$20 val.	1	8		8		26	12		5 00	3 00		Gasoline
		1889	7,000	$15 val.	$15 val.	5	2		9		26	12					Electric
Bellingham	Laundry	1910	5,000			2	8	30	9	9	26	12	26	3 40	2 25	1 50	Electric
		1888	1,500			9	12	8	9	10	25	12	22	3 00		1 40	Electric
S.	Laundry	1889	35,000	$200 val.	$175 val.	16		8	8	10	28	12	23			1 00	Electric
Bel		1891	8,000			6	15		10		26	12		8 00	2 50		Steam
	Beer and ice	1908	5,000	100 bls. b'r 30 tons ice	40 bls. b'r 10 tons ice	6	7		10		28	12			2 00		Steam
Bellingham	Flour and feed	1907	250,000	50 tons		15	10		8		26	12		3 00	2 50		Steam
			60,000			1	12		10		26	12		5 00	2 50		Electric

Location	Product	Year	Capital	Output	Output value	Empl.	Power
	Sprgs, mattresses	1909	7,500	100 springs / 100 mattr	50 springs / 50 mattr		Electric
Bellingham	... products	1904	15,000			5	Steam
Bellingham	Wood products	1904	15,000	$250 val.	$250 val.	1	Electric
Bellingham	Wood products	1906	10,000	$125 val.	$125 val.	7	Electric
	Wood products	1906	5,000			14	Electric
Carlisle	Canned salmon	1902	300,000	2500 cases		6	S. and G.
		1899	250,000	2500 cases	1500 cases	2	Steam
		1905	50,000	2000 cases		100	S. and E.
		1898	80,000	cases		75	Steam
		1909	25,000	cases		15	
		1880	50,000	50000		150	Steam
		1906	20,000	12-page prs	11,000 / 12-page prs		Electric

WHITMAN COUNTY.

Location	Product	Year	Capital	Output	Output value	Empl.	Power
	Flr and feed	1905	$30,000	125 bbls.	50 bbls.	2	Wr
	Flour and feed	1905	25,000	125 lbs.	90 bbls.	1	elec
	Flour and feed	1901	25,000	100 lbs.	50 bbls.	1	Wr
	Flour and feed	1905	25,000	125 lbs.	65 bbls.	1	Wr
Winona	Flr and feed	1903	20,000	100 lbs.	100 bbls.	1	Electric
	Flour and feed	1907	18,000	100 lbs.	100 bbls.	2	Wr
	Flour and feed	1892	16,000	125 bbls.	125 bbls.	1	S. rl l.
Oakesdale	Flr and feed	1906	14,000	75 lbs.	35 bbls.	3	elec
	Flr and feed	1897	12,000	$00 wl.	$70 val.		elec
	Laundry	1900	10,000	$83 wl.	$66 val.	14	elec
	Laundry	1900	7,000	$00 val.	$50 val.	1	elec
Palouse	Laundry	1903	6,500	$25 wl.	$50 val.	2	elec
	elr and cd		6,000	50 lb. b'r	15 bls. b'r	10	tam
		1908	50,000	5 tns ice	5 tons ice		Steam
				20 lbs.	8 bbls.		l. and S.

WA.

Location	Product	Year	Capital	Output	Output value	Empl.	Power
	Wagons	1905	40,000	125,000 ft.	125,000 ft.	5	Steam
Colfax	Office fixtures, etc	1900	6,000	100,000 ft.	100,000 ft.	3	Electric
Colfax		1897	20,000				Electric

NY.

Location	Product	Year	Capital	Output	Output value	Empl.	Power
North Yakima	Lumber	1902	$125,000	125,000 ft.	125,000 ft.	31	Steam
North Yakima	Lumber	1902	15,000			12	Steam
North Yakima	General millwork	1907	40,000			42	Steam
North Yakima	Iron	1907	9,000			4	Electric
North Yakima	Beer	1904	50,000	75 bbls.	75 bbls.		Steam
North Yakima	Laundry	1908	40,000	$200 val.	$175 val.	5	Steam
North Yakima	Laundry	1900	20,000			3	Electric
North Yakima	Flour and feed	1876	85,000	300 bbls.	300 bbls.	6	W. and E.

TABLE NO. 2.—STATISTICS OF MANUFACTURES.

Summaries by Counties and Industries for all Plants Reported.

Goods Manufactured or Handled	Total number of pl'nts	Total capital invested in plant	Total daily capacity	Total daily output	Total males employed Skil'd	Un-skil'd	Total fe-males em-pl'y'd	Aver. hours per day Males	Fe-males	Aver. days per mo., males	Aver. mos. per year	Aver. days per mo., fe-males	Aver. wages, males Skilled	Un-skilled	Aver. wages, fe-males	Kind of power used Electric	Steam	Water
ADAMS COUNTY.																		
Flour and feed......	2	$140,000	800 bbls.	*300 bbls.	6	18	......	10	......	26	10½	......	$3 50	$2 50	......	2	......	......
ASOTIN COUNTY.																		
Flour and feed......	3	$42,500	250 bbls.	198 bbls.	15	20	......	12	......	26	8	......	$3 25	$2 50	......	......	2	......
Lumber	1	100,000	30,000ft.	25,000ft.	5	15	......	10	......	26		......	3 50	2 25	......	......	1	1
BENTON COUNTY.																		
Laundries	3	$831,000			6	5	24	10	10	26	12	21	$2 87	$2 41	$1 58	1	2	
Miscellaneous	2	115,000			4	8	......	12	......	27	12		8 37	2 50				1
CHEHALIS COUNTY.																		
Shingles	25	*$902,000	*4,290,000	‡3,555,000	345	223	......	10	......	23	10	......	$4 08	$2 30	......	1	22	......
Lumber	19	2,578,000	2,250,000ft.	2,050,000ft.	497	1,426	1	10	9	24	11	12	3 83	2 25	$2 00	......	19	......
Wood products	9	†295,000			154	88	88	9½	9½	25	12	......	3 80	2 21	......	4	5	......
Machinery	5	114,500			37	19	2	9½	10	26	12	24	3 40	2 47	......	5	......	......
Laundries	5	48,000			21	2	78	10	10	25	12	24	3 30	2 50	1 68	5	......	......
Miscellaneous	7	*582,000			188	98	31	9	8	29	8	25	3 50	2 25		......	7	......

*Two not reported.   †One not reported.   ‡Three not reported.

CHELAN COUNTY.

Product															
Flour and feed	2	$90,000	550 bbls.	350 bbls.	5	15	10	96	10	....	$4 00	$2 50	....	1	1
Lumber	2	*$350,000	225,000ft.	225,000ft.	93	105	10	25	9	22	8 00	2 12	$1 40	8	2
Miscellaneous	9	95,000	....	....	9	13	10	26	10	....	8 88	2 16	....	....	2

CLALLAM COUNTY.

Product															
Shingles	14	$61,500	785,000	708,000	78	88	10	22	8	30	$4 00	$2 41	....	....	13
Miscellaneous	2	89,000	12,000ft.	....	9	35	10	24	7	20	8 50	2 37	....	....	2

CLARKE COUNTY.

Product															
Lumber	15	*$848,000	620,000ft.	†485,000ft.	157	227	10	23	10	27	$3 64	$2 48	$1 75	1	15
Laundries	3	*$20,000	....	....	18	1	9	25	12	25	2 75	....	1 81	1	8
Miscellaneous	7	*335,000	....	....	89	119	10	25	11	28	8 14	2 11	1 10	2	5

COLUMBIA COUNTY.

Product															
Flour and feed	3	$105,000	560 bbls.	560 bbls.	15	8	10	20	11	....	$3 00	$2 50	....	1	16
Miscellaneous	2	45,000	....	....	4	3	10	25	11	....	4 25	2 25	....	1	18

COWLITZ COUNTY.

Product															
Lumber	16	*$388,000	507,000ft.	418,000ft.	96	287	10	24	10	....	$3 32	$2 36	....	1	16
Shingles	13	342,000	1,800,000	1,560,000	159	98	10	24	9	....	4 09	2 51	....	....	18

DOUGLAS COUNTY.

Product															
Flour and feed	2	$45,000	350 bbls.	225 bbls.	9	9	11	26	11	....	$3 25	$2 50	....	1	1
Lumber	1	6,000	12,000ft.	12,000ft.	4	10	....	26	5	....	3 50	2 50	....	1	1

FERRY COUNTY

Product															
Lumber	6	$51,000	212,000ft.	157,000ft.	31	57	10	23	9	25	$3 34	$2 54	....	....	5

FRANKLIN COUNTY.

Product															
Laundry	1	$10,500	$400 val.	....	2	8	10	25	12	....	$2 50	$1 66	$1 50	....	1

* One not reported.   † Three not reported.

GARFIELD COUNTY.

Goods Manufactured or Handled	Total number of plants	Total capital invested in plant	Total daily capacity	Total daily output	Skil'd	Un-skil'd	Total females employ'd	Males	Fe-males	Aver. days per mo., males	Aver. mos. per year	Aver. days per mo., fe-males	Skilled	Un-skilled	Aver. wages, fe-males	Electric	Steam	Water
Flour and feed	1	$20,000	125 bbls.	100 bbls.	2	3		10		26	8		$4 00	$3 00				1

GRANT COUNTY.

Goods Manufactured or Handled	Total number of plants	Total capital invested in plant	Total daily capacity	Total daily output	Skil'd	Un-skil'd	Total females employ'd	Males	Fe-males	Aver. days per mo., males	Aver. mos. per year	Aver. days per mo., fe-males	Skilled	Un-skilled	Aver. wages, fe-males	Electric	Steam	Water
Flour and feed	1	$100,000	500 bbls.	500 bbls.	2	13		10		25	10		$4 00	$2 50				1

JEFFERSON COUNTY.

Goods Manufactured or Handled	Total number of plants	Total capital invested in plant	Total daily capacity	Total daily output	Skil'd	Un-skil'd	Total females employ'd	Males	Fe-males	Aver. days per mo., males	Aver. mos. per year	Aver. days per mo., fe-males	Skilled	Un-skilled	Aver. wages, fe-males	Electric	Steam	Water
Shingles	8	*$335,400	590,000	†380,000	66	26		10		24	11		$4 08	$2 54			7	
Lumber	2	*7,000	190,000ft.	140,000ft.	6	322		10		23	12		4 25	2 28		1	2	
Miscellaneous	4	1,067,000			138	320	14	10	10	25	12	24	3 81	2 87	$1 30		4	

*One not reported. † Three not reported.

ISLAND COUNTY.

Goods Manufactured or Handled	Total number of plants	Total capital invested in plant	Total daily capacity	Total daily output	Skil'd	Un-skil'd	Total females employ'd	Males	Fe-males	Aver. days per mo., males	Aver. mos. per year	Aver. days per mo., fe-males	Skilled	Un-skilled	Aver. wages, fe-males	Electric	Steam	Water
Shingles	2	$11,000	*125,000	125,000	12	6		10		20	12		$3 50	$2 50			2	
Lumber	1	4,000	10,000ft.	5,000ft.	3	2		9					3 50	2 50			1	

KING COUNTY.

Goods Manufactured or Handled	Total number of plants	Total capital invested in plant	Total daily capacity	Total daily output	Skil'd	Un-skil'd	Total females employ'd	Males	Fe-males	Aver. days per mo., males	Aver. mos. per year	Aver. days per mo., fe-males	Skilled	Un-skilled	Aver. wages, fe-males	Electric	Steam	Water
Shingles	88	*1,061,600	6,055,000	†5,168,000	474	506	2	10	10	24	10	30	$3 89	$2 40	$1 89	2	37	
Lumber	57	†3,402,900	3,283,540ft.	†2,731,000ft.	1,050	2,298	3	10	10	24	11	30	3 30	2 30	2 02	4	56	
Wood products	33	§786,700			469	199	34	9	9	25	12	26	3 42	2 16	2 11	22	11	
Machinery	30	$4,860,200			722	679		9		25	12		3 85	2 28		29		
Laundry	12	471,800	‡$2,700 val.	‖$2,140 val.	80	214	439	10	10	26	12	26	3 08	2 07	1 68	2	11	
Flour, cereals, feed	9	$1,175,500			152	198	20	10	8	26	12	25	3 74	2 65	1 75	7	1	
Brick, clay products	7	829,000			101	244	1	10	8	26	12		3 28	2 34		4	1	
Beer	3	2,254,500	1,750 bbls.	980 bbls.	34	150		8		28	12		8 50	3 68		8	2	
Ice	2	215,000			25			8		30	12		8 44			2	1	

Crackers and candy	2	250,000	......	25	88	46	131	9	10	24	12	21	3 99	1 70	I 23	1	2
Packinghouse prod.	2	101,500	......	88	191	11		10	10	26	12	28	3 25	2 00	1 50	1	1
Printing	8	*110,000	......	180	10	45		9		26	12	25	3 89	2 00	1 89	8	
Wool and leather	8	130,000	......	32	30			9		26	12		2 83	2 16	......	2	1
Wall plaster	2	40,000	70 tons	2	9					26	12		3 50	2 37	......	2	
Miscellaneous	17	$4,664,700	40 tons	355	408	310		9		26	12	26	3 60	2 23	1 77	14	3

* One plant not reported. † Five plants not reported. ‡ Four plants not reported. § Two plants not reported. ‖ Three plants not reported.

KITSAP COUNTY.

Shingles	4	$65,750	*130,000	15	27			10	22	10	21	4 19	3 25	......		4
Lumber	5	†818,750	475,000ft.	114	355			10	25	11		4 02	2 10	1		4
Ship builders	1	300,000	‡350,000ft.	125	75	1	8	8	26	12	26	4 50	2 25	$2 50	1	

* Two not reported. † Two not reported. ‡ One not reported.

KITTITAS COUNTY.

Lumber	3	$27,500	*29,000ft.	15	34		10	25	9		3 92	2 62		8	3
Miscellaneous	6	†127,000	63,000ft.	28	14	9	8	28	2	24	2 98	2 00	$1 00	8	4

* Two not reported. † Four not reported.

KLICKITAT COUNTY.

Lumber	2	$7,500	*80,000ft.	6	9		10	29	6		3 00	2 50		2
Miscellaneous	2	31,000	†20,000ft.	8	2	4	10	26	12	20	2 75	2 50	$1 20	1

* One not reported. † Four not reported.

LEWIS COUNTY.

Shingles	12	$144,995	*1,459,000	189	97		10	22	11		4 16	2 58			12
Lumber	37	3,477,300	†1,707,000ft.	333	1,187	1	10	22	11	9	3 37	2 15		2	35
Wood products	11	217,800	2,187,000ft.	156	248		10	22	11		8 15	2 00	$2 00		11
Machinery	2	50,000	......	37	11		9	25	12		4 00	2 88		2	
Laundry	2	8,250	......	2	5	20	10	29	12	20	2 88	2 50	1 23	1	1
Miscellaneous	4	†95,000	......	19	112	15	10	25	12	25	8 30	2 16	1 60	8	

* One not reported. † Four not reported. ‡ One not reported.

LINCOLN COUNTY.

Goods Manufactured or Handled	Total number of pl'nts	Total capital invested in plant	Total daily capacity	Total daily output	Total males employed Skil'd	Un-skil'd	Total fe-males em-pl'y'd	Aver. hours per day Males	Fe-males	Aver. days per mo., males	Aver. mos. per year	Aver. days per mo., fe-males	Aver. wages, males Skilled	Un-skilled	Aver. wages, fe-males	Elec-tric	Steam	Water
Flour and feed	8	$374,000	3,100 bbls.	2,750 bbls.	44	77	......	10	......	26	9	......	$3 57	$2 43	$1 40	5	3	......
Miscellaneous	2	38,500	......	......	7	20	6	10	10	26	8	22	3 50	2 50		1	2	

MASON COUNTY.

Goods Manufactured or Handled	Total number of pl'nts	Total capital invested in plant	Total daily capacity	Total daily output	Total males employed Skil'd	Un-skil'd	Total fe-males em-pl'y'd	Aver. hours per day Males	Fe-males	Aver. days per mo., males	Aver. mos. per year	Aver. days per mo., fe-males	Aver. wages, males Skilled	Un-skilled	Aver. wages, fe-males	Elec-tric	Steam	Water
Shingles	4	$38,400	345,000	300,000	32	22		10		23	11		$4 46	$2 70			4	
Machine shop	2	14,000			10	10		10		26	12		3 75	2 44			2	

OKANOGAN COUNTY.

Goods Manufactured or Handled	Total number of pl'nts	Total capital invested in plant	Total daily capacity	Total daily output	Total males employed Skil'd	Un-skil'd	Total fe-males em-pl'y'd	Aver. hours per day Males	Fe-males	Aver. days per mo., males	Aver. mos. per year	Aver. days per mo., fe-males	Aver. wages, males Skilled	Un-skilled	Aver. wages, fe-males	Elec-tric	Steam	Water
Lumber	1	$5,000	20,000 ft.	20,000 ft.	4	12		10		22	4		$3 50	$2 50			1	

* One plant not reported.

PACIFIC COUNTY.

Goods Manufactured or Handled	Total number of pl'nts	Total capital invested in plant	Total daily capacity	Total daily output	Total males employed Skil'd	Un-skil'd	Total fe-males em-pl'y'd	Aver. hours per day Males	Fe-males	Aver. days per mo., males	Aver. mos. per year	Aver. days per mo., fe-males	Aver. wages, males Skilled	Un-skilled	Aver. wages, fe-males	Elec-tric	Steam	Water
Lumber	20	*1,816,000	1,472,000 ft.	1,135,000 ft.	290	1,008		10		24	11		$3 70	$2 15			20	
Shingles	9	145,500	1,168,000	1,148,000	117	49		10		24	10		3 98	2 36			9	
Wood products	8	160,000			24	36	32	10	9	26	12	26	3 08	1 92	$1 38		8	
Canned salmon	2	*15,300	1600 cases	780 cases	58	29	8	10		26	6	7	3 03	2 25	1 00		3	
Miscellaneous	3	73,000			16	16	5	10	9	25	12	20	3 66	2 50			3	

* One plant not reported.

PIERCE COUNTY.

Goods Manufactured or Handled	Total number of pl'nts	Total capital invested in plant	Total daily capacity	Total daily output	Total males employed Skil'd	Un-skil'd	Total fe-males em-pl'y'd	Aver. hours per day Males	Fe-males	Aver. days per mo., males	Aver. mos. per year	Aver. days per mo., fe-males	Aver. wages, males Skilled	Un-skilled	Aver. wages, fe-males	Elec-tric	Steam	Water
Lumber	*34	$389,200	2,213,000 ft.	*1,651,000 ft.	*605	1,628	10	10	9	25	10	24	$3 31	$2 13	$1 50	5	31	1
Shingles	21	1,108,500	2,465,000	*2,470,500	346	361	1	10	10	25	9	29	3 86	2 36		1	21	
Wood products	12	698,000			179	589	24	10	10	24	12	24	3 14	2 01	1 42	4	8	
Machinery	10	34,060			330	746	4	9	8	24	12	25	3 55	2 16	2 10	6	4	
Flour, cereals, feed	6	120,000			88	182	9	10	9	26	12	28	3 22	2 04	1 67	4	3	
Furniture	6	27,000			200	165	77	10	9	25	12	25	2 88	2 05	1 50	3	2	
Laundry	9	29,000	$1,520 val.	$1,150 val.	143	48	20	10	10	25	12	22	2 48	1 98	1 41	4	7	
Miscellaneous	14	†208,000			589	405	50	3	9	26	12	26	3 39	2 20	1 43	11	5	

* One plant not reported. † Three plants not reported.

SAN JUAN COUNTY.

Goods Manufactured or Handled	Total number of pl'nts	Total capital invested in plant	Total daily capacity	Total daily output	Total males employed Skil'd	Un-skil'd	Total females em-ploy'd	Aver. hours per day Males	Fe-males	Aver. days per mo. males	Aver. mos. per year	Aver. days per mo. fe-males	Aver. wages males Skilled	Un-skilled	Aver. wages fe-males	Electric	Steam	Water
Canned salmon	1	$20,000	2000 cases	750 cases	6	35	35	10	5	30	5	19	$2 18	......	$0 90	......	......	1

SKAGIT COUNTY.

Goods Manufactured or Handled	Total number of pl'nts	Total capital invested in plant	Total daily capacity	Total daily output	Total males employed Skil'd	Un-skil'd	Total females em-ploy'd	Aver. hours per day Males	Fe-males	Aver. days per mo. males	Aver. mos. per year	Aver. days per mo. fe-males	Aver. wages males Skilled	Un-skilled	Aver. wages fe-males	Electric	Steam	Water
Lumber	26	*966,500	1,425,000ft.	1,284,000ft.	263	524	1	10	10	25	11	30	$3 42	$2 23	......	......	26	......
Shingles	50	†760,000	5,961,000	5,640,700	560	351	1	10	10	24	9	30	4 25	2 50	$1 25	......	50	......
Canned salmon	4	251,000	10,000 cases	6,958 cases	98	157	100	10	10	26	6½	23	3 88	2 56	2 37	......	4	......
Laundry	4	24,300	$250 val.	$155 val.	9	4	32	10	10	24	12	20	2 81	2 22	1 31	......	4	......
Wood products	2	79,000	$185 val.	$185 val.	38			10		25	12		3 00			......	4	......
Machinery	2	23,000	$185 val.	$185 val.	24	9		10		26	12	28	3 50	2 50		......	2	......
Miscellaneous	5	947,000			72	146	11	10	10	23	10	28	2 87	2 06	1 87	1	4	......

* Six plants not reported. † Two plants not reported.

SKAMANIA COUNTY.

Goods Manufactured or Handled	Total number of pl'nts	Total capital invested in plant	Total daily capacity	Total daily output	Total males employed Skil'd	Un-skil'd	Total females em-ploy'd	Aver. hours per day Males	Fe-males	Aver. days per mo. males	Aver. mos. per year	Aver. days per mo. fe-males	Aver. wages males Skilled	Un-skilled	Aver. wages fe-males	Electric	Steam	Water
Lumber	1	$35,000	40,000ft.	35,000ft.	20	25	......	10	......	25	9	......	$3 00	$2 65	......	......	1	......

SNOHOMISH COUNTY.

Goods Manufactured or Handled	Total number of pl'nts	Total capital invested in plant	Total daily capacity	Total daily output	Total males employed Skil'd	Un-skil'd	Total females em-ploy'd	Aver. hours per day Males	Fe-males	Aver. days per mo. males	Aver. mos. per year	Aver. days per mo. fe-males	Aver. wages males Skilled	Un-skilled	Aver. wages fe-males	Electric	Steam	Water
Shingles	158	*2,842,689	21,015,000	†17,209,000	1,517	1,209	15	10	9	24	9	26	$4 12	$2 45	$1 30	......	158	......
Lumber	67	†2,686,346	‡3,747,000ft.	||2,612,000ft.	901	1,719	9	10	8	24	9½	26	3 50	2 27	1 75	......	67	......
Laundries	6	**52,000	$315 val.	**$397 val.	46	5	68	9	9	26	12	23	2 72	2 00	1 51	5	6	......
Machinery	7	**157,000			268	162	3	9	8	26	12	26	3 71	2 30	1 72	8	2	......
Wood products	5	166,000			106	109	3	10	8½	24	12	25	2 98	2 25		2	2	......
Meat, lard, etc.	2	**3,000			3	1		10		24	10		2 77	2 00		4		......
Miscellaneous	7	$155,000			210	53	30	10	10	24	10	24	3 07	2 20	1 85	4	3	......

* Eight plants not reported. † Fourteen plants not reported. ‡ Five plants not reported. § Three plants not reported. || Ten plants not reported.
** One plant not reported.

SPOKANE COUNTY.

Goods Manufactured or Handled	Total number of pl'nts	Total capital invested in plant	Total daily capacity	Total daily output	Total males employed Skil'd	Un-skil'd	Total females em-ploy'd	Aver. hours per day Males	Fe-males	Aver. days per mo., males	Aver. mos. per year	Aver. days per mo., fe-males	Aver. wages, males Skilled	Un-skilled	Aver. wages, fe-males	Elec-tric	Steam	Water
Lumber	25	$824,000	*1,195,000ft	†1,070,000ft	318	474	......	10	......	25	10	......	$3 54	$2 18	......	8	21	1
Shingles	9	†155,000	390,000	370,000	45	21	......	10	......	25	10	......	3 67	2 45	......	8	6	...
Wood products	18	435,600	......	......	390	230	......	10	......	25	12	......	3 45	2 20	......	14	4	...
Flour and feed	5	368,500	......	......	23	37	......	10	......	25	11	......	3 68	2 50	......	8	...	2
Laundries	15	343,000	$3,825 val.	$2,465 val.	80	126	460	10	10	26	12	24	3 02	2 88	$1 49	6	9	...
Clay products	5	428,000	......	......	128	257	......	10	......	26	12	......	3 62	2 87	......	2	8	...
Beer	8	1,290,000	1100 bbls.	450 bbls.	72	16	......	8	......	26	12	......	4 00	3 50	......	3	8	...
Machinery	14	1,048,000	......	......	415	485	......	9	......	26	12	......	3 73	2 65	......	...	14	...
Miscellaneous	30	3,065,000	......	......	349	465	165	9	9	26	12	25	3 20	2 23	1 60	23	6	1

* Six plants not reported. † Seven plants not reported. ‡ One plant not reported.

STEVENS COUNTY.

Goods Manufactured or Handled	Total number of pl'nts	Total capital invested in plant	Total daily capacity	Total daily output	Total males employed Skil'd	Un-skil'd	Total females em-ploy'd	Aver. hours per day Males	Fe-males	Aver. days per mo., males	Aver. mos. per year	Aver. days per mo., fe-males	Aver. wages, males Skilled	Un-skilled	Aver. wages, fe-males	Elec-tric	Steam	Water
Lumber	31	1500	1,363,000ft.	1,127,000ft.	226	586	8	10	......	24	7	30	$3 65	$2 41	$1 50	1	29	1
Brick	1	400,000	95 tons	70 tons	70	75	......	10	......	29	12	......	3 50	2 25	......	...	1	...

* One plant not reported.

THURSTON COUNTY.

Goods Manufactured or Handled	Total number of pl'nts	Total capital invested in plant	Total daily capacity	Total daily output	Total males employed Skil'd	Un-skil'd	Total females em-ploy'd	Aver. hours per day Males	Fe-males	Aver. days per mo., males	Aver. mos. per year	Aver. days per mo., fe-males	Aver. wages, males Skilled	Un-skilled	Aver. wages, fe-males	Elec-tric	Steam	Water
Shingles	6	$885,000	765,000	*595,000	78	38	......	10	......	23	9	......	$3 95	$2 35	......	...	6	...
Lumber	15	975,000	985,000ft.	†715,000ft.	202	341	......	10	......	23	11	......	3 55	2 29	......	...	14	...
Stone quarry	2	175,000	......	......	28	49	......	10	......	26	10	......	4 55	2 50	......	8	2	...
Miscellaneous	3	180,000	......	......	34	34	......	8	......	26	12	......	3 58	2 56	......	...	2	...

* One not reported. † No not reported.

WAHKIAKUM COUNTY.

Goods Manufactured or Handled	Total number of pl'nts	Total capital invested in plant	Total daily capacity	Total daily output	Total males employed Skil'd	Un-skil'd	Total females em-ploy'd	Aver. hours per day Males	Fe-males	Aver. days per mo., males	Aver. mos. per year	Aver. days per mo., fe-males	Aver. wages, males Skilled	Un-skilled	Aver. wages, fe-males	Elec-tric	Steam	Water
Canned salmon	5	*$123,000	†2200 cases	‡189 cases	7	66	3	8	10	26	5	26	$2 68	$1 50	......	...	5	...
Miscellaneous	2	22,000	......	......	23	24	......	10	......	24	10	......	3 25	2 50	......	...	2	...

* Two plants not reported. † One plant not reported. ‡ Four plants n ot reported.

WALLA WALLA COUNTY.

Mill work	5	$120,000			48	48	26	12		$3 80	$2 35		5	
Flour and feed	6	*$204,000			21	55	25	10	8	3 71	2 41		4	
Machinery	8	300,000			100	77	26	12	8	3 87	2 14		3	
Laundries	3	58,000			9	16	26	12	8	3 51	2 73	$2 62	3	
Beer	3	275,000	185 bbls.		11	3	26	10	2	3 87	3 00	1 86		
Miscellaneous	2	165,000	70 bbls.		22	39	28	9	10	3 87	2 50	2 80	2	2

* One plant not reported.

WHATCOM COUNTY.

Shingles	100	*1,061,750	6,785,000	†5,459,000	813	436	21	10	10	$4 00	$2 40	$1 28		100
Lumber	28	†1,497,500	1,198,000††	†1,082,000††	290	746	25	10	8	3 28	2 21	1 90	7	28
Machinery	8	*188,000	$110 val.	$86 val.	61	41	26	9	9	3 72	2 14	1 25		3
Laundry	8	49,000	$200 val.	‖$175 val.	22	22	26	12	10	3 00	2 25	1 30	4	3
Wood products	4	45,000	$375 val.	$340 val.	54	29	24	12	10	2 86	1 81		1	
Canned salmon	5	656,000	7850 cs s'l'n		191	302		5¼	7¾	3 50	2 35	1 90	2	5
Printing	2	50,000			50	66	26	12	8	3 62	2 30	2 46	1	
Miscellaneous	4	317,500			30	81	26	12	8	3 45	2 31	1 50	2	2

* One plant not reported. † Six plants not reported. ‡ Four plants not reported. § Three plants not reported. ‖ Two plants not reported.

WHITMAN COUNTY.

Flour and feed	9	$185,000	*875 bbls.	†615 bbls.	16	20	26	9	11	$3 80	$2 22		5	
Laundry	4	29,500	$408 val.	$236 val.	12	17		12	10	3 08	1 66		2	2
Beer	2	90,000	70 bbls.	23 bbls.	10	10	23	12	9	4 25	2 50	$1 40	1	2
Miscellaneous	2	26,000			11	4	26	12	10	3 90	2 25		1	

* One plant not reported. † One plant not reported.

YAKIMA COUNTY.

Lumber	2	$140,000	225,000 ft.	225,000 ft.	23	48	26	11	10	$4 44	$2 38		2	2
Laundry	2	60,000	*$200 val.	†$175 val.	6	8	26	12	10	3 35	2 00	$1 65	1	1
Miscellaneous	4	134,000			62	82	26	12	10	3 30	2 08		2	2

* One plant not reported. † One plant not reported.

—15

TABLE NO. 3.—STATISTICS OF MANUFACTURES.

Summary for the State by Counties.

COUNTIES	Total number of plants reported	Total capital invested in plant	Total males employed Skilled	Total males employed Un-skilled	Total females employed	Aver. hours per day Males	Aver. hours per day Females	Aver. days per mo., males	Aver. mos. per year	Aver. days per mo., females	Aver. wages, males Skilled	Aver. wages, males Unskilled	Aver. wages, females	Kind of power used Electric	Kind of power used Steam	Kind of power used Water
Adams	2	$140,000	6	18	..	10	..	28	10¼	..	$3.50	$2.50	..	2	..	1
Asotin	4	142,500	90	36	24	11	..	28	8	21	3.87	2.37	$1.58	..	8	1
Benton	5	146,000	10	8	..	..	..	26½	12	..	3.12	2.45	1.81	1	2	..
Chehalis	70	4,327,500	1,232	1,851	24	9½	10	25	11	20	3.64	2.33	1.40	15	58	..
Chelan	7	585,000	46	43	110	10	9	26	10	22	3.61	2.29	..	4	5	..
Clallam	10	100,500	87	78	15	10	10	28	7½	25	3.75	2.39	..	8	15	..
Clarke	25	1,008,000	294	446	11	10	9½	24	10	26	3.17	2.27	1.38	1	23	..
Columbia	5	160,000	19	11	61	10	..	25	7½	..	3.68	2.37	..	..	1	..
Cowlitz	19	725,000	245	335	..	10	..	24	9½	..	3.73	2.43	1.50	1	29	..
Ferry	6	61,000	31	57	12	10	..	23	9	25	3.34	2.54	..	1	6	..
Franklin	1	10,500	2	3	..	10	..	25	12	..	2.50	1.68	..	..	1	..
Garfield	1	20,000	2	8	..	10	..	26	8	..	4.00	2.00	..	..	1	..
Grant	1	100,000	2	18	..	10	10	25	10	24	4.05	2.50	1.30	1	1	..
Jefferson	14	1,109,400	200	669	14	10	..	24	12	..	3.50	2.50	..	..	13	..
Island	3	15,000	15	8	..	9½	9	20	12	29	3.50	2.31	1.70	98	130	2
King	220	17,343,400	8,789	5,167	996	9	9	24	11	29	4.24	2.20	2.50	6	8	1
Kitsap	10	684,500	254	457	1	9	8	25½	11	24	4.05	2.61	1.00	3	7	1
Kittitas	9	545,000	41	88	9	9	..	24½	10	30	2.83	2.00	1.20	..	3	..
Klickitat	4	38,500	9	11	4	10	9	24	9	24	3.46	2.29	1.61	6	62	..
Lewis	6	8,998,275	686	1,660	36	10	9	26	12	26	3.54	2.47	1.40	6	5	..
Lincoln	10	412,500	61	97	6	10	10	24	8½	22	4.11	2.57	..	..	1	..
Mason	6	62,400	42	32	12	10	..	26	4	18	3.50	2.50	1.19	..	37	..
Okanogan	..	5,000	4	12	40	10	9	23	10	24	3.49	2.28	1.57	38	81	1
Pacific	37	2,209,800	495	1,131	385	10	9	25	11	19	3.22	2.57	.90	..	1	..
Pierce	112	8,941,700	2,980	4,074	35	10	5	25	5	28	2.13	2.08	1.70	1	92	..
San Juan	1	20,000	6	35	205	10	10	19	9	20	3.39	2.94	..	1	..	..
Skagit	93	3,050,800	1,059	1,191	128	10	9	25	11	25	3.00	2.65	1.66	14	238	3
Snohomish	252	6,026,995	3,049	3,248	625	10	9½	25	9½	24½	3.27	2.21	1.54	57	68	1
Spokane	124	7,985,100	1,810	2,111	3	10	..	25	10	30	3.54	2.49	1.53	..	80	..
Stevens	32	977,500	296	611	..	10	..	24	7½	..	3.57	2.43	..	8	24	..
Thurston	29	1,415,000	880	457	90	10	..	25	10	26	2.94	2.00	2.29	7	7	..
Wahkiakum	7	145,000	20	90	57	9	10	25	7½	25	3.68	2.57	1.64	17	2	2
Walla Walla	22	1,122,000	211	236	278	9½	9	26	10¼	24	3.63	2.21	1.40	16	140	..
Whatcom	154	8,766,780	1,501	1,730	40	10	10	23	11	28	3.73	2.15	1.65	6	6	8
Whitman	17	380,000	49	61	65	10	10	26	11	22	3.78	2.04	..	8	5	1
Yakima	8	864,000	91	108	..	..	..	..	12	..	3.69	2.04	..	..	..	..
Grand totals and averages	**1,880**	**$98,161,170**	**18,984**	**26,141**	**3,194**	**9**	**9**	**23**	**10**	**24**	**$3.67**	**$2.36**	**$1.56**	**206**	**1,110**	**30**

NEW INDUSTRIES ESTABLISHED SINCE JANUARY 1, 1909.

TABLE 1.

BENTON COUNTY.

Town or City	Goods Manufactured or Handled	Date when est'b'lished	Capital invested in plant	Daily capacity	Daily output	Males employed Skil'd	Un-skil'd	Fe-males em-pl'y'd	Hours per day Males	Fe-males	Days per mo., males	Mos. per year	Days per mo., fe-males	Wages, Males Skilled	Un-skilled	Wages fe-males	Kind of power used
Kennewick	Laundry	1909	$15,000	$125 val.	$42 val.	3	2	10	10	10	26	12	24	$3 00	$3 00	$1 60	Steam
Kennewick	Laundry	1909	12,000			2	1	10	10	10	26	12	20	2 75	1 50	1 50	S. and E.

CHEHALIS COUNTY.

Town or City	Goods Manufactured or Handled	Date when est'b'lished	Capital invested in plant	Daily capacity	Daily output	Males employed Skil'd	Un-skil'd	Fe-males em-pl'y'd	Hours per day Males	Fe-males	Days per mo., males	Mos. per year	Days per mo., fe-males	Wages, Males Skilled	Un-skilled	Wages fe-males	Kind of power used
Aberdeen	Shingles	1909	$70,000	75,000	75,000	15	50		10		25	11		$3 50	$2 25		team
Kuhn	Shingles	1909	16,000	70,000	70,000	7	4		10					4 25	2 50		8am
Aberdeen	Shingles	1910	15,000	120,000	120,000	13			10		25	12		4 00			Eltric
Elma	Shingles	1910	5,000	90,000	90,000	9	5		10		30	12		4 50	3 00		Steam
Elma	Shingles	1909	5,000	40,000	35,000	6	10		10		20	11		4 00	3 00		team
	Lumber	1909	150,000	100,000ft.	95,000ft.	20	60		10		28	12		5 00	2 25		team
Aberdeen	Wood products	1909	100,000	30,000ft.	30,000ft.	40	20		10		25	12		3 50	2 00		Steam
Hoquiam	Wood products	1909	60,000	500 boards	350 broads	30	20		10		26	12		2 50	2 00		Electric
Aberdeen	Wood products	1909	40,000			30	5		10		25	12		2 75	1 75		Steam
Hoquiam	Wood products	1909		lbs	lbs	20	25		10		26			2 75	2 15		Eltic
Elma	Laundry	1909	7,000	$25 val.	$0 val.	5		4	10	10	26	12	26	4 00		$1 50	Steam
Hoquiam	Hay, flour, grain	1910		8 tons	2 tons	2			8		26	12		3 00			Steam

OLALLAM COUNTY.

Town or City	Goods Manufactured or Handled	Date when est'b'lished	Capital invested in plant	Daily capacity	Daily output	Males employed Skil'd	Un-skil'd	Fe-males em-pl'y'd	Hours per day Males	Fe-males	Days per mo., males	Mos. per year	Days per mo., fe-males	Wages, Males Skilled	Un-skilled	Wages fe-males	Kind of power used
Port Angeles	Shingles	1910	$5,000	60,000	60,000	6	8		10		20	8		$4 35	$2 25		Steam
Port Crescent	Shingles	1910	5,000	90,000	90,000	12	6		10		25			5 00	2 75		Steam
Port Angeles	Shingles	1909	4,000	35,000	35,000	8	2		10		24	7		4 00	3 00		Steam
Port Angeles	Shingles	1910	3,000	30,000	30,000	4	1		10			9		4 00	2 00		Steam
Port Angeles	Shingles	1909	2,500	60,000	10,000	4	4		10		25	9		4 00	2 50		Steam
Port Angeles	Shingles	1909	2,000	50,000	40,000	5	4	1	10		25	9		4 00	2 50		Steam

OLARKE COUNTY.

Town or City	Goods Manufactured or Handled	Date when est'b'lished	Capital invested in plant	Daily capacity	Daily output	Males employed Skil'd	Un-skil'd	Fe-males em-pl'y'd	Hours per day Males	Fe-males	Days per mo., males	Mos. per year	Days per mo., fe-males	Wages, Males Skilled	Un-skilled	Wages fe-males	Kind of power used
Heisson	Lumber	1909	$20,000	50,000ft.	50,000ft.	6	20		10		24	12		$3 00	$2 25		Steam
Vancouver	Laundry	1909	10,000	$100 val.	$75 val.	6		15	8	8	28	12	25	3 00		$1 40	Steam
Vancouver	Laundry	1909				6		18	10	10	25	12	28	2 75		1 40	Steam
Vancouver	Machinery	1910	7,000			4			9			12		4 00			Steam

COLUMBIA COUNTY.

Town or City	Goods Manufactured or Handled	Date when est'b'lished	Capital invested in plant	Daily capacity	Daily output	Males employed		Fe-males em-pl'y'd	Hours per day		Days per mo., males	Mos. per year	Days per mo., fe-males	Wages, Males		Wages to fe-males	Kind of power used
						Skil'd	Un-skil'd		Males	Females				Skilled	Un-skilled		
Dayton	Wagons	1909	$10,000	......	......	2	2	......	10	......	26	12	......	$3 50	$2 50	......	Electric
					COWLITZ COUNTY.												
Kalama	Lumber	1909	$90,000	85,000ft.	85,000ft.	29	30	......	10	......	28	12	......	$3 25	$1 12	......	Steam
Kelso	Lumber	1909	40,000	40,000ft.	6,000ft.	3	5	......	10	......	24	10	......	4 00	2 25	......	Steam
Castle Rock	Lumber	1910	4,000	10,000ft.	10,000ft.	2	5	......	10	......	25	......	......	4 00	2 75	......	Steam
Castle Rock	Lumber	1910	4,000	25,000ft.	20,000ft.	6	8	......	10	......	25	......	......	3 50	2 50	......	Steam
Kelso	Shingles	1910	12,000	100,000	100,000	8	5	......	10	......	29	12	......	4 70	2 50	......	Steam
					FERRY COUNTY.												
Karamin	Lumber	1909	$5,000	40,000ft.	30,000ft.	4	8	......	10	......	25	10	......	$3 00	$2 50	......	Electric
Barstow	Lumber	1909	6,000	22,000ft.	22,000ft.	8	13	......	10	......	29	8	......	3 00	2 50	......	Steam
Barstow	Lumber	1909	4,500	15,000ft.	15,000ft.	8	5	......	10	......	20	8	......	3 00	2 50	......	Steam
					ISLAND COUNTY.												
......	Shingles	1909	$6,000	100,000	100,000	8	6	......	10	......	25	10	......	$3 50	$2 50	......	Steam
	Shingles	1909	5,000	25,000	25,000	4	......	......	10	......	20	8	......	3 00	......	......	Steam
					JEFFERSON COUNTY.												
Port Townsend	Shingles	1909	$40,000	60,000	......	8	8	......	10	......	26	10	......	$4 00	$3 50	......	Steam
Quilcene	Shingles	1909	4,200	75,000	75,000	9	2	......	10	......	22	12	......	4 00	2 50	......	Steam
Center	Shingles	1909	2,000	60,000	60,000	8	7	......	10	......	24	11	......	4 10	3 50	......	Steam
					KING COUNTY.												
Seattle	Shingles	1909	$10,000	125,000	185,000	10	9	......	10	......	24	9	......	$3 75	$2 50	......	Steam
Sherwood	Shingles	1910	6,000	60,000	60,000	9	8	......	10	......	24	10	......	4 25	2 75	......	Steam
Seattle	Shingles	1910	900	25,000	17,000	3	1	......	10	......	20	8	......	4 00	2 00	......	Steam
Algona	Lumber	1909	20,000	30,000ft.	25,000ft.	7	12	......	10	......	20	12	......	3 50	2 30	......	Steam

Location	Product	Year	Capital	Output	Output 2								Wage hi	Wage lo		Power
Seattle	Lumber	1909	10,000	20,000ft.	15 ft.	7	7	10		24	12		3 00	2 25		Steam
Seattle	Wood products	1909	25,000	$100 val.		20	10	9		28	12		3 60	2 00		Steam
Seattle	Wood products	1909	10,000	$100 val.	$50 val	13	1	9		23	12		3 50	1 00		Electric
Seattle	Wood products	1910	6,000	$00 val.	$25 val	9	3	9		26	10		3 50			Electric
Seattle	Wood products	1910	5,000	$50	$35 val.	8	2	9		24	12		4 50	2 25		Electric
Seattle	Machinery	1909	1,800	Wal.	$100 val.	8	2	9		28	12		3 75	1 75		Electric
Seattle	Machinery	1910	15,000			4	6	10		24	12		3 00	2 50		Electric
Seattle	Laundry	1909	15,000	750 hp heat		3	1	10	10	30	12	30	8 25	1 50	$1 00	Electric
Seattle	Ice, steam heat	1909		90 tons ice		9	11	8		30	12					Electric
KITSAP COUNTY.																
Colby	Shingles	1909	$4000	10,000		4	10	10		20	10		$5 00	$2 25		Steam
Colby	Shingles	1909	1,750	50,000	50,000	2	9	10		24	11		4 25	2 00		Steam
Colby	Lumber	1909	15,000	25,000ft.	25,000ft.	4	10	10		30	10		5 00	2 25		Steam
Colby	Lumber	1909	3,750	25,000ft.	25,000ft.	4	19	10		24	11		4 25	3 00		Steam
KITTITAS COUNTY.																
Ellensburg	Lumber	1910	$10,00	20,000ft.	14,000ft.	5	9	10		26	8		$4 00	$3 00		Steam
LEWIS COUNTY.																
Centralia	Shingles	1910	$12,000	120,000	100,000	10	5	10		20	10		$4 00	$8 50		Steam
Chehalis	Shingles	1910	5,000	90,000	90,000	9	5	10		30	12		4 50	8 00		Steam
Chehalis	Lumber	1909	3,500	10,000ft.	10,000ft.	2	6	10		30			2 75	2 00		Steam
Chehalis	Wood products	1910	3 000		260 colums	20	15			25			2 50			Steam
MASON COUNTY.																
Shelton	Shingles	1909	$14,000	95,000	85,000	7	8	10		25			$5 00	$2 50		Steam
PACIFIC COUNTY.																
Raymond	Wood products	1910	$100,000	$1500 val.	$1500 val.	17	4	10	10	25	10	25	$2 75	$1 75	$1 25	Steam
Raymond	Shingles	1909	15,000	140,000	140,000	20		10		26	10		4 00			Steam
Francis	Shingles	1910	15,000	160,000		14	20	10		24	10		4 00	2 75		Steam
South Bend	Shingles	1910	10,000	110,000	110,000	18	7	10		22	10		4 25			Steam
PIERCE COUNTY.																
Milton	Lumber	1909	$50	20,000ft.	20,000ft.	14	16	10		26	12		$2 50	$2 25		Steam
Tacoma	Lumber	1910	10,000	35,000ft.	25,000ft.	7	8	10		26	12		3 00	2 25		Electric

PIERCE COUNTY—Continued.

Town or City	Gs mfd or mfd	Date when est'b-lished	Capital invested in plant	Daily capacity	Daily output	Males Skil'd	Males Un-skil'd	Fe-males em-pl'y'd	Hours Males	Hours Fe-males	Days per mo., males	Mos. per year	Days per mo., fe-males	Wages Males Skilled	Wages Males Un-skilled	Wages fe-males	Kind of power used
Orting	lbr	1910	$7,000	20,000ft.	15,000ft.	5	10		10		24			$3 25	$2 25		Steam
Gig Harbor	lbr	1910	3,000	10,000ft.	3,000ft.	2	1		10					3 00	2 00		Steam
	lbr	1909	3,000			10	2		10		26	12		3 00	1 50		1 mle
National	lbs	1909	10,000	100,000	100,000	8	4		10		26	10		4 50			Steam
	lbd	1910	4,000	100,000	90,000	11	5		10		20	8		4 00	2 50		t am
	Shingles	1910	5,000	25,000	25,000	4			10		24	8		3 75			Steam
	Shingles	1910	3,000	30,000	25,000	4	1		10		22			2 50	2 50		team
	lbs	1910	1,000	25,000	25,000	20	7		10					2 50			Steam
	wd	1909	12,000	150 beds		5	8		9		26	12		2 75	2 00		Mle
	wd	1909	1,000			2	2		10		26	12		3 00	3 00		Mle
	wd	1910	12,000			25	18				25	9		3 00	2 25		Electric
	wd rock	1909	12,000	400 tons	200 tons	4		7	8		25	12	24	2 25			mle
	dry	1909	10,000	$100 val.	$90 val.	25	1		10	10	26	12		3 00	2 50	$1 80	ten
	Cereals	1910	5,000	35 bbls.	10 bbls.	1			10								mle

SKAGIT COUNTY.

Town or City	Gs mfd or mfd	Date when est'b-lished	Capital invested in plant	Daily capacity	Daily output	Males Skil'd	Males Un-skil'd	Fe-males em-pl'y'd	Hours Males	Hours Fe-males	Days per mo., males	Mos. per year	Days per mo., fe-males	Wages Males Skilled	Wages Males Un-skilled	Wages fe-males	Kind of power used
	lbr	909	$55,000	50,000ft.	50,000ft.	8	32		10		26	11		$4 00	$2 50		Steam
	lber	910	15,000	20,000ft.	15,000ft.	4	20		10		26	12		4 00	2 00		team
	lbr	909	8,000	8,000ft.	8,000ft.	5	2		10		26	11		2 75	2 25		Steam
	lbs	910		16,000ft.	13,000ft.	4	6		10		26			3 25	2 50		Steam
	lber	910		50,000ft.	50,000ft.	17	12		10		24			3 50	2 00		Steam
	lber	910		125,000ft.	100,000ft.	15	7		10		26	10		3 50	2 00		Steam
	lber	910		16,000ft.	13,000ft.	4	6		10		24	10		3 25	2 50		Skm
	shles	909	35,000	200,000	200,000	17	8		10		26			5 00	3 50		Steam
	shles	908	32,000	225,000	225,000	18	9		10		24			3 25	2 50		Steam
	shles	1910	11,000	90,000	60,000	6	4		10		24			8 75	3 00		Steam
	shles	909	8,000	90,000	65,000	9	5		10		20	9		4 30	2 25		Steam
	shles	90	6,400	65,000	65,000	6	4		10		20	8		4 00	2 30		Steam
	Shingles	90	6,000	60,000	60,000	5	3		10					4 00	2 40		Steam
M. Vernon	wd	1910	7,000			8			10	10	25	12		4 00	2 75		team

SNOHOMISH COUNTY.

Town or City	Gs mfd or mfd	Date when est'b-lished	Capital invested in plant	Daily capacity	Daily output	Males Skil'd	Males Un-skil'd	Fe-males em-pl'y'd	Hours Males	Hours Fe-males	Days per mo., males	Mos. per year	Days per mo., fe-males	Wages Males Skilled	Wages Males Un-skilled	Wages fe-males	Kind of power used
Granite Falls	Shingles	1910	$75,000	250,000	5900	10	16		10		25			$3 50	$2 50		ten
Everett	Shingles	1909	37,500	300,000	270,000	18	14		10		24	10					team

Granite Falls	es	909	$25,000	130,000	130,000	10	6		10		20	10	4 00	2 25	Steam
	Shingles	99	20,000	150,000	150,000	10	13	15	10		24	4 90	3 00		tam
	es	99	20,000	90,000	90,000	10	6	8	11		22	5 50	2 50		tam
Clipper	es	99	20,000	160,000	180,000	10	10	3				3 50	2 50		Steam
ke	ber	99	20,000	175,000	175,000	10	8	15	10		26	2 50	2 50		tam
en	An	99	17,500	120,000	120,000	10	6	10	9		26	4 50	2 65		tam
Gl	An	99	15,000	140,000	140,000	10	7	13			23	3 00			tam
Index	es	999	15,000	80,000	100,000	10	5	2				3 20	2 00		tam
Monroe	es	99	16,000	25,000	65,000	10		12	12		29	4 50	2 25		tam
	Mn	99	14,000	125,000	100,000	10	4	10	12		25	4 00	2 50		tam
	An	99	14,000	100,000	100,000	10	4	2	4		24	5 00	2 50		tam
	es	909	12,500	30,000	140,000	10	1	13	6		25	3 75	2 25		tam
Granite Falls	es	99	11,600	140,000	180,000	10	4	3	10		26	4 00	2 25		tam
Go	es	909	10,000	130,000	100,000	10		6	10		25	3 25	2 75		tam
	Mn	90	10,000	70,000	70,000	10		22		30		4 25		$1 85		tam
	Mod	99	9,000	100,000	90,000	10	5	9	9			4 00	2 50		tam
	Shingles	90	8,000	100,000	100,000	10	4	9			24	3 85	2 00		tam
	Shingles	90	7,500	125,000	80,000	10	5	2	9		20	3 66	2 50		tam
	Shingles	999	6,000	30,000	30,000	10	2	6				3 60	2 50		tam
	Shingles	999	6,000	55,000		10	3	6		10		4 00	2 50	$1 33		tam
	es	90	5,200	60,000	60,000	10	9	6				4 00	2 50			tam
	es	1909	5,000	100,000	100,000	10	4	8				4 50	2 75			tam
	es	999	5,000	60,000	60,000	10	2	8				4 00	2 50			tam
	es	909	4,000	50,000	50,000	10	3	6				3 50	2 00			tam
	Kn	90	75,000	90,000	90,000	10	7	9		30		3 85	2 50	30	Steam
	tki	90	70,000	60,000t.	60,000ft.	10	34	20		25		3 15	2 75			tam
	le	90	38,500	17,500t.	25,000ft.	10	10	8	9			3 60	2 25			tam
Granite	es	90	20,000	34,000t.	40,000ft.	10	26	29		10	26	3 50	2 35			tam
	ed	90	20,000		40,000ft.	10	20	7	10			3 60	2 80			tam
ek	Es	90	20,000	70,000t.	30,000ft.	10	17	5				4 00	2 50			tam
Est	Is	90	17,500	12,000t.	12,000ft.	10						2 50				tam
	le	90	15,000	25,000t.	25,000ft.	10		30	12		23		2 65			tam
ke	iger	90	15,000	40,000t.	50,000ft.	10	15	6	4		25	3 50	2 25			tam
Gold	Mn	1909	12,500	30,000t.	40,000ft.	10	14	27			24	4 00	2 25			tam
	Me	999	10,000	25,000t.	25,000ft.	10	9	5			24	3 75	2 25			tam
	eh	99	7,500	23,000t.	23,000ft.	10	4	8				4 00				tam

SPOKANE COUNTY.

Spokane	hr	90	$8,000	20,000ft.	30,000ft.	10	5	4			25	$3 75	$2 35		Electric
Spokane	hr	90	4,000			10	8	4			26	3 50	2,50		Steam

SPOKANE COUNTY—Continued.

Town or City	Gs Mf or Hf	Date when est'b'lished	Capital invested in plant	Daily capacity	Daily output	Males employed Skill'd	Males employed Un-skill'd	Fe-males em-ploy'd	Hours per day Males	Hours per day Fe-males	Days per mo., males	Mos. per year	Days per mo. fe-males	Wages, Males Skilled	Wages, Males Un-skilled	Wages fe-males	Kind of power used
Sp	Mr	1910	$2,000	25,000ft.	15,000ft.	2	4		9		26	8		$3 00	$2 50		Steam
Sp	Wd	1909	35,000			9	7		9		26	12		3 50	2 00		Steam
Spo	Wd products	1909	10,000			8	4		10		26			2 75	1 75		Electric
Spo	Wd	1909	5,000			2			9		26			4 25			Electric
Sp	Wd	1909	5,000			10	2		9		26	12		3 00	2 25		Electric
Sp	Wd	1909	4,000			3	1		10		26	12		3 25	2 50		Electric
Si	Wd	1909	600			1		20	10	10	26	12	24	4 00		$1 95	Electric
Si	Ry	1909	26,000	$200 val.	$150 val.	4	6	22	10	10	26	12	25	3 50	2 50	1 50	Steam
de	Bdry	1909	10,000	$150 val.	$125 val.	5	7		10		26	12		3 75	1 50		Steam
Ford	Brick	1909	38,000	40000 brick	33000 brick	5	30		10		24	5		4 00	2 00		Steam
de	Ce dres	1909	10,000	25,000ft.		18	1	8	10	9	26	12	26	3 25	2 25	2 00	Electric
de	Mfs, sprgs	1909	15,000			15	7		10		26	12		3 00	2 25		Electric
de	Mfy.	sprgs	7,000			10	4		9		26	12		3 25	2 00		Electric

STEVENS COUNTY.

Town or City	Gs Mf or Hf	Date when est'b'lished	Capital invested in plant	Daily capacity	Daily output	Males employed Skill'd	Males employed Un-skill'd	Fe-males em-ploy'd	Hours per day Males	Hours per day Fe-males	Days per mo., males	Mos. per year	Days per mo. fe-males	Wages, Males Skilled	Wages, Males Un-skilled	Wages fe-males	Kind of power used
Ione	Mr	1910	$200,000	50, 000ft.	50, 000ft.	25	100		10		26	12		$5 00	$2 50		Electric
Clayton	Lumber	1910	20,000	20, 000ft.	140, 000ft.	12	8		10		26	12		3 25	2 50		Steam
Echo	Mr	1909	16,000	50, 000ft.	50, 000ft.	9	32		10		26			3 75	2 25		Steam
Newport	Mr	1909	8,000	30, 000ft.	30, 000ft.	2	9		10		24	7		8 00	2 25		Steam
Colville	Mr	1909	7,000	30, 000ft.	18, 000ft.	4	5		10		28	4		2 45	2 25		Steam
Colville	Mr	1909	5,000	30, 000ft.	25, 000ft.	2	3		10		30	8		8 50	2 25		Steam
Chewelah	Mr	1909	4,500	25, 000ft.	20, 000ft.	5	9		10		28			3 25	2 00		Steam
Colville	Mr	1909	3,000	25, 000ft.	25, 000ft.	3	18		10		28	9		3 75	2 50		Steam
Colville	Mr	1909	2,000	25, 000ft.	25, 000ft.	2	8		10		28	8		3 25	2 50		Steam
Blue Creek	Lumber	1909	2,000		18,000ft.	4	6		10		20	4		3 25	2 25		Steam

SKAMANIA COUNTY.

Town or City	Gs Mf or Hf	Date when est'b'lished	Capital invested in plant	Daily capacity	Daily output	Males employed Skill'd	Males employed Un-skill'd	Fe-males em-ploy'd	Hours per day Males	Hours per day Fe-males	Days per mo., males	Mos. per year	Days per mo. fe-males	Wages, Males Skilled	Wages, Males Un-skilled	Wages fe-males	Kind of power used
Stevenson	Mr	1909	$35,000	40,000ft.	35,000ft.	20	25		10		25	9		$3 00	$2 65		Steam

THURSTON COUNTY.

Town or City	Gs Mf or Hf	Date when est'b'lished	Capital invested in plant	Daily capacity	Daily output	Males employed Skill'd	Males employed Un-skill'd	Fe-males em-ploy'd	Hours per day Males	Hours per day Fe-males	Days per mo., males	Mos. per year	Days per mo. fe-males	Wages, Males Skilled	Wages, Males Un-skilled	Wages fe-males	Kind of power used
Tenino	Mr	1909	$200,000	75,000ft.	60,000ft.	15	30		10		15	12		$3 00	$2 00		Steam
Grand Mound	Mer	1910	8,000	25,000ft.	25,000ft.	10	13		10		20	8		4 00	2 50		Steam
Rochester	Mr	1909	7,000	20,000ft.	20,000ft.	5	4		10					3 50	2 50		Steam

WALLA WALLA COUNTY.

Walla Walla	Feed	1909	$80,000	300 tons		18 tons	8	11	10		26	8	$5 00	$2 50	Electric
Walla Walla	Feed	1909	14,000	25 tons			1	4	10			8	4 00	2 50	Electric

WHATCOM COUNTY.

Maple Falls	Shingles	1909	$20,000	100,000	100,000		10	5	10		24	8	$4 00	$2 50	Steam
Maple Falls	Shingles	1909	10,000	75,000	75,000		8	5	10		25	9	5 00	3 00	Steam
Maple Falls	Shingles	1909	5,000	50,000	50,000		10	5	10		24	10	350	3 00	Steam
Lynden	Shingles	1909	5,000	5,000	70,000		8	8	10		25	10	40	2 50	Steam
Ufr	Shingles	1910	4,000	50,000	50,000		6	8	10		22		50	2 50	Steam
Lynden	Shingles	1910	4,000	75,000	70,000		9	2	10			10	400	2 25	Steam
Bellingham	Shingles	1909	3,500	30,000	30,000		5	1	10				375	2 25	Steam
...	...	1909	3,000	50,000	50,000		7		10		25	10	3 50	2 00	Steam
Goshen	Lumber	1910	80,000	100,000ft.	100,000ft.		10	80	10		26	12	8 00	250	Steam
Sumas	Lumber	1909	22,000	25,000ft.	25,000ft.		6	14	10				3 50	2 25	Steam
Ferndale	Lumber	1909	10,000	40,000ft.	30,000ft.		8	10	8		25	12	375	1 75	Steam
Deming	Lumber	1909	10,000	20,000ft.	15,000ft.		5	13	10		25	11	3 00	2 00	Steam
Blaine	Lumber	1910	6,000	20,000ft.	20,000ft.		2	9	10		20	9	3 00	2 00	Steam
Bellingham	Machinery	1910	3,000	7,000ft.			2	3	9		23		3 25	2 50	Steam
Bellingham	Sprgs, mattresses	1909	1,500	$15 val.	$15 val.						25	12			Electric
			7,500	100 springs	50 springs		8	5	8	8	25	12	3 00	2 00	Electric
Bellingham	Canned salmon	1909	26,000	100 mttr.	50 mttr.	per season	26	22	10	10	25	20	8 00	1 50	Steam

NEW INDUSTRIES ESTABLISHED SINCE JANUARY 1, 1909.

TABLE No. 2.—Showing a summary by counties of all industries reported.

Goods Manufactured or Handled	Total number of plants	Total capital invested in plant	Total daily capacity	Total daily output	Total males employed — Skilled	Total males employed — Un-skilled	Total fe-males em-ploy'd	Aver. hours per day — Males	Aver. hours per day — Fe-males	Aver. days per mo., males	Aver. mos. per year	Aver. days per mo., females	Aver. wages, males — Skilled	Aver. wages, males — Un-skilled	Aver. wages, fe-males	Kind of power used — Steam	Kind of power used
BENTON COUNTY.																	
Laundry	2	$17,000	......	......	4	8	20	10	10	26	12	22	$2 87	$2 25	$1 55	1	1 S.-E.
CHEHALIS COUNTY.																	
Shingles	5	$111,000	395,000	390,000	50	60	......	10	......	28	12	......	$4 05	$2 69	......	4	1 E.
Wood products	4	200,000	......	......	120	70	......	10	......	26	12	......	2 88	1 98	......	2	2 E.
Miscellaneous	8	157,000	......	......	27	60	4	10	10	26	12	......	4 00	1 50	$1 50	3	
OLALLAM COUNTY.																	
Shingles	6	$21,500	325,000	295,000	34	20	......	10	......	23	8	......	$4 28	$2 50	......	5	
CLARKE COUNTY.																	
Laundry	2	$10,000	......	......	12	20	38	9	9	25	12	25	$2 87	......	$1 40	2	
Miscellaneous	2	27,000	......	......	10	......	2	9	......	25	12	......	3 50	$2 25	......	2	
COLUMBIA COUNTY.																	
Wagons	1	$10,000	......	......	2	2	......	10	......	26	12	......	$3 50	$2 50	......	......	1 E.
COWLITZ COUNTY.																	
Lumber	4	$138,000	180,000ft.	121,000ft.	31	48	......	10	......	24	11	......	$3 69	$2 10	......	4	
Shingles	1	12,000	100,000	100,000	8	5	......	10	......	26	12	......	4 70	2 50	......	1	
FERRY COUNTY.																	
Lumber	3	$18,500	77,000ft.	77,000ft.	10	21	......	10	......	22	8	......	$3 00	$2 50	......	2	1 E.

ISLAND COUNTY.

Product																
Shingles	2	$11,000	125,000	125,000	12	6	10		23	11		$3 50	$2 50		2	

JEFFERSON COUNTY.

Product																
Shingles	3	$162,000	195,000	115,000	22	12	10		23	11		$4 08	$2 50		8	

KING COUNTY.

Product																
Shingles	8	$25,000	210,000	202,000	22	9	10		23	9		$4 00	$2 59		8	3 E.
Lumber	2	$30,000	50,000ft.	40,000ft.	14	25	10		23	12		$3 25	$2 28		3	2 E.
Wood products	4	$46,000			45	16	9		28	12		$3 58	$1 83		1	
Machinery	2	$7,400			7	8	9		25	12		$4 13	$2 13			
Miscellaneous	2	$30,000			6	1	9	10	30	12	30	$3 13	$1 50	$1 00	1	1 E.

KITSAP COUNTY.

Product																
Shingles	2	$18,750	60,000	50,000	6	19	10		22	10		$4 68	$2 18		2	
Lumber	2	$18,750	50,000ft.	25,000ft.	8	29	10		22	10		$4 63	$2 13		2	

KITTITAS COUNTY.

Product																
Lumber	1	$10,000	20,000ft.	14,000ft.	5	9	10		26	8		$4 00	$3 00		1	

LEWIS COUNTY.

Product																
Shingles	2	$17,000	210,000	190,000	19	10	10		20	11		$4 25	$2 75		2	
Miscellaneous	2	$6,500			22	21	10		22			$2 63	$2 00		2	

MASON COUNTY.

Product																
Shingles	1	$14,000	95,000	85,000	7	3	10		25			$5 00	$2 50		1	

PACIFIC COUNTY.

Product																
Shingles	3	$40,000	410,000	250,000	52	7	10		24	10		$4 08	$2 75		3	
Wood products	1	$100,000			17	4	10	20	25		25	$2 75	$1 75	$1 25	1	

PIERCE COUNTY.

Goods Manufactured or Handled	Total number of plants	Total capital invested in plant	Total daily capacity	Total daily output	Total males employed Skilled	Total males employed Un-skilled	Total females em-ploy'd	Aver. hours per day Males	Aver. hours per day Females	Aver. days per mo., males	Aver. mos. per year	Aver. days per mo., females	Aver. wages, males Skilled	Aver. wages, males Un-skilled	Aver. wages, females	Kind of power used Steam	Kind of power used
Lumber	5	$385,000	85,000ft.	63,000ft.	38	32	...	10	...	25	12	...	$2 95	$2 05	...	3	2 E.
Shingles	5	23,000	280,000	265,000	31	17	...	10	...	23	9	...	3 69	2 50	...	5	3 E.
Wood products	3	23,000	...	...	27	10	...	9	...	26	12	...	2 75	2 00	...	...	2 E.
Miscellaneous	3	27,000	...	...	30	19	7	9	10	26	11	24	2 75	2 38	$1 30	1	

SKAGIT COUNTY.

Goods Manufactured or Handled	Total number of plants	Total capital invested in plant	Total daily capacity	Total daily output	Total males employed Skilled	Total males employed Un-skilled	Total females em-ploy'd	Aver. hours per day Males	Aver. hours per day Females	Aver. days per mo., males	Aver. mos. per year	Aver. days per mo., females	Aver. wages, males Skilled	Aver. wages, males Un-skilled	Aver. wages, females	Kind of power used Steam	Kind of power used
Lumber	7	$78,000	285,000ft.	249,000ft.	57	85	...	10	...	26	11	...	$3 46	$2 25	...	7	
Shingles	6	98,400	730,000	675,000	61	31	...	10	...	22	9	...	4 23	2 60	...	6	
Wood products	1	7,000	...	...	3	...	...	10	...	25	12	...	4 00	...	...	1	

SNOHOMISH COUNTY.

Goods Manufactured or Handled	Total number of plants	Total capital invested in plant	Total daily capacity	Total daily output	Total males employed Skilled	Total males employed Un-skilled	Total females em-ploy'd	Aver. hours per day Males	Aver. hours per day Females	Aver. days per mo., males	Aver. mos. per year	Aver. days per mo., females	Aver. wages, males Skilled	Aver. wages, males Un-skilled	Aver. wages, females	Kind of power used Steam	Kind of power used
Shg's	29	$428,000	3,195,000	2,880,000	241	147	2	10	9	24	9	30	$3 30	$2 46	...	28	
Lumber	12	821,000	410,000ft.	856,000ft.	150	159	...	10	...	24	9	...	3 58	2 42	...	11	

SPOKANE COUNTY.

Goods Manufactured or Handled	Total number of plants	Total capital invested in plant	Total daily capacity	Total daily output	Total males employed Skilled	Total males employed Un-skilled	Total females em-ploy'd	Aver. hours per day Males	Aver. hours per day Females	Aver. days per mo., males	Aver. mos. per year	Aver. days per mo., females	Aver. wages, males Skilled	Aver. wages, males Un-skilled	Aver. wages, females	Kind of power used Steam	Kind of power used
Lumber	3	$14,000	55,000ft.	35,000ft.	10	17	...	10	...	26	9	...	$3 40	$2 45	...	3	1 E.
Wood products	6	39,600	...	...	33	14	...	9	...	26	12	...	3 54	2 13	...	1	5 E.
Laundry	2	36,000	...	...	9	13	42	10	10	26	12	24	3 13	2 00	$1 67	1	
Mrell	4	70,000	...	...	54	42	3	10	9	26	10	26	3 38	2 25	...	1	3 E.

STEVENS COUNTY.

Goods Manufactured or Handled	Total number of plants	Total capital invested in plant	Total daily capacity	Total daily output	Total males employed Skilled	Total males employed Un-skilled	Total females em-ploy'd	Aver. hours per day Males	Aver. hours per day Females	Aver. days per mo., males	Aver. mos. per year	Aver. days per mo., females	Aver. wages, males Skilled	Aver. wages, males Un-skilled	Aver. wages, females	Kind of power used Steam	Kind of power used
Lumber	10	$267,500	5,850,000ft.	501,000ft.	68	188	...	10	...	24	7	...	$3 45	$2 38	...	9	1 E.

SKAMANIA COUNTY.

Goods Manufactured or Handled	Total number of plants	Total capital invested in plant	Total daily capacity	Total daily output	Total males employed Skilled	Total males employed Un-skilled	Total females em-ploy'd	Aver. hours per day Males	Aver. hours per day Females	Aver. days per mo., males	Aver. mos. per year	Aver. days per mo., females	Aver. wages, males Skilled	Aver. wages, males Un-skilled	Aver. wages, females	Kind of power used Steam	Kind of power used
Lumber	1	$35,000	40,000ft.	35,000ft.	20	25	...	10	...	25	9	...	$3 00	$2 65	...	1	

THURSTON COUNTY.

Goods Manufactured or Handled	Total number of plants	Total capital invested in plant	Total daily capacity	Total daily output	Total males employed Skilled	Total males employed Un-skilled	Total females em-ploy'd	Aver. hours per day Males	Aver. hours per day Females	Aver. days per mo., males	Aver. mos. per year	Aver. days per mo., females	Aver. wages, males Skilled	Aver. wages, males Un-skilled	Aver. wages, females	Kind of power used Steam	Kind of power used
Lumber	3	$215,000	120,000ft.	105,000ft.	30	47	...	10	...	18	10	...	$3 50	$2 38	...	3	

WALLA WALLA COUNTY.

Feed	2	$94,000			4	15	10		26	8		$4 50	$2 50			2 E.

WHATCOM COUNTY.

Shingles	8	$54,500	505,000	495,000	63	27	10		24	10		$4 08	$2 59		8
Lumber	6	151,000	212,000ft.	190,000ft.	96	129	10		24	11		8 25	2 17		6
Miscellaneous	3	34,500			31	27	9	9	25	12	26	8 00	1 75	$1 50	1
															2 E.

NEW INDUSTRIES ESTABLISHED SINCE JANUARY 1, 1909.

TABLE No. 3.—Final summaries by counties for all industries reported

COUNTIES	Total number of plants	Total capital invested in plant	Total males employed — Skilled	Total males employed — Unskilled	Total females employed	Aver. hours per day — Males	Aver. hours per day — Females	Aver. days per mo., males	Aver. mos. per year	Aver. days per mo., females	Aver. wages, males — Skilled	Aver. wages, males — Unskilled	Aver. wages, females	Kind of power used — Steam	Kind of power used — Electric	Kind of power used — Steam and electric
Benton	2	$17,000	4	8	20	10	10	26	12	22	$2 87	$2 25	$1 55	1		1
Chehalis	12	518,000	197	199	4	10	10	25	12		3 64	2 30	1 50	9	8	
Clallam	6	21,500	34	20		10		28	8	25	4 28	2 25		5		
Clarke	4	87,000	22	20	38	9	9	25	12		3 19	2 25	1 40	4	1	
Ella	1	10,000	2	2		10		26	12		3 50	2 50		5		
Cowlitz	5	150,000	39	56		10		25	12		4 20	2 33		2		
Ferry	8	18,500	10	21		10		22	8		3 00	2 50		8		
Island	2	11,000	12	6		10					3 50	2 50		7		
...mon	8	162,000	22	12	11	10	10	23	11	30	4 08	2 50	1 00	4		
King	18	188,400	94	59		9		25	12	90	3 90	2 08		4	6	
Kitsap	4	37,500	14	48		10		22	10		4 08	2 13		5		
...lias	1	10,000	5	9		10		26	8		4 00	3 00		2		
Lewis	4	23,500	41	31		10		21	11		3 44	2 38		1		
...mon	1	14,000	7	8		10		25			5 00	2 50		1		
Pacific	4	140,000	69	11	20	10	10	25	10	25	3 42	2 25	1 25	9	7	
Pierce	16	111,000	196	78	7	10	10	26	11	24	3 04	2 23	1 30	14		
...it	14	183,400	121	116		10		24	9		3 90	2 43		39		
...mish	41	749,000	391	306	2	10	9	28	12	30	3 67	2 44	1 67	6		
Eye	15	179,600	108	88	45	10	10	24	7	25	2 90	2 21		9	9	
Stevens	10	287,500	68	98		10		24	9		3 45	2 38		9	1	
...lla	1	85,000	90	25		10		25	10		3 00	2 66		8		
Thurston	8	215,000	30	47		10		18	8		3 50	2 88			2	
...lla Walla	2	94,000	4	5		10		26	11		4 50	2 50			2	
Whatcom	17	240,000	130	188	22	9	9	24	11	26	3 43	2 27	1 50	15		
Grand totals and averages	184	$3,882,900	1,568	1,626	164			24	10	26	$3 67	$2 39	$1 39	145	31	1

STATISTICS OF STEAM RAILROADS

STATISTICS OF STEAM RAILROADS.

NORTHERN PACIFIC RAILWAY COMPANY.

NUMBER OF MEN EMPLOYED IN EACH DEPARTMENT, WITH DAILY OR MONTHLY WAGES PAID.

DEPARTMENTS.	Number of employes....	*Number of days per month......	Wages per day or month......	Number of hours per day....	REMARKS
Conductors—passengers	81	......	$4 99	10	
Conductors—freight	224	......	3 97	10	
Engineers—passengers	103	......	5 37	10	
Engineers—freight	179	......	7 35	10	
Engineers—switch	59	......	3 96	10	
Firemen—passengers	103	......	3 58	10	
Firemen—freight	179	......	4 88	10	
Firemen—switch	58	......	2 63	10	
Brakemen—passengers	132	......	2 63	10	
Brakemen—freight	460	......	2 81	10	
Switchmen—yard	307	......	3 74	10	
Flagmen	148	......	1 82	12	
Engine hostlers	23	......	3 35	12	
Machinists	224	......	3 92	9	
Machinist helpers	128	......	2 21	9	
Boiler makers	55	......	3 94	9	
Boiler maker helpers.................	78	......	2 32	9	
Blacksmiths	58	......	3 46	9	
Blacksmith helpers	111	......	2 22	9	
Car builders	72	......	3 02	10	
Car repairers	436	......	2 32	10	
Car oilers	98	......	2 47	10	
Coach painters	52	......	2 59	10	
Bridge and building painters........	8	....	2 74	10	
Bridge and building carpenters.......	509	......	2 79	10	
Bridge and building helpers..........	28	......	2 25	10	
Section foremen	287	......	2 24	10	
Section men	2,908	......	1 69	10	
Freight house men....................	480	......	1 94	10	
Train dispatchers	58	......	4 70	8	
Train masters	10	......	5 54	8	
Telegraph operators	329	......	2 39	9	
Office help	755	......	2 42	9	
Electricians	7	......	3 52	10	
Engineers—stationary	7	......	2 26	10	
Firemen—stationary	4	......	2 48	12	
Station agents	171	......	2 50	10	
Street car conductors................	......	......	....	....	
Street car gripmen..................	......	......	....	....	
Street car motormen.................	......	......	....	....	
Other help	1,586	......	2 41	10	
Totals...........................	10,454	......	....	....	

* It is not practicable to say how many days per month each employe averages.

—16

GREAT NORTHERN RAILWAY—CASCADE DIVISION:
NUMBER OF MEN EMPLOYED IN EACH DEPARTMENT, WITH DAILY OR MONTHLY WAGES PAID.

DEPARTMENTS.	Number employed	Number of days each month.	Wages per day or month.	Number of hours per day.	REMARKS.
Conductors — passengers	13 regular / 3 extra	Calendar month / As opportunity permits	$150	Average about 8 hours	Paid by schedule, 10 per cent higher over mountains.
Conductors — freight	28 / 6		$3.83 per 100 miles / $4.18 per 100 miles / $4.02 per 100 miles	Not over 16 hours	$5 difference account less than 1 year svc.
Brakeman — passenger	5 / 13		$81.50 / $76.50	Average about 8 hours	All paid by schedule, make time depending on amt. of business.
Brakeman — freight	6 / 42 regular / 39 extra		$2.81, $2.97, $2.68, $2.56 and $2.97 per 100 miles	Not over 16 hours	
Switchmen — yard	36	Calendar	$2.56	10 hours	
Flagman	1	Calendar		10 hours	
Engineers — passenger	15			Not over 16 hours	
Firemen — passenger	15				
Engineers — freight	88				
Firemen — freight	102				
Firemen — switch.	11	6 working days per wk.	$3.10 per day	11 hours	
Engine hostlers	11	6 or'ing days	42c per hour.	10 hours	
Machinists	6	6 working days	$110 per mth	10 hours	Paid overtime for Sundays.
Boiler makers	13	6 working days	$90 per month	10 hours	
Boiler maker helpers	1	6 working days	$60 per mth	10 hours	
Blacksmiths	2	6 working days	3c per hour.	10 hours	
Car repairers	3	6 working days	22c per hour.	10 hours	
Bridge carpenters	9	6 working days	$2.40 per dy	10 hours	
Bridge helpers	43	6 working days	$2.75 per dy	10 hours	
Section foremen	39	6 working days	$2.00 per day	10 hours	{1, $80; 2, $75; 1, $72.50; 10, $70; 17 $65; 27, $90 per month}
Section men	58		$60 to $80 per month	10 hours	
	1		$1.00 per day	10 hours	
	136		$1.25 per day	10 hours	
	129		$1.30 per day	10 hours	
	212		$1.20 per day	10 hours	
	196		$1.50 per day	10 hours	
Freight house men	44	Working month	$50 to $100 per mnth	8 hours	
Train dispatchers	5		$140	11 hours	
Telegraph operators	47 / 10 / 6		$65 / $70 / $75	8 hrs	
Office help	1		$60	6 hours	
Electricians	47		$50 to $125	10 hours	
Agents	1 / 12		$90 / $85 to $200	10 hours	Exclusive agents.

GREAT NORTHERN RAILWAY—EASTERN WASHINGTON.

NUMBER OF MEN EMPLOYED IN EACH DEPARTMENT, WITH DAILY OR MONTHLY WAGES PAID.

DEPARTMENTS.	Number employed.	Number of days each month.	Wages per day or month.	Number of hours per day	REMARKS.
Conductors—passenger	8	20	$140 month	10 hours	
Conductors—freight	45	20	$125 month	16 hours	
Brakemen—passenger	15	20	$72.50 mth	10 hours	
Brakemen—freight	100	30	$75 month	16 hours	
Switchmen—yard	{ 22 foremen, 44 helpers }	30	$3.20 day / $2.90 day	10 hrs.	
Flagmen	1	30 and 31	$45 month	10 hrs.	
Engineers—passenger	12	30	$4.25 per 100 miles	12 hrs.	
Engineers—freight	54	30	$4.50 per 100 miles	12 hrs.	
Engineers—switch	12	30	$3.30 per 100 miles	12 hours	
Engineers—stationary					
Engine hostlers	8	30 and 31	$2.70 day	10 hours	
Machinists	15	26	$3.70 day	10 hours	
Boiler makers	4	26	$3.70 day	10 hours	
Blacksmiths	2	26	$3. 90day	10 hours	
Blacksmith helpers	2	26	$1. 90day	10 hours	
Car builders	25	26 and 30	$60 to $70 month	12 hrs.	
Car repairers					
Car oilers					
........ters					
building painters	24	26	$2.75 and $3.00 day	10 hours	
building carpenters	30	26	$2.25 and $2.50 day	10 hours	
building helpers	54	30	$60 mth	10 hours	
Section men	350	26	$1.35 dy / $1.50 day	10 hours	{ $1.35 for Japs / $1.50 for white men }
Freight house men	60	30 and 31	$2.25 day	10 hours	
Train dispatchers	3	30 and 31	$60 to $100 month	8 hours	
Telegraph operators and agents	60	30 and 31	$30 mth / $60 to $90 mth	9 to 12 hours	
Office help	67	30 and 31	$40 to $100 mth	10 hours	

OREGON RAILROAD & NAVIGATION COMPANY.

NUMBER OF MEN EMPLOYED IN EACH DEPARTMENT, WITH DAILY OR MONTHLY WAGES PAID.

DEPARTMENTS.	Number of employed.	Number of days each month.	Wages per day or month.	Number of hours per day.
Conductors—passengers	5	30	$140 00	10
Conductors—freight	27	30	3 45	10
Brakemen—passenger	10	30	81 20	10
Brakeman—freight	47	30	2 56½	10
Switchmen—yard	13	30	2 80	10
Flagmen	2	30	1 50	12
Engineers—passengers	15	28	4 25	8
Engineers—freight	36	28	4 25	10
Engineers—switch	7	30	3 10	10
Engineers—stationary	2	30	1 90	11
Engine hostlers	8	30	2 50	11
Machinists	13	26	3 10	9
Boiler makers	3	26	3 10	9
Blacksmiths	2	26	3 10	9
Blacksmith helpers	2	26	2 10	10
Car builders	19	30	2 25	10
Car repairers	...	...	...	...
Car oilers	...	...	...	...
Car painters	2	26	2 50	10
Bridge and building painters	59	26	2 50	10
Bridge and building carpenters	1	26	2 25	10
Bridge and building helpers	61	30	57 50	10
Section men	239	26	1 75	10
Section men	48	30	55 00	10
Freight house men	3 Trick, 2 Chief	30	130, 150 and 135	8
Telegraph ...	40	30	60 00	12
Office help	62	30	65 00	10

COLUMBIA & PUGET SOUND RAILROAD COMPANY.

NUMBER OF MEN EMPLOYED IN EACH DEPARTMENT, WITH DAILY OR MONTHLY WAGES PAID.

DEPARTMENTS.	Number of employed.	Number of days each month.	Wages per day or month.	Number of hours per day.	REMARKS.
Conductors—passenger	1	30	$140.00 mnth	8	
Conductors—freight	4	30	$3.85 day	10	
Brakemen—passenger	1	30	$90.00 month	8	
Brakemen—freight	8	30	$2.65 day	10	
Switchmen—yard	6	30	1, $125 month; 2, $3.20 day; 2, $3.40 day; 1, $3.10 day	10	
Flagmen	1	30	$50.00 mnth	12	
Engineers—passenger	2	30	41c hour	8	
Firemen—passenger	2	30	24½c hur	8	
Engineers—freight	4	30	47½c hour	10	
Firemen—freight	4	30	30c hour	10	
Engineers—switch	2	30	37½c hour	10	
Firemen—switch	2	30	22½c hour	10	
Engine hostlers	2	30	$2.70 day	12	
Machinists	6	26	40c hour	9	
Boiler makers	3	26	1, $150 month; 2, 40 and 50c hour.	9	
Blacksmiths	3	26	1, 40c hour; 2, 36c hour	9	
Blacksmith helpers	3	26	35c hour	9	
Car builders	5	26	1, $100.00 mnth; 4, 30c hour	9	
Car repairers	5	26	1, 30c hour; 4, 29c hour	9	
Car oilers	1	29	17½c hour	9	
[illegible]	2	26	1, $90.00 mnth; 1, 43½c hour.	8	
Bridge and building carpenters	28	26	30c hour	10	
Bridge and building helpers	19	26	25c hour	10	
Section men	10	30	$70.00 month	10	
Section men	White 36	26	$1.75 day	10	
Section men	Japs 17	26	$1.50 day	10	
Freight house men	2	26	1, $75.00 month; 1, 20c hour	9	
Train dispatchers	3	30	$115.00 month	9	
Telegraph operators and station agents	8	30	$25.00 to $165.00 month	10	
Office help—station	5	30	$55.00 to $85.00 mnth	10	
Engineers—stationary	2	30	1, $110.00 month; 1, $90.00 month	12	
Firemen—stationary	2	30	$2.40 day	12	
Office help—general office clerks	7	26	$85.00 month, average.	8¾	

BELLINGHAM BAY & BRITISH COLUMBIA RAILROAD COMPANY.

NUMBER OF MEN EMPLOYED IN EACH DEPARTMENT, WITH DAILY OR MONTHLY WAGES PAID.

DEPARTMENT.	Number of employes.	Number of days per month.	Wages per day or month.	Number of hours per day.	REMARKS.
Conductors—passenger	2	71	$3.60 day	10	
Conductors—freight	5	108	$3.60 day	10	
Engineers—passenger	3	70	$3.60; $3.90 day	10	Size of engine regulates pay
Engineers—freight	3	108	$3.90; $4.25 day	10	Size of engine regulates pay
Engineers—switch	4	31	$3.25 $3.50 day	11	Size of engine regulates pay
Fireman—passenger	2	37	$2.46 day	10	
Fireman—freight	3	108	$2.45; $2.75 day	10	Size of engine regulates pay
Fireman—switch	2	31	$2.25 day	11	
Brakeman—passenger	2	72	$2.75 day	10	
Brakemen—freight	6	151	$2.75 day	10	
Switchmen—yard	5	60	$2.75 day	11	
Flagmen					
Engine	1	31	$65 month	10	
Machinists	4	91	$4.00 day	9	
Machinist	2	35	$3.25 day	10	
Boiler					
Boiler helpers	1	21	$3.25 day	9	
Blacksmiths	1	14	$2.25 day	10	
Blacksmith helpers	3	67	$3.00 to $4.00 day	9	
Car	2	55	$2.50 day	10	
Car	2	45	$2.25 day	10	
Car	1	22	$3.00 day	9	
Bridge and building	5	108	$4.00 day	10	
Bridge and building	12	154	$2.75 day	10	
Bridge and building helpers	10	289	$60.00 to $75.00 month	10	
men	106	1,200	$2.00; $2.50 day	10	
men	9	243	$50.00 to $85.00 mth.	11	
dispatchers	1	31	$100.00 mth	9	
men	1	31	$125.00 month	9	
Telegraph operators	13	306	$20.00 to $100.00 month	8 to 12	
Office help					
Electricians	1	15	$4.00 day	10	
Engineers—stationary	1	10	$2.50 day	10	
Firemen—stationary	9	279	$20.00 to $100.00 month	11	Location regulates pay
Station agents					
Street car					
Street car gripmen					
Street car motormen					
help	5	29	$2.25 to $3.00 day	10	
Totals	238	3,925			

CHICAGO, MILWAUKEE & PUGET SOUND RAILWAY AND TACOMA EASTERN RAILWAY.
NUMBER OF MEN EMPLOYED IN EACH DEPARTMENT, WITH DAILY OR MONTHLY WAGES PAID.

DEPARTMENT.	Number of employes.	Number of days per month.	Wages per day or month.	Number of hours per day.	REMARKS.
Conductors—passenger	8	15 to 30	$135.00 to $150.00 mth	12	
Conductors—freight	98	30	$3.80 to $4.00 per day	12	
Engineers—passenger	11	30	$4.30 per day	10	
Engineers—freight	160	30	$4.80 per day	10	
Engineers—switch	13	30	$3.75 per day	10	
Firemen—passenger	11	30	$3.10 per day	10	
Firemen—freight	160	30	$3.25 per day	10	
Firemen—switch	13	30	$2.50 per day	10	
Brakemen—passenger	8	30	$75.00 to $85.00 mth	12	
Brakemen—freight	186	30	$2.58 to $4.45 per day	12	
Switchmen—yard	24	30	$4.00 per day	11	
Flagmen	1	30	$50.00 per mth	12	
Engine hostlers	11	30	$2.05 per day	12	
Machinists	53	27 to 30	$3.96 per day	9	
Machinist helpers	17	27 to 30	$2.07 per day	9	
Boiler makers	24	27 to 30	$3.915 per day	9	
Boiler maker helpers	28	27 to 30	$2.16 per day	9	
Blacksmiths	19	27 to 30	$3.87 per day	9	
Blacksmith helpers	18	27 to 30	$2.25 per day	9	
Car builders	40	27 to 30	$2.75 per day	9	
Car repairers	97	30	$2.50 per day	10	
Car oilers and apprs.	23	30	$1.02 per day	11	
Coach painters and helpers	9	27	$2.50 per dy	9	
Bridge and building painters	37	28	$2.65 per day	10	
Bridge and building carpenters	829	28	$3.00 per day	10	
Bridge and building helpers	219	28	$2.50 per day	10	
Section foremen and extra gangs	81	30	$70.00 to $150.00 mth	10	
Section men and xtra gangs	1,629	30	$1.75 to $1.85 per dy	10	
Freight house men	35	30	$90.00 to $125.00 month	10	
Train dispatchers	12	30	$90.00 to $160.00 mth	8	
Train men	2	30	$175.00 per month		
Office help	46	30		8 to 12	
Electricians	250	27 to 31	$25 to $900.00 per mth	8 to 12	
Engineers—stationary	3		$100.00 per mth	9	
Firemen—stationary	2		$65.00 per mth	12	
Station agents	10	30	$70.00 per month	12	
Street car conductors	36	30	$65.00 to $200.00 month	10 to 12	
Street car gripmen					
Street car motormen					
Other help	266	26 to 31	$30.00 to $140.00 month	9 to 12	
Totals	4,513				

SPOKANE, PORTLAND & SEATTLE RAILWAY COMPANY.

NUMBER OF MEN EMPLOYED IN EACH DEPARTMENT, WITH DAILY OR MONTHLY WAGES PAID.

REMARKS.	Number of employed.	Number of days each month.	Wages per day or month.	Number of hours per day.
Conductors—passenger	4	23	$185.00 month	9
Conductors—freight	2	26	$4.18 per 100 miles	11
Brakemen—passenger	6	23	$75.00 month	9
Brakemen—freight	4	26	$2.59 per 100 miles	11
Switchmen—yard				
Flagmen				
Engineers—passenger	5	23	$4.10 per 100 miles	9
Firemen—passenger	6	23	$2.70 per 100 miles	8
Engineers—freight	2	26	$4.90 per 100 miles	11
Firemen—fr-ight	2	26	$3.25 per 100 miles	11
Engineers—switch				
Firemen—switch				
Engine hostlers	1	31	$90.00 per month	10
Engine hostler helpers	1	31	$2.25 day	10
Machinists				
Boiler makers				
Blacksmiths				
Blacksmith hlprs				
Car builders	1	31	$85.00 month	10
Car inspectors	4	31	$2.40 day	10
Car repairers				
Car men				
Sash painters				
Bridge and building painters	1	31	$90. mth	10
Bridge and building foremen	21	26	$275 day	10
Bridge and building carpenters	18	26	$2.25 day	10
Bridge and building helpers	40	31	$65.00 mth	10
Section men	84	31	$1.20 day	10
	170	27	$1.30 day	10
	18	27	$1.50 day	10
Freight house men	4	31	$135.00 month	8
Train dispatchers	13	31	$65.00 month	9
Telegraph operators	40	31		8
Office help				

OREGON & WASHINGTON RAILROAD COMPANY.

NUMBER OF MEN EMPLOYED IN EACH DEPARTMENT, WITH DAILY OR MONTHLY WAGES PAID.

DEPARTMENTS.	Number of employes	Number of days per month	Wages per day or month	Number of hours per day	REMARKS.
Conductors—passenger	7	27	$150 00	7½	
Conductors—freight	14	31	124 00	10	
Engineers—passenger	9	20	161 89	7½	
Engineers—freight	18	31	144 77	10	
Engineers—switch	6	31	116 25	10	
Firemen—passenger	9	20	118 00	7½	
Firemen—freight	24	31	107 26	10	
Firemen—switch	6	31	77 50	10	
Brakemen—passenger	14	27	78 70	7½	
Brakemen—freight	28	31	84 63	10	
Switchmen—yard	18	31	120 90	10	
Flagmen					
Engine hostlers	5	31	96 10	10	
Machinists	7	27	113 40	10	
Machinists helpers	4	27	64 80	10	
Boiler makers	2	27	117 45	10	
Boiler maker helpers	2	27	64 80	10	
Blacksmiths	2	27	91 80	10	
Blacksmith helpers	2	27	64 80	10	
Car builders					
Car repairers	5	27	64 80	10	
Car oilers					
Coach painters					
Bridge and building painters					
Bridge and building carpenters	7	27	76 41	10	
Bridge and building helpers					
Section foremen	2	27	72 50	10	
Section men	8	27	54 00	10	
Freight house men	8	31	61 40	10	
Train dispatchers					
Train masters	1	27	150 00	10	
Telegraph operators	8	31	76 67	9	
Office help	130	27	90 20	8	
Electricians					
Engineers—stationary					
Firemen—stationary					
Station agents	8	27	121 25	10	
Street car conductors					
Street car gripmen					
Street car motormen					
Other help	409	27	75 85	10	
Totals	758	27.4	86 45	9.5	

SPOKANE INTERNATIONAL RAILWAY COMPANY.

NUMBER OF MEN EMPLOYED IN EACH DEPARTMENT, WITH DAILY OR MONTHLY WAGES PAID.

DEPARTMENTS.	Number of employes.	Number of days per month.	Wages per day or month.	Number of hours per day.	REMARKS.
Conductors—passengers	4	Full month	$150.00 per month	Aver. 5½	Work 3 days out of 4; double, 1 day
Conductors—freight	7	Full month	$3.85 and $4.23 per day	Aver. 12	Wages per 100 miles
Engineers—passengers	4	Full month	$4.21 per day	Aver. 5½	Wages per 100 miles
Engineers—freight	7	Full month	$4.00, $4 90, $5.39 day	Aver. 12	Wages per 100 miles
Engineers—switch	2	Full month	$3.75 per day	10	
Firemen—passengers	4	Full month	$2.90 per day	Aver. 5½	Wages per 100 miles
Firemen—freight	8	Full month	$3.25, $3.57, $2.80 day	Aver. 12	Wages per 100 miles
Firemen—switch	2	Full month	$2.25 per day	10	
Brakemen—passengers	4	Full month	$81.50 per month	Aver. 5½	Work 3 days out of 4; double, 1 day
Brakemen—freight	16	Full month	$2.50 and $2.80 per day	Aver. 12	Wages per 100 miles
Switchmen—yard	7	Full month	$2.90 and $3.70 per day	10	
Flagmen					
1 ... ...rs	2	Full month	$3.00 per day	10	
...s	5	26	44c per hour	9	
...s helpers	3	26	25c per hour	9	
Boiler ...rs	1	26	45c per hour	9	
Boiler maker ...rs	2	26	25c per hour	9	
Blacksmiths	2	26	45c and 33c per hour	9	
Blacksmith helpers	1	26	25c per hour	9	
Car builders	8	26	30c per hour	9	
Car repairers	8	26	27½c per hour	9	
Car oilers	2	26	25c per hour	9	
...h painters	2	26	35c and 30c per hour	9	
Bridge and building ...rs	8		$4.00, $3.50, $3.00 day	10	
Bridge and building ...eters	3		$2.75 and $2.50 per day	10	
Bridge and building helpers	3	26	$1.75, $2.00, $2.25 day	10	
Section ...men	15	Full month	$75, $70, $65 month	10	
Section men	110	26 to 30	$1.75, $2.00, $2.25 day	10	
...ght house- men	18	26	$65.00 to $80.00 month	10	
...n ...rs	4	Full month	$160, $115, $110 month	8	
...h ...rators	8	Full month	$65.00 to $75.00 month	9	
...ce help	8	26 to 30	$65.00 to $125.00 month	8 to 10	Supt's office and station only
Electricians					
Engineers—stationary					
Firemen—stationary					
Station agents ...rs	7	Full month	$65.00 to $125.00 month	9 to 13	
Street car ...rs					
Steet car ...m					
Street car motormen					
Other help					

ILWACO RAILROAD COMPANY.

NUMBER OF MEN EMPLOYED IN EACH DEPARTMENT, WITH DAILY OR MONTHLY WAGES PAID.

DEPARTMENTS.	Number of employes	Number of days per month.	Wages per day or month.	Number of hours per day.	REMARKS.
Conductors—passengers and freight	2	28 to 31	$92.50 per month	10	
Engineers—passengers and freight	3	28 to 31	$100.00 per month	10	
Engineers—switch					
Firemen—passengers and freight	2	28 to 31	$70.00 per month	10	
Firemen—switch					
Brakemen—passengers and freight	4	29 to 31	$65.00 per month	10	
Switchmen—yard					
Flagmen					
Engine hostlers	2	28 to 31	$60.00 per month	12	
Machinists	1	31	$3.00 per day	10	
Machinist helpers	1	31	$2.25 per day	10	
Boiler makers					
Boiler maker helpers					
Blacksmiths					
...th helpers	1	31	$2.50 per day	10	
... cars					
... cars					
Car oilers					
...h painters					
Bridge and building painters					
Bridge and building carpenters					
Bridge and building helpers					
Section foremen	10	31	$60.00 per month	10	
Section men	10	26	$2.00 per day	10	
Freight house men					
...in dispatchers					
...in masters					
Telegraph operators	1	31	$70.00 per month	10	
Office help					
Electricians					
Engineers—stationary					
Firemen—stationary					
Station agents	9	31	$25.00 to $70.00 month	10	Nine agents during summer season; five agents balance of year.
Street car conductors					
Street car gripmen					
Street car motormen					
Other help					
Totals	87				

WENATCHEE VALLEY & NORTHERN RAILWAY COMPANY.

NUMBER OF MEN EMPLOYED IN EACH DEPARTMENT, WITH DAILY OR MONTHLY WAGES PAID.

DEPARTMENTS.	Number of employes.	Number of days per month.	Wages per day or month.	Number of hours per day.	REMARKS.
Conductors—passengers	2	30	35c per hour	12	
Conductors—freight					
Engineers—passengers	2	30	45c per hour	12	
Engineers—freight					
Engineers—switch					
Firemen—passengers	2	30	30c per hour	12	
Firemen—freight					
Firemen—switch					
Brakemen—passengers	3	30	27½c per hour	12	
Brakemen—freight					
Switchmen—yard					
Flagmen					
Engine hostlers					
Machinists					
Machinist helpers					
Boiler makers					
Boiler maker helpers					
Blacksmiths					
Blacksmith helpers					
Car builders					
Car repairers	2	30	25c per hour	12	
Car painters	1	30	22½c per hour	12	
Bridge and building painters					
Bridge and building carpenters					
Bridge and building helpers					
Section foremen					
Section men					
Freight house men					
Train	1	30	40c per hour	12	
Train					
Telegraph operators					
Office help					
Electricians					
Engineers—stationary					
Firemen—stationary					
Station agents					
Street car conductors					
Street car					
Street car motormen					
Other help					

PORT TOWNSEND SOUTHERN RAILROAD COMPANY.

NUMBER OF MEN EMPLOYED IN EACH DEPARTMENT, WITH DAILY OR MONTHLY WAGES PAID.

DEPARTMENTS.	Number of employes.	Number of days each month.	Wages per day or month.	Number of hours per day.
Conductors—passengers	1	26	$125.00 month	10
Conductors—freight				
Brakemen—passengers				
Brakemen—freight				
Switchmen—yard				
Flagmen				
Engineers—passengers	1	26	$80.00 month	10
Fireman—passengers	1	26	$80.00 month	10
Engineers—freight				
Firemen—freight				
Engineers—switch				
Firemen—switch				
Engine h ailers				
Machinists				
Boiler mkrs				
Blacksmiths				
Blacksmith helpers				
Car bldrs				
Car repairers				
Car lers				
h painters				
Bridge and building painters				
Bridge and building carpenters				
Bridge and building helpers				
Section fmen	1	26	$75.00 month	10
Section men	10	26	$1 25 day	10
Freight hse men				
n ailrs				
Telegraph operators				
Electricians				
Engineers—stationary				
Firemen—stationary				
Office help				
Other labor				

Engineer and fireman do car repairing when necessary for which extra pay is allowed. Conductor acts as brakeman. Power brakes on coaches.

STATISTICS OF STREET
RAILWAYS

STATISTICS OF STREET RAILWAYS.

SEATTLE ELECTRIC COMPANY.

NUMBER OF MEN EMPLOYED IN EACH DEPARTMENT, WITH DAILY OR MONTHLY WAGES PAID.

DEPARTMENTS.	Number of employes.	Number of days per month.	Wages per day or month.	Number of hours per day.	REMARKS.
Machinists	18	26	$3.25 to $3.50 per day	9	
...hs	8	26	$3.25 to $3.75 per day	9	
...ith helpers	4	26	$2.50 per day	9	
Car builders	73	28	$2.25 to $3.00 per day	9	
Car repairers	32	28	$2.25 per day	9	
Car ...rs					
...ch ...rs	12	26	$3.00 per day	10	
Bridge and building painters					
Bridge and building ...prs	10	26	$75.00 per mth	10	
Bridge and building ...hs	125	28	$2.00 per day	10	
Section ...men					
...en men					
Freight ...use ...m	8	28	$80.00 per month	8	
Train ...prs					
Telegraph ...bars					
...ce help	540	30	25c to 32c per hour	10	
...et car (...ars	80	30	25c to 33c per hour	10	
...et car ...men	460	30	25c to 32c per hour	10	
Street car motormen	20	28	27c to 41c per hour	8 to 10	
Electricians	18	26	$80.00, $100 m	8	
Engineers—stationary	32	28	$80.00, ..., $100 m	8	Boiler men { Firemen, Coal passers, Water tenders
Firemen—stationary	150	26	$2.25 per day	8½	
Office help					
Other help					

PUGET SOUND ELECTRIC RAILWAY.

NUMBER OF MEN EMPLOYED IN EACH DEPARTMENT, WITH DAILY OR MONTHLY WAGES PAID.

DEPARTMENTS.	Number of employes.	Number of days per month.	Wages per day or month.	Number of hours per day.	REMARKS.
Conductors—passengers	19	30	$80.00 to $110.00 month.	10 to 12	Interurban service to Seattle.
Conductors—freight	3	30	$80.00 to $110.00 month.	10 to 12	Interurban service to Seattle.
Motormen—passengers	19	30	$90.00 to $120.00 month.	10 to 12	Interurban service to Seattle.
Motormen—freight	3	30	$90.00 to $120.00 month.	10 to 12	Interurban service to Seattle.
Engineers—switch					
Firemen—passengers					
Firemen—freight					
Firemen—switch					
Brakemen—passengers	20	30	$65.00 to $80.00 month.	10 to 12	Interurban service.
Brakemen—freight	9	30	$70.00 to $85.00 month.	10 to 12	Interurban service.
Switchmen—yard					
Flagmen					
Engine hostlers					
Machinists	8	26	$75.00 to $90.00 month.	9	
Boiler makers	4	26	$60.00 to $70.00 month.	9	
Boiler maker helper					
Blacksmiths	3	26	$75.00 to $90.00 month.	10	
Smith helpers	3	26	$60.00 to $70.00 month.	10	
Car repairs	67	30	$60.00 to $70.00 month.	10 to 12	
Car repairers	4	30	$60.00 to $70.00 month.	10 to 12	
Car cleaners	8	26	$70.00 to $85.00 month.	10	
Bridge repairers	22	28	$60.00 to $90.00 month.	11	
Bridge and building					
Bridge and building helpers					
Section foremen	16	30	$75.00 per month.	10	
Section men	149	26	$50.00 per month.	10	
Freight men	11	28	$55.00 per month.	10	
Train men	3	30	$100.00 per month.	8	
Train masters	2	30	$125.00 per month.		
Ticket and agents	8	30	$60.00 to $75.00 month.	10 to 12	
Office help	44	26	$85.00 to $100.00 month.	10 to 12	
Electricians	8	30	$70.00 to $80.00 month.	8¾	
Engineers—stationary	17	30	$70.00 to $80.00 month.	9	
Firemen—stationary	4	30	$60.00 to $65.00 month.	8 to 9	
Street car conductors	117	30	$60.00 to $80.00 month.	10 to 13	See telegraph operators.
Street car gripmen	8	30	$60.00 to $80.00 month.	10 to 13	
Street car motormen	109	30	$90.00 to $90.00 month.	10 to 13	
Other help	20	30	$50.00 to $75.00 month.	8 to 10	
Totals	708		$1,915.00 to $2,510.00...	Av. 10½	

—1 7

TACOMA RAILWAY & POWER COMPANY.

NUMBER OF MEN EMPLOYED IN EACH DEPARTMENT, WITH DAILY OR MONTHLY WAGES PAID.

DEPARTMENTS.	Number of employes.	Number of days each month.	Wages per day or month.	Number of hours per day.
Conductors—passengers				
Conductors—freight				
Brakemen—passenger				
Brakemen—freight				
Switchmen—yard				
Flagmen				
Engineers—passengers				
Firemen—passenger				
Engineers—freight				
Firemen—freight				
Engineers—switch				
Firemen—switch				
Engine hostlers	6		$2.50 to $3.50 day	9
Boiler makers				
Blacksmiths	2		$3.25 to $3.50 day	9
Blacksmith hprs	2		$2.50 day	10
Car builders	7		$2.50 to $2.75 day	10
Car repairers	32		$1.50 to $2.50 day	10
Car oilers	5		$2.00 to $2.25 day	10
Car painters	2		$2.25 to $2.75 day	
Bridge and building painters				
Bridge and building cars				
Bridge aud building helpers				
Section men	11		$70.00 month	10
Section men	157		$1.75 day	10
Freight				
Train dispatchers				
help operators				
Street car conductors	128		24c to hr.	av. 11 hrs.
Street car gripmen	5		3hr.	av. 11 hrs.
Street car motormen	122		hr.	av. 11 hrs.
Electricians	6			
Engineers—stationary	1		$120.00 month	12
Firemen—stationary	2		$70.00 to $30.00	12

THE WASHINGTON WATER POWER COMPANY.

NUMBER OF MEN EMPLOYED IN EACH DEPARTMENT, WITH DAILY OR MONTHLY WAGES PAID.

DEPARTMENTS.	Number of employes.	Number of days per month.	Wages per day or month.	Number of hours per day.	REMARKS.
Conductors—passengers	8	31	35c per hour	11	Interurban
Conductors—freight	8	26	35c per hour	10	Interurban
Motormen—passengers	8	31	35c per hr.	11	Interurban
Motormen—freight	2	26	35c per hour	10	Interurban
Electricians	25	26	50c per hour	9	
	35	26	40c per hour	9	
	40	26	40c per hour	9	
	6	26	53.8-9c per hour	9	
	10	26	44c per month	9	
Electrician helpers	10	31	$100 per month.	9	
Brakemen—passengers	50	26	27.7-9c per hour.	11	Interurban
Track gang	9	31	25c per hour.	9	
cars	3	26	$65.00 per mth	9	
Flagmen	15	31	27.7-9c per hour.	10	
	6	26	27.7-9c per hour.	9	
Moulders and foundrymen	6	26	37½c per hour.	9	
	7	26	35c per hour.	9	
	5	26	27½c per hour.	9	
Machinists	20	26	40c per hour.	8	
	15	28	37½c per hour.	9	
	20	26	35c per hour.	9	
	6	26	30c per hour.	9	
Mach helprs	20	26	27½c per hour.	9	
	12	26	22½c per hour.	9	
Boiler makrs	3	28	37½c per hour.	9	
Boiler maker helpers	4	26	25c per hour.	9	
Blacksmiths	5	26	40c per hour.	9	
	8	26	30.8-9c per hour.	10	
Blacksmith helpers	5	26	35c per hour.	10	
	6	26	30c per hour.	10	
Car repairers	10	26	27½ per month.	10	
	1	31	$150 per mth.	10	
	10	31	30c per hour.	10	
	12	31	27½c per hour.	10	
	10	31	25c per hour.	10	
Coach painters	6	31	20c per hour.	10	
	1	31	$110 per mth	9	
	4	26	35c per hour.	9	
	4	26	30c per hour.	9	

THE WASHINGTON WATER POWER COMPANY—Continued.

DEPARTMENTS.	Number of employes.	Number of days per month.	Wages per day or month.	Number of hours per day.	REMARKS.
Coach ...rs	8	26	25c per hr	9	
Building ...ars	3	26	20c per hr	9	
	1	31	$110 per mth	10	
...ng carpenters	10	26	30c per hr	10	
	10	26	27½c per hr	10	
	30	26	40c per hr	10	
Carpenter helpers	25	26	37½c per hour	9	
	40	26	27½c per hr	9	
...n foremen	2	31	25c per hr	9	
...n men	8	26	$80.00 per mth	8	
Stenographers	1	26	27 7-9c per mth	8	
	7	26	$125 per month	8	
	1	26	$75 per mth	10	
Freight ... em.	1	31	$60 per mth	10	
	1	31	$80.00 per mth	10	
...in dis ...ars	1	31	$70.00 per mth	10	
	20	31	$100.00 per month	9	
	10	31	$85.00 per mth	9	
	6	31	$80.00 per month	9	
	14	31	$80.00 per month	9	
Office help	10	31	$45.00 per mth	9	
	20	31	$100.00 per mth	9	
	10	31	$125.00 per mth	9	
	5	31	$70.00 per month	9	
Engineers—stationary	4	31	$60.00 per mth	12	
(day)	1	31	$1.00 per mth	12	
...stationary (night)	1	31	$50.00 per mth	8	
	8	31	$85.00 per mth	8	
	4	31	$65.00 per mth	10	
...n agents	2	31	$8.00 per day	10	
	1	31	$2.75 per day	10	
	1	31	$75.00 per month	9	
Street car ...rs	150	31	$80.00 per mth	8	
...e ...rs	1	31	$85.00 per month	8	
	3	26	$76.25 per mth	9	
Street car motormen	150	31	$50.00 per month	9	
...lp: Laborers	350	26	$35.00 per month	8	
... hrs	140	26	$76.25 per day	9	
Janitors	4	26	$2.50 per day	10	
			$70.00 per mth	8	

PUGET SOUND INTERNATIONAL RAILWAY & POWER COMPANY, LESSEE, EVERETT PROPERTY.

NUMBER OF MEN EMPLOYED IN EACH DEPARTMENT, WITH DAILY OR MONTHLY WAGES PAID.

DEPARTMENTS.	Number of employés.	Number of days each month.	Wages per day or month.	Number of hours per day.
Conductors—passengers				
Conductors—freight				
Brakemen—passenger				
Brakemen—freight				
Switchmen—yard				
Flagmen				
Engineers—passengers				
Firemen—passenger				
Engineers—freight				
Firemen—freight				
Engineers—switch				
Firemen—switch				
Engine hostlers				
Machinists	1		$300 per 4th	8
Boiler makers	1		$3.00 per day	8
Blacksmiths	1		$1.75 per day	8
Car builders				
Car	2		$2.75 per day	10
Car	1		$1.75 per day	10
Car builders	1		$3.50 per day	10
Bridge and building painters	1		$3.00 per day	8
Bridge and building carpenters				
Bridge and building helpers				
Track men	30		$2.00 per day	10
Line men	3		$3.85 per day	9
Freight				
Telegraph operators	20		18c to 27c per hour	10
Street car conductors	21			
Street car gripmen	11		18c to 27c per hour	10
Street car men	2		$3.35 per day	8
Electricians	10		$90.00 per month	9
Engineers—stationary	13		$2.50 per day	9
Firemen—stationary	4		$70.00 per month	9
The help			$60.00 per month	9
Other labor				

WHATCOM COUNTY RAILWAY & LIGHT COMPANY.

NUMBER OF MEN EMPLOYED IN EACH DEPARTMENT, WITH DAILY OR MONTHLY WAGES PAID.

DEPARTMENTS.	Number of employes.	Number of days per month.	Wages per day or month.	Number of hours per day.	REMARKS.
Conductors—passenger	2	28	$3.12 per day	12	
Conductors—freight					
Engineers—passenger	2	28	$3.12 per day	12	
Engineers—freight	1	28	$3.12 per day	12	
Engineers—switch					
Firemen—passenger					
Firemen—freight					
Firemen—switch					
Brakemen—passenger	1	28	$3.00 per day	12	
Brakemen—freight	1	30	$1.50 per day	10	
Switchmen—yard					
Flagmen					
Engine hostlers	1	26	$3.65 per day	10	
Machinists					
Machinist helpers					
Boiler makers					
Boiler maker helpers					
Blacksmiths					
Blacksmith helpers					
Car builders	1	26	$3.00 per day	10	
Car repairers	1	26	$3.00 per day		
Car painters					
Bridge and building painters					
Bridge and building					
Bridge and building men					
Section men	10		$2.25 per day		
Section house men					
Train dispatchers					
cars					
Tel graph operators					
Office help					
Electricians			$2.50 per day		Total office expense charged proportionately to "Railway," "Light," and "Gas."
Engineers—stationary					
Firemen—stationary					Power purchased
Station agents					
Street car conductors			$2.50 per day		
Street car gripmen					
Street car motormen			$2.40 per day		
Other help ar cleaner					

GRAYS HARBOR RAILWAY & LIGHT COMPANY.

NUMBER OF MEN EMPLOYED IN EACH DEPARTMENT, WITH DAILY OR MONTHLY WAGES PAID.

DEPARTMENTS.	Number of employes.	Number of days each month.	Wages per day or month.	Number of hours per day.
Conductors—passenger				
Conductors—freight				
Brakemen—passenger				
Brakemen—freight				
Switchmen—yard				
Flagmen				
Engineers—passenger				
Firemen—passenger				
Engineers—freight				
Firemen—freight				
Firemen—switch				
Engine hostlers				
Machinists	2	26	40c and 50c per h'r	8
Boiler ...				
Blacksmiths				
Blacksmith helpers				
Car barn men	2	26	27c and 32c per h'r	10
Car ...				
Car oilers	1	26	43 3-4c per hour...	8
Bridge ad building carpenters	1	26	$75.00 per month.	10
Bridge ad building	3	29	$2.00 per day....	10
Bridge ad building				
...house man				
...in dispatchers	10	30	25c to 30c per hour	8 to 10
Telegraph ...				
Street car gripmen	10	30	Same as conduct's	8 to 10
Street car motormen	13	28	25c to 45c per hour	8
Electricians ad bl ...	3	30	$90 to $125 month	8
Engineers—stationary	4	30	$70.00 per month.	12
Firemen—stationary	4	26	$75 to $85 month.	12
...dp ...	10	26	$2.00 to $3.50 day	9
...				10

OLYMPIA LIGHT & POWER COMPANY.

NUMBER OF MEN EMPLOYED IN EACH DEPARTMENT, WITH DAIL OF MONTHLY WAGES PAID.

DEPARTMENTS.	Number of employes.	Number of days each month.	Wages per day or month.	Number of hours per day.
Conductors—passenger				
Conductors—freight				
Motormen—passenger	1	25	$65.00 per month.	
Motormen—freight				
Switchmen—yard				
Flagmen				
Engineers—passenger				
Firemen—passenger				
Engineers—freight				
Firemen—freight				
Engineers—switch				
Firemen—switch				
Engine hostlers				
Machinists				
Boiler makers				
Blacksmiths				
Blacksmith helpers				
Car ꓸꓸrs	1	25	$75.00 per month.	9
Car repairers				
Car ꓸꓸrs				
Coach painters				
Bridge and ꓸꓸg painters				
Bridge and building carpenters				
Bridge and building helpers	1	25	$70.00 per ꓸꓸnth.	9
Section men				
Car ꓸse men	1	30	$65.00 per month.	10
Train dispatchers				
Telegraph ꓸꓸrs				
ꓸce help				
Street car conductors	4	30	22c ꓸr bur	10
Street car ꓸen	4	30	22c to 25c ꓸr bur	10
Electricians	2	25	$80.00 ꓸr ꓸnh.	9
Engineers—stationary	3	30	$70.00 ꓸr ꓸnh.	8
Firemen—stationary				
Office help	3	25	$70.00 ꓸr ꓸnh.	8
Other labor—linemen	5	25	$65 ꓸd $70 mth	9

WALLA WALLA VALLEY RAILWAY COMPANY.

NUMBER OF MEN EMPLOYED IN EACH DEPARTMENT, WITH DAILY OR MONTHLY WAGES PAID.

DEPARTMENTS.	Number of employes.	Number of days per month.	Wages per day or month.	Number of hours per day.	REMARKS.
Conduct rs—passenger	1	.....	25c to 30c per hour....	.....	According to time of service
Conductors—freight	1	.....	25c to 30c per hour....	.....	According to time of service
Brakemen—freight	1	28	27 per hr.......	10	
Machinists	1	28	$125.00 per month....	8	
Machinist helpers	2	30	30c per bur.......	10	
Car repairers	2	30	25c per hour.......	10	
Section foen	8	28	$60, $65 and $80 mnth.	.....	
Section men	12	28	25c per hour.......	9	
Night house men	1	28	$60 per month.......	12	
Train wirs	1	30	$95.00 per month....	10	
Station agts	2	30	$80 and $85 per mth.	.....	
Street car conductors	14	30	25c to 30c per hour..	.....	According to time of service
Street car motormen	14	30	25c to 30c per hour..	.....	According to time of service
Other help	16		25c and 40c per hour..	9	Extra section men and linemen
Totals	70				

SEATTLE, RENTON & SOUTHERN RAILWAY.

NUMBER OF MEN EMPLOYED IN EACH DEPARTMENT, WITH DAILY OR MONTHLY WAGES PAID.

DEPARTMENTS.	Number of men employed.	Number of days each month.	Wages per day or month.	Number of hours per day.	REMARKS.
Machinists—car builders	11	26	.....	.....	One at $100 per month; 1 at $65 per month; 1 at $60 per month; 1 at 40c per hour; 1 at 35c per hour; 1 at 24c per hour; 4 at 20c per hour.
Section foremen	2	28	$65.00 per month.	.....	
Section men	14	26	22½c per hour.....	.....	Twenty-one at 24c per hour; 9 at 22c per hour; 1 at $75 per month; 1 at $20 per month.
Street car conductors—motormen	32	30	.....	.....	
Electricians	1	30	$70.00 per month.	.....	
Office help	4	28	$87.50 per month.	.....	Average.

NORTH YAKIMA & VALLEY RAILWAY COMPANY.

NUMBER OF MEN EMPLOYED IN EACH DEPARTMENT, WITH DAILY OR MONTHLY WAGES PAID.

DEPARTMENTS.	Number of employes.	Number of days per month.	Wages per month.	Number of hours per day.	REMARKS.
Conductors—passengers and freight (mixed)	2	26	$108.00 per month	10	
Engineers—passengers and freight (mixed)	2	26	$3.50 per day	10	
Engineers—switch					
Firemen—passengers and freight (mixed)	2	26	$2.25 per day	10	
Firemen—switch					
Brakemen—passengers and freight mixed	3	26	$2.25 per day	10	
Switchmen—yard					
Flagmen					
Engine ...	2	26	$2.00 per day	10	
Machinists					
Machinist helpers					
Boiler makers					
Boiler maker helpers					
Blacksmiths					
Blacksmith helpers					
Carpenters	1	26	$2.50 per day	10	
Car repairers					
Car oilers					
Bridge and building	2	26	$3.00 per day	10	Temporary
Bridge and building					
Bridge and building helpers					
Section men	3	26	$75.00 per month	10	Partly construction
Section men	90	26	$2.15 per day	10	Partly construction
Freight house men					
Train ...					
Train ...					
Office ...	2	26	$95.00 per month	8	
Office help					
Engineers—stationary					
Firemen—stationary	1	26	$85.00 per month	10	
Street car ...					
Street car gripmen					
Street car motormen					
Other dispatch	3	26	$108.00 per month	8	Engineering department
Totals	111	312			

STATISTICS OF TELEGRAPH
COMPANIES

STATISTICS OF TELEGRAPH COMPANIES.

THE WESTERN UNION TELEGRAPH COMPANY.

NUMBER OF MEN EMPLOYED IN EACH DEPARTMENT, WITH DAILY OR MONTHLY WAGES PAID.

DEPARTMENTS.	Number of employes.	Number of days per month.	Wages per month.	Number of hours per day.
Managers .... (Average)	20	28	$75 57	8
Chief operators ...... (Average)	15	28	108 00	8
Telegraph operators ..... (Average)	90	28	78 00	8
Office help ...... (Average)	110	28	47 00	8
Other help ...... (Average)	78	28	38 00	8

POSTAL TELEGRAPH & CABLE COMPANY.

NUMBER OF MEN EMPLOYED IN EACH DEPARTMENT, WITH DAILY OR MONTHLY WAGES PAID.

DEPARTMENTS.	Number of employes.	Number of days per month.	Wages per day or month.	Number of hours per day.	REMARKS.
Telegraph operators and chiefs......	91	24 to 27	$40.00 to $125.00...	7½ to 9	
Office help (clerks)...............	29	24 to 27	$15.00 to $90.00....	8 to 9	Have included combination linemen [and managers under managers.
Managers*......................	57	......	$65.00 to $75.00....	8 to 9	
Linemen	4	24 to 27	$15.00 to $140.00...	8 to 9	
Total...............	121				

*This includes railway offices where station agent or operator is our manager. Where salary is as small as $15.00, which is at only one office, very little work is done for the company and the office is maintained chiefly as a test station. Most of our managers work on commission.

NOTE: We employ a few extra operators at Seattle and Spokane, but the number varies and they do not get in full time. This list gives regular employes.

CONVICT LABOR

CONVICT LABOR.

The problem of giving employment to the state convict labor is being worked out in Washington on a very successful, and withal an eminently humane basis. The convicts are being used in the rock crushing plants operated by the state and in the work of actual road construction and the results have been all that was anticipated.

Through the state's policy in dealing with this question, the convicts are given healthful employment in the open air, which in itself is conceded to be an important reformatory influence. Moreover the improvements made in the public highway system are of a permanent nature and will be of lasting benefit to the entire state. It should be noted also that the work is of a character that does not interfere with the interests of free labor, as it has always been difficult to secure men for this class of public improvements.

Influences at Work in the Interests of Labor

INFLUENCES AT WORK IN THE INTERESTS OF LABOR.

It is undoubtedly true that at no previous time have there been so many and such powerful agencies at work with a view to improving general labor conditions in this country and incidentally seeking to preserve peaceful relations between employers and wage earners. Recognition of the importance of these problems is widespread, and their solution is commanding the attention and assistance of patriotic citizens and students of economic conditions in all walks of life.

The federal government is taking an active lead in the van of this movement, through the national Labor Bureau which has been an important factor in the adjustment of numerous grave industrial disturbances. Closely allied to the work of the federal authorities is that carried on by the various state Bureaus of which there are at present, 33 in active operation. These Bureaus perform a variety of functions, governed largely by the conditions to be met in the several states. In the states which have important manufacturing interests, the Labor Bureaus are usually charged with the work of factory inspection and the collection of industrial statistics. This work, with the enforcement of sanitary laws and other enactments designed for the protection of wage earners make up the more important duties performed by the Bureaus, which duties, however, in most of the states are annually being widened in scope.

Having in view the same general objects as the national and state Bureaus, and largely supplementing their work, there has been organized an association of public spirited citizens known as the National Civic Federation. The work of this organization is national in its scope, one of its important purposes being to establish branches in all of the large industrial centers of the country. The membership is extremely representative, and among its officers will be found the names of leaders in the industrial, commercial, financial and professional life of the country as well as many of the men who are the recognized spokesmen of organized labor.

One of the leading objects is to provide a common meeting ground for labor and capital where views may be interchanged and free expression of opinion given. Also to exert the influence of the organization for the prevention of strikes and other industrial disturbances and the settlement of all such difficulties by peaceful means wherever it may be possible.

The Civic Federation is proceeding on the theory that employer and employee have a common interest in the preservation of industrial peace throughout the country and an active campaign of education having this end in view is being carried out. The results are manifesting themselves in a widespread interest in the work of the organization and endorsement of its principles.

In the light of what is being accomplished through the foregoing and other agencies that are working along similar lines, it is perhaps not too much to anticipate the arrival of the time when the strike and lockout and other weapons commonly employed in the battles between labor and capital will give way to some peaceful method of settlement, based upon a reasonable recognition of the rights of all parties at interest.

Opinions of the Attorney General.

OPINIONS OF THE ATTORNEY GENERAL.

The following opinions relating to labor laws and their enforcement have been rendered by the Attorney General on request of this Department.

Discriminations Against Labor.

June 25, 1910.

Hon. C. F. Hubbard, Labor Commissioner, Olympia, Wash.:

DEAR SIR—Your favor of the 20th, inst. addressed to the Attorney General and reading as follows has been referred to me for reply:

"I wish to submit for your written opinion the following question:

"Is it a misdemeanor under the state law (see Sec. 130, Criminal Code) for employers of labor to conspire or agree together and post notices, in their various shops in which they employ labor, during a strike, to the effect that hereafter none but non-union labor will be employed, or in other words is it a misdemeanor under the present law to discriminate against laborers, simply because they belong to a labor union, to the extent of depriving them of employment, unless they withdraw from their trades union?"

This office is of the opinion that the facts set forth in your inquiry do not constitute a crime under Section 130 of the Criminal Code, Session Laws of 1909 (Section 2382 Rem. & Bal. Code).

Under this section in order to constitute a conspiracy it is necessary for two or more persons to conspire to prevent another from exercising a lawful trade or calling by *force, threats* or *intimidation.* The mere fact that several employers agree that they will employ in their establishments none but non-union labor does not within itself constitute a crime. Employers of labor have a perfect right to employ or engage such kind or character of labor as they desire, just as laboring men have an equally perfect right to work or refuse to work in certain establishments. The crime is complete within the purview of the statute, only when employers of labor by *force, threats* or *intimidation* prevent others from exercising any lawful trade or calling. This is equally true of employees and they offend against the statute, only when they employ force, threats or intimidation. A conspiracy is a combination of two or more persons by a concerted action to accomplish a criminal or unlawful purpose, or some purpose not in itself criminal or unlawful, by criminal or unlawful means. It is not apparent how the acts of employers as indicated in your letter could possibly come within this universally accepted definition of conspiracy.

Speaking on this general question our Supreme Court has said as follows:

"It is true that a man, not under contract obligations to the contrary, has the right to quit the service of another at any time he sees fit, and may lawfully state, either publicly or privately, the grievances felt by him which gave rise to his conduct. And that rgiht which one man may exercise singly, many may lawfully agree, by voluntary association, to exercise jointly. But one man singly, nor any number of men jointly, having no legitimate interests to protect, may not ruin the business of another by maliciously inducing his patrons and other persons not to deal with him. Men cannot lawfully jointly congregate about the entrance of one's place of business, and there, either by persuasion, coercion, or force, prevent his patrons and the public at large from entering his place of business or dealing with him. To destroy his business in this manner is just as reprehensible as it is to physically destroy his property. Either is a violation of a natural right, the right to own, and peaceably enjoy, property."

39 Wash. Jensen vs. Cooks' & Waiters' Union.

This same reasoning may be applied to the acts of employers and necessarily results in the conclusion that so long as employers use no force, threats or intimidation to prevent others from exercising a lawful trade or calling, and so long as they conduct their establishments in a lawful manner, they are privileged under the law to employ either union or non-union men as they may choose.

You are therefore advised, without extending this opinion further, that the facts set forth in your inquiry do not constitute a crime within the scope of Section 2382 Rem. & Bal's. Code.

Yours very truly,

GEO. A. LEE,
Assistant Attorney General.

REPORTS OF OPERATORS.

September 20, 1910.

Hon. Charles F. Hubbard, Labor Commissioner, Olympia, Wash.:

DEAR SIR—You inquire of this office what recourse, if any, you have against the owner, proprietor or manager of any factory, workshop, mill, machine or other establishment where labor is employed, who refuse or neglect to fill out and return to your office the statistical blanks furnished by the Labor Commissioner, in violation of Sec. 6554, Rem. & Bal. Code, which requires such report to be returned to your office.

In reply we beg to refer you to the succeeding section, 6555, Rem. & Bal. Code, which provides that the Commissioner of Labor shall have the power to issue subpoenas, administer oaths and take testimony in all matters relating to the duties required by the statute of the Labor Commissioner, such testimony to be taken in some suitable place and witnesses to be subpoenaed under the order and direction of the Labor Commissioner. If there is a refusal to testify, such refusal constitutes a misdemeanor, and under the statute is subject to a fine or imprisonment. In our opinion if any person or corporation required by the statute to fill out the blanks sent by your office refuses or neglects so to do, your relief and recourse would be under sec. 6555, and we would advise that you would have the right to subpoena the officers of the delinquent or derelict corporation, and compel them under oath to disclose the information that they would otherwise incorporate in the blanks sent by your office. We believe that this would be a sure and speedy remedy, and that this section of the statute was enacted in order that your office might compel obedience from derelict persons and corporations who fail or neglect to comply with the provisions of sec. 6554, Rem. & Bal. Code.

Yours very truly,

GEO.. A. LEE,
Assistant Attorney General.

Supreme Court Decisions Affecting Labor

SUPREME COURT DECISIONS AFFECTING LABOR.

[No. 7561. Department One. July 16, 1909.]

IDA BUSH, *Respondent*, v. INDEPENDENT MILL COMPANY, *Appellant*.

Master and Servant—Negligence—Appliance—Proximate Cause.
Master and Servant—Injuries—Death of Servant—Performance of
Duty—Question for Jury.
Same—Cause of Death—Evidence—Sufficiency—Question for Jury.
Master and Servant—Assumption of Risks—Duty of Servant.
Same—Duties of Servant—Evidence—Materiality.
Trial—Instructions—Burden of Proof.
Master and Servant—Contributory Negligence—Two Ways—Momentary Forgetfulness—Question for Jury.
Trial—Instructions.

Appeal from a judgment of the superior court for Pierce county,
Reid, J., entered April 21, 1908, upon the verdict of a jury rendered in
favor of the plaintiff, in an action for the death of an employee, caught
by a set-screw upon a revolving shaft. Affirmed.

Hudson & Holt, for appellant.
Garvey & Kelly, for respondent.

GOSE, J.—The respondent, plaintiff below, is the widow of John Bush,
deceased, who died on the 9th day of October, 1907, from an injury sustained
on the 17th day of June of the same year. The complaint
charged, in addition to the facts stated, that on the 17th day of June,
1907, and for some months prior thereto, the appellant was the owner
of and engaged in operating a sawmill; that on the day stated the deceased
was in its employ as a filer and oiler of the machinery and
boxes on the upper deck of the mill; that there was a revolving shaft
on the upper deck of the mill about nine feet from the main floor; that
there was a collar attached to the shaft by means of an unguarded, projecting
set-screw; that the set-screw could have been effectively guarded;
that, while engaged in his regular employment, the clothing of the deceased
was caught on the set-screw; that the deceased was thrown to
the main floor with such violence that his back was broken, resulting in
his death on the date heretofore stated. The giving of the statutory
notice of the injury was also alleged. The appellant pleaded affirmatively
that the injury of the deceased was due to his own negligence,
and that it was his duty to properly safeguard the machinery. The case
was tried to the jury, which returned a general verdict for the respondent
in the sum of $3,200, and made the following special findings:

"Interrogatory 2. Did he know that the set-screw was over the shaft
and set-screw on which his clothing was caught? Answer: The evi-

dence did not show that he was injured while stepping over the shaft but it did show that he was caught by said set-screw.

"Interrogatory 2. Did he know that the set-screw was there, and that it projected? Answer: Yes.

"Interrogatory 3. Where was he going and what was he doing at the time he was caught by the set-screw? Answer: The evidence did not show where he was going or what he was doing at the time he was caught by the set-screw.

"Interrogatory 4. Was there a plank laid to the right looking north, of the timber for the boxing and end of the shaft, as shown in defendant's exhibit No. 4? Answer: Yes. One 8-inch plank.

"Interrogatory 5. If you find that at the time of the injury to John Bush there was a plank lying to the right, looking north, of the timber for the boxing and end of the shaft as shown in defendant's exhibit No. 4, then state whether the plank or planks leading from the ladder to the platform of the canting gear were so placed that a person coming along them could step as safely and conveniently to the said plank lying to the right of the timber for the boxing and end of the shaft, as he could to the plank or planks lying to the left of the said timber and end of the shaft? Answer: No.

"Interrogatory 6. Do you find from the evidence that there was a guard or protection placed over the set-screw complained of in this case, and that John Bush removed it and failed to replace it? Answer: No."

This appeal is taken from a judgment entered upon the general verdict. The evidence shows that the appellant had not complied with the factory act. Laws 1905, page 164.

The appellant, at the time of the injury, was operating a sawmill in a one and one-half story building. The principal machinery was on the lower floor. The canting gear was on the upper deck, and was operated by the sawyer at his post on the lower floor, by a rod attached to the line shaft on the upper deck. The end of the shaft rested on a timber about eight inches square. There was a collar attached to the shaft by a projecting set-screw, about five-eighths of an inch in length. There was a pulley about thirty inches in diameter between the canting gear and the collar. The distance between the pulley and the set-screw was about eleven and one-half inches. There was no floor on the upper deck. A ladder, extending from the main floor to the upper deck, afforded the only way of going from the one to the other. One of the duties of the deceased was to oil the boxing of the canting gear and the line shaft when the machinery was in operation. Just before the accident and while the machinery was in operation, the deceased took an oil can and ascended the ladder to the upper deck, presumably for the purpose of oiling the boxing. There were three eight-inch boards leading from the ladder to the line shaft, one of which passed to the right of the timber on which the shaft rested. The other two passed to the left side of the timber.

After the deceased had been thrown to the lower floor, the machinery was stopped and an investigation of the cause of the accident was made.

The right leg of the deceased's overalls had been torn off, and was wound around the shaft at the point of the projecting set-screw. There was a tear in the leg of the overalls, some ten or twelve inches from the bottom and toward the back part of the leg. The oil can was found a few feet from the set-screw, in a slanting position, and a part of the oil had run out. No one saw any part of the accident except the falling of the body.

There were two ways of passing the boxing on the shaft to reach the canting gear; one by walking on the eight-inch plank and passing to the right of the east end of the shaft, then turning west to the canting gear. There was evidence tending to show that this way was impracticable, owing to the narrowness of the plank, and because there were scantling lying across it, and because the height of the ceiling made it necessary to go in a stooping posture. The other way was to walk on the two eight-inch planks and step over the shaft at the east side of the pulley. There was evidence tending to show that this was dangerous, because the shaft and set-screw were raised about sixteen or eighteen inches above the plank, and also on account of the pulley, which was about eleven and one-half inches from the set-screw. The evidence tended to show that both ways were used in going to the canting gear. The deceased at the time of the accident chose the latter way. The evidence tended to show that, when the latter way was used, the party crossing the shaft would take hold of a vertical rod, step over the shaft, turn to the left, and walk to the canting gear. This was the nearer way. The evidence clearly shows that a sunken or safety set-screw without a head could have been used, and that there would have been no danger in stepping over the shaft. This method was adopted shortly after the accident.

Numerous errors have been assigned, and the discussion has taken a wide range in the appellant's brief; but the view we take of the case will make it unnecessary to separately consider each of the assignments. It must be conceded that a sunken or a safety set-screw could have been used, and that, if it had been used, there would have been no danger in stepping over the line shaft on the upper deck. The proximate cause of the injury—that is, the efficient cause without which the accident would not have occurred, was the failure of the appellant to use a sunken set-screw.

The appellant first urges that the evidence does not show that the deceased was injured while in the performance of his duty. There is no force in this position. It is conceded that it was a part of his duty to oil the boxing on the canting gear and line shaft, and that he did so eight or ten times a day. We have seen that he ascended the ladder with the oil can in his hand, presumably for the purpose of discharging this duty. It was, therefore, a question of fact for the jury to determine whether he was engaged in the performance of his duty when he was injured.

It is next urged that the cause of the accident is so involved in doubt that there can be no recovery. An issuable fact may be proven by direct or circumstantial evidence, or by the two combined. We have seen, that it was the duty of the deceased to oil the boxing on the upper deck; that he did so eight or ten times each day; that he had gone to the upper deck with the oil can; that in order to reach the canting gear he had to pass the line shaft; that there was boxing on the line shaft which he was required to oil; that he was seen to fall with great velocity from the upper deck; that his back was broken from the violence of the fall; that his right trousers' leg had been torn from his body and was wound around the shaft at the set-screw; that there was a rent in the cloth, showing that it had been caught in the set-screw; that the oil can was found a few feet distant from the shaft, partially overturned; and that part of the oil had run out. The cause of the accident was therefore removed from the field of speculation, if doubt can be removed in this class of cases. The jury had no difficulty in determining the cause of the accident, and we do not feel disposed to either raise or adopt a doubt which would have no support in the evidence.

It is next contended that the deceased was employed as a millwright, and that, as such, it was his duty to safeguard the set-screw. Numerous cases are cited in support of this contention. The position would be sound were it not for the fact that it finds no support in the evidence. It is true that one or two witnesses testified that he was the millwright and that such was his duty. However, the true relation of the deceased to the operation of the mill is shown by the testimony of Frank Isley, the foreman of the mill, who employed and instructed the deceased as to his duties. He testified as follows:

"Question: Did he [meaning the deceased] report to you if he was going to make any change or alteration of any kind? Would he consult with you at first about it? Answer: Yes, sir. Q. Why would he do that? A. To get my permission to do so."

He further testified, that he knew of the unguarded condition of the set-screw; that it was dangerous to pass between the pulley and the set-screw; and that he never directed the deceased to protect it. It is true that he stated that a hood had been placed over the set-screw before the deceased commenced work, and that the deceased had removed it. This testimony was contradicted by other witnesses, and we have seen that the jury found that the deceased did not remove it.

The appellant asked one Jackson, a witness, to state the duties of a millwright. An objection was sustained to this line of evidence, which is urged as error. The court pertinently remarked that what this man did was the proper inquiry. We have already shown, by an excerpt from the testimony of the foreman, that this line of evidence was immaterial. It was not important what were the duties of a millwright in other mills. The question was, what was the duty of the deceased in this mill. The evidence clearly shows that he filed the saws and oiled the machinery on the upper deck; that he could not make any change or alteration without the permission of the foreman, and that the latter knew of the defect which caused the injury, and did not direct it to be safeguarded. This case is, therefore, clearly distinguishable from *Woellen v. Lewiston-Clarkston Co.*, 49 Wash. 405, 95 Pac. 493, and kindred cases.

The court gave the following instruction, to which error is assigned:

"Now, I want to make clear to you, if I can, this matter of burden of proof. If the testimony in a case were equally balanced, just as much testimony, credible testimony, on one side as on the other, then it is the duty of the court or jury to decide against the person who has the burden upon him, because by the burden means that he must show to the satisfaction, and if it is evenly balanced, then of course the person who has had the burden has not overcome that; so that when I say the burden of proof in the main case of showing that the deceased lost his life by being caught on a set-screw that was unguarded, is upon the plaintiff, it means that they must make it out to your satisfaction or by a fair preponderance of the evidence; likewise, when I say the burden of proof of showing negligence upon his own part, which has proximately caused his death, is upon the defendant, they must make that out to your satisfaction, by a fair preponderance of the evidence." The instruction is correct, under the rule announced in *Carstens v. Earles*, 26 Wash. 676, 67 Pac. 404, and *Hart v. Niagara Fire Ins. Co.*, 9 Wash. 620, 38 Pac. 213, 27 L. R. A. 86.

The appellant contends in his brief, and earnestly contended in the oral argument, that the deceased was guilty of contributory negligence, and that for this reason there should be a reversal of the judgment. It contends that the plank leading to the right of the shaft, to which reference has been made, afforded a safe way to reach the canting gear. The jury upon competent evidence has disposed of this contention. The only danger that could arise from walking on the two eight-inch planks leading to the left, and stepping over the shaft, was from the presence of the pulley and the set-screw. The injury did not come from the pulley. Can it be said, as a matter of law, that it was negligence for the deceased to step over the set-screw, which was elevated some sixteen or eighteen inches above the timbers upon which he was walking? We have seen that both ways were used by different persons in going to the canting gear, and that the projecting set-screw was the only danger. It is true that the jury found that the deceased knew of the existence of the set-screw. We have seen that the shaft containing the collar and set-screw was placed upon a timber eight inches in width. There are two reasons why we cannot declare as a matter of law that it was negligence for the deceased to step over the set-screw. The first is that, whilst injury might result therefrom, the act was not necessarily a negligent one. The other, and perhaps the stronger one, is that the law does not require a person engaged in the performance of duty to constantly keep his mind on some defective piece of machinery. To do so would place too great a burden on the human mind. In *Hall v. West & Slade Mill Co.*, 39 Wash. 447, 81 Pac. 915, the respondent's cloth-

—19

ing was caught upon an unguarded set-screw with which he came in contact in a moment of forgetfulness, while handling a heavy piece of timber between two parallel lines of rollers located about four feet apart. Speaking to the question of contributory negligence, at page 451, the court said:

"But it will hardly do to say that an employee is guilty of contributory negligence for merely working in a dangerous place when he does not assume the risk of injury for working therein. It is true that in such cases contributory negligence and assumption of risk approximate, and it is difficult to draw a line between them, but we think that, to convict an employee of contributory negligence for working in a place where he does not assume the risk of injury, it must be shown that he did not use care reasonably commensurate with the risk to avoid injurious consequences; in other words, that it was some negligent act of his own that caused his injury, and not alone the dangers of his situation."

In the *Hall* case the injured party testified that he came in contact with the unguarded machinery in a moment of forgetfulness, and in the instant case the injured party did not testify, but it was a legitimate and reasonable inference that the jury had a right to deduce from the testimony, that the deceased did momentarily forget the existence of the set-screw. Such inference is indeed strengthened because, as we have said, the act of stepping over was not necessarily negligent. See, also, *Rector v. Bryant Lumber etc. Co.*, 41 Wash. 556, 84 Pac. 7; *Erickson v. McNeeley & Co.*, 41 Wash. 509, 84 Pac. 3.

There was no error in the instruction that the testimony was conflicting upon certain points. It merely stated an actual fact. Nor did the court err in refusing to give the requested instructions. The instructions given in their entirety clearly stated the governing law. Other minor questions are suggested, which we have examined and conclude are without merit.

The judgment will be affirmed with costs to the respondent.

RUDKIN, C. J., and FULLERTON, J., concur.

CHADWICK, J. (concurring)—The risk was clearly assumed, and but for the factory act respondent could not recover. Upon the merits of the case, the only defense that could be set up is that of contributory negligence. This issue was resolved against appellant by the jury. I therefore concur in the result reached by Judge Gose.

MORRIS, J. (concurring)—I concur solely upon the answers to the first and third interrogatories. If deceased was caught on the set-screw while attempting to step over the shaft, on his way to oil the canting gear, as contended for by appellant, I think he would be guilty of such contributory negligence as would bar a recovery. Such an act would not be the act of an ordinarily prudent man, and to my mind, reasonable minds could not differ in reaching a like conclusion. But the jury having specially found that the evidence did not show deceased was injured while stepping over the shaft, and that the evidence did not show where he was going, such finding is controlling, and I cannot interpose a contradictory finding and say he was caught while in the act of stepping over the shaft on his way to oil the canting gear. For this reason alone I concur.

[No. 7938. Department Two. November 16, 1909.]

ARCHIE BENNER, *Respondent*, v. WALLACE LUMBER & MANUFACTURING COMPANY, *Appellant*.

Master and Servant—Negligence of Master—Defective Appliance—Guards—Factory Act.
Same—Assumption of Risks.
Master and Servant—Appliances—Guarding Machinery—Factory Act —Prima·Facie Case—Instructions—Harmless Error.

Appeal from a judgment of the superior court for Snohomish county, Neterer, J., entered June 29, 1908, upon the verdict of a jury rendered in favor of the plaintiff, in an action for personal injuries sustained by an employee in a shingle mill. Affirmed.

Roberts & Hulbert, for appellant.
Lyter & Folsom and *S. G. Murray*, for respondent.

CROW, J.—This action was originally commenced by Archie Benner, an infant, by Mary Benner, his guardian *ad litem*, against the Wallace Lumber & Manufacturing Company, a corporation, to recover damages for personal injuries sustained. Prior to the trial the plaintiff attained his majority, and now prosecutes the action. From a judgment in his favor the defendant has appealed.

The appellant owns and operates a shingle mill in Snohomish county, in which the respondent, a young man about twenty years of age, was employed as a shingle packer. The mill was equipped with three knot saws, and occasionally the appellant directed the respondent to operate one of them. He had worked on the saw at different times, to the total amount of seventeen and one-half days. The saw was adjusted on an arbor immediately in front of, and about eighteen inches from, the sawyer. Slightly above the saw was a shelf or table, on which were the shingles which were to be trimmed by the sawyer. The edge of the table, when properly constructed, so extended over the saw as to leave only a small portion thereof exposed, thus serving as a safeguard for the protection of the sawyer. Immediately in front of the sawyer, and slightly below the level of the table, was a sliding carriage upon which he placed the shingles he intended to trim. He then pushed the carriage under the table, carrying the shingles against the saw and trimming them. The sawyer was compelled to reach over the table for the shingles, and in doing so passed his hand above the level of the saw.

On the morning of the accident, appellant's foreman directed him to operate the knot saw. About three o'clock in the afternoon, as respondent withdrew his hand after reaching over the table for shingles, it in some manner came in contact with the saw, and was severely injured. In his complaint and on the trial, he contended that the appellant was guilty of negligence in failing properly to safeguard the saw, and that he was injured by reason thereof.

The first, and as we regard it, the controlling contention made by the appellant, is that the trial court erred in denying its motion for a directed verdict. It contends that the saw had been properly guarded, but that the guard had been removed and replaced from time to time by appellant's employees, certain other knot sawyers, for their own convenience in performing their work. There was evidence tending to show that, when the saw was first installed and the table was first constructed, some years prior to the accident, the edge of the table had been sufficiently extended to constitute a practical safeguard. It was further shown that, from time to time, the knot sawyers would chop out or saw off the edge of the table, leaving greater portions of the saw exposed; that other knot sawyers, before commencing work, would nail on a band or cleat to again extend it and more securely guard the saw, and that the various sawyers, from time to time, made these changes according to their own ideas.

Appellant therefore contends that, when it, as the master, had properly constructed the table to serve as a guard, it had discharged its full duty, and that if the sawyers thereafter removed, changed, or added to the guard, the appellant was not guilty of negligence in failing to install or maintain the same. This contention cannot be sustained. Whenever a master employs a servant, or changes the character of his work, it is the master's duty, at the inception of and during such employment, to furnish the servant a reasonably safe place in which to work, and to also comply with the requirements of the factory act in properly safeguarding saws and other dangerous machinery, where guards are practical. Whether an employee has wilfully changed, removed, or destroyed a proper safeguard, provided by the master, might become a material issue if such servant, being injured, should attempt to recover damages. But no such issue is now before us. There is ample evidence in the record to show that, when the appellant directed the respondent to commence work on the saw, it was not then properly guarded, a fact the master should have known, and that by reason of the absence of a proper guard, the respondent was injured. A reckless or negligent servant might wilfully remove a proper guard that had been provided by the master. Another servant more cautious and conservative might himself voluntarily perform the duty of the master by restoring the guard before commencing his work. The respondent did neither. He was under no obligation to provide or change the guard. He commenced work upon the saw in obedience to the order of the master, and the only question to be determined is whether it could be, and was then, guarded as required by the factory act. As above stated, the appellant introduced considerable evidence to show that it was the custom of knot sawyers to repeatedly change, remove, or add to the guard, to suit their own convenience, and in substance contended that, when it had once properly safeguarded the saw it had discharged its duty, and that the custom of the employees constituted a. sufficient excuse to relieve it of any charge of negligence resulting from its subsequent failure to restore the guard. The statute not only · requires that guards be provided, but also that they be *maintained* in use. Laws 1907, p. 448, ch. 205, § 1.

The appellant cites *Johnston v. Northern Lumber Co.*, 42 Wash. 230, 84 Pac. 627, and *Daffron v. Majestic Laundry Co.*, 41 Wash. 65, 82 Pac. 1089, and contends, on the authority of those cases, that it is relieved from liability for negligence by reason of the fact that it had properly safeguarded the saw. There is a marked difference between the facts of the case at bar and those of the cases cited. In the *Johnston* case the guard· had not been changed or removed. It had been in use for a number of years. It had not only been properly installed, but had been also maintained. The servant had been working at the machine with the same guard during all of that time. The contention there made was that some guard other than the one actually used should have been adopted. In the *Daffron* case it appeared that a proper guard had been provided. Here the fact seems to be that no practical or proper guard whatever was provided for the knot saw, at the particular time the respondent went to work, or during the time he continued at work. If the appellant could excuse its neglect by relying upon the action of the knot sawyers in changing or removing the guards, such a defense would be equivalent to withdrawing from the jury the vital issue whether the saw was properly guarded when used by the respondent, and substituting in lieu thereof an immaterial inquiry into the custom of knot sawyers who had preceded respondent in operating the saw. The statute does not contemplate or permit any such defense or excuse. There was abundant evidence to sustain the jury in finding that a practical guard .could be provided, that it was not provided at the time the respondent commenced work, and that as a result thereof he was injured. The motion for a directed verdict was properly denied.

The trial court instructed the jury on the defense of assumption of risk pleaded by the appellant. After the jury had retired, the respondent promptly interposed an exception to the giving of this instruction. Thereupon the jury were recalled, and the trial judge withdrew the defense from their consideration as not being an issue in the case. The appellant has assigned error upon the withdrawal of the instruction. The controlling issue of fact in· this case was whether the knot saw could be and was guarded. The only ground of negligence alleged was appellant's failure to guard. If appellant had· guarded there could be no recovery. If the saw could not be guarded, appellant was in no event negligent. Assumption of risk was not an issue in the case. If appellant had failed to provide proper guards when practicable, the defense could not be interposed. *Hall v. West & Slade Mill Co.*, 39 Wash. 447, 81 Pac. 915.

The mill had been inspected by the deputy labor commissioner, who issued a certificate which the appellant posted in compliance with the requirements of the statute. The certificate was admitted in evidence, and the deputy who made the inspection appeared as a witness for appellant and testified as to what he considered necessary to constitute a proper safeguard, and stated the condition in which he found the mill. The appellant in writing requested, with others, the following instructions No. 19:

"You are instructed that under the law of this state that if the operator of a mill has his mill inspected by the labor commissioner or one of his deputies and receives a certificate of inspection and posts the same in his mill, that this certificate is *prima facie* evidence that the factory act has been complied with and that the machinery and appliances have been constructed and maintained in a reasonably safe condition. In other words, the law requires the operator of a mill to have his mill inspected by the state labor commissioner of this state and whenever this is done and a certificate is issued to the owner of a mill and the certificates are posted in the mill the presumption is that the mill operator has complied with the law with reference to the guards and other matters and that the mill is in a proper condition and that the operator has furnished and maintained reasonable and proper safeguards; so, if you should find in this case that the defendant company had its mill inspected by the state labor commissioner or his deputy and that the commissioner had issued a certificate of inspection, copies of which certificates were posted in the mill, then I instruct you that this was *prima facie* evidence of the defendants having complied with the factory act. It is *prima facie* evidence that the knot-saws in question in this case were reasonably and properly guarded, and I further instruct you that if the defendant in this case had complied with the factory act in regard to the furnishing of reasonable safeguards then I instruct you that the plaintiff cannot recover and your verdict must be for the defendant; you are instructed also that even if the defendant failed to comply with the factory act in furnishing a reasonable and proper safeguard, yet if the plaintiff himself was guilty of negligence he cannot recover and your verdict must be for the defendant."

This instruction was not given, nor did the trial judge give any other instruction relating to the inspection by the deputy, and the posting of his certificate. Appellant has assigned error upon the refusal of the instruction requested. In the order denying the motion for new trial, the trial judge said:

"The defendant in support of its motion for a new trial urges two reasons: . . . 2nd. That the court refused to give the defendant's requested instruction No. 19. The instruction as requested should not have been given; it was not error to refuse it. Was it error not to give an instruction covering the certificate of inspection? If the court's attention has been actually called to the fact, or if the exception to the instruction as given had been actually taken at the time, the court perhaps would have recalled the jury so as to preclude all possibility of error; the question now is, was prejudicial error committed? The deputy labor commissioner was present in court and testified fully as to the facts upon which his conclusion was based in issuing this certificate of inspection. The reason for the rule to make the certificate *prima facie* evidence was overcome by his testimony in court. The certificate could not be stronger than the testimony upon which it was based; and this was before the jury, and must be weighed as other evidence. If the testimony was absent, and the certificate was present, a different condition would exist. The certificate would not be admissible in evidence, unless made so by the legislature, because the examination was *ex parte*, and the defendant would be deprived of the facts before the jury upon which the certificate is based. The instructions given preclude all possibility of error. The burden in the case at no time shifted; it at all times remained with the plaintiff. It was incumbent upon the plaintiff to show by a fair preponderance of the evidence that the machinery was not guarded, and that it could be guarded, and all the facts being before the jury, and the court having instructed the jury, as in this case, it is inconceivable how error could be predicated upon the record as it stands in this case, conceding that the requested instruction was proper. The motion for a new trial is denied, and exception noted."

Some question arises in our minds as to whether the appellant is in a position to predicate error upon any of the instructions given or refused. The record shows that no exceptions were taken by it until after the jury had returned its verdict; that by stipulation the parties agreed that its exceptions might be taken at any time prior to the hearing of the motion for a new trial, and that written exceptions were subsequently made by the appellant. In view of the fact that the respondent has raised no question as to the sufficiency of these exceptions, and that in any event we find no prejudicial error in giving or refusing instructions, we will, without deciding, assume for the purposes of this case that the appellant's exceptions were, under the circumstances, sufficient.

On the record before us, we are constrained to hold that no prejudicial error was committed by the trial judge in failing to give the requested instruction upon the effect of the certificate as evidence. If no evidence other than the certificate had been introduced to show the safeguarding of the saw or to dispute the same, it would upon proper request have been the duty of the trial judge to instruct the jury that such certificate was *prima facie* evidence of compliance on the part of appellant with the requirements of the factory act. During the trial much evidence was introduced by the respondent to show that as a matter of fact the saw was not properly safeguarded, while the appellant introduced evidence not only of other witnesses but also of the inspector himself to show that it was safeguarded. This being true, no issue as to the existence of a *prima facie* case was before the jury for its consideration. Although it would have been proper for the trial judge to give an instruction upon this subject, we fail to see how his omission to do so constituted prejudicial error or could have affected the verdict, in the light of the issues framed by the pleadings and the evidence introduced at the trial. The issuance and posting of the certificate was not disputed, and it is not at all improbable that the jury would give more consideration to the potency of the certificate as evidence of a performance of statutory duty by the appellant than if they had been told that it constituted *prima facie* evidence only.

Other exceptions have been taken to instructions given and refused. We have carefully examined the instructions given by the trial judge, and find that they fully, clearly and correctly state all questions of law applicable to the issues in this case which, under the pleadings and evidence, were proper for the consideration of the jury. The evidence is abundantly sufficient to show that the knot saw could have been, but was not, safeguarded, that for the want of any guard the respondent was injured, and that he was not guilty of contributory negligence.

The judgment is affirmed.

RUDKIN, C. J., MOUNT, PARKER, and DUNBAR, JJ., concur.

[No. 8023. Department Two. July 29, 1909.]

FRANK R. WARD, *Respondent*, v. NATIONAL LUMBER & BOX COMPANY, *Appellant.*

Master and Servant—Guarding Machinery—Factory Act—Statutes—Construction—Ejusdem Generis.
Master and Servant—Contributory Negligence—Question for Jury.
Same—Obvious Dangers.
Same—Assumption of Risks—Giving Notice of Danger to Master.

Appeal from a judgment of the superior court for Chehalis county, Irwin, J., entered January 8, 1909, upon the verdict of a jury rendered in favor of the plaintiff for personal injuries sustained by an employee in a factory. Affirmed.

W. H. Abel and *A. M. Abel,* for appellant.
Govnor Teats, Hugo Metzler, and *Leo Teats,* for respondent.

DUNBAR, J.—This is an appeal by the National Lumber & Box Company, from a judgment rendered against it in the sum of $2,000, in a suit brought by respondent, Frank B. Ward, for personal injuries received by him in its employ. The injury was the loss of his left hand, which was cut and torn off between the grease cup and friction wheel while he was lubricating a bearing.

The friction wheel drives the set works to the double cut-off saw.

In order to oil ,the bearing, it was necessary to mount a ladder and walk along a plank. The friction wheel revolved upon a shafting. The boxing of the shaft was fastened to a timber, known as a bridge tree. The oiler had to go in a stooping position, reach through between two horizontal timbers, and oil the bearing. To lubricate this bearing, there was an oil extension pipe and patent cup, the pipe being between two and three feet long, fastened in the boxing, and extending therefrom to where the oiler stood. There was also a patent grease cup fastened in the boxing, consisting of a pipe about six inches long, with cup attached, screwed into the boxing at a distance of about three-fourths of an inch from the spokes of the friction wheel.

Ward had used the oil cup for the purpose of lubricating this bearing for about three weeks before the accident, when he found the grease cup placed there, as he supposed, for him to use; and from that time until the accident he did use the grease cup to lubricate the bearing. He testified that he had been instructed to economize the oil, as it was very expensive, and to use the grease when it could be used, and that he was undertaking to follow out what he supposed was the will and desire of his employers in using the grease instead of the oil. In turning the grease cup, his hand was sucked in, as he says, by the wheel, and was cut off.

The case was tried to a jury. At the close of the respondent's case, motion was made for nonsuit, which motion was overruled. The case went to trial. The defense introduced testimony in support of its contention that the respondent had been guilty of negligence, and had assumed the risk, and that there was no negligence on the part of the appellant. The motion was repeated at the end of the whole case, and refused, and the case submitted to the jury, with the verdict mentioned above, viz., the sum of $2,000, for which judgment was entered.

There are two principal contentions of the appellant in this case, viz.: (1) That the factory act does not in terms require friction wheels to be guarded, and that therefore the respondent should be charged with the assumption of risk in operating a machine which was noticeably dangerous; and (2) that the respondent was guilty of contributory negligence in operating said machine in the way he did operate it.

The factory act provides for reasonable safeguards for all vats, pans, trimmers, cut-off, gang-edger, and other saws, planers, cogs, gearings, belting, shafting, couplings, set-screws, live rollers, conveyors, mangles in laundries and machinery of other or similar description. The enacting clause is: "An act providing for the protection of employees in factories, mills or workshops where machinery is used." Laws 1903, page 40. The act further provides for ventilation and sanitary conditions, guarding of trapdoors and hatchways, etc.; so that it will be seen from a reading of the act that the evident intention of the legislature was to protect operatives in factories in every manner and in every particular in which they could be protected, consistent with the reasonable operation of the particular factory which was engaged in business. The appellant invokes the rule of *ejusdem generis*, and insists that the friction wheel, not being specified in the factory act and not being of the same kind or genus as any of the machinery specially mentioned, does not fall under the head of machinery of other or similar description, and that therefore the assumption of risk attaches in this kind of a case. Considering the whole scope of the factory act and the evident intention of the legislature, we are unable to reach the conclusion contended for by the appellant. There is no doubt that the general rule is that the general word must take its meaning and be presumed to embrace only things or persons of the kind designated in the specific words; but, as is said in 26 Am. & Eng. Ency. Law (2d ed.), p. 610, the object of the rule in question being not to defeat but to ascertain and effectuate the legislative intent, it will not be applied where the application would be in the face of the evident meaning of the framers of the law. In other words, the maxim has no application where there is no room for construction but only when the meaning is not apparent from the language itself; and it is also said,

"Nor does the rule obtain where the specific words signify subjects greatly different from one another, for here the general expression might very consistently add one more variety; in such case, the general term must receive its natural and wide meaning."

This is peculiarly the case under our statute, where the specific words signify subjects greatly different from one another, vats, pans, trimmers, cut-off, gang-edger and other saws, planers, cogs, gearings, belting, shafting, coupling, set-screws, live rollers, conveyors, mangles in laundries, etc., all or nearly all, being machinery or parts of machinery of different character. We think, in the face of the statute, it would be doing violence to the evident intention of the legislature to hold that the duty to guard the machinery in question was not imposed upon the millowner; and the testimony is undisputed that this machine could have been guarded without affecting the efficiency of its operation.

It is also strenuously contended that the respondent was guilty of contributory negligence in using a machine which was manifestly dangerous, and in using it in the manner in which he did use it. A persistent attempt was made during the trial of the cause, as shown by the record, to show that it was negligence for the respondent to take hold of the cup with his left hand instead of his right; but outside of the fact that there is nothing to indicate that the cup could not be manipulated as safely with the left hand as with the right, the testimony of all the respondent's witnesses, as well as his own testimony, was to the effect that it would have been inconvenient to have used his right hand owing to the manner in which the cup had to be approached by the oiler. We are speaking now exclusively of the testimony of the respondent, any conflicting testimony on that subject which was submitted by the appellant having been submitted to the discretion of the jury; and assuming that the testimony of the respondent was true, we are unable to determine that the use of this machine in the way in which it was used was contributory negligence as a matter of law.

Nor is it reasonable to our minds to impute to the respondent the knowledge of the dangerous condition of the machine to such an extent that it was apparently too dangerous to be used with safety, when the undisputed testimony shows that it had been used by the respondent for three weeks prior to the accident, and when it had been established, in the condition in which it existed, by the appellant itself. It could scarcely be said with reason that the minds of reasonable men could not differ on that subject, when the machine was conceived and constructed by the appellant, and placed there for practical operation by its employees.

There is some contention by the appellant that it was the duty of the oiler to report to the appellant when the machinery was found in a dangerous condition. But this duty and instruction certainly did not have reference to the original construction of the mill and arrangement of the machinery; but only to any machinery that had become dangerous by misplacement or accident of any kind.

On the whole we are unable to find any reversible error in the record, and the judgment will therefore be affirmed.

Rudkin, C. J., Mount, Crow, and Parker, JJ., concur.

[No. 8178. Department Two. October 29, 1909.]

Frank Hoseth, *Respondent*, v. Preston Mill Company, *Appellant*.

Appeal—Review—Record—Evidence—Presumptions.
Appeal—Review—Evidence—Question for Jury.
Appeal—Review—Harmless Error.
Appeal—Review—Correction of Error—Trial—Instructions.
Master and Servant—Negligence—Acts of Vice Principal—Assistance in Work.

Appeal from a judgment of the superior court for King county, Tallman, J., entered January 11, 1909, upon the verdict of a jury rendered in favor of the plaintiff, in an action for personal injuries sustained by a signalman employed in a logging camp. Affirmed.

Shank & Smith, for appellant.
Vince H. Faben and *Martin J. Lund*, for respondent.

Dunbar, J.—This appeal is from a judgment rendered upon the verdict of a jury in the sum of $5,000, in an action for personal injuries. This action has been in this court upon a former appeal, and is reported in 49 Wash. 682, 96 Pac. 423, where the following brief statement of the case is presented, which we will adopt:

"This action was instituted in the court below to recover damages for personal injuries. At the time of receiving the injuries complained of, the plaintiff was in the employ of the defendant in one of its logging camps, and was standing near a cable extending from the logging engine out into the forest, for the purpose of transmitting signals from the men in the forest to the engineer. In transmitting the signals, the plaintiff stood within ten or twelve feet of a large stump to which a snatch block was anchored for the purpose of holding the cable in place. The snatch block was fastened to the stump by a lead line which was wrapped one and one-half times around the stump, and a swamp hook attached to the end of the line was hooked or fastened into the body of the stump. While the plaintiff was occupying this position, the strain on the cable caused the swamp hook at the end of the lead line to give way, and the hook or line struck him, fracturing his leg and arm. The specific acts of negligence charged in the complaint were the use of a defective and inadequate hook, and the failure to securely fasten the hook in the stump. The answer denied the negligence charged in the complaint, and alleged affirmatively contributory negligence on the part of the plaintiff and negligence of a fellow servant."

The judgment was reversed for the reason that an instruction as to damages caused by a fall from crutches three months after the original injury, to the effect that plaintiff is not guilty of negligence if using the leg before complete recovery with the permission of the physician, in the absence of bad faith, and may recover for injuries incurred while walking around in good faith, is erroneous in failing to require reasonable care in the plaintiff, and is not cured by a contradictory instruction on the subject of contributory negligence. Upon a retrial of the cause, the verdict above mentioned was obtained, and judgment was entered, and the case is here again on appeal.

It is insisted that there is no evidence whatever to show who set the swamp hook at the time of the injury to the plaintiff. The hooktender, Mr. McCormick, at the time of both trials was dead. In the absence of proof, the presumption must be that, in the orderly and usual conduct of the business, the hook was set by a tender duly authorized by the defendant company. It is stated by the appellant that there is a sharp conflict in the testimony between the plaintiff and the skid-road man, the doctor and the nurses who attended him during his injuries, and other witnesses offered by the defense, and this conflict of testimony is largely set forth. With a sharp conflict of testimony, or indeed any substantial conflict of testimony, this court has no concern, questions of that kind being submitted entirely to the jury; so that it is not necessary to discuss in this opinion questions involving the conflict of testimony.

The first assignment is that the court erred in allowing plaintiff to introduce evidence, over objection, that plaintiff was inexperienced and was not warned by defendant or its employees. In addition to the fact that this affected only the question of contributory negligence, and that there is no testimony whatever tending to show contributory negligence on the part of the plaintiff, the admission of this testimony could be at least only immaterial, and not in any way prejudicial. Moreover, this court, at the request of the appellant, instructed the jury directly upon this point, as follows:

"You are instructed that plaintiff does not charge in his complaint and cannot recover for any acts of negligence and carelessness of defendant, or any of its servants, in and about any other thing, or in any other manner than that of the selection and use of the swamp hook, and the manner in which it was fastened in the stump by defendant's foreman or under his immediate supervision."

On the point raised in relation to the testimony of want of warning, introduced by the plaintiff, the court instructed as follows:

"You are further instructed that plaintiff has not charged in his complaint, and cannot recover for any act of carelessness or negligence of its foreman by reason of the failure to warn the plaintiff of any danger to which he was subjected by reason of the performance of the work he was directed to do. Even though you should find from the evidence that the injury to plaintiff was caused by the failure of defendant to warn the plaintiff of danger to which he might be subjected, yet you cannot find a verdict for the plaintiff by reason thereof."

Notwithstanding this instruction, it is insisted by the appellant that the error was not cured by said instruction. But the trial of a lawsuit cannot be conducted in every particular in exact accord with prescribed rules. Many slight errors are liable to creep in, and the best that can be done is for the court to correct the error and remedy the inadvertence as nearly as possible. In this case this attempt was made by the court, and we think that the direct, positive, and explicit instruction of the court in this case substantially cured the error committed, if error it was in the first instance.

It is also alleged that the court erred in instructing the jury as follows:

"If you shall find from the evidence in the case that the swamp hook was insecurely and improperly fastened to the stump and by reason thereof liable to give way and fall out, and to cause injury to the plaintiff, and that the plaintiff did not know these facts and could not have known them under the circumstances, by the exercise of reasonable care and caution, and that such facts were known to defendant's foreman in charge of the plaintiff, or by the use of reasonable care could have been known by him and that the foreman failed to remedy the defect and failed to have the swamp hook properly fastened and that such defect on the part of defendant's foreman was the cause of such injury to plaintiff, then you should find a verdict for the plaintiff."

As presenting the opposite doctrine, the appellant asked that the following instructions be given by the court, which was by the court refused, which refusal is assigned as error here:

"I instruct you, gentlemen of the jury, that the master owes a duty to its servant to use reasonable care to provide reasonably safe tools and appliances with which to prosecute the work undertaken, and if injury is caused to the servant by reason of the master's failure to perform that duty, and while the servant is using due care, then the master is liable for damages for injuries so caused. If you shall find from a fair preponderance of the evidence before you that the injuries to plaintiff complained of were caused by the use of the swamp hook that was too small or inadequate for the work for which it was used, and in addition thereto that defendant was careless and negligent in the selection of the swamp hook, and while the plaintiff was using due care, then your verdict should be given for the plaintiff. But you are instructed that if the defendant in this case used due and reasonable care in the selection of a reasonably safe swamp hook, then defendant has performed its entire duty which it owed to the plaintiff in this respect, and plaintiff cannot recover any damages resulting from the use of the size and the kind of hook used."

The twelfth instruction asked for contains substantially the same idea. The argument of the appellant in support of its assignments is that, when a master has used due and reasonable care in the selection of reasonably safe tools and appliances, and the furnishing of a safe place in which the servant is to work, he has performed his entire duty, and cannot be liable for any injuries arising from the conduct of his business; that it is not his duty to see that such tools are properly adjusted in the ordinary conduct of the business of the master; that it is not the duty of the master to follow every servant about and see that he does not place an instrumentality or a combination of instrumentalities, or the place, temporarily, where the servants are working, in a dangerous condition. The fault of this argument, as applied to this particular case, is that there is no question of fellow servant involved here, or the question of the master following servants around to see that they properly use instrumentalities which are furnished to them by the master; because, under the former rulings of this court, the hooktender is the *alter ego* of the master, and therefore it is the master himself who is performing his own duty in the management of the instrumentalities employed in the performance of the work.

In the cases cited by the appellant to sustain this contention, the injury was either the result of the action of a fellow servant, or the plaintiff was engaged in work under his own control and as a representative of the master, as in the case of *Anderson v. Inland Telephone etc. Co.*, 19 Wash. 575, 53 Pac. 657, 41 L. R. A. 410. That the hooktender here was performing a nondelegable duty of the master, see *Sullivan v. Wood & Co.*, 43 Wash. 259, 86 Pac. 629, 117 Am. St. 1047; *Goldthorpe v. Clark-Nickerson Lum. Co.*, 31 Wash. 467, 71 Pac. 1091.

We have examined the other instructions complained of, but in the light of the whole instruction given by the court, which was extremely fair and presented every defense available under the law to the appellant with no uncertain qualifications, the instructions given being more favorable, as we view them, to the appellant than they were to the respondent, we think no error was committed in the giving or refusing of instructions.

As to the claim of excessive damages allowed, we are unable to reach the conclusion from the testimony that the verdict of the jury and the judgment of the court in this respect ought to be interfered with by this court. The judgment is therefore affirmed.

.. RUDKIN, C. J., MOUNT, CROW, and PARKER, JJ., concur.

[No. 7776. Decided June 28, 1909.]

THE STATE OF WASHINGTON *on the Relation of John D. Atkinson, Attorney General, Respondent,* v. NORTHERN PACIFIC RAILWAY COMPANY, *Appellant.*

Master and Servant—Railroads—Hours of Service—Statutes—Construction—Federal Statute Superseding State Legislation.

Appeal from a judgment of the superior court for Thurston county, Linn, J., entered December 4, 1907, in favor of the plaintiff, upon sustaining a demurrer to the answer, in a prosecution for the violation of a statute regulating the hours of service of railway employees. Affirmed.

Geo. T. Reid and *J. W. Quick* for appellant.

John D. Atkinson, J. B. Alexander and *W. V. Tanner* for respondent.

FULLERTON, J.—The legislature of the State of Washington at its session of 1907 passed an act (Laws 1907, p. 25, ch. 20) regulating the hours of service of railroad employees. By the act it was made unlawful for any common carrier operating a railroad to require or permit any of its employees engaged in or connected with the movement of its trains to remain on duty for a longer period than sixteen consecutive hours, except in certain specified instances. A violation of the act was made a misdemeanor, subjecting the offending carrier to a penalty of not less than one hundred nor more more than one thousand dollars for each offense, to be recovered in a suit brought by the attorney general on a duly verified information being filed with him showing that a violation of the act had occurred. This act, as it had no emergency clause, went into effect on June 12, 1907.

On March 4, 1907, the Congress of the United States passed an act on the same subject-matter. U. S. Stat. at Large, p. 1415, ch. 2939. In this act, among other provisions, it was made unlawful for any common carrier, its officers or agents, to require or permit any employee to be or remain on duty for a longer period than sixteen consecutive hours, under a penalty not to exceed five hundred dollars for each and every violation, to be recovered by suit brought by the United States district attorney in the district court of the United States having jurisdiction in the locality where the act was committed, on satisfactory evidence being lodged with the district attorney that there has been a violation of the act. It was expressly provided, however, that this act should "take effect and be in force one year after its passage," or on March 4, 1908.

On August 26, 1907, the attorney general of the State of Washington brought the present action against the appellant, charging it with a violation of the state statute in the operation of one of its freight trains between Seattle and Sedro-Woolley, both points being within the State of Washington. In the complaint it was averred that the train left the terminal station at Seattle at 6:30 a. m. of July 3, 1907, and reached effect and be in force one year after its passage," or on March 4, 1908. being on the way nineteen hours and forty-five minutes, during which time the employees in charge of the train, to-wit, the engineer, fireman, · two brakemen, and the conductor, were required to be on continuous duty. Judgment was demanded for one thousand dollars, the maximum amount of the penalty.

The appellant answered admitting the specific charge that it had at the time mentioned required its employees to work continuously for a period of nineteen hours, but denied that it was thereby guilty of violating any state statute. It then set out affirmatively that it was a common carrier engaged in carrying interstate as well as intrastate commerce; that the freight train on which its employees were engaged at the time complained of was carrying various and sundry articles of merchandise shipped from points without the state to points within the State of Washington; various and sundry articles of merchandise shipped from points within the State of Washington to points without such state; and various and sundry articles of merchandise shipped through the state from points without the state to other points without the state. It then set out the act of Congress of March 4, 1907, above mentioned, and averred that it was governed in relation to the number of hours it might require its employees to remain continuously on duty, by that statute, and that the statute of the state regulating such hours of labor was not, at the time alleged in the complaint of the plaintiff, applicable to that particular train, or the employees engaged therein; and claimed immunity from the penalties imposed thereby. A demurrer was interposed and sustained to the answer, whereupon the appellant elected to stand thereon and refused to plead further. Judgment was thereupon entered against it for the full amount of the penalty, and this appeal taken therefrom.

Counsel for the appellant concede that it is within the power of the state, in the absence of Congressional legislation on the subject, to enact laws operative within the boundaries of the state regulating the number of hours an employee of a railroad company can be required to remain on continuous duty, even though the railroad company may be a common carrier engaged in interstate commerce. On the other hand, it is conceded by the state that the power of the Congress to regulate interstate commerce in plenary, and that, as an incident to this power, the Congress may regulate by legislation the instrumentalities engaged in the business, and may prescribe the number of consecutive hours an employee of a carrier so engaged shall be required to remain on duty; and that when it does legislate upon the subject, its act supersedes any and all state legislation on that particular subject. In fact, these propositions can hardly be said to be debatable in the state courts, since the Federal courts, whose decisions are authoritative on questions of this character, have repeatedly announced them as governing principles in determining the validity of regulative legislation concerning carriers of interstate commerce. *Escanaba etc. Transp. Co. v. Chicago*, 107 U. S. 678, 2 Sup. Ct. 185, 27 L. Ed. 442; *Morgan etc. S. S. Co. v. Louisiana Board of Health*, 118 U. S. 455, 6 Sup. Ct. 1114, 30 L. Ed. 237; *Nashville etc. R. Co. v. Alabama*, 128 U. S. 96, 9 Sup. Ct. 28, 32 L. Ed. 352; *Gladson v. Minnesota*, 166 U. S. 427, 17 Sup. Ct., 627, 41 L. Ed. 1064; *Lake Shore etc. R. Co. v. Ohio*, 173 U. S. 285, 19 Sup. Ct. 465, 43 L. Ed. 702; *Erb v. Morasch*, 177 U. S. 584, 20 Sup. Ct. 819, 44 L. Ed. 897.

Since, therefore, both the Congressional and state statutes relate to the same subject-matter, and purport to regulate the same specific acts, it is manifest that the Congressional statute superseded the state statute at some point of time, determined by the determination of the status of the Congressional act between the time of its enactment on March 4, 1907, and the time it became actively operative on March 4, 1908. If it had the effect of a law during the period it remained in suspension, then manifestly the state statute never went into effect, in so far as it related to roads engaged in interstate commerce; while, on the other hand, if it became effective as a law at the expiration of the year, the state statute became effective as against roads engaged in interstate commerce, on June 12, 1907, and continued in force until March 4, 1908, and was operative at the time the acts here complained of were committed.

The general rule is that a statute speaks from the time it goes into effect, whether that time be the day of its enactment or some future day to which the power enacting the statute has postponed the time of its taking effect.

"A law must be understood as beginning to speak at the moment it takes effect, and not before. If passed to take effect at a future day, it must be construed as if passed on that day, and ordered to take immediate effect." *Rice v. Ruddiman*, 10 Mich. 125.

"A statute passed to take effect at a future day must be understood as speaking from the time it goes into operation and not from the time of passage. Thus, the words 'heretofore,' 'hereafter,' and the like, have reference to the time the statute becomes effective as a law, and not to the time of passage. Before that time no rights may be acquired under it, and no one is bound to regulate his conduct according to its terms; it is equivalent to a legislative declaration that the statute shall have no effect until the designated day." 26 Am. & Eng. Ency. Law (2d ed.), p. 565.

See, also, *Price v. Hopkin*, 13 Mich. 318; *Grant v. Alpena*, 107 Mich. 335, 65 N. W. 230; *Galveston etc. R. Co. v. State*, 81 Tex. 572; *Jackman v. Garland*, 64 Me. 133; *Evansville etc. R. Co. v. Barbee*, 59 Ind. 592.

Applying this principle to the question before us, it seems clear that the Federal statute did not speak as a statute until after March 4, 1908, the date on which it went into effect; for if a law passed to take effect at a future day must be construed as if passed on that day, and if, prior to the time it goes into effect, no rights can be acquired under it and no one is bound to regulate his conduct according to its terms, it is idle to say that it has the effect of a statute between the time of its passage and the time of its taking effect. A statute cannot be both operative and inoperative at the same time. It is either a law or it is not a law, and, without special words of limitation, when it goes into effect for one purpose it goes into effect for all purposes. So with this statute, it cannot be a law between the day of its passage and the day it is made to go into effect, for the purpose of superseding the state statute, and not a law for any other purpose. Undoubtedly the Federal legislature could have so framed its act as to supersede state legislation on the subject-matter involved, and at the same time have given the carriers effected a year within which to regulate their business to meet the changed conditions, but it did not do this; it postponed the operation of the entire act for one year after its passage, leaving the field open for state legislation during that period, and this being true, it follows as of course that the act did not suspend or supersede the state legislation on the same subject-matter on any principle of paramount right of legislation until the end of the year.

These propositions have seemed to us so self-evident as scarcely to admit of debate. Our attention, however, has been called to two recent cases which maintain the contrary view. The first is *State v. Chicago etc. R. Co.* (Wis.), 117 N. W. 686. The state statute there before the court was one limiting the number of hours a telegraph operator might be required by the company to remain on continuous duty at the station of a railroad company engaged in interstate commerce. The court held the statute invalid on two grounds, first, that the "restriction of the hours of labor of telegraph operators engaged in moving interstate trains or traffic is a field of legislation denied to the state by the Federal constitution," and second, that the statute "is in conflict with and in negation of the act of Congress." Discussing the latter question, the court used this language:

"Not less obviously the act of Congress declared a policy that interstate railroads should have a reasonable time in which to adjust their business to the new restrictions, by postponing the date when the law should become operative for one year after its passage, thus indicating that such period of time was so necessary to reasonable convenience of interstate commerce. Indeed, this latter implication is not only clear from the act, but made the more certain by reference to the debates and reports of committeees attending the consideration and passage of the law of Congress. Hence a state provision to the effect that the time for such preparation and adjustment should be restricted to the 1st of January, 1908, as contained in chapter 575, p. 1188, Laws of 1907, is in direct conflict with the policy of Congress."

The second case is *State v. Missouri Pac. R. Co.*, 212 Mo., 658, 111 S. W. 500. The state statute before the court was similar to that in question in the former case. The decision was rested on the ground that the Federal statute had superseded the state enactment, the court saying:

"We must construe the Federal act by reading into dry letter its manifest spirit and purpose. Its dry letter reads that it shall not go into effect for one year. What was the meaning of, the object to be subserved by, that suspension of the operation of the law? What, ex‹ cept to preserve the equities of the situation by impliedly giving common carriers engaged in interstate commerce one year in which to get a supply of experienced telegraph and telephone operators and trainmen to carry on their business without interruption and hindrance, and otherwise adjust their business affairs to the shorter hours required by that act? When broadly judged, the Federal law must be construed as a notice (in the nature of a caveat) to all state Legislatures, first, that Congress has occupied the ground by its statutory regulations; second, that in its high wisdom it has prescribed and marked out a transition or preparatory period of one year (a sort of truce period). Now with such broad and wise purposes read into the Federal act shall any state Legislature thereafter sit in judgment upon the wisdom of such truce period, and say, in effect, 'We deem it too long and too liberal'? Shall it say, in effect, 'We see you have suspended your act for one whole year; we find by mathematical-computation there is left six months or so which we may cover by a state law, and accordingly we shall pass a law giving shorter hours than yours that will be good at least from June 14, 1907, until March 4, 1908'? If the one law grants, by necessary implication, a breathing spell, shall the other take it away? If the one chalks out a policy, may the other rub it out? In our opinion the comity that should exist between state and Federal legislative power prohibits our taking that ungracious and narrow view."

But we are unable to concur in the conclusion reached in these cases. The effect of the decisions is to make the statute speak from the time of its enactment instead of from the time it was made to become a law, thus giving it an effect that the power that enacted it did not give to it. Nor do we think there is any such question of comity involved as requires the courts to hold the state statutes inoperative. That Congress had entered the field of legisation on this subject, and that a state statute on the same subject could at most have but a short life, must indeed have been a persuasive argument before the state legislature against the passage of such an act, but it has no force in the courts. The court must take the statutes as it finds them, and can rightfully refuse to give them force only when they violate some positive principle of government laid down in the fundamental law. Statutes are not to be overturned on mere principles of comity.

The cases where this precise question is involved seem not to be many. Indeed the only one called to our attention, other than the two just referred to, where the direct question was presented is *Larrabee v. Talbott*, 5 Gill. (Md.) 426. By the seventeenth section of the bankruptcy act of 1841, which was passed on August 19 of that year, it was expressly provided that the act should take effect only from and after the first day of February, 1842. It was claimed that the insolvent laws of Maryland were superseded in their operation between the date of the passage of the act and the date it went into effect. The court denied the claim, using this language:

"The late bankrupt law of the United States was passed on the 19th day of August, 1841; but it was expressly provided by the seventeenth section of the statute, that it should take effect only from and after the first day of February, 1842. This is equivalent to declaring that the act should have no effect until that day; and therefore, there is no foundation for the point made by the counsel for the appellant; that the insolvent laws of Maryland were suspended in their operation by the Bankrupt Act of the United States, at the period when the proceedings of Rogers & Frick under those laws were commenced and consummated. At that time, the Bankrupt Act was not in force, and there could have been no conflict between the national and state legislation upon this subject.

"In *Ex parte Eames*, 2 Story Rep. 325, Mr. Justice Story said:

" 'That as soon as the Bankrupt Act went into operation, in February, 1842, it *ipso facto* suspended all action on future cases, arising under the state insolvent laws, where the insolvent persons were within the purview of the Bankrupt Act. I say future cases, because very different considerations would or might apply, where proceedings under any state insolvent laws were commenced, and were in progress before the Bankrupt Act went into operation. It appears to me, that both systems cannot be in operation, or apply at the same time to the same persons; and where the state and national legislation, upon the same subject, and the same persons, come in conflict, the national laws must prevail and suspend the operation of the state laws. This as far as I know, has been the uniform doctrine maintained in all the courts of the United States.' "

This decision seems to us more in consonance with correct principles than the more recent cases above cited, and we follow it in preference to them.

The judgment is affirmed.

RUDKIN, C. J., GOSE, DUNBAR, CROW, PARKER, MOUNT, CHADWICK, and MORRIS, JJ., concur.

Labor Laws of Washington

LABOR LAWS OF WASHINGTON.

CHAPTER I.

BUREAU OF LABOR.

1. Appointment of Commissioner—Bureau of Labor.

A Commissioner of Labor shall be appointed by the Governor, and said Commissioner of Labor, by and with the consent of the Governor, shall have power to appoint and employ such assistants as may be necessary to discharge the duties of said Commissioner of Labor; and said Commissioner of Labor, together with the Inspector of Coal Mines, shall constitute a Bureau of Labor. On the first Monday in April in 1897, and every four years thereafter, the Governor shall appoint a suitable person to act as Commissioner of Labor, and as factory, mill and railroad inspector, who shall hold office until his successor is appointed and qualified. (L. '05, Sec. 1, Chap. 83).

2. Duties of Commissioner.

It shall be the duty of such officer and employes of the said Bureau to cause to be enforced all laws regulating the employment of children, minors and women, all laws established for the protection of the health, lives, and limbs of operators in workshops, factories, mills and mines, on railroads, and other places, and all laws enacted for the protection of the working classes, and declaim it a misdemeanor on the part of the employers to require as a condition of employment the surrender of any rights of citizenship, laws regulating and prescribing the qualifications of persons in trades and handicrafts, and similar laws now in force or hereafter to be enacted. It shall also be the duty of officers and employes of the Bureau to collect, assort, arrange and present in biennial reports to the legislature, on or before the first Monday in January, statistical details relating to all departments of labor in the state; to the subjects of corporations, strikes, or other labor difficulties; to trade unions and other labor organizations and their effect upon labor and capital; and to such other matters relating to the commercial, industrial, social, educational, moral, and sanitary conditions of the laboring classes, and the permanent prosperity of the respective industries of the state as the Bureau may be able to gather. In its biennial report the bureau shall also give account of all proceedings of its officers and employes which have been taken in accordance with the provisions of this act, or of any other acts herein referred to, including a statement of all violations of law which have

been observed, and the proceedings under the same, and shall join
with such accounts and such remārkś, suggestions and recommendations as the commissioner may deem necessary. (Sec. 2, P. 132, '01).

3. Female Deputy Inspector.

The Commissioner of Labor shall appoint one female as assistant
Commissioner of Labor, and such female assistant shall have charge,
under the direction of the Commissioner of Labor, of the enforcement
of all laws relating to the health, sanitary conditions, surroundings,
hours of labor and all other laws affecting the employment of female
wage-earners. She shall receive a salary of twelve hundred dollars per
annum and shall be allowed her actual and necessary expenses in the
performance of her duties as such assistant. Such salary and expenses to be paid in the same manner as other expenses of the office of
Commissioner of Labor. (Chap. 227, P. 815, '09).

NAVIGATION LAW.

4. Inspectors Appointed.

The Commissioner of Lábor shall be charged with the administration of the provisions of this act, shall employ the necessary inspectors
to enable him to carry said provisions into effect, and shall exercise
supervision over them in the performance of their duties.

5. Report to Governor.

The commissioner shall on or before the first day of January in each
year, make a verified report to the Governor, containing a detailed statement of the names and number of vessels examined and licensed, the
name and number of vessels to which licenses were refused and stating
the reasons for the refusal, the names and number of persons examined
and licensed, the names and number to whom licenses were refused and
stating the reasons therefor, and may include in such report any other
information he may deem desirable. (Chap. 200, P. 425, L. '07).

6.

That a sum of one thousand dollars ($1,000.00) be appropriated, in
addition to fees and fines collected, for the inspection of steam vessels, and vessels or boats operated by machinery, navigating the waters
within the jurisdiction of this state, éxcepting vessels which [are sub-
ject] to inspection under the laws of the United States. (Chap. 159, P.
634, '09).

7. Operator or Owner to Make Reports.

It shall be the duty of every owner, operator, or manager of every
factory, workshop, mill, mine, or other establishment where labor is employed, to make to the Bureau, upon blanks furnished by said Bureau,
such reports and returns as the said Bureau may require, for the
purposes of compiling such labor statistics as are authorized by this
chapter, and the owner or business manager shall make such reports.

and returns within the time prescribed therefor by the Commissioner of Labor, and shall certify to the correctness of the same. In the reports of said Bureau no use shall be made of the names of individuals, firms, or corporations supplying the information called for by this section, such information being deemed confidential, and not for the purpose of disclosing personal affairs, and any officer, agent, or employe of said Bureau violating this provision shall be fined in the sum not to exceed five hundred dollars, or being imprisoned for not more than one year. (Sec. 3, P. 133, '01).

8. Witnesses to Be Examined.

The Commissioner of the Bureau of Labor shall have the power to issue subpoenas, administer oaths, and take testimony in all matters relating to the duties herein required by such Bureau, such testimony to be taken in some suitable place in the vicinity to which testimony is applicable. Witnesses subpoenaed and testifying before any officer of the said Bureau shall be paid the same fees as witness before a superior court, such payment to be made from the contingent fund of the Bureau. Any person duly subpoenaed under provisions of this section [who] shall wilfully neglect or refuse to attend or testify at the time and place named in the subpoena, shall be guilty of a misdemeanor, and, upon conviction thereof, before any court of competent jurisdiction, shall be punished by a fine not less than twenty-five dollars, or more than one hundred dollars, or by imprisonment in the county jail not exceeding thirty days. (Sec. 4, P. 134, '01).

9. Power to Inspect.

The Commissioner of Labor, the Coal Mine Inspector, or any employe of the Bureau of Labor, shall have power to enter any factory, mill, mine, office, workshop, or public or private works at any time for the purpose of gathering facts and statistics such as are contemplated by this act, and to examine into the methods of protection from danger to employes, and the sanitary conditions in and around such buildings and places and make a record thereof, and any owner or occupant of said factory, mill, mine, office, or workshop, or public or private works or his agent or agents, who shall refuse to allow an inspector or employe of the said Bureau to enter, shall be deemed guilty of a misdemeanor, and, upon conviction thereof, before any court of competent jurisdiction, shall be punished by a fine of not less than twenty-five dollars nor more than one hundred, or be imprisoned in the county jail not to exceed ninety days, for each and every offense. (Sec. 5, P. 134, '01).

10. Records of Office, Treated How.

No report or return made to the said Bureau in accordance with the provisions of this act, and no schedule, record, or document gathered or returned by the Commissioner or Inspector thereof, such reports, schedules, and documents being declared public documents. At the expiration of the period of two years above referred to in this section, all records, schedules, and papers accumulating in the said Bureau that may be considered of no value by the Commissioner, may be destroyed: Provided, The authority of the Governor be first obtained for such destruction. (Sec. 6, P. 135, '01).

11. Reports to Be Printed and Distributed.

The biennial reports of the Bureau of Labor, provided for by section 2 above, shall be printed in the same manner and under the same regulations as the reports of the executive officers of the state: Provided, That not less than five hundred copies of the report shall be distributed, as the judgment of the Commissioner may deem best. The blanks and other stationery required by the Bureau of Labor in accordance with the provisions of this act shall be furnished by the Secretary of State, and shall be paid for from the printing fund of the state. (Sec. 7, P. 135, '01).

12. Salary of Commissioner.

The salary of the Commissioner of Labor, provided for in this act, shall be twenty-four hundred ($2,400) per annum, and shall be allowed his actual and necessary traveling and incidental expenses; and any assistant of said Commissioner of Labor shall be paid for each full day service rendered by him, such compensation as the Commissioner of Labor may deem proper, but no such assistant shall be paid to exceed four ($4.00) dollars per day, and his actual necessary traveling expenses. (Chap. 203, Sec. 8, P. 445, '07).

CHAPTER II.

ARBITRATION.

13. Commissioner to Advise.

It shall be the duty of the State Labor Commissioner upon application of any employer or employe having differences, as soon as practicable, to visit the location of such difference and to make a careful inquiry into the cause thereof and to advise the respective parties, what, if anything, ought to be done or submitted to by both to adjust said dispute, and should said parties then still fail to agree to a settlement through said Commissioner, the said Commissioner shall endeavor to have said parties consent in writing to submit their differences to a board of arbitration to be chosen from citizens of the state as follows, to-wit: Said employer shall appoint one and said employes acting through a majority, one, and these two shall select a third, these three to constitute the board of arbitration and the findings of the said board of arbitration to be final. (Sec. 1, P. 71, '03).

14. Commissioner as Moderator.

The proceedings of said board of arbitration shall be held before the Commissioner of Labor, who shall act as moderator or chairman, without the privilege of voting, and who shall keep a record of the proceedings, issue subpoenas and administer oaths to the members of said board, and any witness said board may deem necessary to summon. (Sec. 2, P. 71, '03).

15. Sheriff to Serve Process.

Any notice or process issued by the board herein created, shall be served by the sheriff, coroner, or constable to whom the same may be directed, or in whose hands the same may be placed for service. (Sec. 3, P. 71, '03).

16. Compensation of Arbitrators.

Such arbitrators shall receive five dollars per day for each day actually engaged in such arbitration and the necessary traveling expenses, to be paid upon certificates of the Labor Commissioner out of the fund appropriated for the purpose or at the disposal of the Bureau of Labor applicable to such expenditure. (Sec. 4, P. 71, '03).

17. Statements From Contestants.

Upon the failure of the Labor Commissioner, in any case, to secure the creation of a board of arbitration, it shall become his duty to request a sworn statement from each party to the dispute of the facts upon which their dispute and their reasons for not submitting the same to arbitration are based. Any sworn statement made to the Labor Commissioner under this provision shall be for public use and shall be given publicity in such newspapers as desire to use it. (Sec. 5, P. 72, '03).

18. Appropriation.

There is hereby appropriated out of the state treasury from funds not otherwise appropriated the sum of *three thousand dollars, or so much thereof as may be necessary, to carry out the provisions of this act. In case the funds herein provided are exhausted and either party to a proposed arbitration shall tender the necessary expenses for conducting said arbitration, then it shall be the duty of the State Labor Commissioner to request the opposite party to arbitrate such differences in accordance with the provisions of this act. (Sec. 6, P. 72, '03).

CHAPTER III.

SAFEGUARDS AGAINST INJURY.

19. Safety Appliances to Be Provided and Maintained.

That any person, firm, corporation or association operating a factory, mill or workshop where machinery is used shall provide and maintain in use, belt shifters or other mechanical contrivances for the purpose of

---

* 1,000. Chap. 212, p. 490, '07·

throwing on or off belts on pulleys while running, where the same are practicable with due regard to the nature and purpose of said belts and the dangers to employes therefrom; also reasonable safeguards for all vats, pans, trimmers, cut-off, gang-edger, and other saws, planers, cogs, gearings, belting, shafting, coupling, set screws, live rollers, conveyors, mangles in laundries and machinery of other or similar description, which it is practicable to guard, and which can be effectively guarded with due regard to the ordinary use of such machinery and appliances, and the dangers to employes therefrom, and with which the employes of any such factory, mill or workshop are liable to come in contact while in the performance of their duties; and if any machine or any part thereof, is in a defective condition, and its operation would be extra hazardous because of such defect, or if any machine is not safeguarded as provided in this act, the use thereof is prohibited, and a notice to that effect shall be attached thereto by the employer or inspector immediately on receiving notice of such defect or lack of safeguard, and such notice shall not be removed until said defect has been remedied or the machine safeguarded as herein provided. (Sec. 1, Chap. 205, L. '07).

20. Ventilation.

Every factory, mill or workshop where machinery is used, and manual labor is exercised by the way of trade for the purposes of gain within an enclosed room (private houses in which the employes live, excepted) shall be provided in each work room thereof with good and sufficient ventilation and kept in a cleanly and sanitary state, and shall be so ventilated as to render harmless, so far as practicable, all gases, vapors, dust or other impurities, generated in the course of the manufacturing or laboring process carried on therein; and if in any factory, mill or workshop any process is carried on in any enclosed room thereof, by which dust is generated and inhaled to an injurious extent by the persons employed therein, conveyors, receptacles or exhaust fans, or other mechanical means, shall be provided and maintained for the purpose of carrying off or receiving and collecting such dust.

21. Places of Danger to Be Guarded.

The openings of all hoist-ways, hatch-ways, elevators, and well-holes and stairways in factories, mills, workshops, storehouses, warerooms or stores, shall be protected where practicable, by good and sufficient trapdoors, hatches, fences, gates or other safeguards, and all due diligence shall be used to keep all such means of protection closed, except when it is necessary to have the same open that the same may be used.

22. Duty of Commissioner to Make Inspection.

It shall be the duty of the Commissioner of Labor, by himself or his duly appointed deputy, to examine as soon as may be after the passage of this act, and thereafter annually and from time to time, all factories, mills, workshops, storehouses, warerooms, stores and buildings and the machinery and appliances therein contained to which the provisions of this act are applicable for the purpose of determining whether they do conform to such provisions, and of granting or refusing certificates of approval, whether requested to do so or not. (Sec. 4, Chap. 205, '07).

23. **Application for Inspection, Acknowledgment of, Effective as Certificate Until Inspection Is Made.**

Any person, firm, corporation or association carrying on business to which the provisions of this act are applicable, shall have the right to make written request to said Commissioner of Labor to inspect any factory, mill or workshop, and the machinery therein used, and any storehouse, wareroom or store, which said applicant is operating, occupying or using, and to issue his certificate of approval thereof; and said Commissioner of Labor by himself, or his deputy, shall forthwith make said inspection. Upon receiving such application, the Commissioner of Labor shall issue to the person making the same, an acknowledgment that such certificate has been applied for, and thirty days after such acknowledgment, by said Commissioner of Labor, and pending the granting of such certificate, such acknowledgment shall have the same effect as such certificate, till the granting of such certificate by said Commissioner of Labor: Provided, Said applicant has not been notified by an inspector what alterations or repairs are necessary: Provided, The Commissioner of Labor by himself or deputy shall make such examination annually whether requested to do so or not. (Sec. 5, Chap. 205, '07).

24. **Defective or Unguarded Equipment to Be Reported by Employes.**

Any employe of any person, firm, corporation or association shall notify his employer of any defect in, or failure to guard the machinery, appliances, ways, works and plants, with which or in or about which he is working, when any such defect or failure to guard shall come to the knowledge of any said employe, and if said employer shall fail to remedy such defects then said employe may complain in writing to the Commissioner of Labor of any such alleged defects in or failure to guard the machinery, appliances, ways, works and plants, or any alleged violation by such person, firm, corporation or association, of any of the provisions of this act, in the machinery and appliances and premises used by such person, firm, corporation or association, and with or about which such employe is working, and upon receiving such complaint, it shall be the duty of the Commissioner of Labor, by himself or his deputy, to forthwith make an inspection of the machinery and appliances complained of.

25. **Copies of Certificates to Be Kept Posted—Fees to Be Paid—Work to Be Done within Thirty Days After Notice—Procedure—Civilly Liable for Inspection Fee.**

Whenever upon examination or re-examination of any factory, mill or workshop, store or building, or the machinery or appliances therein to which the provisions of this act are applicable, the property so examined and the machinery and appliances therein conform in the judgment of said Commissioner of Labor to the requirements of this act, he shall thereupon issue to the owner, lessee or operator of such factory, mill or workshop or to the owner, lessee or occupant of any such storeroom, wareroom or store, a certificate to that effect, and such certificate shall be prima facie evidence as long as it continues in force of compliance on the part of the person, firm, corporation or association to whom it is issued, with the provisions of this act. Such certificate may be revoked by said Commissioner of Labor at any time upon written notice to the person, firm, corporation or association holding the same, whenever in his opinion after re-examination, conditions and circumstances have so changed as to justify the revocation thereof. A copy of said certificate shall be kept posted in a conspicuous place on every floor of all factories, mills, workshops, storehouses, warerooms or store to which the provisions of this act are applicable. If, in the judgment of said Commissioner of Labor, such factory, mill or workshop, or the machinery and appliances therein contained, or such storehouse, warehouse or store does not conform to the requirements of this act, he shall forthwith, personally or by mail, serve on the person, firm, corporation or association operating or using such machinery or appliances, or occupying such premises, a written statement of the requirements of said Commissioner of Labor, before he will issue a certificate as hereinbefore provided for; said requirements shall be complied with, within a period of thirty days after said requirements have been served as aforesaid and thereupon the said Commissioner of Labor shall forthwith issue such certificate; but if the person, firm or corporation operating or using said machinery and appliances or occupying such premises shall consider the requirements of said Commissioner of Labor unreasonable and impracticable or unnecessarily expensive, he may within ten days after the requirements of said Commissioner of Labor have been served upon him appeal therefrom or from any part thereof, to three arbitrators to whom shall be submitted the matter and things in dispute, and their findings shall be binding upon said applicant and upon the Commissioner of Labor. Such appeal shall be in writing, addressed to the Commissioner of Labor, and shall set forth the objection to his requirements, or any part thereof, and shall mention the name of one person who will serve as the representative of said applicant calling for arbitration. Immediately upon the receipt of such notice of appeal, it shall be the duty of the Commissioner of Labor to appoint a competent person as arbitrator resident in the county from which such appeal comes, and to notify such person so selected, and also the party appealing stating the cause of the arbitration, and the place, date and time of meeting. These two arbitrators shall select the third, and as soon thereafter as practicable, give a hearing on the matters of said appeal, and the findings of these arbitrators by a majority vote, shall be reported to the

Commissioner of Labor, and to the applicant, and shall be binding upon each. The expense of such arbitration shall be borne by the party calling for the arbitration; and if said arbitrators sustain the requirements of said Commissioner of Labor or any part thereof, said applicant shall within thirty days, comply with the findings of said arbitrators, and thereupon said Commissioner of Labor shall issue his certificate as hereinbefore provided (in section four of this act), but if said arbitrators shall sustain such appeal or any part thereof, the same shall be binding upon said Commissioner of Labor; and any such person, firm or corporation or association shall within thirty days, after the finding of the board of arbitrators, comply with the requirements of the Commissioner of Labor, as amended by said arbitrators, if so amended as herein provided for, and thereupon said Commissioner of Labor shall forthwith issue to any such person, firm, corporation or association, his certificate as provided for in section four of this act: Provided, however, That before any certificate shall be issued by said Commissioner of Labor as provided for in this act, the person, firm, corporation or association which has complied with the provisions of this act, shall pay to the Commissioner of Labor of the State of Washington, an annual fee of ten dollars (providing that any person, firm, corporation or association, employing not to exceed five persons in said factory, mill or workshop shall pay a fee of five dollars), and take his receipt therefor: It is further provided, That the withholding of such certificate shall not excuse such person, firm, corporation or association from obtaining the same and paying the required inspection fee, and the person, firm, corporation or association inspected shall likewise be civilly liable for such inspection fee.

Upon presentation of said receipt to said Commissioner of Labor, or his deputy, he shall forthwith issue said certificate as in this act provided. Said fee shall entitle the person, firm, corporation or association paying the same, to any and every inspection of any factory, mill, workshop, wareroom or store, and the machinery and appliances contained therein, owned and operated by the party paying said fee, that may be necessary, for a period of one year subsequent to its payment; and all moneys collected for licenses and fines, under the provisions of this act, shall be paid into the state treasury and be converted into a special factory inspection fund, from which special fund shall be paid the deputy factory inspectors required to enforce the provisions of this act. Said deputy factory inspectors shall be paid from the special factory inspection fund, upon the presentation of vouchers properly signed by the Labor Commissioner in the same manner in which other employes of the state are paid. (Sec. 7, Chap. 205, '07).

26. Violation of Law—Damages Limited to Sum of $7,500.

Any person, firm, corporation or association who violates or omits to comply with any of the foregoing requirements or provisions of this act, and such violation or omission shall be the proximate cause of any injury to any employe, shall be liable in damages to any employe who sustains injuries by reason thereof: Provided, The amount of damages which any one person may recover in an action for or on account of injuries received by reason of any alleged violation of any of the provisions of this act, is hereby expressly limited to the sum of seven thousand five hundred dollars.

27. Action for Damages—Notice to Be Given.

No action for the recovery of compensation for injury under this act shall be maintained unless notice of the time, place and cause of injury is given to the employer within six months, and the action is commenced within one year from the occurrence of the accident causing the injury. The notice required by this action shall be in writing, signed by the person injured, or by some one in his behalf; but if from mental or physical incapacity it is impossible for the person injured to give the notice within the time provided in this section he may give the same within ninety (90) days after such incapacity is removed, and in case of death without having given the notice because of mental or physical incapacity, his executor, or administrator may give such notice within thirty days after his appointment.

28. Common Law Action May Be Brought.

Nothing in this act contained shall prevent any person from bringing an action under any other statute or act or at common law for any personal injuries received by him; and in that event the certificate provided for herein shall not be admitted in evidence in such suit or action.

29. Penalty for Non-Compliance.

Any person, firm, corporation or association who violates or fails to comply with any of the provisions of this act or to pay for and obtain the certificate of inspection shall be deemed guilty of a misdemeanor, and upon conviction thereof shall be punished by a fine of not less than twenty-five dollars nor more than one hundred dollars. (Sec. 11, Chap. 205, '07).

30. Copy of Law to Be Kept Posted.

A copy of this act, together with the name and address of the Commissioner of Labor, printed in a legible manner, shall be kept posted in a conspicuous place on each floor of every factory, mill, workshop, storehouse, wareroom or store, and at the office of every public and private work to which the provisions of this act are applicable, upon the same being supplied to the operators, owners, lessee, or occupants, of such places with sufficient copies thereof by the Commissioner of Labor.

31. Former Acts Repealed.

That an act entitled "An act providing for the protection of employes in factories, mills, or workshops where machinery is used, and providing for the punishment of the violation thereof," approved March 6, 1903, and all acts and parts of acts in conflict herewith shall be and the same hereby are repealed.

CHAPTER V.
LAWS GOVERNING STREET CARS.

32. Competent Men Required.

Hereafter street railway or street car companies, or street car corporations, shall employ none but competent men to operate or assist as conductors, motor men, or grip men upon any street railway or street car line in this state. (Sec. 1, P. 215, '01).

33. Who Deemed Competent.

A man shall be deemed competent to operate or assist in operating cars or dummies usually used by street railway or street car companies, or corporations, only after first having served at least three days under personal instruction of a regularly employed conductor, motor màn, or grip man on a car or, dummy in actual service on the particular street railway or street car line for which the service of an additional man or additional men may be required: Provided, That during a strike on the street car lines the railway companies may employ competent men who have not worked three days on said particular street car line. (Sec. 2, P. 215, '01).

34. Penalty.

Any violation of section twenty-nine hereof by the president, secretary, manager, superintendent, assistant superintendent, stockholder or other officer or employe of any company or corporation owning or operating any street railway or street car line or any receiver of street railway or street car company, or street railway or street car corporations appointed by any court within this state to operate such car line shall, upon conviction thereof, be deemed guilty of a misdemeanor, and subject the offender to such offense to a fine in any amount not less than fifty dollars nor more than two hundred dollars, or imprisonment in the county jail for a term of thirty days, or both such fine and imprisonment at the discretion of the court. (Sec. 3, P. 215, '01).

35. Vestibules Required.

All corporations, companies, or individuals owning, managing or operating any street railway or line in the State of Washington, shall provide, during the rain or winter season, all cars run or used on its or their respective roads with good, substantial, and sufficient vestibules, or weather guards, for the protection of the employes of such corporation, company, or individual. (Sec. 1, P. 360, '95).

—21

36. How Constructed.

The vestibules or weather guards, provided for in the preceding section, shall be so constructed as to protect the employes of such company, corporation, or individual from the wind, rain, or snow. (Sec. 2, P. 360, '95).

39. Penalty.

Any such street railway company, corporation, or individual, as mentioned in the preceding sections, failing to comply with the provisions of this act, shall forfeit and pay to the State of Washington a penalty of not less than fifty dollars nor more than two hundred and fifty dollars for each and every violation of this act, and each period of ten days that any such company, corporation, or individual shall fail to comply with the provisions of this act, or for each car used by such corporation, company, or individual not in conformity with this act, and all moneys collected under and by virtue of the provisions of this act shall be paid into the common school fund of the State of Washington. (Sec. 3, P. 360, '95).

38. Duty of Prosecuting Attorney.

It shall be the duty of the prosecuting or county attorneys of the various counties of this state to see that the provisions of this article are complied with. (Sec. 4, P. 361, '95).

39. Ten Hours on Street Cars.

No person, agent, officer, manager, or superintendent, or receiver of any corporation, or owner of street cars shall require his or its gripmen, motor men, drivers, or conductors to work more than ten hours in any twenty-four hours. (Sec. 1, P. 192, '95).

40. Penalty.

Any person, agent, officer, manager, superintendent, or receiver of any corporation, or owner of street car or cars, violating any of the provisions of section 39 above shall, upon conviction thereof be deemed guilty of a misdemeanor, and be fined in any sum not less than $25 nor more than $100 for each day in which such gripmen, motormen, driver, or conductor in the employ of such person, agent, officer, manager, superintendent, or receiver of such corporation or owner is required to work more than ten (10) hours during each twenty-four (24) hours, as provided in section 39 above, and it is hereby made the duty of the prosecuting attorney of each county of this state to institute the necessary proceedings to enforce the provisions of this article. (Sec. 2, P. 193, '95).

41. Fenders on All Cars.

Every street car used or run on any street car line in the State of Washington shall be provided with good and substantial aprons, pilots, or fenders, and which shall be so constructed as to prevent any person from being thrown down and run over or caught beneath or under such car. (Sec. 1, P. 281, '97).

42. Penalty.

The owners or managers operating any street car line failing to comply with the provisions of this article shall forfeit and pay to the State of Washington a penalty of not less than twenty-five dollars for each and every violation of this article and each car run shall be considered a separate violation of this act and every period of five days shall be deemed a separate violation of this article; and all moneys collected under and by virtue of this article shall be paid into the common school fund. (Sec. 2, P. 282, '97).

43. Prosecuting Attorney's Duty.

It shall be the duty of the prosecuting attorneys of the various counties of this state to see that the provisions of this article are complied with. (Sec. 3, P. 282, '97).

CHAPTER VI.

REGULATING THE PRACTICE OF BARBERING.

44. Must Have Certificate—Exception.

It shall be unlawful for any person to follow the occupation of barber in any incorporated city or town in this state, unless he shall have first obtained a certificate of registration as provided in this article: Provided, however, That nothing in this article shall apply to or affect any person who is now engaged in such occupation except as hereinafter provided. (Sec. 1, P. 349, '01).

45. Barbering Defined.

Shaving the face, or cutting the hair or the beard of any person either for hire or reward, shall be construed as practicing the occupation of barbering within the meaning of this article. (Sec. 2, P. 349, '01).

46. Board of Examiners.

A Board of Examiners, to consist of three persons, is hereby created to carry out the purposes and enforce the provisions of this article. Said board shall be appointed by the Governor, the appointees to be chosen from practical barbers who have at least five years prior to their appointment followed the occupation, and have been residents of the State of Washington for two years. Each member of the said board shall serve for a term of three years, and until his successor is appointed and qualified, except in the case of the first board, who shall serve one, two and three years respectively. (Sec. 3, P. 349, '01).

47. Officers of Board.

Said board shall elect a president, secretary, and treasurer, shall have a common seal, and shall have power to administer oaths. The headquarters of said board shall be the place of residence of the secretary. (Sec. 4, P. 349, '01).

48. Treasurer to Give Bond.

The treasurer of said board shall give surety bond to be approved by and deposited with the Auditor of this state, in the sum of one thousand dollars, and said board shall take the oath provided by law for public officers. The costs of said bond shall be paid out of the funds in the hands of the treasurer. (Sec. 5, P. 349, '01).

49. Compensation of Board.

Each member of said board shall receive a compensation of five dollars per day for actual services and actual expenses incurred in attending the meetings of the board. All moneys shall be paid out of the fund in the hands of the treasurer, and in no event shall any money be paid out of the state treasury. (Sec. 6, P. 350, '01).

50. Biennial Report.

Said board shall report to the Governor of this state biennially a full statement of the receipts and disbursements of the board during the preceding two years, a full statement of its doings and proceedings, and such recommendation as may seem proper. (Sec. 7, P. 350, '01).

51. Examination—Where and When Held.

Said board shall hold public examinations at least four times a year in different cities of this state, at such times and places as it may determine, notice of such meetings to be sent to the various applicants by mail, at least ten days before the meetings are to be held. (Sec. 8, P. 350, '01).

52. Certificates Issued Without Examination.

Every person now engaged in the occupation of barber in cities of the first, second, or third class in this state shall within ninety days after the approval of this act file with the secretary of said board an affidavit setting forth his name, residence, and length of time during which and the places where he has practiced such occupation, and shall pay to the secretary of said board one dollar, and a certificate entitling him to practice said occupation for one year shall thereupon be issued to him. (Sec. 9, P. 350, '01).

53. Examination, How Conducted—Fee.

To obtain a certificate of registration under this article, any person except those mentioned in section 52 above, shall make application to said board, and shall pay to the secretary an examination fee of five dollars, and shall present himself at the meeting of the board for examination of applicants. The board shall examine such person, and being satisfied that he is above the age of eighteen years, of good moral character, free from contagious or infectious disease, has studied the trade for two years as an apprentice under or as a qualified and practicing barber in this state, or other states, and is possessed of the requisite skill to properly perform all the duties, including his ability in the preparation of the tools used, shaving, cutting of the hair and beard, and all the various services incident thereto, and has sufficient knowledge concerning the common diseases of the face and skin to avoid the aggravation and spreading thereof in the practice of his trade, his name shall be entered by the board in a register hereinafter provided for and a certificate of registration shall be issued to him authorizing him to practice said trade in this state, for one year. All certificates shall be renewed each year, for which renewal, a fee of fifty cents shall be paid. All persons making application for examina- tion under the provisions of this article, shall be allowed to practice the occupation of barber until the next meeting as designated by said board. (Sec. 10, P. 350, '01).

54. Apprentice.

Nothing in this article shall prohibit any person from serving as. an apprentice in said trade under a barber authorized to practice under this article: Provided, That in no barber shop shall there be more than one apprentice to each registered barber and all apprentices shall be registered with the secretary of said board, for which registration no fee shall be paid. (Sec. 11, P. 351, '01).

55. Certificates on Examination.

Said board shall furnish to each person who has successfully passed examination, a certificate of registration, bearing the seal of the board and the signature of its president and secretary certifying that the holder thereof is entitled to practice the occupation of barber in this state, and it shall be the duty of the holder of such certificate to post the same in a conspicuous place in the shop. (Sec. 12, P. 351, '01).

56. Register to Be Kept.

Said board shall keep a register in which shall be entered names of all persons to whom certificates are issued under this article, and said register shall be at all times open to public inspection. (Sec. 13, P. 351, '01).

57. Certificates May Be Revoked.

Said board shall have power to revoke any certificate of registration granted by it under this article, for (a) conviction of crime, (b) drunk- enness, (c) having or imparting any contagious disease, or (d) for doing work in an unsanitary or filthy manner: Provided, That before any certificate shall be revoked the holder thereof shall have notice in writing of the charge or charges against him, and shall at a day specified in said notice, at least five days after the service thereof, be given a public hearing and full opportunity, to produce testimony in his behalf, and to confront the witnesses against him. Any person whose certificate has been so revoked may after expiration of ninety days upon application have the same re-issued to him upon satisfactory showing that disqualification has ceased. (Sec. 14, P. 351, '01).

58. Health Regulations—Penalties.

Any person practicing the occupation of barber in any city of the first, second, or third class in this state, without having first obtained a certificate of registration as provided in this article, or falsely pretending to be practicing such occupation under this article, or who uses, or allows towels to be used on more than one person before such towels have been laundered; or razors, lather, or hair brushes on more than one person before same shall have been sterilized, or in violation of any of the provisions of this article, and every proprietor of a barber shop who shall wilfully employ a barber who has not such a certificate, shall be guilty of a misdemeanor and upon conviction thereof shall be punished by a fine of not less than ten dollars nor more than one hundred dollars, or by imprisonment in the county jail not less than ten days nor more than ninety days, or both. (Sec. 15, P. 352, '01).

CHAPTER VII.

PUBLIC WORK TO BE PERFORMED IN WORKING DAYS OF EIGHT HOURS EACH.

59. Eight Hours on Public Works.

That it is a part of the public policy of the State of Washington that all work "by contract or day labor done" for it or any political subdivision created by its laws, shall be performed in work days of not more than eight hours each, except in cases of extraordinary emergency. No case of extraordinary emergency shall be construed to exist in any case where other labor can be found to take the place of labor which has already been employed for eight hours in any calendar day. (Sec. 1, P. 51, '03).

60. Contracts to Contain Clause.

All contracts for work for the State of Washington, or any political subdivision created by its laws, shall provide that they may be canceled by the officers or agents authorized to contract for or supervise the execution of such work, in case such work is not performed in accordance with the policy of the state relating to such work. (Sec. 2, P. 51, '03).

61. Duty of Officers.

It is made the duty of all officers or agents authorized to contract for work to be done in behalf of the State of Washington, or any political subdivision created under its laws, to stipulate in all contracts as provided for in this act, and all such officers and agents, and all officers and agents entrusted with the supervision of work performed under such contracts, are authorized, and it is made their duty, to declare any contract canceled, the execution of which is not in accord-ance with the public policy of this state as herein declared. (Sec. 3, P. 51, '03).

62. (3322b) Hours Constituting Day's Labor.

Hereafter eight hours in any calendar day shall constitute a 'day's work on any work done for the state or any county or municipality within the state, subject to conditions hereinafter provided.

63. Public Contract, Work Governed By.

All work done by contract or sub-contract on any building or im-provements or works on roads, bridges, streets, alleys or buildings for the state or any county or municipality within this state, shall be done under the provisions of this act: Provided, That in cases of extraordi-nary emergency, such as danger to life or property, the hours for work may be extended, but in such case the rate of pay for time employed in excess of eight hours of each calendar day, shall be one and one-half times the rate of pay allowed for the same amount of time during eight hours' service. And for this purpose this act is made a part of all contracts, sub-contracts or agreements for work done for the state or any county or municipality within the state.

64. Penalty.

Any contractor, sub-contractor, or agent of contractor or sub-con-tractor, foreman or employer who shall violate the provisions of this act, shall be deemed guilty of misdemeanor and upon conviction shall be fined in a sum not less than twenty-five dollars nor more than two hundred dollars, or with imprisonment in the county jail for a period of not less than ten days nor more than ninety days, or both such fine and imprisonment, at the discretion of the court.

(Approved March 13, 1899; L. 1899, P. 163).

65. Bonds on Public Work to Pay Laborers.

Whenever any board, council, commission, trustees or body acting for the state or any county or municipality or any public body shall contract with any person or corporation to do any work for the state, county or municipality, or other public body, city, town or district, such board, council, commission, trustees or body shall require the person or persons with whom such contract is made to make, execute and deliver to such board, council, commission, trustees or body a good and sufficient bond with two or more sureties, or with a surety company as surety, conditioned that such person or persons shall faithfully per-form all the provisions of such contract and pay all laborers, mechanics and sub-contractors and material men, and all persons who shall sup-ply such person or persons, or sub-contractors, with provisions and supplies for the carrying on of such work, all just debts, dues and demands incurred in the performance of such work, which bond shall be filed with the county auditor of the county where such work is performed or improvement made, except in cases of cities and towns, in which cases such bond shall be filed with the clerk or comptroller thereof, and any person or persons performing such services or furnishing material to any sub-contractor shall have the same right under the provision of such bond as if such work, services or material was furnished to the original contractor. (Chap. 207, P. 716, '09).

66.

If any board of county commissioners of any county, or mayor and common council of any incorporated city or town, or tribunal transacting the business of any municipal corporation shall fail to take such bond as herein required, such county, incorporated city or town, or other municipal corporation, shall be liable to the persons mentioned in the first section of this act, to the full extent and for the full amount of all such debts so contracted by such contractor. (Chap. 207, P. 717, '09).

67.

The bond mentioned in section 1 of this act shall be in an amount equal to the full contract price agreed to be paid for such work or improvement, and shall be to the State of Washington, except in cases of cities and towns, in which cases such municipalities may by general ordinance fix and determine the amount of such bond and to whom such bond shall run: Provided, The same shall not be for a less amount than twenty-five per cent. (25%) of the contract price of any such improvement, and may designate that the same shall be payable to such city, and not to the State of Washington, and all such persons mentioned in said section 1 of this act shall have a right of action in his, her, or their own name or names on such bond, for the full amount of all debts against such contractor, or for work done by such laborers or mechanics, and for materials furnished or provisions and goods supplied and furnished in the prosecution of such work, or the making of such improvements: Provided, That such person shall not have any right of action on such bond for any sum whatever, unless within thirty (30) days from and after the completion of the contract with and acceptance of the work by the board, council, commission, trustees, or body acting for the state, county or municipality, or other public body, city, town or district, the laborer, mechanic or sub-contractor, or material man, or person claiming to have supplied materials, provisions or goods for the prosecution of such work, or the making of such improvement, shall present to and file with such board, council, commission, trustees or body acting for the state, county or municipality, or other public body, city, town or district, a notice in writing in substance as follows:

To (here insert the name of the state, county or municipality or other public body, city, town or district):

Notice is hereby given that the undersigned (here insert the name of the laborer, mechanic or sub-contractor, or material man, or person claiming to have furnished labor, materials, or provisions for or upon such contract or work) has a claim in the sum of.........dollars (here insert the amount) against the bond taken from......... (here insert the name of the principal and surety or sureties upon such bond) for the work of.........(here insert a brief mention or description of the work concerning which said bond was taken).

                                (Here to be signed).................

Such notice shall be signed by the person, or corporation making the claim or giving the notice; and said notice after being presented and filed shall be a public record open to inspection by any person: Provided further, That any city may avail itself of the provisions of this act, notwithstanding any charter provisions in conflict herewith: And provided further, That any city or town may impose any other or further conditions and obligations in such bond as may be deemed necessary for its proper protection in the fulfillment of the terms of the contract secured thereby. (Chap. 207, P. 717, '09).

68. Providing for the Employment of Convicts on State Roads.

All convicts confined and not otherwise employed shall be employed under authority of the State Board of Control in charge of the Superintendent of the penitentiary or of such other persons in the employ of the state as the State Board of Control shall direct, in the building of state roads in this state. All expenses of whatsoever nature incurred through such employment shall be paid from the fund appropriated by the state legislature for the construction of the particular road or roads upon which such convicts may be employed. The places where and the manner in which work shall be performed upon state roads by such convicts shall be designated by the State Highway Board. (Chap. 93, P. 173, '07).

69. An Act Relating to Elections.

At all elections where national, state, county or municipal officers are elected, the polls shall be opened at eight o'clock a. m. and closed at eight o'clock p. m.: Provided, That in precincts outside of incorporated towns and cities the hour of opening of said polls shall be nine o'clock a. m., the hour of closing seven o'clock p. m. (Chap. 235, P. 581, '07):

FEMALES.

LIMITING HOURS OF EMPLOYMENT.

70. Ten Hours for Females.

That no female shall be employed in any mechanical or mercantile establishment, laundry, hotel, or restaurant in this state more than ten hours during any day. The hours of work may be so arranged as to permit the employment of females at any time so that they shall not work more than ten hours during the twenty-four. (Sec. 1, P. 118, '01).

71. Seats to Be Provided.

Every employer in establishments where females are employed shall provide suitable seats for them and shall permit the use of such seats by them when they are not engaged in the active duties for which they are employed. (Sec. 2, P. 119, '01).

72. Penalty.

Any employer, overseer, superintendent, or other agent of any such employer who shall violate any of the provisions of. this article, shall, upon conviction thereof be fined for each offense in a sum not less than ten dollars nor more than twenty-five dollars. (Sec. 3, P. 119, '01).

.73. Seats for Females.

It shall be the duty of very agent, proprietor, superintendent, or employer of female help in stores, offices, or schools within the State of. Washington to provide for each and every such employe a chair, stool, or seat, upon which such female worker or workers shall be allowed to rest when their duties will permit, or when such rest shall or does not interfere with a faithful discharge of their incumbent duties. (Sec. 1, P. 104, '89-'90).

See section 64, supra.

74. Penalty.

A violation of any of the provisions of the preceding section shall be deemed a misdemeanor, and upon conviction thereof by any court of competent jurisdiction, shall subject the person offending to a fine of not less than ten dollars nor more than fifty dollars. (Sec. 2, P. 104, '89-'90).

EMPLOYMENT OF FEMALES.

75. All Avenues Open.

That hereafter in this state every avenue of employment shall be open to women; and any business, vocation, profession, and calling followed and pursued by men may be followed and pursued by women, and no person shall be disqualified from engaging in or pursuing any business, vocation, profession, calling, or employment on account of sex: Provided, That this section shall not be construed so as to permit women to hold public offices. (Sec. 1, P. 519, '89-'90).

EXCEPTION.

76. Employment in Certain Places Prohibited.

No female person shall be employed in any capacity in any saloon, beer hall, bar room, theater, or place of amusement, where intoxicating liquors are sold as a beverage, and any person or corporation convicted of so employing, or of participating in so employing, any such female person shall be fined not less than five hundred dollars; and any person so convicted may be imprisoned in the county jail for a period of not less than six months. (Sec. 1, P. 177, '95).

77. Employment of Minors Prohibited.

Every person who shall employ, or cause to be employed, exhibit or have in his custody for, exhibition or employment any minor actually or apparently under the age of eighteen years; and every parent, relative, guardian, employer or other person having the care, custody, or control of any such minor, who shall in any way procure or consent to the employment of such minor—

1. In begging, receiving alms, or in any mendicant occupation; or,

2. In any indecent or immoral exhibition or practice; or,

3. In any practice or exhibition dangerous or injurious to life, limb, health or morals; or,

4. As a messenger for delivering letters, telegrams, packages or bundles, to any known house of prostitution or assignation;

Shall be guilty of a misdemeanor.

78. Employment of Children.

Every person who shall employ, and every parent, guardian or other person having the care, custody or control of such child, who shall permit to be employed, by another, any male child under the age of fourteen years or any female child under the age of sixteen years at any labor whatever, in or in connection with any store, shop, factory, mine, or any inside employment not connected with farm or house work, without the written permit thereto of a judge of a superior court of the county wherein such child may live, shall be guilty of a misdemeanor. (P. 947, L. '09).

78. Penalty.

Any employer, or any overseer, superintendent, or agent of such person, telegraph company, telephone company or messenger company who shall violate any of the provisions of this act shall, upon conviction thereof, be fined for each offense not less than ten dollars nor more than five hundred dollars, or be imprisoned in the county jail not to exceed six months, or by both such fine and imprisonment. (Chap. 128, P. 238, '07).

79. Not to Be Employed Under Fifteen Years During School Months.

All parents, guardians and other persons in this state having or who may hereafter have immediate custody of any child between eight and fifteen years of age shall cause such child to attend the public schools of the district in which the child resides for the full time which such school may be in session, or shall attend a private school for the same time, unless the child is physically or mentally unable to attend school, has already attained a reasonable proficiency in the branches required by law to be taught in the first eight grades of public schools of this state as provided by the course of study of the said school, is otherwise being furnished with the same education, or has been excused from such attendance for some other sufficient reason, by the superintendent of the schools of the district in which the child resides, if there be such a superintendent, and, in all other cases, by the county superintendent of common schools. Proof of absence from public school or approved private school shall be prima facie evidence of a violation of this section.

No child under the age of fifteen years shall be employed for any purpose by any corporation, person or association of persons in this state during the hours which the public schools of the district in which such child resides are in session, unless the said child shall present a certificate from a school superintendent, as provided for in section one of this act, excusing the said child from attendance in the public schools and setting forth the reason for such excuse, the residence and age of the child, and the time for which such excuse is given. Every owner, superintendent, or overseer of any establishment, corporation, company or person employing any such child shall keep such certificate on file so long as such child is employed by him, her or it. The form of said certificate shall be furnished by the Superintendent of Public Instruction. Proof that any child under fifteen years of age is employed during any part of the period in which public schools of the district are in session, shall be deemed prima facie evidence of a violation of this section.

80. Penalty.

Any person violating any of the provisions of either of the two preceding sections shall be fined not more than twenty-five dollars. Attendance officers shall make complaint for violation of the provisions of this act, to a justice of the peace or to a judge of the superior court.

81. Truant Officers.

To aid in the enforcement of this act, attendance officers shall be appointed and employed as follows: In incorporated city districts the board of directors shall annually appoint one or more attendance officers. Any attendance officer may be a sheriff, deputy sheriff, constable, a city marshal, or a regularly appointed policeman. In all other districts the county superintendent shall act as attendance officer, and he shall also have authority to appoint one or more assistant attendance officers to aid him in the performance of his duties as attendance officer. The compensation of the attendance officer in such city districts shall be fixed and paid by the board appointing him. The attendance officer shall be vested with police powers, the authority to make arrests and serve all legal processes contemplated by this act, and shall have authority to enter all stores, mills, shops or other places in which children may be employed, for the purpose of making such investigations as may be necessary to the enforcement of this act. The attendance officer is authorized to take into custody the person of any child between eight and fifteen years of age, who may be a truant from school, and to conduct said child to his parents, for investigation and explanation, or to the school which he should properly attend. The attendance officer shall institute proceeedings against any officer, parent, guardian, person, company or corporation violating any provision in this act, and shall perform such other services as the superintendent of schools or the board of directors may deem necessary. The attendance officer shall keep a record of his transactions, for the inspection and information of the board of directors and the city and county superintendent, and shall make a detailed report to the superintendent of the city or of the county, as often as the same may be required.

82. Who May Arrest.

Any attendance officer, sheriff, deputy sheriff, marshal, policeman, or any other officer authorized to make arrests in the city or district, shall arrest without warrant a child who, under the provisions of this act is required to attend school, such child being then a truant from instruction at the school which he or she is lawfully required to attend, shall forthwith deliver a child so arrested either to the custody of a person in parental relation to the child or to the teacher from whom the child is then a truant, or, in case of habitual and incorrigible truants, shall bring him or her before a justice of the peace. The justice of the peace shall, if he be convinced that the child so arrested is an habitual truant or that the child is guilty of wilful and continual disobedience to the school rules and regulations or laws, or that the conduct of the child is pernicious and injurious to the school, bind the child over to the superior court with a view to his commitment to the state reform school or other school for incorrigibles.

83. Census Required.

It shall be the duty of the district clerk or secretary, at the beginning of each school year, to provide the teacher with a copy of the last census of school children taken in his school district: Provided, That if there be a principal·or city superintendent in such district, the clerk or secretary shall make such census report to him, and it shall be the duty of each teacher to report to the proper truant officer, all cases of truancy or incorrigibility in his or her school, immediately after the offense or offenses shall have been committed: Provided further, That if there be a principal the report shall be made to him and by him transmitted to the truant officer: And provided further, That if there be a city superintendent, the principal shall transmit such report to said city superintendent, who shall transmit such report to the proper truant officer of his district.

84. Jurisdiction of Courts.

In cases arising under this act all justices' courts, municipal courts and superior courts in the State of Washington shall have concurrent jurisdiction.

85. Duty of County Attorney.

The county attorney shall act as attorney for the complainant in all court proceedings relating to the compulsory attendance of children as required by this act.

86. Notice by County Superintendent.

The county superintendent shall, on or before the 15th day of August, 1907, by printed circular or otherwise, call the attention of all school district officers to the provisions of this act, and to the penalties prescribed for the violation of its provisions, and he or she shall require the clerk of every school district to make a report annually hereafter, to him or her, verified by affidavit, stating whether or not the provisions of this act have been faithfully complied with in his district. Such reports shall be made upon blanks to be furnished by the Superintendent of Public Instruction and shall be transmitted to the county superintendent at the time the district clerk is required to make his annual report to the county superintendent. Any district clerk who shall make a false report relating to the enforcement of the provisions of this act shall be deemed guilty of a misdemeanor, and upon conviction in a court of competent jurisdiction shall be fined not less than twenty-five dollars nor more than one hundred dollars; and any district clerk who shall refuse or neglect to make the report required by this section, shall be personally liable to his district for any loss which it may sustain because of such neglect or refusal to report.

87. School Funds Withheld.

If the clerk of any school district shall fail to make the report required by the provisions of section nine (9) of this act, or if he shall report that the provisions of this act have not been faithfully complied with, or if the county superintendent shall personally know that the provisions of this act have not been complied with in good faith in any school district, it shall be the duty of the county superintendent to withhold during the next succeeding school year and until such district shall have complied with the provisions of this act in good faith, twenty-five per cent. of all state school funds to which such district would have been entitled had it complied with the provisions of this act in good faith. He shall report the facts to the county treasurer, who shall return the money so withheld to the state treasurer, and be by him returned to the current school fund of the state.

88. Penalty.

Any superintendent, teacher, or attendance officer, who shall fail or refuse to perform the duties prescribed by this act shall be deemed guilty of a misdemeanor and, upon conviction thereof, be fined not less than twenty or more than one hundred dollars: Provided, That in case of a district officer, such fine shall be paid to the county treasurer and by him placed to the credit of the school district in which said officer resides, and in case of other officers such fine shall be paid to the county treasurer and by him placed to the credit of the general school fund of the county.

89. Fines Applied, How.

All fines except as otherwise provided in this act shall inure and be applied to the support of the public schools in the district where such offense was committed.

90. Officers Not Liable for Costs.

No officer performing any duty under any of the provisions of this act, or under the provisions of any rules that may be passed in pursu-ance hereof, shall in any wise become liable for any costs that may ac-crue in the performance of any duty prescribed by this act. (Chap. 231, P. 567, '07).

91. School Holidays.

No teacher shall be required to teach school on Saturdays or on Labor Day, Thanksgiving Day and the day immediately following Thanksgiving Day, Christmas, New Year's or Fourth of July, or on Memorial, commonly called "Decoration Day": Provided, That no re-duction from the teacher's time or salary shall be made by reason of the fact that a school day happens to be one of the days referred to in this section as a day on which school shall not be taught. (Chap. 59, P. 98, '07).

SUNDAY CLOSING.

92. Places for Sale or Trade of Goods to Be Closed.

It shall be unlawful for any person or persons of this state to open on Sunday for the purpose of trade or sale of goods, wares, and mer-chandise, any shop, store or building, or place of business whatever: Provided, That this section shall apply to hotels only in so far as the sale of intoxicating liquors is concerned, and shall not apply to drug stores, livery stables, or undertakers. Any person or persons violating this section shall be guilty of a misdemeanor, and on conviction thereof shall be fined in any sum not less than twenty-five dollars nor more than one hundred dollars. (Sec. 26, P. 127, '91).

ADDITIONAL PROVISION.

93. Barbering Prohibited.

That it shall be unlawful for any person, persons, or corporation to carry on the business of barbering on Sunday. (Sec. 1, P. 68, '03).

94. Penalty.

Any person or persons violating the provisions of the foregoing sec-tion shall be guilty of a misdemeanor and upon conviction thereof shall be punished by a fine of ten dollars or imprisonment in the county jail for five days for the first offense, and by a fine of not less than twenty-five dollars nor more than fifty dollars, or imprisonment in the county jail for not less than ten days nor more than twenty-five days for the second and each subsequent offense. (Sec. 2, P. 68, '03).

95. Fraud by Employment Agency.

Every employment agent or broker who, with intent to influence the action of any person thereby, shall misstate or misrepresent verbally, or in any writing or advertisement, any material matter relating to the demand for labor, the conditions under which any labor or service is to be performed, the duration thereof or the wages to be paid therefor, shall be guilty of a misdemeanor. (Chap. 249, Sec. 372, P. 1005, '09).

CHAPTER VIII.

HEALTH.

REGULATION OF BAKE SHOPS.

96. Bakeries to Be Sanitarily Constructed.

All buildings or rooms occupied as biscuit, bread or cake bakeries shall be drained or plumbed in a manner conducive to the proper healthful and sanitary condition thereof, and constructed with air shafts and windows or ventilating pipes sufficient to insure ventilation as the Commissioner of Labor shall direct, and no cellar or basement, not now used as a bakery, shall hereafter be used and occupied as a bakery and a cellar or basement heretofore occupied as a bakery shall, when once closed, not be re-opened for use as a bakery. (Sec. 1, P. 258, '03).

97. Toilet Rooms Separate From Bake Shops.

Every such baker shall be provided with a proper wash room and water closet, or closets, apart from the bake room or rooms where the manufacturing of such products is conducted; and no water closet, earth closet, privy or ash pit shall be within or communicate directly with a bake shop. (Sec. 2, P. 259, '03).

98. Size of Room.

Every room used for the manufacture of flour or meal food shall be at least eight feet in height; the side walls of such room shall be plastered or wainscoted, the ceiling plastered or ceiled with lumber or metal, and if required by the Commissioner of Labor, shall be white-washed at least once in three months; the furniture and utensils of such room shall be so arranged as to be easily moved in order that the furniture and floor may at all times be kept in proper healthful sanitary condition. (Sec. 3, P. 259, '03).

99. Store Room to Be Kept Dry.

The manufactured flour or meal food products shall be kept in perfectly dry and airy rooms, so arranged that the floors, shelves, and all other facilities for storing the same can be easily and perfectly cleaned. (Sec. 4, P. 259, '03).

100. Sleeping Room to Be Separate.

The sleeping places for persons employed in a bakery shall be kept separate from the room or rooms where flour or meal food products are manufactured or stored. (Sec. 5, P. 259, '03).

101. Commissioner of Labor to Issue Certificate, When.

After an inspection of a bakery has been made by the Commissioner of Labor and it is found to conform to the provisions of this chapter, said commissioner shall issue a certificate to the owner or operator of such bakery, that it is conducted in compliance with all the provisions of this chapter, but where orders are issued by said commissioner to improve the condition of a bakery, no such certificate shall be issued until such order and the provisions of this chapter have been complied with. (Sec. 6, P. 259, '03).

102. Notice to Owner.

The owner, agent, or lessee of any property affected by the provisions of this chapter, shall, within thirty days after the service of notice upon him, of an order issued by the Commissioner of Labor requiring any alterations to be made in or upon such premises, comply therewith, or cease to use or allow the use of such premises as a bake shop; such notice shall be in writing and may be served upon such owner, agent, lessee, either personally or by mail, and a notice by registered letter, postage prepaid, mailed to the last known address of such owner, agent or lessee shall be deemed sufficient for the purposes of this chapter. (Sec. 7, P. 259, '03).

103. Diseased Person Not Permitted to Work in Shop.

No employer shall require, permit or suffer any person to work in his bake shop who is affected with tuberculosis, or with scrofulous diseases, or with any venereal disease, or with any communicable skin affection or contagious disease and no person so affected shall work or remain in a bake shop. Every employe is hereby required to maintain himself and his employes in a clean and sanitary condition while engaged in the manufacture, handling or sale of such food products. (Sec. 8, P. 260, '03).

104. Child Under Sixteen Years Prohibited.

No employer shall require, permit or suffer any person under sixteen years of age to work in his bake shop between the hours of eight o'clock in the evening and five o'clock in the morning. (Sec. 9, P. 260, '03).

105. Penalty.

Any person who violates the provisions of this chapter or refuses to comply with the requirements of the Commissioner of Labor, as provided herein, shall be guilty of a misdemeanor, and on conviction thereof before any court of competent jurisdiction, shall be fined not less than twenty-five nor more than fifty dollars or imprisonment not more than ten days for the first offense; and shall be fined not less than fifty nor more than one hundred dollars and imprisonment not less than ten nor more than thirty days for each offense after the first. (Sec. 10, P. 260, '03).

106. Wages Exempt.

Current wages or salary to the amount of one hundred dollars ($100.00) for personal services rendered by any person having a family

—22

dependent upon him for support, shall be exempt from garnishment, and where it appears upon the trial, or by answer of the garnishee, when not controverted as hereinafter provided, that the garnishee is indebted to the defendant for such current wages or salary for an amount not exceeding one hundred dollars ($100.00) the garnishee shall be discharged as to such indebtedness: Provided, That if the garnishment be founded upon a debt for actual necessaries furnished to the defendant or his family or his dependents no exemption shall be allowed in excess of ten dollars ($10.00) out of each week's wages or salary, whether said wages or salary are paid, or to be paid, weekly, bi-weekly, monthly or at other intervals, and whether there be due the defendant wages for one week or a longer period: Provided, however, That said exemption shall in no event be allowed out of wages or salary for a longer period than four (4) consecutive weeks: And provided further, That no money due or earned as wages or salary shall be exempt from garnishment in lieu of any other property. The provisions of this section shall apply to actions in the superior court or before justice of the peace, and shall govern exemptions of wages or salary to the exclusion of all other statutes or parts of statutes. (Chap. 210, P. 477, '07).

107. No Exemption Against Certain Claims.

That from and after the passage of this section, no property shall be exempt from execution for clerk's, laborer's, or mechanic's wages earned within this state, nor for actual necessaries, not exceeding fifty dollars in value or amount furnished to the defendant or his family within sixty days preceding the beginning of an action to recover therefor, nor shall any property be exempt from execution issued upon a judgment against an attorney or agent on account of any liability incurred by such attorney or agent to his client or principal on account of any moneys or other property coming into his hands from or belonging to his client or principal: Provided, That nothing herein shall be construed as repealing or in any wise effecting the next preceding section, relative to the exemptions in garnishment suits. (Sec. 1, P. 135, '03).

CHAPTER IX.

MISCELLANEOUS.

ARTICLE I. BLACKLISTING.

108. Blacklisting, Penalty for.

Every person in this state who shall wilfully and maliciously, send or deliver, or make or cause to be made, for the purpose of being delivered or sent or part with the possession of any paper, letter, or writing, or with any letter or writing, with or without name signed thereto, or signed with a fictitious name, or with any letter, mark or other designation, or publish or cause to be published any statement for the purpose of preventing any other person from obtaining employment in this state or elsewhere, and every person who shall wilfully and maliciously "blacklist" or cause to be "blacklisted" any person or persons, by writing, printing, or publishing, or causing the same to be done the name, or mark, or designation representing the name of any person in any paper, pamphlet, circular, or book, together with any statement concerning persons so named, or publish or cause to be published that any person is a member of any secret organization, for the purpose of preventing such person from securing employment, or who shall wilfully and maliciously make or issue any statement or paper that will tend to influence or prejudice the mind, of any employer against the person of such person seeking employment, or any person who shall do any of the things mentioned in this section for the purpose of causing the discharge of any person employed by any railroad or other company, corporation, individual, or individuals, shall, on conviction thereof, be adjudged guilty of misdemeanor and punished by a fine of not less than one hundred dollars nor more than one thousand dollars, or by imprisonment in the county jail for not less than ninety days nor more than one year, or by both such fine and imprisonment. (Sec. 1, P. 34, '99).

WAGES TO BE IN LAWFUL MONEY.

109. Providing for the Payment of Wages.

، That it shall not be lawful for any corporation, person or firm engaged in manufacturing of any kind in' this state, mining, railroading, constructing railroads, or any business or enterprise of whatsoever kind in this state, to issue, pay out or circulate for payment of wages of any labor, any order, check, memorandum, token or evidence of indebtedness, payable in whole or in part otherwise than in lawful money of the United States, unless the same is negotiable and redeemable at its face value, without discount, in cash or on demand, at the store or other place of business of such firm, person or corporation when the same is issued, and the person who, or company which may issue any such order, check, memorandum, token or other evidence of indebtedness shall upon presentation and demand redeem the same in lawufl money of the United States. And when any laborer performing work or labor as above shall cease to work whether by discharge or by voluntary withdrawal the wages due shall be forthwith paid either in cash or by order redeemable in cash at its face value on presentment at bank, store, commissary, or other place in the county where the labor was performed: Provided, Such order may be given payable in another county when the place of payment is more convenient of access to the employe. (Sec. 1, Chap. 112, '05).

110. Regulating Assignment of Wages.

No assignment of, or order for, wages to be earned in the future to secure a loan of less than three hundred dollars, shall be valid against an employer of the person making said assignment or order unless said assignment or order is accepted in writing by the employer, and said assignment or order, and the acceptance of the same, have been filed and recorded with the county auditor of the county where the party making said assignment or order resides, if a resident of the state, or in which he is employed, if not a resident of the state.

No assignment of, or order for, wages to be earned in the future shall be valid, when made by a married man, unless the written consent of his wife to the making of such assignment or order is attached thereto. (Chap. 32, P. 52, '09).

111. Providing for Labor Liens on Certain Property.

Every person, firm or corporation who has expended labor, skill, or material on any chattel, at the request of its owner, or authorized agent of the owner, shall have a lien upon such chattel for the contract price for such expenditure, or in the absence of such contract price, for the reasonable worth of such expenditure for a period of one year from and after such expenditure, notwithstanding the fact that such chattel be surrendered to the owner thereof: Provided, however, That no such lien shall continue after the delivery of such chattel to its owner as against the rights of third persons who may have acquired an interest in, or the title to, such chattel in good faith, for value, and without actual knowledge of the lien. (Chap. 166, P. 626, '09).

112. Notice of Lien to Be Given.

In order to make such lien effectual the lien claimant shall within ninety days from the date of delivery of such chattel to the owner file in the office of the auditor of the county in which such chattel is kept a lien notice, which notice shall state the name of the claimant, the name of the owner, a description of the chattel upon which the claimant has expended labor, skill or material, the amount for which a lien is claimed, and the date upon which such expenditure was completed, which notice shall be signed by the claimant, or some one in his behalf, and may be in substantially the following form:

CHATTEL LIEN NOTICE.

........................Claimant,

         against

........................Owner.

Notice is hereby given that.................has and claims a lien upon (here insert description of chattel), owned by.................
for the sum of...................dollars, for and on account of labor, skill and material expended upon said...............which was completed upon the........day of.................190...

                      ....

                               Claimant.

(Sec. 2, Chap. 72, '05).

113. Person in Possession of Property Deemed to Be Owner.

Every person who is in possession of a chattel, under an agreement for the purchase thereof, whether the title thereto be in him, or his vendor, shall, for the purposes of this act, be deemed the owner thereof, and the lien of 'a person expending material, labor or skill thereon shall be superior to and preferred to the rights of the person holding the title thereto, or any lien thereon antedating the time of expenditure of the labor, skill or material thereon by a lien claimant, to the extent that such expenditure has enhanced the value of such chattel. (Sec. 3, Chap. 72, '05).

114. Enforcement of Lien.

The lien herein provided for may be enforced against the owner of and all persons having an interest in any such chattel by notice and sale in the same manner that a chattel mortgage is foreclosed, or by decree of any court in this state, exercising original equity jurisdiction in the county wherein such chattel may be, or in action commenced within nine months after the filing of such lien notice and if no such action be commenced within such time such lien shall cease. (Sec. 4, Chap. 72, '05).

115. Filing of Lien With County Auditor.

Upon presentation of such lien notice to the auditor of any county, and the payment to him of fifteen cents, he shall file the same, and endorse thereon the time of the reception, the number thereof, and shall enter the same in a suitable book or file (but need not record the same). Such book or file shall have herewith an alphabetical index, in which the county auditor shall index such notice by noting the name of the owner, name of lien claimant, description of property, date of lien (which shall be the date upon which such expenditure of labor, skill or material was completed), date of filing and when released, the date of release. (Sec. 5, Chap. 72, '05).

116. Liens on Certain Work.

Every person performing labor upon or furnishing material to be used in the construction, alteration or repair of any mining claim, building, wharf, bridge, ditch, dike, flume, tunnel, well, fence, machinery, railroad, street railway, wagon road, aqueduct to create hydraulic power or any other structure or who performs labor in any mine or mining claim or stone quarry has a lien upon the same for the labor performed or material furnished by each, respectively, whether performed or furnished at the instance of the owner of the property subject to the lien or his agent; and every contractor, subcontractor, architect, builder or person having charge of the construction, alteration or repair of any property subject to the lien as aforesaid, shall be held to be the agent of the owner for the purposes of the establishment of the lien created by this chapter: Provided, That whenever any railroad company shall contract with any person for the construction of its road, or any part thereof, such railroad company shall take from the person with whom such contract is made a good and sufficient bond, conditioned that such person shall pay all laborers, mechanics, and material men, and persons who supply such contractors with provisions, all just dues to such persons or to any person to whom any part of such work is given, incurred in carrying on such work, which bond shall be filed by such railroad company in the office of the county auditor in each county in which any part of such work is situated. And if any such railroad company shall fail to take such bond, such railroad company shall be liable to the persons herein mentioned to the full extent of all such debt so contracted by such contractor. (Sec. 1, Chap. 116, '05).

117. Land Where Property Situated Subject to Lien.

The lot, tract or parcel of land upon which the improvement is made or the property is situated, subject to the lien created by section one of this act, or so much thereof as may be necessary to satisfy the lien and the judgment thereon, to be determined by the court on rendering judgment in a foreclosure of the lien, is also subject to the lien to the extent of the interest of the person or company, who in his or its own behalf, or who, through any of the persons designated in section one to be agent of the owner or owners caused the performance of labor, or the construction, alteration or repair of the property. (Sec. 2, Chap. 116, '05).

CHAPTER X.

MINING.

118. State Districted—Appointment of Inspector.

For the purpose of this act, this state shall be divided into inspection districts, each district to contain not less than ten nor more than sixty coal mines, each district to be under the supervision of an inspector of coal mines, the manner of whose appointment shall be as follows: Provided, That there shall be appointed but one inspector until sixty coal mines shall be in operation in this state. The Governor shall upon the recommendation of a board, to be by him selected and appointed for the purpose of examining candidates for appointment to the office of mine inspector under the provisions of this act, appoint a properly qualified person or persons to fill the office of inspector of coal mines for this state. The commissions of said inspector or inspectors shall be for the term of four years, and inspectors shall be at all time subject to removal from office for neglect of duty or malfeasance in the discharge of their duties. Said board shall consist of one practical coal miner, one owner or operator of a coal mine, and one mining engineer, all of whom shall be sworn to a faithful discharge of their duties. The said inspectors shall be citizens of the State of Washington, and shall have had at least five years' practical experience in coal mining. Such person or persons so appointed as inspector shall devote their entire time to the duties of the office, and shall possess other qualifications at present defined by the laws of the State of Washington and not inconsistent with the provisions of this act. Each of such inspectors shall give bond in the sum of two thousand dollars, with sureties to be approved by a judge of a superior court of the county in which he resides, conditioned for the faithful performance of his duties, and take an oath (or affirmation) to discharge his duties impartially and with fidelity, to the best of his knowledge and ability. The salary of each of such inspectors shall be twenty-four hundred (2,400) dollars per annum, and he shall be allowed his actual and necessary traveling expenses while in the performance of his duties under the provisions of this chapter, and the Auditor of the state is hereby authorized and directed to draw his warrant on the State Treasurer in favor of each of such inspectors for the amount due them for their salaries monthly, to be paid out of any moneys in the treasury not otherwise appropriated. (Chap. 77, P. 130, '07).

119. Term of Board and Time of Meeting.

The Board of Examiners provided in the next preceding section, shall be appointed by the Governor and shall hold office for four years. They shall meet immediately after the passage of this chapter, at the state capital, for the purpose of examining candidates for the office of mine inspector under the provisions of this chapter, and at such times thereafter when notified by the Governor that from any cause the office of mine inspector has or is about to become vacant. They shall receive as compensation five dollars per day while actually and necessarily employed, and five cents per mile for distance necessarily traveled. (Sec. 2, P. 59, '97).

120. Coal Mine Defined, Penalty.

No coal mine shall be considered a coal mine for the purpose of enumeration in a district to increase the number of inspectors unless ten or more are employed at one time in or about the mine, nor shall mines employing less than ten men be subject to the provisions of this chapter. It shall be the duty of the owner, agent, or operator of any mine employing less than ten men in or about said mine to immediately notify the inspector when ten men or more are employed at any one time, said notice to be given within one week. Failure on the part of any owner, agent or operator to comply with this provision shall render the offender liable to a fine of not less than twenty dollars or more than one hundred dollars, with an additional penalty of five dollars per day for each day said notice is neglected to be given. (Sec. 6, P. 61, '97).

121. Inspector's Duty.

It shall be the duty of the inspector of mines to enforce the provisions of this chapter, and of all other acts for the regulation of coal mines, in accordance with section 117, and any infringement of the provisions of this chapter shall subject the offender to the same penalties as are provided in sections 119 and 131, unless otherwise provided for in this act. (Sec. 7, P. 61, '97).

122. Maps to Be Made by Operator.

(a) That the operator of every coal mine in this state shall make, or cause to be made, an accurate map or plan on tracing linen of such mine, drawn to a scale not smaller than one hundred feet to the inch, and as much larger as practicable, on which shall appear the name of the state, county and township in which the mine is located, the designation of the mine, the name of the company or owner, the certificate of the mining engineer or surveyor as to the accuracy and date of the survey, the north point and the scale to which the drawing is made.

(b) Every such map or plan shall correctly show the surface boundary lines of the coal rights pertaining to each mine, and all section or quarter section lines or corners within the same; the lines of town lots and streets; the tracks and sidetracks of all railroads and the location of all wagon roads, rivers, streams, ponds, buildings, landmarks and principal objects on the surface.

(c) For the underground workings said maps shall show all shafts, slopes, tunnels or other openings to the surface or to the workings of a contiguous mine; all excavations, entries, rooms and cross-cuts; the location of the fan and the direction of the air currents; the location of pumps, hauling engines, engine planes, abandoned works, fire walls and standing water; and the boundary line of any surface outcrop of the seam.

(d) A separate and similar map, drawn to the same scale in all cases, shall be made of each and every seam worked in any mine, and the maps of all such seams shall show all shafts, inclined planes or other passageways connecting the same.

(e) A separate map shall also be made of the surface whenever the surface buildings, lines or objects are so numerous as to obscure the details of the mine workings if drawn upon the same sheet with them, and in such case the surface map shall be drawn on transparent cloth or paper, so that it can be laid upon the map or underground workings and thus truly indicate the local relation of lines and objects on the surface to the excavations of the mine.

(f) Each map shall also show by profile drawing and measurements, in feet and decimals thereof, the rise and dip of the seam from the bottom of the shaft, slope or drift in either direction to the face of the workings.

(g) The original or true copies of all such maps shall be kept in the office of the mine, and the true copies thereof shall also be furnished to the State Inspector of Mines. The maps so delivered to the inspector shall be the property of the state, and shall remain in the custody of said inspector during his term of office, and be delivered by him to his successor in office; they shall be kept at the office of the inspector, and be open to the examination of all persons interested in the same, but such examination shall be made only in the presence of the inspector, and he shall not permit any copies of the same to be made without the written consent of the operator or the owner of the property.

(h) An extension of the last preceding survey of every mine in active operation shall be made once in every twelve months, prior to July first of every year, and the results of said survey, with the date thereof, shall be promptly and accurately entered upon the original maps and all copies of the same, so as to show all changes in plan or new work in the mine, and all extensions of the old workings to the most advanced face or boundary of such workings, which have been made since the last preceding survey. The said changes and extensions shall be entered upon the copies of the maps in the hands of the said inspector.

(i) When any coal mine is worked out or is about to be abandoned or indefinitely closed, the operator of the same shall make or cause to be made a final survey of all parts of such mine, and the results of the same shall be duly extended on all maps of the mine and copies thereof, so as to show all excavations and the most advanced workings of the mine, and their exact relation to the boundary or section lines on the surface.

(j) The State Inspector of Mines may order a survey to be made of the workings of any mine, and the results to be extended. (Chap. 117, P. 406, '09).

123. Failure to Furnish Map.

Whenever an operator of any mine shall neglect or refuse or for any cause not satisfactory to the Mine Inspector fail for the period of three months to furnish said inspector the map or plan of such mine, or a copy thereof, or of the extensions thereto as provided for in section 1 of this act, such operator shall be deemed guilty of a misdemeanor, and upon conviction thereof shall be fined not less than ten dollars nor more than one hundred dollars, and shall stand committed to the county jail until such fine is fully paid, and in addition thereto the inspector is hereby authorized to make or cause to be made an accurate plan or map of such mine at the cost of the owner thereof, and the cost of the same may be recovered from the operator in an action at law brought in the name of the inspector for his use. (Chap. 117, P. 406, '09).

124. Two Openings, at Least, for Escape Must Be Provided.

It shall not be lawful for the owner, agent or operator of any coal mine to employ any person to work within said coal mine, or to permit any person to work in said mine, unless they are in communication with at least two (2) openings in case such mine [is] to be worked by shaft or slope, which openings, shafts, or slopes shall be separated by natural strata by a distance of not less than one hundred (100) feet at the mouth of such opening, except that in mines already opened such distance may be less, if, in the judgment of the Mine Inspector, one hundred (100) feet is impracticable. If the mine be

worked by drift, two (2) openings not less than one hundred (100)
feet apart shall be required, except in drift mines heretofore opened,
where the Mine Inspector shall deem such distance impracticable: Provided, however, That an aggregate number not exceeding twenty-four
(24) persons may be employed in the mine at any one time until the
second opening shall be reached and made available, which said second
opening the Mine Inspector shall cause to be made without unnecessary
delay, and in case of furnace ventilation being used before the second opening is completed, the furnace shall not be placed within
forty (40) feet of the foot of the shaft, slope, or drift, and shall be well
secured so as not to be a source of danger by fire, by brick, stone, or
walls made of other fireproof material of sufficient thickness, while
such second opening is being driven and until the same is completed.
(Chap. 117, P. 406, '91).

125. Provisions for Speedy Exit in Case of Danger.

All escapement shafts shall be equipped with stairways or ladders
having landing places or platforms at reasonable distances apart, as in
the judgment of the Mine Inspector they should be constructed for
easy traveling, or, in lieu thereof, such hoisting apparatus as will enable the employes in the mine to make safe and speedy exit in case
of danger. The escapement shaft, ropes and machinery used for
hoisting or lowering employes out of or into said mine shall be kept in
a 'safe condition and inspected at least once in each twenty-four (24)
hours by a competent person employed in whole or in part for that
purpose and a record of such examination shall be entered by the
person making the same in a book to be kept at the mine for that
purpose and said book must always be produced for examination at the
request of the inspector. At all points where the passageway to the
escapement shaft and other places of exit is intersected by other
roadways or entries, conspicuous signboards, subject to the approval
of the State Mine Inspector, shall be placed indicating the direction it
is necessary to take in order to reach such place of exit. (Chap. 117,
P. 406, '09).

126. Number and Names of Persons Entering Mines.

Where a mine has only one means of ingress and egress, daily record must be kept by the owner or person in charge of said mine, showing the actual number and the names of each and every person entering the mine for any purpose whatever, and should a greater number
of persons than twenty-four be allowed in the mine, under any circumstances, at any time, it shall be the duty of any judge of the superior court of the county in which said mine is situated, when it shall
be shown to the satisfaction of said court that more than twenty-four
persons were allowed in said mine at any one time, to issue an order
closing said mine until a second opening is completed. (Sec. 3, P. 59,
'97).

127. Ventilation to Be Provided.

The owner, agent, or operator of every coal mine, whether operated by shafts, slopes, or drifts, shall provide in every coal mine a good and sufficient amount of ventilation for such persons and animals as may be employed therein, the amount of air in circulation to be in no case less than one hundred cubic feet per minute for each man, boy, horse, or mule employed in said mine, and as much more as the inspector may direct, and said air must be made to circulate through the shafts, levels, stables, and working places of each mine, and on the traveling roads to and from all such working places. Every mine shall be divided into districts or splits, and not more than seventy-five persons shall be employed at any one time in each district or split: Provided, That where the inspector gives permission in writing a greater number than seventy-five men, but not to exceed one hundred men, may be employed in each of said splits: Provided also, That in all mines already developed, where, in the opinion of the mining inspector, the system of splitting the air cannot be adopted except at extraordinary or unreasonable expense, such mine or mines will not be required to adopt said split air system, and the owner or operator of any coal mine shall have the right of appeal from any order requiring the air to be split, to the examining board provided for in section 101 of this chapter, and said board shall, after investigation, confirm or revoke the orders of the mining inspector. Each district or split shall be ventilated by a separate and distinct current of air, conducted from the downcast through said district, and thence to the upcast. On all main roads where doors are required, they shall be so arranged that when one door is open the other shall remain closed, so that no air shall be diverted. In all mines where fire-damp is generated, every working place shall be examined every morning with a safety lamp by a competent person, and a record of such examination shall be entered by the person making the same in a book to be kept at the mine for that purpose, and said book must always be produced for examination at the request of the inspector. (Sec. 4, P. 59, '97).

128. Measurement of Air.

The quantities of air in circulation shall be ascertained with an anemometer; such measurements shall be made by the superintendent, inside foreman or his assistant, at least once a week at the inlet and outlet airways, also at or near the face of each gangway, and at the nearest cross-heading to the face of the inside and outside chamber, breast or pillar where men are employed: Provided, That no heading shall be driven more than sixty feet from the face of each chamber, breast or pillar, unless for the reason that he deem the same impracticable the inspector gives permission in writing to extend the distance beyond sixty feet. A record of all measurements herein provided for shall be entered in a book to be kept for that purpose, and said book must always be produced for examination at the request of the inspector. It shall be the duty of the Mine Inspector, whenever he shall visit said mine, to make a careful measurement of the quantities of air in circulation therein, said measurements to be made at the places hereinabove indicated. Any superintendent, inside foreman or his assistant, who shall neglect or fail to comply with the provisions of this section, or who shall make any false report in regard to air measurements, shall be guilty of a misdemeanor, and upon conviction thereof, shall be fined in any sum not less than ten dollars nor more than fifty dollars, and shall stand committed to the county jail until such fine is fully paid. (Chap. 57, P. 101, '09).

129. Sufficient Air.

Whenever the inspector shall find men working without sufficient air or under any unsafe conditions he shall at once notify the superintendent of the mine, or in his absence the person immediately in charge thereof, in writing of the facts, and such superintendent or person in charge shall at once remove such men from such places where such conditions exist. At the expiration of one (1) year from and after the passage of this act, it shall not be lawful to use a furnace for the purpose of ventilating any coal mine in the state. (Sec. 9, P. 158, '91).

130. Machinery Breaking Down.

If at any time the ventilating machinery should break down or otherwise cease operation, or if it is found by the person for the time being in charge of the mine, or any part thereof, that by reason of noxious gases prevailing in said mine, or such part thereof, or of any cause whatever, the mine or the said part is dangerous, every workman shall be withdrawn from the mine, or such part thereof as is so found dangerous, and a competent person, who shall be appointed for the purpose, shall inspect the mine or such part thereof as is so found dangerous, and if the danger arises from inflammable gas, shall inspect the same with a locked safety lamp, and in every case shall make a true report of the condition of such mine, or the part thereof, and a workman shall not, except in so far as is necessary for inquiring into the cause of danger, or for the removal thereof, or for exploration, be readmitted into the mine, or such part thereof as was so found dangerous, until the same is stated in such report not to be dangerous. Every such report shall be recorded in a book which shall be kept at the mine for that purpose, and shall be signed by the person making the same. (Sec. 8, P. 61, '97).

131. Fan Breaking Down—Repairs.

The engineer in charge of any ventilating fan or apparatus must keep the same running as the manager of the mine directs in writing. In case of accident to the boiler or fan machinery, he shall immediately notify the mine manager or foreman. If ordinary repairs of the fan or machinery become necessary, he must give timely notice to the mine manager or foreman and await his instructions before stopping it. He shall also examine, at the beginning of each shift, all the fan bearings, stays, and other parts, and see that they are kept in perfect working order. He shall not stop the fan except on the order of the mine manager or foreman, unless it should become impossible to run the fan or necessary to stop it to prevent destruction. He shall then at once' stop it and notify the mine manager or foreman immediately and give immediately warning to persons in the mine. (Sec. 9, P. 62, '97).

132. Bore-Holes to Be Provided—When and How.

The owner, agent, or operator of any coal mine shall provide that bore-holes shall be kept twenty (20) feet in advance of the face of each and every working place, and if necessary on both sides when driving towards an abandoned mine or part of a mine suspected of containing inflammable gases or being inundated with water. (Sec. 14, P. 160, '91).

133. Signals—Cages, How to Be Furnished.

The owner, agent or operator of every coal mine operated by shaft or slope shall provide suitable means of signaling between the bottom and top thereof, subject to the approval of the mine inspector, and shall also provide in all shafts safe means of hoisting and lowering persons in a cage covered with boiler iron, so as to keep safe as far as possible persons descending into or ascending out of such shaft, and such cage shall be furnished with guides to conduct it through such shaft with a sufficient brake on every drum to prevent accident in case of the giving out or breaking of the machinery, and such cage shall be furnished with safety catches (to be approved by the Mine Inspector), intended and provided as far as possible to prevent the consequences of cable breaking or the loosening or disconnecting of the machinery, and no props or rails shall be lowered in a cage while men are descending into or ascending out of said mine, and such owner, agent or operator shall also provide in all slopes, safe means for raising and lowering persons therein: Provided, That in shafts less than one hundred feet in depth the owner, agent or operator shall provide such means for raising and lowering persons as may be approved by the Mine Inspector. .(Chap. 105, P. 204, '07).

134. Regulations for Hoisting and Lowering.

No owner, agent, or operator of any coal mine operated by shaft or slope shall place in charge of any engine whereby men are lowered into or hoisted from the mine any other than competent, experienced, and sober engineers and firemen, and they shall be not less than eighteen (18) years of age. No person shall ride upon a loaded cage or car used for hoisting purposes in any shaft or slope, and in no case shall more than twelve (12) persons ride on any cage or car at one time in any such shaft. Nor shall more than five (5) persons for each and every ton's capacity of the hoisting apparatus ride in any cage or car at any one time in any such slope, excepting in the case of persons employed as rope riders or couplers, nor shall any coal be hoisted out of any

coal mine while persons are descending into such mine, notice of
which shall be kept posted at said mine. The number of persons permitted to ascend out of or descend into any coal mine at one time shall
be determined by the inspector, and such persons shall not be lowered
or hoisted more rapidly than six hundred (600) feet per minute.
Whenever a cage load of persons shall come to the bottom to be hoisted
out, who have finished their day's work or otherwise been prevented
from working, an empty cage shall be given them to ascend, except in
mines having slopes or provided with stairways in escapement shafts.
(Sec. 19, P. 162, '91).

135. Age Limit of Employes.

No boy under the age of sixteen years and no female of any age
shall be employed or permitted to be in any mine for the purpose of
employment therein, nor shall a boy under the age of fourteen years be
employed or permitted to be in or about the outside structures or
workings or the colliery for the purpose of employment: Provided,
That this prohibition shall not affect the employment of boys of suitable
age in an office or in the performance of clerical work at the colliery.
When an employer is in doubt as to the age of any boy applying for employment in or about a mine or colliery, he shall demand and receive
proof of the age of such boy by certificate from the parents or guardian
of such boy before he shall be employed.   (Chap. 117, P. 407, '09).

136. Boilers to Be Examined—Signals.

All boilers used in generating steam in and about coal mines shall
be kept in good order, and the owner, agent, or operator, as aforesaid,
shall have said boilers examined and inspected by a competent person
as often as once every six (6) months, and the result of such examination shall be certified in writing· to the Mine Inspector, and every
steam boiler shall be provided with a steam gauge, water gauge, and
safety valves. All underground self-acting or engine planes on which
coal cars are drawn and persons travel shall be provided with some
proper means of signaling between the stopping places and the end of
said planes, and sufficient places of refuge shall be provided at the sides
of said planes, the same to be not more than sixty (60) feet apart and
extend six (6) feet at right angles from the rail: Provided, however,
That such places of refuge shall not be required in mines where a separate traveling road is provided for employes.   (Sec. 18, P. 161, '91).

137. What Must Be Done in Case of Explosion or Accident.

Whenever by reason of any explosion or other accident in any coal
mine, or the machinery connected therewith, loss of life or serious
personal injury shall occur, it shall be the duty of the person having
charge of such mine or colliery to give notice thereof forthwith to
the inspector of the district, and, if any person is killed thereby, to the
coroner of the county, who shall give due notice of the inquest to be
held. If the coroner shall determine to hold an inquest the Mine In-

spector shall be allowed to testify and offer such testimony as he may deem necessary to thoroughly inform the said inquest of the cause of the death, and the said inspector shall have authority at any time to appear before such coroner and jury and question or cross-question any witness, and in choosing a jury for the purpose of holding such inquest, it shall be the duty of the coroner to empanel a jury, no one of whom shall be directly or indirectly interested. It shall be the duty of the inspector upon being notified as herein provided, to immediately repair to the scene of the accident and make such suggestions as may appear necessary to secure the future safety of the men, and if the results of the explosion or accident do not require an investigation by the coroner, he shall proceed to investigate and ascertain the cause of the explosion or accident and make a record thereof which he shall file as provided for, and to enable him to make the investigation he shall have power to compel the attendance of persons, to testify and administer oaths or affirmations. The cost of such investigation shall be paid by the county in which the accident occurred, in the same manner as costs of inquests held by coroners or justices of the peace are paid. (Sec. 15, P. 160, '91).

138. Powers of Inspectors—Provisions to Stop Dangerous Mines From Being Worked.

It shall be lawful for the inspectors provided for in this chapter to enter into and examine and inspect any and all coal mines and machinery belonging thereto within their respective districts at all reasonable times either day or night; but they shall not hinder or obstruct the necessary workings of such coal mines, and the owner, agent or operator of every such coal mine is hereby required to furnish all necessary facilities for the entering and making of such examination and inspection, and if the said owner, agent or operator shall refuse to permit such inspection the inspector shall file his affidavit setting forth such refusal with the judge of the superior court of the county in which said mine is situated, and obtain an order from such judge commanding such owner, agent or operator so refusing as aforesaid, to permit such examination and inspection and furnish such necessary facilities for the examination and inspection of such coal mine, or in default thereof to be adjudged as in contempt of court and punished accordingly; and if the said inspector shall, after examination of any coal mine and the works and machinery pertaining thereto, find the same to be worked contrary to the provisions of this chapter, or unsafe for the workmen therein employed, said inspector shall, through the prosecuting attorney of the county in which said mine is located, or any attorney in the case of the refusal of such prosecuting attorney to so act, in the name and on behalf of the state proceed against the owner, agent or operator of such coal mine by injunction without bond after giving at least two days' notice to such owner, agent or operator, and said owner, agent or operator shall have the right to appear before the judge to whom the application is made, who shall hear

the same on affidavits and such other testimony as may be offered in
support as well as in opposition thereto; and if sufficient cause appear the court or judge, in term time or in vacation, by order shall prohibit the further working of any portion or portions of any such coal
mine in which persons may be unsafely employed, and the further use
of such unsafe machinery, contrary to the provisions of this chapter,
until the same shall have been made safe and the requirements of this
chapter have been complied with, and the court shall award such costs
in the matter of said injunction as may be just, but any such proceedings so commenced shall not prejudice any other remedy permitted by
law for enforcing the provisions of this chapter. (Sec. 8, P. 157, '91).

139. Citation to Inspector for Neglect of Duty—Costs.

Upon a petition signed by not less than ten reputable citizens who
shall be miners, mine owners, or lessees of mines, to the superior
court of any county in the proper district, with the affidavit of one or
more of said petitioners attached, setting forth that any inspector of
mines neglects his duty or is incompetent, or that he is guilty of malfeasance in office or any act tending to the injury of miners or operators of mines, the judge of such superior court shall issue a citation
in the name of the state to the said inspector to appear on not less
than fifteen (15) days' notice, upon a day fixed before said court, at
which time the court shall proceed to inquire into and investigate the
allegations of the petitioners. If the court find that said inspector is
neglectful of his duties or that he is guilty of malfeasance in office the
court shall certify the same to the Governor, who shall declare the
office of said inspector vacant and proceed in compliance with the provisions of this act to supply the vacancy. The costs of said investigation shall, if the charges are sustained, be imposed upon the inspector,
but if the charges are not sustained they shall be imposed upon the pe-
tioners, and the payment of such cost shall be enforced by the proper
action brought in the name of and on behalf of the state by the prosecuting attorney of the county wherein such investigation is had.
(Sec. 7, P. 156, '91).

140. Offenses Defined.

Any miner, workman, or other person who shall knowingly injure
any water gauge, barometer, air course, or bratice, or shall obstruct
or throw open any air ways, or carry any lighted lamp or matches into
places that are worked by the light of safety lamps, or shall handle or
disturb any part of the machinery of the hoisting engine or open a
door in the mine and not have the same closed again, whereby danger
is produced, either to the mine or those that work therein, or who
shall enter into any part of the mine against caution, or who shall interfere with or intimidate, or attempt to interfere with or intimidate,
any engineer, fireman, or other employe employed in or about such
mine, in the discharge of his duty or performance of his labor, or,
who shall disobey any order given in pursuance of this chapter, or who

shall do any wilful act whereby the lives and health of persons working in the mine, or the security of the mine or mines or the machinery thereof is endangered, shall be deemed guilty of a misdemeanor, and upon conviction thereof shall be punished by a fine of not more than two hundred ($200) dollars nor less than fifty ($50) dollars, or by imprisonment in the county jail for a term not exceeding six (6) months nor less than three months, or by both such fine and imprisonment, in the discretion of the court. (Sec. 21, P. 163, '91).

141. Owner to Furnish Timber.

The owner, agent, or operator of any coal mine shall keep a sufficient supply of timber at any such mine where the same is required for use as props, so that the workmen may at all times be able to properly secure the said workings from caving in, and it shall be the duty of the owner, agent, or operator to send down into the mine all such props when required, the same to be delivered at the entrance of the working place. (Sec. 10, P. 158, '91).

142. Steam Pumps. ·

At all mines where coal is hoisted by steam power from shaft or slope, having no other means of ingress or egress than that afforded to persons employed therein by such hoisting apparatus by way of such shaft or slope, there shall be provided within ninety (90) days next after the first day of May, A. D. 1891, a steam pump or other power, conveniently situated, and a sufficient supply of water and hose always ready for use in any part of the buildings, chutes, or constructions within a radius of fifty (50) feet of said coal hoisting shaft or slope; and if the person in charge of such coal shaft or slope shall refuse or neglect to comply with the provisions of this chapter, then the inspector of coal mines for the district in which the said shaft or slope is situated shall proceed, through the prosecuting attorney in the county in which said shaft or slope is situated, or any attorney in case of the refusal of the prosecuting attorney to so act, in the name and on behalf of the state against the owner, agent, or operator of said shaft or slope by injunction without bond, after giving at least two (2) days' notice to such owner, agent, or operator, and the said owner, agent, or operator shall have the right to appear before the judge to whom the application is made, who shall hear the same on affidavits and such other testimony as may be offered in support as well as in opposition thereto, and if it be found that the owner, agent or operator of said shaft or slope has refused or neglected to comply with the provisions of this chapter, the court or judge, in term time or in vacation, by order shall prohibit the further working of any such coal shaft or slope until the owner, agent, or operator shall have complied with the provisions of this chapter. (Sec. 11, P. 159, '91).

—23

143. Stretchers Must Be Provided for Injured Workmen.

It shall be the duty of the owner, superintendent, or operator of any coal mine to keep at the mouth of the drift, shaft, or slope, or at such other place as may be designated by the Mine Inspector, stretchers properly constructed for the purpose of carrying away any miner or employe working in or about such mine who may in any way be injured in or about his employment.   (Sec. 13, P. 161, '91).

144. Main Doors in Mine—How to Be Placed.

All main doors in any coal mine shall be so placed that whenever one door is open another which has the same effect upon the same current of air shall be and remain closed, and thus prevent any temporary stoppage of the current.   (Sec. 17, P. 161, '91).

145. Printed Rules, Etc., Must Be Kept Posted About Mines.

All owners or operators of coal mines within the state shall keep posted in a conspicuous place about their mines printed rules, submitted to and approved by the district mining inspector, regulating the duties of persons employed in or about said mines or collieries.   (Sec. 20, P. 163, '91).

146. Right-of-Way Between Mines.

When two or more coal mines are so located as to allow the said mines to be connected by permanent entries between, and the land or mining right lying between such mine is owned by any person or persons with whom the owner or owners of said mine or mines are unable to agree for the purchase of the right-of-way for the connecting entry or entries, between such mines, and the right to maintain and use such entry as a connecting entry is claimed, such owner or owners of any such coal mine or mines, or either of them, may acquire such right or title in the manner that may be now or hereafter provided by any law of eminent domain.   (Sec. 2239, 1 Hill's Code).

147. Tools.

The use of iron needles and iron tampting bars not tipped with five inches of copper is hereby declared unlawful. Any failure on the part of a coal miner, or an employe of any coal mine, to conform to the terms and requirements of this chapter shall subject such miner or employe to a fine of not less than five ($5) dollars or more than twenty-five ($25) dollars, with costs of prosecution, for each offense, to be recovered by civil suit before any justice of the peace; said fines, when collected, to be paid into the treasury of the county when the offense was committed, to the credit of the fund provided for the payment of the county inspector of mines.   (Sec. 2240, 1 Hill's Code).

148. Output of Coal to Be Weighed and Credited to Employe.

It shall be unlawful for any mine owner, lessee, or operator of coal mines in the State of Washington employing miners at bushel or ton rates, or other quantity, to pass the output of coal mined by said miners over any screen or other device which shall take any part from the value thereof before the same shall have been weighed and duly credited to the employe sending the same to the surface, and accounted for at the legal rate of weights as fixed by the laws of the State of Washington. (Sec. 1, P. 414, '91).

149. Oath of Coal Weighman—Rights of Employes.

The weighman employed at any mine shall subscribe an oath or affirmation before a justice of the peace, or other officer authorized to administer oaths, to do justice between employer and employe, and weigh the output of coal from the mines as herein provided. The miners employed by or engaged in working for any mine owner, operator, or lessees, or any mine in this state, shall have the privilege, if they desire, of employing at their own expense a check-weighman who shall have like rights, powers, and privileges in the weighing of coal as the regular weighman and be subject to the same oath and penalties as the regular weighman. Said oath or affirmation shall be kept conspicuously posted in the weigh office, and any weigher of coal, or person so employed, who shall knowingly violate any of the provisions of this and the preceding section shall be deemed guilty of a misdemeanor, and upon conviction shall be punished by a fine of not less than twenty-five ($25.00) dollars nor more than one hundred ($100.00) dollars for each offense, or by imprisonment in the county jail for a period not to exceed thirty (30) days, or by both such fine and imprisonment, proceedings to be instituted in any court having jurisdiction therein. (Sec. 2, P. 414, '91).

150. Punishment for Certain Provisions.

Any person violating any of the provisions of this chapter other than those mentioned in section 123, shall be guilty of a misdemeanor, and upon conviction thereof shall be fined in any sum not more than five hundred ($500) dollars nor less than two hundred ($200) dollars. (Sec. 22, P. 163, '91).

151. Sale of Coal Mines Reported.

Any mine owner transferring any coal mine shall immediately report such sale to the Inspector of Mines, giving the name or names of the purchaser or purchasers and the address or addresses of the same. The purchaser or purchasers of any such coal mine shall also immediately report to the Inspector of Mines giving the officers and superintendent of such coal mine with their addresses. Failure to make such report shall constitute a misdemeanor and upon conviction thereof, the said seller or purchaser shall be subject to a fine of not to exceed one hundred dollars, and not less than ten dollars, or by imprisonment not to exceed thirty days in the county jail, or by both such fine and imprisonment. (Chap. 105, P. 204, '07).

152. Safety Cage In Mining Shaft—Regulations.

It shall be unlawful for any person or persons, company or companies, corporation or corporations to sink or work through any vertical shaft at a greater depth than one hundred and fifty feet, unless the said shaft shall be provided with an iron-bound safety cage, to be used in the lowering and hoisting of the employes of such person or persons, company or companies, corporation or corporations. The safety apparatus, whether consisting of eccentrics, springs or other devices, shall be securely fastened to the cage, and shall be of sufficient strength to hold the cage loaded at any depth to which the shaft may be sunk, provided the cable shall break. The iron bonnet aforesaid shall be made of boiler sheet iron of a good quality, of at least three-sixteenths of an inch in thickness, and shall cover the top of the cage in such a manner as to afford the greatest protection to life and limb from any matter falling down said shaft. (Sec. 7, P. 123, '89-'90).

153. Penalty.

Any person or persons, company or companies, corporation or corporations, who shall neglect, fail, or refuse to comply with the provisions of the next preceding section, shall be guilty of a misdemeanor, and upon conviction thereof, shall be fined not less than five hundred ($500) dollars nor more than one thousand ($1,000) dollars. (Sec. 8, P. 123, '89-'90).

This and the next preceding sections are modified, if not repealed, by sections 133 and 116 respectively.

154. Application.

Nothing contained in the two preceding sections shall be so construed as to prevent recovery being had in a suit for damages for injuries sustained by the party so injured, or his heirs or administrator or administratrix, or any one else now competent to sue in an action of such character. (Sec. 9, P. 123, '89-'90).

155. Regulating the Use of Lamps In Coal Mines.

In every working of a coal mine approaching any place where there is likely to be an accumulation of explosive gases, or in any working where there is imminent danger from explosive gases, no light, lamp or fire other than a magnetic locked, air locked or lead locked safety lamp shall be allowed or used, except by mine superintendents, mine foremen or their assistants, gas-testers, fire-bosses or shot-lighters, who may use such lamps as may be approved by the State Mine Inspector. Whenever safety lamps are required in any mine they shall be the property of the owner of said mine, and a competent person, who shall be appointed for the purpose, shall examine every safety lamp immediately before it is taken into the workings for use, and ascertain it to be clean, safe and securely locked, and safety lamps shall not be used until they have been so examined and found safe, clean and securely locked.

Whenever the operator or operators of any mine may be using safety lamps other than magnetic locked, air locked or lead locked lamps, the said operator or operators shall procure and put in use the said magnetic locked, air locked or lead locked lamps and cease the use of other lamps within six months from the time this act shall go into effect. Where non-magnetic lighting safety lamps are not in use, the operator or operators shall provide stations in safe places for relighting safety lamps.

For the violation of any of the provisions of this act the operator or operators of any mine shall be deemed guilty of a misdemeanor, and upon conviction thereof may be fined in any sum not less than fifty dollars nor more than two hundred dollars and in addition thereto the State Mine Inspector shall have authority and it shall be his duty to close such mine until the provisions of this act shall be complied with. Any man opening or tampering with one of said safety lamps or found with matches or any lighting device other than safety lamps, shall be guilty of a misdemeanor and upon conviction thereof for the first offense he shall be fined not less than ten dollars ($10.00) nor more than one hundred dollars ($100.00) and for the second offense he shall be fined not less than two hundred dollars ($200.00) or imprisonment for a term of not more than one year. (Chap. 55, P. 99, '09).

156. Eight-Hour Day for Coal Miners in Underground Work.

It shall be unlawful for any person, firm, or corporation operating any coal mine within the State of Washington, to cause any employee to remain at his place of work, where the same is situated underground, for more than eight (8) hours, exclusive of one-half ($\frac{1}{2}$) hour for lunch, in any one calendar day of twenty-four (24) hours. Any person, firm or corporation, or the agent of any person, firm or corporation violating the provisions of this section shall be guilty of a misdemeanor, and upon conviction shall be fined in any sum not less than ten dollars ($10.00) or more than one hundred dollars ($100.00) for each offense.

It shall be unlawful for any person in the employ of any person, firm, or corporation operating any coal mine, within the State of Washington, to wilfully remain at, or in his working place, where the same shall be underground, to exceed eight (8) hours, exclusive of one-half ($\frac{1}{2}$) hour for lunch, in any one calendar day of twenty-four (24) hours. Any person violating the provisions of this section shall be guilty of a misdemeanor, and upon conviction shall be fined in any sum not less than five dollars ($5.00) or more than twenty dollars ($20.00) for each offense.

The provisions of this act shall not apply to, or prohibit engineers, rope-riders, motormen, cagers, or others necessarily employed in transporting men in and out of the mine: Provided, however, That all persons so employed shall not work more than ten (10) hours in any one calendar day: And provided further, That this act shall not be con-

strued to prohibit extra hours of employment underground, necessitated
by a weekly change of shift, or where rendered necessary by reason of
any accident, or for the purpose of making unavoidable repairs, or
for the protection of property or human life.

It shall be the duty of the State Inspector of Coal Mines to enforce
the provisions of this act. (Chap. 220, P. 749, '09).

CHAPTER XI.

AN ACT RELATING TO TRADE MARKS.

157. Trade Marks of Unions Protected—Violation Defined.

Whenever any person, or any association or union of workingmen
has heretofore adopted or used, or shall hereafter adopt or use, and has
filed as herinafter provided any label, trade-mark, term, design, device
or form of advertisement for the purpose of designating, making
known or distinguishing any goods, wares, merchandise or other product of labor, as having been made, manufactured, produced, prepared,
packed or put on sale by such person or association or union of workingmen or by a member or members of such association or union, it
shall be unlawful to counterfeit or imitate such label, trade-mark,
term, design, device or form of advertisement, or to use, sell, or offer
for sale, or in any way utter or circulate any counterfeit or imitation
of any such label, trade-mark, term, design, device or form of advertisement. (Sec. 1, P. 65, '97).

158. Violation Further Defined—Penalty.

Whoever counterfeits or imitates any such label, trade-mark, term
design, device, or form of advertisement, or sells, offers for sale, or in
any way utters or circulates any counterfeit or imitation of any such
label, trade-mark, term, design, device, or form of advertisement; or
keeps or has in his possession, with intent that the same shall be sold
or disposed of, any goods, wares, merchandise or other products of
labor, to which or on which any such counterfeit or imitation is
printed, painted, stamped or impressed; or knowingly sells or disposes
of any goods, wares, merchandise or other product of labor contained
in any box, case, can or package, to which or on which any such
counterfeit or imitation is attached, affixed, printed, painted, stamped
or impressed; or keeps or has in his possession with intent that the
same shall be sold or disposed of, any goods, wares, merchandise or
other product of labor, in any box, case, can or package, to which or
on which any such counterfeit or imitation is attached, affixed, printed,
painted, stamped or impressed, shall be punished by a fine of not
more than one hundred dollars, or by imprisonment for not more than
three months. (Sec. 2, P. 65, '97).

159. File With Secretary of State—Fee for Recording.

Every such person, association or union, that has heretofore adopted
or used, or shall hereafter adopt or use, a label, trade-mark, term, de-

sign, device or form of advertisement, as provided in section one of this act, may file the·same for record in the office of the Secretary of State by leaving two copies, counterparts or fac-similes thereof, with said Secretary, and by filing therewith a sworn application specifying the name or names of the person, association or union on whose behalf such label, trade-mark, term, design, device or form of advertisement shall be filed, the class of merchandise and the description of the goods to which it has been, or is intended to be appropriated, stating that the party so filing or on whose behalf such label, trade-mark, term, design, device or form of advertisement shall be filed, has the right to the use of the same, that no other person, firm, association, union or corporation has the right to such use either in the identical form or in any such near resemblance thereto as may be calculated to deceive, and that the fac-simile or counterparts filed therewith are true and correct. There shall be paid for such filing and recording, a fee.of two dollars. Said Secretary shall deliver to such person, association or union so filing or causing to be filed any such label, trade-mark, term, design, device or form of advertisement, so many duly attested certificates of the recording of the same as such person, association or union may· apply for, for each of which certificates said Secretary shall receive a fee of one dollar. Any such certificate of record shall, in all suits and prosecutions under this act, be sufficient proof of the adoption of such label, trade-mark, term, design, device or form of advertisement. Said Secretary of State shall not record for any person, union or association, any label, trade-mark, term, design, device or form of advertisement that would probably be mistaken for any label, trade-mark, term, design, device or form of advertisement theretofore filed by or on behalf of any other person, union or association. (Sec. 3, P. 65, '97).

160. Fraudulent Registration—Damages.

Any person who shall, for himself, or on behalf of any other person, association or union, procure the filing of any label, trade-mark, term, design or form of advertisement in the office of the Secretary of State, under the provisions of this act, by making any false or fraudulent representations or declaration, verbally or in writing, or by any fraudulent means, shall be liable to pay any damages sustained in consequence of any such filing, to be recovered by or on behalf of the party injured thereby, in any court having jurisdiction, and shall be punished by a fine not exceeding one hundred dollars or by imprisonment not exceeding three months. (Sec. 4, P. 65, '97).

161. May Enjoin—Counterfeits to Be Destroyed.

Every such person, association or union adopting or using a label, trade-mark, term, design, device or form of advertisement, as aforesaid, may proceed by suit to enjoin the manufacture, use, display or sale of any counterfeits or imitations thereof, and all courts of competent jurisdiction shall grant injunctions to restrain such manufacture, use, display or sale, and may award the complainant in any such suit damages resulting from such manufacture, use, sale or display, as may be by the said court deemed just and reasonable, and shall require the defendants to pay to such person, association or union all profits derived from such wrongful manufacture, use, display or sale; and such court shall also order that all such counterfeits or imitations in the possession or under the control of any defendant in such cause be delivered to an officer of the court, or to the complainant, to be destroyed. (Sec. 5, P. 65, '97).

162. Penalty for Unauthorized Use of Labels, Trade-Marks, Etc.

Every person who shall use or display the genuine label, trade-mark, term, design, device or form of advertisement of any such person, association or union, in any manner, not being authorized so to do by such person, union or association, shall be deemed guilty of a misdemeanor, and shall be punished by imprisonment for not more than three months, or by a fine of not more than one hundred ($100) dollars. In all cases where such association or union is not incorporated, suits under this act may be commenced and prosecuted by an officer or member of such association or union on behalf of and for the use of such association or union. (Sec. 6, P. 65, '97).

163. Unauthorized Use of Name or Seal—Penalty For.

Any person or persons who shall, in any way, use the name or seal of any such person, association or union or officer thereof, in and about the sale of goods or otherwise not being authorized to so use the same, shall be guilty of a misdemeanor, and shall be punishable by imprisonment for not more than three months, or by a fine of not more than one hundred dollars. (Sec. 7, P. 65, '97).

164. Penalty for Defacing or Removing Label, Trade-Mark, Etc.

Any person using the trade-mark so adopted and filed by any other person, or any imitation of such trade-mark, or any counterfeit thereof; or who shall, in any manner mutilate, deface, destroy or remove such trade-mark from any goods, wares, merchandise, article or articles, or from any package or packages containing the same, or from any empty or second-hand package which has contained the same or been used therefor, with the intention of using such empty or second-hand package, or of the same being used to contain goods, wares, merchandise, article or articles, of the same general character as those for which they were first used; and any person who shall use any such empty or second-hand package for the purpose aforesaid, without the consent in writing of the person whose trade-mark was first applied thereto or placed thereon shall, upon conviction thereof, be fined in any sum not less than one hundred dollars, or by imprisonment for not more than three months, and the goods, wares, merchandise, article or articles, contained in any such second-hand package or packages shall be forfeited to the original user of such package or packages whose trade-marks was first applied thereto or placed thereon. The violation of any of the above provisions as to each particular article or package shall be held to be a separate offense. (Sec. 8, P. 65, '97).

165. Word "Person" Defined.

The word "person," in this act, shall be construed to include a person, co-partnership, corporation, association or union of workingmen. (Sec. 9, P. 65, '97).

INDEX

Lightning Source UK Ltd.
Milton Keynes UK
UKHW020311220119
335963UK00014B/1310/P